Thomas Bruce

That bruisin' lad o' Greystone Lodge

A novel

Thomas Bruce

That bruisin' lad o' Greystone Lodge
A novel

ISBN/EAN: 9783337101527

Printed in Europe, USA, Canada, Australia, Japan

Cover: Foto ©Andreas Hilbeck / pixelio.de

More available books at **www.hansebooks.com**

JUPITER. 3?.

CONTENTS

LIST OF ILLUSTRATIONS,

ENGRAVED ON WOOD, BY J. D. FELTER.

PREFATORY NOTE.

THIS work on Mythology, as stated in the first ed.tion, is compiled from various authors,* who have treated the subject either directly or indirectly; and the author is happy to find that the method adopted meets with approbation.

The diligent researches of students and antiquarians have been richly rewarded. Still the subject seems inexhaustible, and is ever gathering fresh interest from the result of new investigations. There is yet much to be learned of the foundations upon which the history of Mythology rests; and Müller remarks, that "this must be left to the highest of all historical sciences—one whose internal relations are scarcely yet dreamt of—the history of the human mind."

---

* Heeren, Müller, Moritz, Millin, Wordsworth, Smith, Anthon, Elmes, &c. &c

INTRODUCTORY NOTICE.

A MYTH is not a fable, neither is mythology the history of fables regarded as mere creations of the imagination, or as introduced merely to supply the chasms which are found in all the early historical records of the human race. It may, on the other hand, be truly said, that this branch of knowledge, extravagant and unsatisfactory as it may seem to some, does actually offer more important truth to the contemplative mind than is often furnished by the most accurate annals belonging to later periods of national life. It is very plausibly contended by some, that modern history, and, above all, that of our own country or period, should have the first place assigned to it in all our institutions of learning, and especially in our common schools. The more modern, on this very account the more valuable. The dullest chapter of recent history, repeating ever the same trite page of hollow diplomacy, and corrupt political intrigue, or stale revolutionary demagoguism, is deemed of more account than that rich nursery of ideas, the old Scandinavian Mythology. The history of the annexation of Texas, or of the Mexican war, is of far more importance, it is thought, and should occupy a far larger space in our historical school books, than those wondrous and eventful periods in the world's life, the early heroic ages of Greece and Rome. And this simply because it is modern—because it is *our own* history–irrespective of the great end of the study as a means of mental culture, and as suggestive of those views which have regard to humanity in its most instructive and most interesting relations.

We cannot stop to controvert these positions, or to maintain by argument those that are opposed to them. The mere statement of the different grounds assumed is enough for any thinking mind. Nothing, we contend, presents a more rich and suggestive field of thought, than the earliest ideas entertained by men in respect to natural and supernatural, moral and theological truth. Not that we would, without much exception, endorse the maxim of Cicero in respect to antiquity—*Quo proprius aberat ab ortu et divina progenie, hoc melius ea quae erant vera cernebat**—but because these fresh, primitive conceptions of the world's early morning may be supposed to present, more truly than any subsequent opinions, the universal consciousness, or spontaneous thought of the race in respect to the first elements of moral, religious, and philosophi-

---

* Tusc. Disp. i. 26. The less its distance from the birth and divine stock of the race, the more clearly it discerned those things that are true.

cal truth. If we would study profoundly the moral sense of mankind, and learn its most truthful and unalloyed decisions, we must go back to periods anterior to those which may be styled either political or philosophical. If we would truly know how deeply the religious element enters into the very constitution of humanity, so as to pervade all the early aspects of its social and political life—if we would rightly estimate how strongly the moral ideas of law, and sin, and retribution, and expiation, have maintained their hold upon the conscience, and how inseparably the thoughts of an invisible world, and of invisible agencies of a higher order than the human, have been associated from the start with all the relations of the present existence—we must go far back in antiquity, and, with the Bible in one hand and the old Mythologies in the other, trace the war between Heaven and Earth, between the strong religious instincts and the ever corrupting and distorting human depravity, between the purity and simplicity of the early theism and that tendency to the physical, the pantheistical, and the atheistical, which the world has ever exhibited, except as it has been from time to time interrupted and turned back by a succession of special divine interpositions.

These first thoughts of our race are most important to us in any view we can take; whether regarded as the result of some universal primitive revelation becoming afterwards gradually more and more corrupted, or as the spontaneous workings of the human soul in the freshest, and, in some respects, the purest and most vigorous period of its existence. Even in this age of physical science, it may be maintained, without extravagance, that these early moral and spiritual developments are of far more importance than the geological changes that are discovered in the material structure of our earth, and that some acquaintance with the primitive agencies at work in the formation of religions, and polities, and languages, may be of more value, even in our common schools, than the boasted knowledge which traces the formation of rocks and strata, and makes such a parade of its utility in the discovery of mines and beds of coal.

Especially is such a view interesting to those who hold—as they conceive, on the best of grounds—that the supernatural actually entered largely into the earliest history of our world, and that the first condition of mankind, instead of being that of the gross, savage state, such as is now witnessed in many parts of our earth, was characterized by a purity, a simplicity, yet, at the same time, an elevation of moral and religious truth, which became lost in the ages that soon succeeded. In support of such a view, strengthened as it is by the best light to be derived from profane history and confirmed by divine revelation, the early mythologies and religions of mankind may be regarded as furnishing the most important evidence. They show the subsequent transitions from this comparatively pure and simple state, to one more physical, more pantheistic, more atheistic, and, of course, more irreligious, although attended with scientific progress, with advance in philosophy, and improvements in the arts and refinements of civilized life.

The thoughts here presented are capable of great expansion. Time and space, how ever, will not permit us to dwell on them. They are simply suggested as evidence of the great value of mythological studies, and an argument for their introduction into all our schools, from the highest to the lowest.

Mythology belongs jointly to the departments of history and philosophy, and is, in fact, the primitive form of both. Under each of these aspects, namely, the historical and the philosophical, we discover the origin of those early transitions which give character to its subsequent developments. In the one, the primitive theology, with its purer, though simpler, ideas of the moral and the supernatural, and its intensely religious notion of the divine nature as one universal God viewed mainly in the relations of Creator, Lawgiver, and Judge, tends to pass over into a mystical pantheism, assuming a mixed political and philosophical aspect; from whence its next descent is into an occult system of physics. In the other, or historical development, there become gradually blended with the old patriarchal traditions of supernatural intervention and of the real displays of divine attributes, the acts of the early heroes and founders of nations, immensely magnified in the refractions of the obscure media through which they have been transmitted, and in this way confounded with the divine realities which lie beyond. Thus the pure belief of one creating, governing, rewarding, and punishing God, which the infancy of the world—in this respect like the infancy of the individual—so easily received in all the grandeur of its simplicity, passed gradually into a polytheism representing the powers of nature; whilst the providential interpositions of the ancient patriarchal Deity who walked with the early races of men, and frequently manifested himself in acts both of benevolence and vengeance, were mingled with the heroic exploits of the deified dead. In this way, too, and from this source, did some of those sublime moral attributes, which are ascribed to this primitive Deity in the Old Testament, come down in the epithets of the poets; their glory indeed obscured—

As when the sun, new risen,
Looks through the horizontal misty air,
Shorn of his beams—

yet still possessing a moral grandeur, giving evidence of an older and holier birth, and often startling the reader by the associations in which they are found, or the strange contrast they present to the historico-mythological actions of the sensual divinities to whom they are immediately ascribed. That reader must, indeed, be morally and spiritually blind, who cannot see, in many of these sublime epithets of Homer and Æschylus, evidences of a far purer origin than those fables of the Cretan Zeus, or the Delian Apollo, or the Theban Bacchus, with which they are profanely mingled.

Thus viewed, mythology comes in time to present itself under three main aspects; by a careful analysis of which, some degree of order may be introduced among those blended elements that would otherwise seem only a chaos of unmeaning and contradictory legends. These may be styled the physical, the historical, and the moral. The origin of the two first we have attempted slightly to trace. The third may be regarded as the still preserved remains of that primitive character from which the others are a degeneracy, or as the relics of the old patriarchal religion, still present as a pervading element, and readily discoverable by any one who is not prejudiced in favor of some exclusively physical or historical theory.

No doubt some theological writers in former times may have gone to an absurd extreme, in endeavoring to trace connections between the Grecian or Egyptian fables and incidents recorded in the Scriptures. There were, it is true, many striking suggestions of this kind which came up very naturally from the stories of Prometheus, of Pandora's box, of the wars of the Gods with the Giants and Titans, of the Golden Age, and of the Flood; but these writers rendered the whole thing absurd by endeavoring to carry out their views in the history of Joshua, of Jephthah, of Samson, and in other cases that presented points of mere casual resemblance. The question, nevertheless, may be rationally entertained, whether the later authorities, especially of the German schools, have not gone very much too far towards the opposite extreme of the exclusively physical hypothesis.

There can be no doubt that this latter aspect is predominant in all ancient mythology. Here was that first travelled road from the supernatural to the natural or pantheistic, which Paul so graphically sets forth. Men did not like to retain the pure knowledge of God. It was too simple and child-like; it had too little of the philosophical. They were drawn to the creature, and worshipped the creature more than the creator, or *in addition* to the creator, as there are some grounds for rendering it. Thus the world *by wisdom* lost the true divine knowledge. The early men, in deifying the powers of nature, followed the same tendency which, in modern times, leads the merely scientific mind to interpose as much of visible cause and effect, or as many secondary agencies as possible, between ourselves and a far off personal Deity. The next most pervading aspect is doubtless that which we have styled the historical, and yet, through the whole, the old moral element plainly manifests itself to all who rightly look for it on the ground of the early historical revelations of the Scriptures and their declarations respecting the course of human depravity.

We may illustrate our meaning by taking the case of the Homeric Zeus. The physical aspect here makes itself quite manifest even in Homer. In Hesiod it is altogether predominant. Elsewhere it is so evident that the merest tyro cannot mistake it. Zeus is the aether—Ζεὺς Αἰθήρ—*the universal pervading fire*, as Héré, or Juno, is the lower atmosphere, Neptune, the liquid element, and Pluto, the earth. To the historical or Cretan Zeus, no careful student of antiquity can be at a loss in ascribing those scandalous actions which so mar some of the pages of Homer, and those unfilial proceedings which so much offended Plato. These had doubtless been transferred from the old dead hero or demi-god, whose exploits some early bard or tradition had first compared to, and then identified with, the divine. Again, with all this, there is no mistaking a higher and older element—a moral elevation which appears in the epithets employed in reference to the Homeric Zeus, and in the general character ascribed in the Iliad to

" the Father of gods and men," so superior to that of the other Homeric divinities, and which must have had a different and purer source. Thus then, it may be said, we have finally blended into one personality, the physical Zeus, the creation of some ancient Orphic and pantheistic mysticism early seeking something more philosophical and poetical than the simple primitive belief; next, the historical Zeus, arising from the corruption of some early Cretan legends; and both of these, in time, superadded to the conception of the old patriarchal Zeus coming down amidst it all, and yet preserving something of the obscured attributes of the ancient universal Deity of the Scriptures.

The author of this volume has undoubtedly made this physical aspect of the ancient mythology very predominant. In so doing she has followed the most of those very learned English and German authorities whom she has taken as her guides. The fact is not mentioned by way of censure; for the whole object of this introductory note is to commend to public notice both the work and the study of which it forms an admirable text book. Our design, therefore, in the present remarks, is merely to suggest a few thoughts which we deem important for the student to carry along with him in the reading of this or any other work on the subject. They are intended to be supplementary, rather than corrective—as falling in harmoniously with the general tenor of the work, rather than as inconsistent with it. It is ever well to carry with us what we have styled the moral, in distinction from the physical aspect of the old mythology; and it might have added to the value of the book, had the author devoted more attention to it throughout, or made it a separate subject of investigation. This, however, must have much enlarged the volume, and might have rendered it too large for the purposes intended, or too ponderous to be conveniently used as a manual in schools.

Again :—it was her avowed design to set forth what may be properly styled the He siodean Mythology, and, accordingly, she takes as her general guide or chart the genealogies of that poet. Now this, it must be confessed. is almost wholly, if not exclusively physical. No one can read it without seeing that the Theogonia is throughout a poetical system of physics. The moral aspect, we have said, enters largely into Homer; though greatly marred by the legendary or historically fabulous, whilst the physical but slightly appears.* In Hesiod, on the other hand, the latter or physical element is all in all. The same may be said of those productions styled the Orphic Hymns, which, although doubtless forgeries, as far as their modern forms are concerned, were, in all probability, imitations derived from a much older system of *poetical philosophy* that formed one of the earliest transitions from what may be styled the personal theology, to pantheism, or the worship of nature. In Hesiod, however, much of the Orphic or mystical aspect is lost, and it all comes out without disguise a mere cos-

---

* It is somewhat visible in the "*far darting Phœbus*" or Apollo. in the mythology of Iris, or the rainbow, and in some things said of the God of fire. and the genealogies of the rivers ; but these, like certain appearances of allegory. seem to come in incidentally in Homer, and not to have been in any case actually designed

mogony, instead of a true theism or even polytheism—in other words, a mere system
of physics. The very first lines, after the formal introduction to the Theogonia, show
.nis beyond doubt.

> Ἤτοι μὲν πρώτιστα Χάος γένετ',αὐτὰρ ἔπειτα
> Γαῖ' εὐρύστερνος, πάντων ἔδος ἀσφαλὲς αἰεὶ,
> Ἐκ Χάεος δ' Ἔρεβός τε, μέλαινά τε Νὺξ ἐγένοντο.
> Νυκτὸς δ' αὖτ' Αἰθήρ τε καὶ Ἡμέρη ἐξεγένοντο.*

They manifest the physical tendency of the poet as clearly as the more moral theology
of Homer is exhibited in one of the introductory lines of the Iliad—

> Διὸς δ' ἐτελείετο βουλῆ—†

No one can mistake as to what is intended by these marriages, and births, and wars,
and alliances, of Heaven, and Earth, and Chaos, and Night, and Day, together with
the genealogies that follow of the clouds, and waters, and winds, and elements, and
springs, and rivers, and seas. It is a fact, too, that the Theogonia was ever viewed in
this light by the ancient philosophers themselves. Aristotle quotes it simply as a
work on physics or cosmogony, and never thinks of giving it any other character.
Plato derives from it the flowing doctrine of the Ionic Materialists, although he traces
this also in some slight respects to Homer. Whilst, however, in the latter it only
appears incidentally, and without apparent design, in Hesiod it forms the prevailing
and controlling idea. In short, the Theogonia, instead of being classed with the poetry
of Homer, would rather take its place among such works as the fragments of Empedocles, or Lucretius De Natura Rerum.

It being, then, the avowed object of the author to set forth the Mythology of Hesiod,
and to take his genealogical lists as a chart or guide in the structural outlines of her
work, it may with truth be said that she has most faithfully and accurately performed
the task she had undertaken. She has consulted and brought forward the best authorities. She has presented, in a very clear manner, the principal physical theories that
have been worked out by German learning and ingenuity; and although many of these
are doubtless fanciful and ungrounded, they nevertheless are valuable as illustrating the
exuberant suggestiveness of the Hesiodean system.

It only remains, in this brief introduction, to point out some of the parts of the
ancient mythology in which moral ideas may be rationally regarded as predominan
notwithstanding the tendency among certain scholars to explain every thing by

---

* " First of all Chaos was born; then broad-breasted Earth, the firm seat of all things. From
Chaos Darkness and black Night were born, and then again from Night came Æther (or the fire)
and Day."—Hesiod, Theogonia, 117.
† "The counsel of Jove (in all these things) was being ' rought to pass." As is signified by the
impe:fec' ause.—Iliad i. 5

physical hypothesis. It is a very common theory, that the physical is earliest, the moral and theological of an after growth. A truer view, we think, reverses this— makes spiritual and moral ideas the more ancient, and the physical tendency, with the historical legendary corruptions, the result of that subsequent degeneracy from man's primitive state, which seems clearly taught in the Old Scriptures, and is described by the Apostle Paul in his Epistle to the Romans.

This moral aspect has been greatly obscured, and yet it remains capable of being traced. In some parts it is so visible that it would seem difficult to mistake it. It may be seen, as has been already observed, in many of the epithets of Zeus employed by Homer and the Grecian tragic poets. It is strongly manifested in that whole department of mythology which has reference to the infernal deities; although upon this much of the physical was afterwards superinduced. It flashes out upon the moral sense in the wondrous fable of the avenging-Furies. It appears in the striking personi fications of Nemesis, of Adrasta, or the *Inescapable*, if we may coin a term, and of the ancient Themis, who is ever represented with the sword and scales and sitting at the right hand of the Eternal Justice in the heavens. It gleams out, amid all that tends to obscure it, in the universal doctrine and practice of sacrifices. It shows itself in the mythology of the Destinies, and in that Grecian doctrine of fate (as it is called) which we contend (and as we think, could prove, if time and space permitted) had far more of the aspect of a stern *moral decree*, than of a *physical necessity*. Μοῖρα, as well as the Latin *Futum*, was the positive divine allotment, the divine *word*, or *decree*, the inexor- able law, or δίκη, inflicting wretchedness for some act of transgression, and coming down with immutable and unrelenting severity from generation to generation; as in some of those awfully wicked families whose descending crimes and woes form so fruitful a subject for the Greek tragic poets. In Homer it is the far-reaching βουλή, mentioned in the very beginning of the Iliad—the *decree* of Jove, made to embrace the whole of the war, together with a long list of subsequent events; to which decree he is represented as sacrificing his individual preferences, and yielding even the tenderest feelings of paternal affection.*

But to dwell on these topics would swell our introductory note beyond its prescribed limits. Our object has been simply to bring before the mind of the student an impor- tant view of the Ancient Mythology, which has been too much excluded from many works on the subject. If carried along in the reading and study of the volume, it will, it is thought, continually verify itself by calling out ideas demanding the most rational assent—at the same time such as might not have occurred had they not been thus sug-

---

* Reference is had to the passage—Iliad xvi. 432—which is frequently quoted in support of the opposite view. Jupiter is represented as debating with himself whether to rescue his son Sarpe- ion, about to be slain, or to yield him as a victim to destiny—πεπρωμένον αἴσῃ. Nothing, we think, can be clearer, than that the poet meant to represent Zeus as having the physical power to go against αἶσα or *right*, but his own βουλή, and ulterior purposes, forbade it.

gested, and the system with which they are connected kept constantly before the mind.

As before remarked, these thoughts are not presented as supplying a deficiency in the treatise, but merely as appropriate introductory matter which could come in better here than among the details and statements of the volume.

With a sincere esteem for the author of this well-executed work, and a strong sense of the importance of the Ancient Mythology as a branch of universal education, the writer would feel highly gratified if any introductory observations he could make should be regarded as adding to the utility of the volume, or as promoting the object for which its extensive circulation would be desirable among our various schools and institutions of learning.

TAYLER LEWIS.

New York University, Sept. 6, 1848

INTRODUCTION.

THE word Mythology is compounded of two Greek words, Muthos, a fable, and Logos, a discourse; and signifies a system of fables, or the fabulous history of the false gods of the heathen world.

Mythology in general is instruction conveyed in a tale. A fable, or mere legend without a meaning, can with little propriety deserve the name. And it is not strictly confined to narrative; signs and symbols are sometimes brought in play; and again, instruction is conveyed by simple ceremonies, or even by material representations.

The first, and most simple, flows from mere metaphor, and is an allegory in embryo; which extended and animated becomes a full-grown piece of perfect mythology. Metaphor is the produce of all nations, especially of the eastern. They have fiery fancies, strong passions, and are much given to taciturnity, and therefore, seldom speak but in dark sayings and mystic parallels; for metaphor is the language of passion, as simile is the effect of a warm imagination, which, when cooled and regulated, explains itself in diffuse and elaborate allegory.

The second sort, fable, and more properly deserving the name of mythology, are the admirable Æsopic tales, retaining the ancient simplicity, but so exquisitely adapted to the peculiar instincts of the birds and beasts employed in the fables, and so justly adapted to life and manners, that the natural La Fontaine's, the polite La Motte's, and the ingenious Gay's imitations, though highly interesting, only serve to show the Phrygian to be inimitable. It is, in effect, the happiest way of conveying instruction. The mind easily perceives the moral, and retains it with the same ease that the memory retains, uneffaced, the imagery in which it was conveyed, and their joint impression is persuasive and lasting.

We are indeed told, that truth, naked truth in sacred matters, is like the sun in its brightness, which mortal eye cannot steadfastly view without being dazzled : but allegory, the picture or semblance of truth, is compared to the Iris, the reflected image of the sun, which we behold with wonder and gaze at with ease. " The mind," says a pious philosopher, " attaches itself with higher satisfaction to the rainbow of fable, than to the resplendent sun of simple truth."

Fable is divided into various kinds; and the following is an example of the instructive, as used for the purpose by a famous orator : When Philip's son, the hereditary enemy of the liberty of Greece, demanded eight of their leading men to be delivered up to him, as the great impediment of mutual amity, " On a time," said Demosthenes to his fellow-citizens, " an embassy came from the wolves to the sheep, assuring them that the dogs by which they were attended were the sole occasion of the war ; wherefore, if they would give them up, all would be well, and end in lasting peace. The sheep were persuaded, gave up the dogs, and henceforth the wolves devoured them at pleasure."

A second sort is political, as the following : When Jupiter heard of the death of his son Sarpedon, in the rage of grief he called Mercury, the messenger of the gods, and gave him orders to go instantly to the Fates, and bring from them the strong box in which the eternal decrees were laid up. Mercury obeyed, went to the sisters, and omitted nothing that a wise and well-instructed minister could say to make them pacify the will of Jove. The sisters smiled, and told him that the other end of the golden chain which secured the box with the unalterable decrees, was so fixed to the throne of Jove, that were it to be unfastened, his master's seat itself might tremble."

A third sort of mythology consists in a material representation of virtue and vice, or instruction conveyed by wood and stone, instead of a tale. Such in some respects are all the badges and ensigns of the gods, when carved or cast in metal ;—and such the secret symbols delivered to the initiated in the several mysteries, which they carefully kept from vulgar eyes, showing them only upon certain signs. The example which best illustrates this material species of mythology, contains at the same time a beautiful moral : It was the temple of Honor, that had no entrance of its own, and the only passage to it was through the temple of Virtue. Happy the man who truly worships in the first, even if the ignorance of his contemporaries prevent him from entering the second ; he will yet. sooner or later, possess the station due to his merit.

But Mythology is a vast and various compound; a labyrinth through which no one thread can conduct us; since all the powers of heaven and earth, whatever is, whatever acts, whatever changes, and whatever remains the same, is, by some image congruent to its peculiar nature, variously painted in the mimic mirror of the universe. The primary great gods represent its principal parts and powers; and the numerous inferior train exhibit either the lesser powers of nature or their influences; or, they belong to human passions, and human transactions as connected with them. The rest are men adopted among the gods, and frequently blended with the original deities.

The course of time since the commencement of the world has been divided into three periods; the unknown, the fabulous, and the historical, which may be considered as the origin of mythological fables. The unknown comprehends all that space which the ancients supposed to have passed since the beginning of things, and of which we have no knowledge. In their opinion, all that was then transacted escaped the keenest sight. The fabulous began with the earliest notices of things; that is, in ancient style, with the births and marriages of the gods, and continued through the heroic ages until records and history introduced certainty and unfabled truth. Then commenced the historical period, which preserves its evidence to the present time.

Instead of this accurate division, the early poets sang, that Saturn (by whom they represent time) lurked long out of sight of heaven, and likewise devoured his own progeny as soon as they were born. This is plainly the unknown period. Jupiter, Saturn's son, together with Juno, Ceres, Pluto, Neptune, and Vesta, were produced without his knowledge, and preserved against his will. They conspired against their relentless parent, seized and bound him with a cord of wool never to be loosed, while almighty Jove holds the reins of government. Here is the fabulous period comprehending the birth and adventures of the gods, and the historical in the conclusion.

Religion, law, and philosophy united, were first taught to mankind in the form of fables; but these ancient fables convey no such ideas to the modern reader "The most ancient theology." says Plutarch, "both of the Greeks and barbarians, was natural philosophy involved in fables, that physically and mystically conveyed the truth to the learned;—as appears from the poems of Orpheus, the Egyptian rites, and the Phrygian traditions." A remark which it is necessary to keep in mind, in order to distinguish the pure, primitive doctrine from

later inventions ; for the regions of fable are wide and fertile, resem
bling Rabelais' iron work island, where swords grew from the trees,
and mushrooms sprang from the earth so exactly under them, that
every ripe sword fell precisely into its own scabbard, without missing
it a hair's breadth.

Nature is the parent of real mythology. She was associated with
philosophy in the great work of civilizing the rude tribes of the early
ages. Her robe of triple tissue, is a monstrous tale of feigned, allegorical personages engaged in action, who speak and act so much in
character, as at once to represent causes and narrate transactions, which
by striking the fancy and winning the heart, convey instruction agreeably to the mind. The history of the creation, or rise of the universe,
that the moderns call natural philosophy, and the ancients theogony,
or the generation of the gods, was the groundwork of the fabric ; the
powers that govern the world furnished the figures, and constitute the
design ; while the human character (moral philosophy), the passions
of men as they glow or languish, become tarnished or bloom with life,
gave a gloss and coloring to the whole. But this system of pure, primitive mythology was corrupted as soon as it spread beyond the nations
with whom it originated, and soon became blended with history, and
historical personages.

One definite source of this corruption proceeded from the method
in which the Greeks received their first ideas of gods and the worship
that was paid to them. The Assyrians and Phœnicians were taught
by the Egyptians ; the Greeks by the Egyptians in the first instance,
and at second hand by the Thracians and Pelasgi ; and the Grecians
in their turn taught the Romans. Mistakes necessarily arose in matters so mysterious, and made still more so by the symbolical manner
of treating them.

Another source of corruption, was the stupidity and superstition of
the vulgar, who often take representations for the things represented.
This corruption was so great even before the age of Heraclitus, that in
speaking of the ordinary worship, he exclaims against its gross abuses :
" The common people," says he, " pray to these statues, just as one
would talk to the walls of a house, knowing nothing who or what are
the gods to whom they are praying."

The perpetual changes of sublunary affairs, the catastrophes of nations, and vicissitudes of dominion, so inevitably absorb the manners,
language, and religion of a country, that no human foresight nor reach

of thought has yet founded an unvaried worship, or established an everlasting state. In vain did the Medes and Persians ordain their immutable statutes; in vain did the great Zoroaster or Dodonean Jove forbid the barbarous mysterious terms to be changed; in vain did the Egyptians or Assyrians institute significant solemn rites, or the Greeks and Romans appoint annual feasts, and enter into societies to perpetuate their celebration. All is obliterated or covered in oblivion. Adonis is no more lost and found in Egypt. Mylitta's temple no longer stands open for the ladies at Babylon; the glorious Olympics are forgotten in Elis; and the birthday of Augustus slips unheeded by, in spite of his temples and Flamens, or the Socii Augustales sacred to his memory.

When, therefore, nothing but the rite remains, whether preserved by stupid practice, or barely recorded in history, and the tradition is lost that should explain it, the allegory loses its meaning, and becomes a subject of criticism and conjecture.

There are many prevailing customs, both in sacred and civil matters, in regard to which there is the same uncertainty. A rite once received is carefully observed, and even spreads when the reasons for its institution have been long forgotten or are quite unknown. A learned father of the Latin church has recorded a complaint of Seneca, that after the example of the wicked Jews (for so he calls them), the greater part of the world have begun to lose the seventh part of their life in idleness, and the neglect of their necessary business; in which custom, the vanquished have given Jaw to the victors. Yet they, the Jews," says he, "know the cause of their own rite, while most of our people are doing that for which they can give no reason."

It is certain that mythology, as it now stands, cannot be fully understood without an accurate knowledge of the religious rites of the several nations from whom the Greeks received their gods; because upon some significant ceremony, referring to the nature or traditional tale of the exploits of the divinity, depends the whole legend, and sometimes the very name of the god himself. As the early Egyptian rites were all established by law, were all recorded, and were all typical and symbolical, the type or symbol, by an easy transition, not only obscurely intimated but directly expressed the thing typified, which was a great source of error. But, besides the original type, any remarkable part of the divine service, any mystical mixture as in the rites of Ceres, any striking posture, as in the feats of Pan, any uncouth garb of the hierophant or priest, was sufficient to fix an epithet, and that epithet gradually grow into a name.

Of the twelve great gods, the greatest, according to the Egyptians, was Pan, or the Universe, to whom the highest honors were paid. Next to him stood Latona or Night; Vulcan was next in dignity; and then Osiris and Isis, and Orus their son. That is, the Universe, comprehending nature and all her powers, was overwhelmed in darkness until the igneous, vivifying spirit broke loose, and dispelled the shade that had for eternal ages been brooding over it; then the sun and moon shone forth, parents of light, presiding over the generation of animals, the vegetation of plants, and the order of the whole. Instead of this, with the Grecian poets, Pan is the son of Mercury and Penelope;— Vulcan of Jupiter and Juno; and Latona, a lady with sable locks, gives birth to Apollo and Diana in Delos, or the Ortygian isle. The Roman poets carried their mythology still a step further from the original, and made it, for the most part, merely legendary ; compiling it from the traditionary tales of the Greeks without regarding their relation to the subject. Their own mythology was rude and simple, like the age in which it rose ; consisting mostly of rural deities, Faunus and Silvanus, Pales and Pomona, Janus, Tellus, and the like.

The original gods of the greatest nations were multiplied, first by the knowledge of the philosophers, and then by the fictions of the poets ; and most of all by the avarice and ambition of the priests, and the superstition of the credulous vulgar. Hence arose the distinction, *Dii majorum et minorum gentium,* gods of the greater and lesser nations. The former were the gods worshipped by the Egyptians, Assyrians, Grecians, and other wise nations ; all agreed in deifying the primogenial parts of the creation ; the latter gods were adopted from obscure people among whom their worship had taken rise.

These, the philosophers and wisest of the priests would not allow to be gods ; such as the Theban Hercules, Æsculapius, Castor and Pollux. because they had once been men. The others were the Cabeirim or mighty gods of the eastern nations ; and the Consentes, that is, the unanimous, or co-operating gods of the Romans, who consented to the deliberations of Jupiter's councils, and were universally worshipped. They were twelve in number, whose names Ennius has briefly expressed in these lines :

Juno, Vesta, Minerva, Ceres, Diana, Venus, Mars,
Mercurius, Iovi, Neptunus, Vulcanus, Apollo.

Their rites and mysteries were particularly famous in the island of Samothrace, Lemnos, and at Eleusis in the neighborhood of Athens. Originally, they were but two, Heaven and the Sun, the only gods of the Ethiopians, from whom Egypt is said to have derived both its religion and learning. These were worshipped in Samothrace, and the Egyptians made them first six, then eight, and long afterwards twelve; at which number the *Dii Cabiri Dicti*, gods called *Cabirs* (or mighty), rested in most nations; and when these deities are explained, and their import examined, the nature of things (the universe) is laid open, rather than the nature of the gods. The powers and parts of the universe were therefore the ancient *Cabir*, or mighty gods; and their mutual connections, operations, and productions were typically represented in the rites and mysteries of their religious worship.

In the contest for power, as related by the poets, Giants are brought in opposition to the gods; and from this mythological fiction it may be inferred, that the ancients did not ascribe to their gods immense magnitude. With them, intellectual power always had the preference over physical strength; and the monstrous beings that Oriental Fancy created, rose into existence only to be vanquished in their own deformity by the divine power of intellect. The beautiful propriety that avoids the monstrous, and assigns due limits to all the subjects represented, is the chief feature in the fine arts of the ancients; and not without reason does the Dorian imagination, in its oldest fiction, make the representation that shapelessness and enormity in form and limits, must necessarily be conquered and destroyed, before beauty and fitness can be established in their proper courses.

The whole fiction of the war of the gods seems to rest on that idea. Uranus, or the widely expanded vault of Heaven, was not to be comprehended in a single image. What Fancy had conceived was still too shapeless and unlimited. To Uranus, even his own children must become dangerous. They must rise against him, and his realm disappear in night and darkness. Even the names of the Titans indicate the want of bounds and limits in nature. Imagination shuns this boundlessness of form, which is necessarily fluctuating and uncertain—the modern deities conquer, and the Titans cease to reign, while their forms retreat as it were into mist, through whi h they are but dimly seen.

Still, they are regarded with veneration, for they are not brought in opposition to the modern gods, like pernicious beings to good and beneficent ones, and as such, deserving of hatred ; but power rose against power, and the vanquished remained great, even in his fall ; though the dominions of the Titans and the government of Saturn imply chaos and confusion, yet at the same time, liberty and equality were connected with them, which must cease under the rule of established power, and the candent bolts of thundering Jove.

Structures for the worship of heathen deities may be considered as among the most ancient monuments of antiquity. As soon as a nation had become in the least degree civilized, they took care to appropriate and consecrate particular spots to the worship of their deities.

In the earliest instances, they were contented with erecting altars in the open air, either of earth or ashes, and sometimes resorted, for purposes of worship, to the depths of solitary woods. At length, they acquired the practice of building cells, or chapels, within the enclosure of which they placed the images of their divinities, and there assembled to offer their supplications, thanksgivings, and sacrifices. These places of worship bore some resemblance to their own dwellings. The Troglodites adored their gods in grottoes; and the people who lived in cabins, erected edifices, the form of which was more or less assimilated to that kind of habitation. Herodotus and Strabo contend that the Egyptians first erected temples to the gods; and the first one erected in Greece, is attributed by Apollonius to Deucalion. Clemens Alexandrinus and Eusebius refer the origin of temples to the sepulchres built for the dead.

According to Pausanias, the oracle of Delphi in remote ages was consulted in a kind of arbor formed of laurels. That of Jupiter at Dodona, at a similar era, rendered its oracles by an old oak, as we learn both from Pausanias and Herodotus. In the vicinity of Magnesia, upon the Meander, was a grotto consecrated to Apollo, wherein was to be seen a very ancient statue of that god.

The first statues erected for the ancient gods hardly deserve the name, being only great stones set on end ; generally square, sometimes conical, sometimes pyramidal, or semicircular, and frequently quite rough, without even the touch of a tool. The oldest statues of Mercury were originally large square stones. The statue of the mother of the gods, brought from Phrygia, was a large black square stone.

The ancient Phœnicians had an image of the sun, which they believed not to have been formed by human art, but to have fallen immediately from heaven. It was a large black stone, round and broad at the base, but diminishing by degrees towards the top, and terminating in a slender point. The Megareans worshipped a large stone in the form of a pyramid, under the name of Apollo. Their more elegant neighbors, the Athenians, worshipped him in human shape, but with a head long and sharp, like a pyramid. A small globe split in two, and one of the halves set on a pole, was a symbol adored by the ancient Peönians.*

When the Greeks, at a subsequent period, surpassed all other people in cultivating the arts, they devoted much time, care, and expense, to the building of temples, rendering them in every way worthy of their destination. In every city of Greece, as well as its environs, and in the open country, was a large number of sacred temples ; and the most costly temple of each place was especially dedicated to its tutelary deity. Instances of this are found in the temple of Minerva at Athens, that of Diana at Ephesus, of Apollo at Delphi, of Jupiter at Olympia, of Venus at Paphos and Cytherea ; and of Jupiter Capitolinus at Rome. At Panionium, was a temple of Jupiter Heliconius erected by the Ionian colonies, and imported into Attica from Asia Minor. The Dorian colonies of Asia Minor had likewise a common sanctuary, the temple of Apollo Triopius. Near to Mylassa was a temple sacred to Jupiter Carius and common to the Carians, the Lydians, and the Mysians. In the territory of Stratonice was the temple of Jupiter Chrysaoreus belonging to the Carians. In the immediate vicinity of these edifices, the people, at fixed seasons, held assemblies for the purpose of sacrificing to the gods ; they also celebrated their fêtes on the same spot, and deliberated respecting the affairs of the entire nation.

---

* Plutarch, in his life of Numa, says, " His regulations concerning images seem likewise to have some relation to the doctrine of Pythagoras, who was of opinion that the First Cause was not an object of sense, nor liable to passion, but invisible, incorruptible, and discernible only by the mind. Thus Numa forbade the Romans to represent the Deity in the form either of man or beast. Nor was there among them formerly any image or statue of the Divine Being. During the first hundred and seventy years, they built temples, indeed, and other sacred domes, but placed in them no figure of any kind, persuaded that it is impious to represent things divine by what is perishable, and that we can have no conception of God, but by the understanding. His sacrifices, too, resembled the Pythagorean worship; for they were without any effusion of blood, consisting chiefly of flour, libations of wine, and other very simple and unexpensive things "

The most ancient Greek temples were very small. The *cella* was barely large enough to contain the statue of the presiding deity of the temple, and occasionally an altar in addition. Even in succeeding ages, when the riches and power, as well as the taste and skill of the Grecian states were augmented, they were not built on a great scale; for their object did not render extent necessary, since the priests alone entered the cella, and the people gathered in masses outside the walls. Exceptions were made in those dedicated to the tutelary divinities of towns, of those of the supreme gods, and of those appropriated to the common use of various communities. But this increased extent was chiefly displayed in the porticoes surrounding the cella, and was again enlarged by the peribolos, or enclosure within a wall, which separated it from the adjoining ground, as a sacred place appertaining to the temple. This enclosure was generally adorned with a profusion of statues, altars, and monuments. Sometimes it contained other smaller temples, or even a grove. The elevation and retirement of these Sacred Enclosures, gave additional beauty, dignity, and sanctity to the temples contained within them.

The Grecian temples had, for the most part, possessions of their own, which served to defray the expenses incurred in the service of the god. These possessions consisted partly in votive presents, which had been consecrated (especially where the divinities of health and prophecy were adored) by the hopes or the gratitude of the suppliants for advice or counsel. We know from several examples, especially from that of the temple of Delphi, that treasures were there accumulated, of more value, probably, than those of Loretto, or any other shrine in Europe. But as they were sacred to the gods, and did not come into circulation, they were for the most part unproductive treasures, possessing no other value than that which they received from the artist.

We could desire more accurate information respecting the administration of the treasures of the temples, for it seems hardly credible that the great stores of unwrought gold and silver should have been left entirely unemployed. But besides these treasures, the temples drew a large part of the revenue from lands which were not unfrequently consecrated to their service. When a new colony was founded, it was usual to devote at once a part of its territory to the gods. These resources were sufficient for the support of the temple, the priests, the various persons employed in the service of the temples, and perhaps the daily sacrifices; yet, the incense and other expenses, the celebration of the festivals with all the costs connected with them, still con-tinued a burden to the public.

The Greeks used three kinds of altars in their mythological worship; one, upon which they burned incense and made libations; another served for their sanguinary sacrifices; and the third received their burnt-offerings and sacred vases. Originally, they were made of heaps of earth, and sometimes of ashes, as that of the Olympian Jupiter, mentioned by Pausanias. There was also an altar of ashes at Thebes, consecrated to Apollo. In process of time, they were formed of brick and stones; such was the material of the famous altar at Delos. They were at first erected in groves, in the highways, and streets, as well as upon the tops of mountains; but after the introduction of temples, they were of course transferred to those edifices.

The form of altars, as well as their height, was various among the ancients; sometimes a perfect cube, which was the most common among the Greeks; at others, a parallelopipedon; sometimes round, at others octangular, triangular, &c., according to the material of which they were formed; and from some ancient medals we find there were altars of a circular form. Those which were constructed of metal, were generally triangular and formed like a tripod; those constructed of brick or stone were mostly cubical, and some have sculptured bases and pedestals like candelabra. According to Pausanias, some were constructed of wood; but by far the greater number that have been preserved to our times, are of marble.

On solemn festivals, the ancients decorated the altars of their deities with leaves or the branches of trees that were sacred to them; as those of Minerva with the olive; Venus with the myrtle; Apollo with the laurel; Pan with the pine, &c. And it was from these temporary decorations, that the ancient sculptors drew those elegant elements of foliage, which embellish the altars of antiquity. On others, that were intended for their sanguinary oblations, and were hollowed at the top to receive the blood of their victims, and the offered libations, are found heads and sculls of animals, vases, paterae,* and other instru-

---

* *Patera.*—A round dish, plate, or saucer. The paterae of the most common kind were small plates of red earthenware, on which an ornamental pattern was drawn, and which were sometimes entirely black.

Numerous specimens of them may be seen in the British Museum, and in other col-lections of ancient fictile vases. The more valuable paterae were metallic, being chiefly of bronze; but every family raised above poverty possessed one of silver, together with

ments; also, vessels of sacrifice mingled with garlands of flowers, such as were used to bind the victims; also, bands and other sacrificial accessories. When inscriptions were added, they alluded to the epoch of their consecration, the names of those who erected them, the motive of their erection, and the name of the deity to whose honor they were dedicated.

Altars as well as temples were considered so sacred by the ancient Greeks, that most of them had the privilege of protecting malefactors and debtors, and even rebellious slaves who fled to them for refuge. Plutarch informs us, that those who killed Cylon and his followers, when holding by the altars, were afterwards stigmatized with the epithets impious and profane; and Justin, in his history, observes, that the murder of Laodamia, by Milo, who had fled to the altar of Diana for protection, was the cause of his death, and of the public calamities of Æolia. In the comedy of Mostellaria, by Plautus, the inviolability of altars and temples appears to have existed among the Romans. Every temple, however, was not a sanctuary; but only those which had been made so by consecration. The first asylum is generally supposed to have been founded at Athens by the Heraclidæ, but some writers assert that there was one previously erected at Thebes, by Cadmus.

Independent of the public altars, the Greeks and Romans had private or domestic altars, which were dedicated to the lares and penates, the household gods of the ancients.

All the nations of antiquity were at some period of their history

a silver salt-cellar. In opulent families there was a plate of gold. These metallic plates were often adorned with figures engraved or embossed upon them. A beautiful specimen of a highly ornamented bronze dish, designed to be used in the worship of Mars, was found at Pompeii. The figures upon it represent Mercury and Apollo engaged in exploring the fates of Achilles and Agamemnon.

The ornamental pateræ sometimes represented leaves of fern, probably diverging from the centre. Gems were set in others. We read also of an amber dish having the countenance of Alexander the Great in the centre, and his history represented on the border. One in the British Museum is of white marble, and was found in the ruins of Hadrian's villa. It is fourteen inches in diameter, and one and three quarters high. It is cut with skill and delicacy, the marble not being much more than a quarter of an inch thick. In the centre is sculptured a female Bacchante, in a long tunic, and holding a scarf which floats over her head. This centre piece is encircled by a wreath of ivy. The decorations indicate the appropriation of the plate to the worship of Bacchus. Plates were sometimes made so as to be used with either side downward. In these, both surfaces were ornamented. Plates were further distinguished by being either with or without a base, a boss in the middle, and having feet and handles.

addicted to the custom of offering sacrifices to the deities whom they worshipped. The origin of the practice is attributed by some to the Phœnicians, and by others to the Egyptians ; while Ovid imagines, from the import of the words *victim* and *hostia*, that no bloody sacrifices were offered before the prevalence of wars, when nations became victorious over their enemies. These, however, are mere hypotheses not borne out by historical research or tradition, and are entitled to little regard.

The principal sacrifices among the Hebrews consisted of bullocks, sheep, and goats ; but doves and turtles were accepted from those who were not able to bring these animals, which were to be perfect and without blemish. The rites of sacrificing were various, and all are minutely described in the books of Moses.

The manner of sacrificing among the Greeks and Romans was as follows. In the choice of a victim they took care that it was without blemish or imperfection, and the bull was to be one that had never been yoked. Having pitched upon a victim, they gilded the forehead and horns, especially if a bull, heifer, or cow ; the head was adorned with a garland of flowers, a woollen infula,* or holy fillet, from which hung two rows of chaplets with twisted ribbons ; on the middle of the body was a kind of stole, which hung down on either side ; the lesser victims were also adorned with garlands, and bunches of flowers, together with white tufts, or wreaths.

The victims thus prepared were brought before the altar, the lesser being driven to the place, and the greater led by a halter ; if they made any struggle, or refused to go, the resistance was considered an ill-omen, and the sacrifice frequently set aside. The victim thus brought, was carefully examined to see that it was without defect ; then the priest, clad in his sacerdotal habit, and accompanied by the sacrificers and other attendants, and being washed and purified according to the ceremonies prescribed, turned to the right and passed round the altar, sprinkling it with meal and holy water, and also sprinkling those who were present. The crier then proclaimed, with a loud voice, "Who is here ?" To which the people replied, " Many and good." The priest

---

* *Infula.*—A flock of white and red wool, which was tightly twisted, drawn into the form of a wreath or fillet, and used by the Romans as an ornament on festive and solemn occasions. In sacrificing, it was tied with a white band to the head of the victim, and also of the priest, more especially in the worship of Apollo and Diana. The torta infula" was worn also by the vestal virgins.

then having exhorted the people to join with him, by saying, "Let us pray," confessed his own unworthiness, acknowledging that he had been guilty of divers sins, for which he begged pardon of the gods, and his hope that they would be pleased to grant his requests, accept the oblations offered them, and send them all health and happiness; and to this general form, the priest added petitions for such particular favors as were then desired. Prayers being ended, he took a cup of wine, and having tasted it himself, caused his assistants to do the like; and then poured forth the remainder between the horns of the victim. The priest or the crier, and sometimes the most honorable person in the company, then killed the beast by knocking it down, or cutting its throat. If the sacrifice was in honor of the celestial gods, the throat was turned up towards Heaven; but if they sacrificed to the heroes or infernal deities, the victim was killed with his throat towards the ground. If by accident the beast escaped the stroke, leaped up after it, or expired with pain and difficulty, it was thought to be unacceptable to the gods. The victim being killed, the priest inspected its entrails and made predictions from them. They then poured wine, together with frankincense, into the fire to increase the flame, and then laid the sacrifice on the altar, which in the primitive times was burnt whole to the gods, and thence called a holocaust; but in after times, only part of the victim was consumed in the fire, and the remainder reserved for the sacrificers; the thighs, and sometimes the entrails were burnt to their honor, and the company feasted upon the rest. During the ceremony, the priest and the person who gave the sacrifice jointly prayed, laying their hands upon the altar. Sometimes musical instruments were played during the time of sacrifice, and on some occasions, the people danced around the altar singing sacred hymns in honor of the gods.

The barbarous practice of human sacrifices followed that of offering brutes. When men had gone so far as to indulge the fancy of bribing their gods by sacrifice, it was natural for them to think of enhancing the value of so cheap an atonement by the cost and variety of the offering; and when oppressed with suffering, they never rested until they had offered what they conceived to be the most precious of all, a human sacrifice.

" It was customary" (says Sanchoniathon) " in ancient times, in great and public calamities, for princes and magistrates to offer the dearest of their offspring in sacrifice to the avenging dæmons." Sanchonia-

thon wrote of Phœnicia. But the practice prevailed in every nation
of which we have received any ancient account. The Egyptians were
addicted to it in the early part of their monarchy; and the Cretans
likewise, who retained it for a longer time. The nations of Arabia did
the same. The people of Dumah, in particular, sacrificed a child every
year; then burying it underneath an altar, made use of it as an idol;
for their religion did not admit of images.

The Persians buried people alive. Amestris, the wife of Xerxes, is
said to have entombed twelve persons alive for the good of her soul.
It would be impossible to enumerate every city or province where these
dire practices obtained. The Cyprians, the Rhodians, the Phocians,
the Ionians, those of Chios, Lesbos, Tenedos, all had human sacrifices.
The natives of the Tauric Chersonesus offered to the goddess Diana
every stranger whom chance threw upon their coast. Hence arose that
just expostulation in Euripides upon the inconsistency of the proceeding; wherein much good reasoning is implied. Iphigenia wonders, as the goddess delighted in blood, that every villain and murderer should be allowed to escape, nay, were driven from the threshold
of the temple; whereas, if an honest man chanced to stray thither, he
was immediately seized and put to death.

The Pelasgi, in times of scarcity, vowed the tenth of all that should
be born to them for a sacrifice, in order to procure plenty. Aristome-
nes, the Messenian, slew three hundred noble Lacedemonians, among
whom was Theopompus the king of Sparta, at the altar of Jupiter at
Ithome. The Lacedemonians, a severe and revengeful people, undoubtedly made ample returns; for they offered the like victims to
Mars. Their festival of the Diamastigosis is well known; when the
Spartan boys were whipped in the sight of their parents, before the
altar of Diana, with such severity that they often expired under the
torture.

The Romans were accustomed to like sacrifices. They not only devoted themselves to the infernal gods, but they constrained others to
submit to the same horrid doom. Hence we read in Titus Livius, that
in the consulate of Æmilius Paulus and Terentius Varro, two Gauls,
a man and a woman, and two Greeks were burned alive, in the ox mar-
ket at Rome, where was a place under ground walled round to receive
them, which had previously been used for the same cruel purpose. He
speaks of it as a sacrifice not properly Roman; that is, not originally
of Roman institution, yet it was frequently practised there by public

authority. Plutarch makes mention of a like instance in the consul-
ship of Flaminius and Furius; and there is reason to think, that all
the principal captives who graced the triumphs of the Romans, were, at
the close of that cruel pageantry, sacrificed at the altar of Jupiter Capitolinus.

The Gauls and Germans were so devoted to this shocking custom,
that no business of any moment was transacted among them without
being prefaced by the blood of men. They were offered up to various
gods; but particularly to Hesus, Taranis, and Thautates. These
deities are mentioned by Lucan, where he enumerates the various nations who followed the fortunes of Cæsar.

The altars of these gods were far removed from the common resort
of men; being generally situated in the depths of the woods, that the
gloom might increase the horror of the scene, as well as to give a reverence to the place and proceeding. The devoted victims were led
thither by the Druids who presided at the solemnity, and performed
the cruel offices of the sacrifice. Tacitus notices the Hermunduri, in
a war with the Catti, wherein they had greatly the advantage, at the
close of which they made one general sacrifice of all that were taken
in battle. The poor remains of the legions under Varrus suffered in
some degree the same fate.

There were many places appropriated to this purpose all over Gaul
and Germany; but especially in the mighty woods of Arduenna, and
the great Hercynian forest; a wild that extended above thirty days'
journey in length. The places set apart for this solemnity were held
in the utmost reverence, and only approached at particular seasons.
Lucan mentions a grove of this sort near Massilia, which even the Roman soldiers were afraid to violate, though commanded by Cæsar. It
was one of those set apart for the sacrifices of the country.

These practices prevailed among all the people of the north, of whatever denomination. The Massagetæ, the Scythians, the Getes, the
Sarmatians, all the various nations upon the Baltic, particularly the
Suevi and Scandinavians, held it as an established principle, that their
happiness and security could be obtained only at the expense of the
lives of others. Their chief gods were Thor and Woden, who they
thought could never be sufficiently glutted with blood. They had
many celebrated places of worship, especially in the island of Rugen,
near the mouth of the Oder, and in Zealand; some, too, were very
famous among the Semnones and Naharvalli. But the one most fre-

quonted, and held in greatest reverence, was at Upsal; where was held every year a grand celebration which continued for nine successive days. During this time they sacrificed animals of all sorts; but human victims were the most numerous and considered the most acceptable.

RELIGION OF ANCIENT GREECE (Heeren).

As the Greeks received most, if not all of their gods from abroad, they of course received them as symbols of natural objects and powers; and the further we look back into the Grecian theogony, the more clearly do their gods appear as such beings. He who reads with tolerable attention the early systems as set forth in Hesiod, cannot mistake this for a moment, nor can it be denied, that there are traces of it in the gods of Homer. That his Jupiter designates the pure ether, his Juno the atmosphere, his Apollo the sun, is obvious in many of his narrations. But it is equally obvious, that his prevailing notion is not the ancient symbolical one, but that his Jupiter is already the ruler of the gods and men; his Juno, the queen of Olympus.

This, then, is the essential peculiarity of the popular religion of the Greeks; they gradually dismissed the symbolical representations, and not only dismissed them, but adopted something more human and more sublime in their stead. The gods of the Greeks were *moral pei sons.*

When we call them moral persons, we do not mean to say that a higher degree of moral purity was attributed to them than humanity can attain (indeed, the reverse is well enough known); but rather, that the whole nature of man, with its defects and its excellences, was considered as belonging to them, with the additional notions of superior physical force, a more delicately organized system, and a more exalted, if not always a more beautiful form. Now these ideas became generally prevalent, and were entertained by the whole people; and thus an indestructible wall of division was raised between the Grecian and foreign gods. The former were moral beings; this was their leading character; they would have been mere names if this had been taken from them; but the gods of the barbarians remained only personifications of certain objects and powers of nature; and hence neither a moral nature nor character belonged to them, although the human shape and certain actions and powers were attributed to them.

Having illustrated the essential difference between the Grecian and foreign gods, and shown in what the transfo:mation of the foreign gods, adopted by the Greeks, consisted, the question arises, how and by what means did that transformation take place ?

By means of poetry and the arts. Poetry was the creating power; the arts confirmed the representations which she had called into being by investing them with visible forms. And here we come to the im· portant step, from which we must proceed in continuing our inquiry.

"Whence each of the gods is descended, whether they have always existed," says the father of history, "and what were their shapes, all this the Greeks have but recently known. Hesiod and Homer, whom I do not esteem more than four hundred years older than myself, are the poets who invented for the Grecians their theogony; gave the gods their titles; fixed their rank and occupations; and described their forms. The poets who are said to have lived before these, lived, as I believe, after them."

This remarkable account deserves a careful attention. The historian expressly remarks that this is his own hypothesis, not the belief of others. He may certainly have been mistaken; but he would hardly express himself so explicitly, unless he had believed himself warranted to do so. We must receive his opinion as the result of such an investigation as could in his age be carried on; and can we do more than he?

He names Homer and Hesiod; and naturally understands by them the authors of the poems which already bore their names: the two great epic poems of Homer, and at last the theogony of Hesiod. The case does not become changed, even if those productions are, agreeably to a modern opinion, the works of several authors. It would only be necessary to say that it was the ancient epic poets of the schools of Homer and of Hesiod, who invented the gods of the Greeks; and per-· haps this manner of expression is the more correct; for it would be difficult to doubt that the successors of those poets contributed their share.

According to Herodotus, these poets were the first to designate the forms of the gods; that is, they attributed to them not merely the human figure, but the human figure in a particular shape. They dis· tinguished, moreover, their kindred, their descent, their occupations; they also fixed the personal relations of each individual; and therefore gave them the epithets which expressed these attributes. But if we collect these observations into one, they signify nothing less than that the poets were the authors of the popular religion, in so far as it was grounded on definite representations of the several divinities.

This is not intended to imply that Homer made it his object to be the creator of a national religion. He only made a poetical use of the previous popular belief. But that poetical spirit, which left nothing indistinctly delineated in the heroes whose deeds he celebrated, bring-ing before our eyes their persons and their characters, effects the same with the gods. He no more invented his divine personages, than he did his heroes; but he gave their character to the one and the other. The circle of his gods is limited to a small number. They are inhabit-ants of Olympus, and if they do not all belong to the same family, they yet belong to the same place; and they usually live together, at least when that is required by the purposes of the poet. Under such circumstances, an inferior poet might have felt the necessity of giving them individuality. And how much more a Homer? But that he executed in so perfect a manner, is to be ascribed to the superiority of his genius.

Thus the popular notions entertained of the gods were first estab-lished by Homer, and established never to be changed. His poems continued to live in the mouths of his nation; and how could it have been possible to efface images which were painted with such strokes and colors? Hesiod is, indeed, named with him; but what are his catalogues of names compared with the living forms of Homer?

In this manner, by means of the epic poets, that is, almost exclu-sively by Homer, the gods of the Greeks were raised to the rank of moral beings possessed of definite characters. As such, they gained life in the conceptions of the people; and however much may have been invented respecting them in the poetry of a later age, no one was permitted to represent them under a figure, or with attributes differ-ent from those which were consistent with the popular belief. We soon perceive the various consequences which this must have had on the civilization and improvement of the nation.

The more a nation conceives its gods to be like men, the nearer does it approach them, and the more intimately does it live with them. According to the earliest views of the Greeks, the gods often wandered amongst them, shared in their business, requited with good or ill in conformity to their recent reception, and especially to the number of gifts and sacrifices with which they were honored. In this manner those views decided the character of religious worship, which received from them not merely its forms, but also its life and meaning. How could this worship have received any other than a cheerful, friendly character? The gods were gratified with the same pleasures as mortals; their delights were the same; the gifts which were offered them were the same which please men; there was a common, a correspondent enjoyment. With such conceptions, it was natural that their holidays should have been joyous. And as their joy was expressed by dance and song, both of these necessarily became constituent parts of their religious festivals.

It is another question: What influence must such a religion have on the morals of a nation? The gods were not represented as pure moral beings, but as swayed by human passions, and liable to human infirmities. At the same time, the Greeks never entertained the idea that their divinities were to be held up as models of virtue; and hence the injury done to morality by such a religion, however warmly the philosophers afterwards spoke against it, could hardly have been so great as we with our prepossessions should at first imagine. If it was not declared a duty to become like the gods, no excuse for the imitation could be drawn from the faults and crimes attributed to them. Besides, these stories were esteemed, even by the vulgar, only as poetical fictions; and they felt little concern about their truth, or want of credibility. There existed, independent of those tales, the fear of the gods as higher beings, who, on the whole, desired excellence, and abhorred and sometimes punished crime. This punishment was inflicted in this world; for the poets and the people of Greece for a long time believed that there was no punishment beyond the grave, except for those who had been guilty of direct blasphemy against the gods. Their system of morals was on the whole deduced from the fear of the gods; that fear also produced the observance of certain duties which were of great practical importance; as for example, the inviolable character of suppliants, who stood under the peculiar protection of the gods; the sanctity of oaths and the like; of which the violation was also considered as a crime against the gods. Thus the popular religion of the Greeks was undoubtedly a support of morality, though not to the same degree as in Christian countries. But that its importance was felt as a means of bridling the licentiousness of the people, is sufficiently clear from the care which the state took during its better days to preserve the popular religion, and from the punishments inflicted on those who corrupted it or denied its gods.

If, however, the influence of popular religion in the moral character of the Greeks should be differently estimated, there is no less room for

doubt as to its influence on taste ; for that was formed entirely by the
popular religion, and continued indissolubly united to it.

By the transformation of the Grecian deities into moral agents, a
boundless field was opened for poetical invention. By becoming hu
man, the gods became peculiarly fitted for poetry. The muse of the
moderns has attempted to represent the Supreme Being in action, which
she could only do by investing him as far as possible with human attributes. The failure of this attempt is well known : it was vain to en
deavor to deceive us with respect to the chasm which lay between oui
more sublime ideas of the Divinity, and the image under which he is
represented. But the case was altogether different in ancient Greece
The poet was not only allowed, but compelled to introduce the gods in
a manner consistent with popular belief, if he would not fail of producing
the desired effect. The great characteristics of human nature were ex
pressed in them ; they were exhibited as so many different archetypes.
The poet might relate of them whatever he pleased ; but he never was
permitted to alter the original characters, whether he celebrated their
own actions or introduced them as participating in the exploits of mortals. Although themselves immortal, they always preserved the human
character, and excited a corresponding interest ; with their weaknesses
and faults they stood nearer to man than if they had been represented
as possessing the perfection of moral excellence.

Thus the popular religion of the Greeks was essentially poetical.
There is no need of a long argument to show that it also decided the
character of Grecian art, by affording an inexhaustible supply of subjects.

On this point a single remark will suffice. Among the nations of
the east, the plastic art not only never created forms of ideal beauty,
but was rather exercised in producing hideous ones. The monstrous
figures of their gods, which we have already mentioned, are proofs of
it. The Grecian artist was secure against any thing similar to this,
when their gods had become not merely physical, but human, moral
beings. He never could have thought of representing a Jupiter or
Juno with ten arms ; he would have destroyed his own work by offending the religious popular notions. Hence he was forced to remain true
to the pure human figure, and was thus brought very near the step
which was to raise him still higher and give ideal beauty to his images.
That step he would probably have taken without assistance ; but the
previous labors of the poets made it more natural and more easy

Phidias found in Homer the idea of his Olympian Jupiter; and the most sublime image in human shape which time has spared to us, the Apollo of the Vatican, may be traced to the same origin.

Besides the popular religion, Greece possessed also a religion of the initiated, preserved in the mysteries. Whatever we may think of these institutions, and whatever idea we may form of them, no one can doubt that they were of a religious nature. They must then have necessarily stood in a certain relation to the religion of a people; but we shall not be able to explain, with any degree of probability, the nature of that relation, until we trace them to their origin.

We must preface this inquiry with a general remark. All the mysteries of the Greeks, as far as we are acquainted with them, were introduced from abroad; and we can still point out the origin of most of them. Ceres had long wandered over the earth before she was received at Eleusis, and erected there her sanctuary. Her secret rites at the Thesmophoria, according to the account of Herodotus, were first introduced by Danaüs, who brought them from Egypt to the Peloponnesus. Whether the rites of Orpheus and Bacchus originally belonged to the Thracians or the Egyptians, they certainly came from abroad. Those of the Curetes and the Dactyli originated in Crete.

It has often been said, that these institutions suffered in process of time many and great alterations; that they commonly degenerated; or, to speak more correctly, that the Grecians accommodated them to themselves. It was not possible for them to preserve among the Greeks the same character which they had among other nations. And here we are induced to ask: What were they originally? How were they introduced and preserved in Greece? And in what relation did they stand to the popular religion?

The answer to these questions is contained in the remarks which we have already made on the transformation and appropriation of foreign gods by the Greeks. Most of those gods, if not all of them, were received as symbolical, physical beings; the poets made of them moral agents; and as such they appear in the religion of the people.

The symbolical meaning would have been lost if no means had been provided to ensure its preservation. The mysteries, it seems, afforded such means. Their great end, therefore, was, to preserve the knowledge of the peculiar attributes of those divinities which had been incorporated into the popular religion under new forms; what powers and objects of nature they represented; how these, and how the universe came into being ; in a word, cosmogonies, like that contained in the Orphic doctrines. But this knowledge, though it was preserved by oral instruction, was perpetuated no less by symbolical representa tions and usages ; which, at least in part, consisted of those sacred traditions and fables of which we have already made mention. "In the temple of Sais," says Herodotus, "representations are given by night of the adventures of the goddess ; and these are called by the Egyptians, mysteries ; of which, however, I will relate no more. It was from thence that these mysteries were introduced into Greece." Admitting this even to be the chief design of the mysteries, it does not follow that it was the only one. Indeed, it is very probable that, in the progress of time, great variety of representations may have arisen in the mysteries ; their original meaning might perhaps be gradually and entirely lost, and another be introduced in its stead.

Those passages may therefore be very easily explained, which import that the mysteries, as has been particularly asserted of those of Eleusis, exhibited the superiority of civilized over savage life, and gave instructions respecting a future life and its nature. For what was this more than an interpretation of the sacred traditions which were told of the goddess, as the instructress in agriculture, of the forced descent of her daughter to the lower world, &c. And we need not be more astonished, if in some of their sacred rites we perceive an excitement carried to the borders of that enthusiastic frenzy, which belonged indeed peculiarly to the east, but which the Greeks were not unwilling to adopt. For we must not omit to bear in mind that they shared the spirit of the east, living as they did on the boundary line between the east and west. As those institutions were propagated further to the west they lost their original character. We know what the Bacchanalian rites became at Rome ; and had they been introduced north of the Alps, what form would they have there assumed ? To those countries it was indeed possible to transplant the vine, but not the service of the god to whom the vine was sacred. The orgies of Bacchus were equally unsuited to the cold soil and inclement forests of the north, and to the character of its inhabitants.

The secret doctrines which were taught in the mysteries, may have degenerated into mere forms and an unmeaning ritual. And yet the mysteries exercised a great influence on the spirit of the nation, not of the initiated only, but also of the great mass of the people ; and perhaps they influenced the latter still more than the former. They preserved the reverence for sacred things, and this gave them their political importance. They produced that effect better than any modern secret societies have been able to do. The mysteries had their secrets, but not every thing connected with them was secret. They had, like those of Eleusis, their public festivals, processions, and pilgrimages, in which none but the initiated took a part, but of which no one was prohibited from being a spectator. Whilst the multitude were permitted to gaze at them, they learned to believe that something sublimer than any thing which they knew was revealed to the initiated; and while the value of that sublimer knowledge did not consist in secresy alone, it did not lose any of its value by being concealed.

Thus, the popular religion and the secret doctrines, although always distinguished from each other, united in serving to curb the people. The condition and the influence of religion on a nation are always closely connected with the situation of those persons who are particularly appointed for the service of the gods, the priests. The regulations of the Greeks concerning them deserve the more attention, since many unimportant subjects of Grecian antiquities have been treated with an almost disproportionate expense of industry and erudition . but with respect to the priesthood of the nation, we are as yet left without an investigation corresponding to the importance of the subject. The very abundance of matter renders it the more difficult, for very little can be expressed in general terms, and many dangers were brought about by time.

During the heroic age, we learn from Homer, that there were priests who seem to have devoted themselves exclusively to that vocation. We readily call to mind Calchas, Chryses, and others. But even in that age such priests appear but seldom; and it does not appear that their influence over the rest of the people was considerable. The sacred rites in honor of the gods were not performed by them alone; they were not even required at the public solemnities. The generals and commanders themselves offer their sacrifices, perform the prayers, and observe the signs which indicated the result of an enterprise. In a word, kings and generals were at the same time priests.

Traces of these very ancient regulations were preserved for a long time among the Greeks. The second archon at Athens, who presided at the public ceremonies of worship, was called the king, because he had to prepare the sacred rites, which were formerly regulated by the kings. He had his assistants : and it was necessary for his wife to be of irreproachable character, as she also had secret religious services to perform. He was, however, like the other archons, annually appointed, and the election was by lot. The priests and priestesses of the several divinities were for the most part chosen by vote. But the priestesses could be married, and the priests seem by no means to have been excluded by their station from participating in the offices and occupations of the citizens. There were some sacerdotal offices which were hereditary in certain families. But the number of them seems to have been inconsiderable. In Athens, the Eumolpidæ possessed the privilege that the hierophant, or first director of the Eleusinian rites, as well as the other three, should be taken from his family. But the place of hierophant could not be obtained except by a person of advanced years; and those other offices were probably not occupied during life, but frequently assigned anew. How far the same was true in other cases is but seldom related. At Delphi, the first of the Greek oracles, the Pythian priestess was chosen from among the women of the city, and was cut off from all intercourse with men. It is hardly probable, from the violent exertions connected with the delivery of the oracles, that the same person could long fill the place. Here, as elsewhere, people were appointed for the service without the temple, and were even educated within its limits. But the service within the temple was performed by the most considerable citizens of Delphi, who were chosen by lot. The sanctuary of Dodona, where the responses of the oracle were made, as at Delphi and in other temples, by priestesses, seems to have belonged to the family of the Selli, of which Homer makes mention; but we have no particular accounts respecting the family.

The regulations respecting priests proposed by Plato in his laws, show most clearly, that the ideas of the Greeks required that the offices of priests should not long be filled by the same persons. " Let the election of the priests," says he, " be committed to the god, by referring the appointment to lot; those on whom the lot falls must submit to an examination. But each priesthood shall be filled for one year, and no longer, by the same person; he who fills it may not be less than sixty years old. The same rules shall apply to the priestesses."

We infer from all this, that though the regulations respecting the priesthood were not the same in all parts of Greece, that office was commonly filled for a limited time only; was regarded as a place of honor (to which, as to the other mysteries, appointments were made by lot after an examination); and was subjected to the same rotation with the rest. They to whom it was intrusted were taken from the class of active citizens, to which they again returned: and even whilst they were priests, they were by no means withdrawn from the regular business of civil life. The priesthood did not gain even that degree of consistency which it had at Rome; where the priests, though they were not separated from secular pursuits, formed separate colleges, like those of the pontiffs and augurs, and the members of them were chosen for life. Since the priesthood then, among the Greeks in general, and in the several states, never formed a distinct order, it could not possess the spirit of a party, and it was quite impossible for any thing like priestcraft to prevail. Religion and public acts of worship were so far considered inviolable, that they were protected by the State; and thus a degree of intolerance was produced which led even to injustice and cruelty. But we do not find that the priests were peculiarly active in such cases. It was the people which believed itself injured; or a political party, or individual demagogues, who had some particular object in view.

As the priests of the Greeks formed no distinct class in society, it is evident that they could have no such secret system of instructions as was possessed by those of Egypt. No such system can therefore be contrasted with the popular religion; instead of it, there were the mysteries; but the initiated were not all of them priests, nor was it necessary for every priest to be initiated into the mysteries. Any person could be admitted to them whose condition in life and behavior were found to deserve the distinction.

These regulations led to important consequences. There was in the nation no separate class which claimed an exclusive right to certain branches of scientific and intellectual education, and preserved that exclusive right by means of written characters, intelligible only to themselves. That which ought to be the common property, and is the noblest common property of mankind, was such among the Greeks. And hence the spirit of philosophy was enabled to develop itself with freedom. The most ancient philosophy of the Greeks, as it appeared at first in the Ionic school, perhaps originally stood in close union with religion, and may indeed have proceeded from it; for who does not perceive the close connection between speculations on the elements of things, and the ancient conceptions of the gods as powers or objects

. of nature? But religion could not long hold philosophy in fetters. It could not prevent the spirit of free inquiry from awakening and gaining strength; and thus it was possible for all sciences which are promoted by that spirit to assume among the Greeks a decided and peculiar character. In the intellectual culture of the east, all scientific knowledge was connected with religion; but as these were kept separate by the Greeks, science gained among them that independent character which distinguishes the west, and which was communicated to the nations of whom the Greeks were the instructors.

As in Greece the priests never formed a distinct order, and still less a caste, religion never was united to the state to the same extent as in other countries. It was sometimes subservient to public policy, but never became its slave. The dry, prosaic religion of the Romans could be used or abused to such purposes; but that of the Greeks was much too poetical. The former seems to have existed only for the sake of the state: and the latter, even when it was useful to the state, appears to have rendered none but voluntary services. The patricians confined the popular religion of Rome within the strict limits of a system; but in Greece religion preserved its freedom of character.

TABLE OF HESIOD'S THEOGONY.

From Chaos.

Earth,
Love,
Erebus,
Night.

From Erebus and Night.

Sunshine or the Sky,
Day.

From Earth.

Heaven,
Hills,
Groves,
Sea.

From Heaven and Earth.

Ocean,
Cœus,
Hyperion,
Japetus,
Rhea,
Themis,
Mnemosyne,
Phœbe,
Tethys,
Saturn,
Brontes, ⎫
Steropes, ⎬ Cyclops.
Arges, ⎭
Cottus, ⎫
Gyges, ⎬ Giants.
Briareus, ⎭
Themis.

From Heaven.

Giants,
Furies,
Wood Nymphs.

From Night.

Destiny,
Fate,
Death,

Sleep,
Dreams,
Momus,
Care.

The Hesperides.

Clotho, ⎫
Lachesis, ⎬ Fates
Atropos, ⎭
Nemesis,
Fraud,
Loose Love,
Old Age,
Strife.

From Strife.

Affliction,
Oblivion,
Famine,
Sorrows,
Combats,
Murders,
Wars,
Slaughters,
Deceits,
Quarrels,
Lies,
License,
Perverted Law,
Injury,
Perjury.

From Sea and Earth.

Nereus,
Thaumas,
Phorcys,
Cete,
Eurybia.

From Nereus and Doris.

Nereids,
Proto,
Eucrate,
Lao,

Amphitrite,
Eudore,
Thetis,
Glauce,
Cymothöe,
Spio,
Thalia,
Melite,
Eulimine,
Agave,
Pasithea,
Erato,
Eunice,
Doro,
Proto,
Pherusa,
Dunamene,
Nisaca,
Actea,
Protomedia,
Doris,
Panope,
Galataen,
Hippothöe,
Hipponöe
Cymodoce,
Cymatologe,
Cumo,
Heione,
Halimea,
Glauconome,
Pontoposea,
Liagore,
Evagore,
Laomedia,
Polynome,
Autonoe,
Lysianassa,
Evarne,
Psamathe,
Menippe,
Neso,
Eupompe,
Themisto,
Pronöe,
Nemertes.

From Thaumas and Electra.

· Iris,
Aello,
Ocypete, } The Harpies

From Phorcys and Ceto.

Pephrido, } The Grææ.
Enyo,
Stheno,
Euryale, } Gorgons.
Medusa,

The Serpent Guard of the Golden Fruit.

Chrysaor,
Echidna.

From Chrysaor and Callirrhoë.

Geryon,
Echidna. ·

From Typhæus and Echidna.

Orthrus,
Cerberus,
Hydra,
Chimæra.

From Orthrus and Chimæra.

Sphinx,
Nemæan Lion.

From Ocean and Tethys.
(*Sons.*)

Nile,
Alpheus,
Eridanus,
Strymon,
Meander,
Ister,
Phasis,
Rhesias,
Achelous,
Nessus,
Rhodius,

Haliacmon,
Granicus,
Simois,
Æsapus,
Hermus,
Sangarius,
Pereus,
Caicus,
Ladon,
Parthenius,
Evenus,
Ardescus,
Scamander.

(*Daughters.*)

Naiads,
Admete,
Pitho,
Doris,
Ianthe,
Urania,
Clymene,
Prymno,
Electra,
Calliroe,
Rhodia,
Hippo,
Pasithoe,
Plexaure,
Clytie,
Melobosis,
Idya,
Thoe,
Xeuxo,
Galaxaure,
Dione,
Circeis,
Polydore,
Ploto,
Perseis,
Innira,
Acaste,
Xanthe,
Petreia,
Telestho,
Metis,
Eurynome,
Crisie,
Menestho,

Europa,
Calypso,
Amphiro,
Eudora,
Asia,
Tyche,
Ocyroe,
Styx,
Oceanides.

From Hyperion and Thea.

Sun,
Moon,
Aurora.

From Crius and Eurybia.

Astræus,
Pallas,
Perses.

From Astræus and Aurora.

West,
North, } Winds.
South,
Lucifer,
Stars.

From Pallas and Styx.

Zeal,
Victory,
Strength,
Force.

From Cœus and Styx.

Latona,
Asteria.

From Perses and Asteria.

Hecate.

From Saturn and Rhea.

Vesta,
Ceres,
Juno,
Pluto,
Neptune,
Jupiter.

From Japetus and Clymene.
Atlas,
Menœtius,
Prometheus,
Epimetheus.

Made by Vulcan and all the Gods.
Pandora.

From Tartarus and Earth.
Typhœus,

From Typhœus.
Pernicious Winds.

From Jove and Themis.
Eunomie, ⎫
Dice, ⎬ Hours.
Irene, ⎭

From Jove and Eurynome.
Aglaia, ⎫
Euphrosyne, ⎬ Graces.
Thalia, ⎭

From Jove and Ceres.
Proserpina.

From Jove and Mnemosyne.
THE MUSES.
Clio,
Melpomene,
Euterpe,
Terpsichore
Erato,
Thalia,
Polymnia,
Urania,
Calliope.

From Jove and Latona.
Apollo,
Artemis.

From Jove and Juno.
Lucina,
Mars,
Hebe.

From Jove.
Minerva.

From Juno.
Vulcan.

From Neptune and Amphitrite.
Triton,
Fear,
Harmonia.

From Jove and Maia.
Hermes.

From Jove and Semele.
Bacchus.

From Jove and Alcmena.
Hercules.

From the Sun and Perses.
Circe,
Ætes.

From Ætis and Idya.
Medea.

From Jason and Ceres.
Plutus.

From Cadmus and Harmonia.
Ino,
Senele,
Agave,
Autonoe,
Polydore.

From Tithonus and Aurora.
Hemathion,
Memnon.

From Jason and Medea.
Medeus.

From Eacus and Psamathe.
Phocus.

From Peleus and Thetis.
Achilles.

From Anchises and Venus.
Æneas.

From Ulysses and Circe.
Agrius,
Latinus.

From Ulysses and Calypso.
Nausithous,
Nausinous.

PART FIRST.

ANCIENT DEITIES,

ANCIENT DEITIES.

CHAOS.

CHAOS (*void space*), a heterogeneous mass, containing all the seeds of nature, was first, according to Hesiod; then came into being the broad-breasted Earth, the gloomy Tartarus, and Love.

The idea of Chaos and Night, divested of poetical imagery, is simply that of unformed matter, eternally existing as the passive principle whence all forms are produced. Whether, besides this Chaotic mass, the ancients supposed an infinite, active, intelligent Principle, who from the first matter formed the universe. is a question which has occasioned much debate.

It is evident from the most cursory review of all the ancient theogonies, that God, the great Creator of all things, is not expressly introduced,; but it is doubted whether the framers of these theogonies meant to exclude him from their respective systems, or indirectly to suppose His existence, and the exertion of His power in giving motion to matter. When divested of allegory and poetry, the sum of the doctrine contained in the ancient theogonies, will, it is conceived, be as follows :—The first matter, containing the seeds of all future beings, existed with God. At length, the divine energy acting upon matter, produced a motion among its parts, by which those of the same kind were brought together, and those of a different kind were separated and by which, according to certain wise laws, the various forms of the material world were produced.

The same energy of emanation gave existence to animals and men as well as the gods who inhabit the heavenly bodies and various other parts. Among men, those who possess a larger portion of divine nature than others, are hereby impelled to great and beneficent actions, and afford illustrious proofs of their divine original. on account of which, they were, after death, raised to a place among the gods, and became objects of religious worship.

From Chaos were produced Earth, Love, Erebus, Night, and the Universe.

TERRA OR EARTH.

Earth was one of the most ancient oracles and deities in mythology. She produced the mountains, the sea, and the heavens.

Eros, or Love, was probably understood by the ancients to be that attractive principle in nature, by which homogeneous bodies are united ; and to this principle, they poetically ascribe the attributes of reason and wisdom, to intimate, that in the formation of the world, all things were constituted by harmonious laws.

According to some mythologists, Love is of all gods the most ancient, and is said to have existed before all generations, and first incited Chaos to bring forth darkness, out of which sprang Ether and Day— and also, that his union with Chaos gave birth to men, the animals which inhabit the earth, and that even the gods themselves were the offspring of Love, before the foundation of the world.

Among the ancients, Love was worshipped with great solemnity, and as his influence was supposed to extend over the dead as well as the living, his divinity was universally acknowledged, and vows, prayers, and sacrifices, were offered to him.

Erebus, properly speaking, is the abode of Night ; in conjunction with which he produced Day. This is the commencement of mythological fictions ;—the opposite extremes of things are brought together ;— from shapelessness and deformity arise form and beauty, and light is made to spring out of darkness.

Ancient mythologists and poets say, that the various parts of which the wondrous world consists, would have lain for ever in the abyss of being, if the breath of the tremendous Erebus, the spirit that dwells in eternal darkness, had not gone forth and put the mass in vital agitation.   Then, the congenial parts began to sever from their heterogeneous associates, and mingle together.   Matter appeared, and inseparable from it, attraction ; different degrees of powers, and all active principles of nature continued and increased.

Order, Figurability, Succession, and Retention, were passive in the genial contest ; but Intention and Aptitude mildly interfered, and begot Providence (or 'oresight), who, being joined with his bride, Meas are (*or perfection*), the daughter of Contemplation, presided over the forming world, called to light the vegetable and animal race, and then crowned his wondrous work with the formation of man.

NOX OR NIGHT.

Night covers and conceals, and for this reason she is made the mother of the horrible, as well as the charming.

From uncreated Night, Daylight arose, by which all formations are developed, and all creatures enjoy life. She is likewise, according to some, the mother of the inexorable Parcæ, of the avenging Nemesis, who punishes hidden crime; of the Furies, who torment the wicked; of Charon, the Ferry-man of Hell; and of the twin brothers, Sleep and Death.

Night is also the mother of Dreams; of the Hesperides, who guard the golden apples;—of Deceit, enveloping himself in darkness;—of malicious censure;—of fretting grief;—of trouble and hunger;—of destructive war;—of duplicity of speech;—and finally, of perjury. Among the children of night are comprised all those things which she conceals; or which Fancy, herself, would fain cover with nocturnal darkness. In night, there is something of which even the gods stood in awe: for Homer says, " When Jupiter was angry at the god of sleep, Night covered him with her veil, and the thunderer restrained his wrath, fearing to offend swift Night."—(Il. xiv. 256.)

The nightly, mysterious darkness, in which something hidden exer-cises superior power and influence over gods and men, was not clear to the conception of the ancient poets. They understood not the supreme, over-ruling power, before which all other powers vanish ; but believed in the hidden rule and authority that were apparent in the many mis-eries which mingled with the happiness of mortals. And as danger, fear, and mystery, have their attractions, as well as light, peace, and security, they delighted in the representations of dreadful events and wasting destruction, allowing their imaginations to stray far away into the dominion of night and the world of shadows.

Night was considered among the ancients as one of their oldest divinities, and was worshipped by them with great solemnity. In the temple of Diana, at Ephesus, was a famous statue of her, to whom, as the mother of the Furies, black sheep were offered in sacrifice; and also a cock. as that bird proclaims the approach of Day during the darkness of Night

On antique gems we find Night represented in a female figure of youthful beauty ; either holding in her arms two handsome boys, Death holding an extinguished torch in his hand, and Sleep with the stem of a poppy ; or sitting beneath a shady tree, distributing poppies to Mor- pheus and his brothers. Morpheus, the son of sleep and the god of dreams, stands before her in youthful beauty, receiving the poppy from her hands, while his brothers are behind her, bent to the ground gath- ering the falling leaves.

It appears from these representations, poetical, as well as plastic, how carefully the ancients endeavored to transform gloom and terror into soothing images. And, on the other hand, what a high conception of tragical subjects, considering the night born, inevitable Fate, as the power that rules over gods and men, and whose old dominion and con- cealed future, lie far beyond the penetration of human knowledge and foresight.

PAN.

Various origins have been given to Pan (or the Universe), one of which is, that he sprang from Chaos ; that is to say, Chaos contained the seeds of all things.

Among the most learned of the ancients, Pan was considered as one of the oldest divinities ; and, according to the Egyptians, and the most learned of the Grecian sages, he had neither father nor mother, but sprang from Demogorgon (the genius of the earth) at the same instant with the fatal Parcæ. A beautiful way of saying that the universe derived its origin from a power unknown to them, and was formed according to the unalterable relations, and eternal aptitude of things, as were the Fates, daughters of Necessity.

The figure of Pan represents the universe, and is a delineation of nature and the rough face which it first wore, while his spotted robe of a leopard's skin represents the starry heavens. His person is a com- pound of various and opposite parts, rational and irrational, a man and a goat; so is the world ;—an all-governing mind and heterogeneous, prolific elements pervade and constitute it.

Pan's symbol of the pipes is most eloquently expressive of nature's divine, harmonious constitution, and of the order and measure that govern all her works, producing that solemn movement called the music of the spheres ; imperceptible indeed to our material organ, but so delightful and pleasing to the ear of the mind. This wondrous reed

on which he incessantly plays, is composed of seven pipes, unequal among themselves, but fitted together in such just proportion as to produce the most unerring and melodious notes, calling forth the echo, which poets have made the object of his love.

The worship and the different functions of Pan, were derived from the mythology of the Egyptians. This deity was one of the eight great gods that they worshipped, ranking before the other gods, which the Romans called Consentes. They regarded him as the emblem of fecundity, and the principle of all things; therefore the Greeks gave him the appellation of Pan. He was worshipped with great solemnity at Mendes.

By the Arcadians he was venerated as the chief of the rural deities. Herdsmen and shepherds are said to have dreaded the sight of Pan, yet they regarded him as the tutelary deity of themselves, and of their flocks and herds, and brought him frequent offerings of milk and honey. Sacrifices were offered to him in a deep cave in the midst of a wood. The Athenians had a statue of him like that of Mars, and in some antique gems and sculptures his figure is nearly as formidable as that of the Medusa.

The worship of Pan seems to have been confined to Arcadia till the time of the battle of Marathon, when Phiedipodde, the Athenian courier, who was sent from Athens to Sparta, whither he went to implore aid against the Persians, was accosted, as he said, by the Arcadian deity Pan, who desired him, on his arrival at home, to assure the Athenians of his good will towards them, and of his regret that his favorable disposition had not been acknowledged by them with due honor and gratitude, and of his intention to be present and assist them in the great conflict in which they were about to engage. This promise having been duly fulfilled by the pastoral deity, obtained for him a shrine in the grotto consecrated to his honor at the north-west corner of the Athenian Acropolis.

Pan is unnoticed both by Homer and Hesiod, but in one of the Homerids his occupations are thus described: "He is lord of the hills and dales: sometimes he ranges along the tops of mountains, sometimes pursues the game in the valleys, roams through the woods, floats along the streams, or drives his sheep into a cave, and there plays on his reeds, music not to be excelled by the bird, who among the leaves of flower-full spring laments, pouring forth her moan, a sweet sounding lay."

> "And with him the clear singing mountain nymphs
> Move quick their feet, by the dark-water'd spring
> In the soft mead; where crocus, hyacinth,
> Fragrant and blooming, mingle with the grass,
> Confused; and sing, while echo peals around
> The mountain's top."

The god meanwhile moves his feet rapidly as he joins in the dance, with the skin of a lynx on his back, and delighted with the sweet song.

In after times, Pan's protection was supposed to extend beyond the herds, and we find him regarded as the guardian of bees, and the giver of success in fishing and fowling.

On the southern slope of Hymettus, a little above the village of Bari, is a subterranean grotto or natural temple dedicated to Pan and the pastoral nymphs. We descend a few steps hewn in the rock, and enter the cave which is lighted from the narrow adit: it is hung with stalactites, and bends itself so as to form two apartments, the one nearly parallel to the other. In ancient days the pipes and reeds of shepherds were suspended as votive offerings on its rocky walls; basins of stone and cups of wood carved with figures and flowers, were here dedicated to the deities of the place; here images of the nymphs stood in their small niches; hither, the first flowers of their gardens, the first ripe ears of their harvests, the first grapes of their vineyards, the first apples of their orchards, were brought as oblations by the shepherds and peasants of Attica. And now, at this day, there remain visible traces of their devotion, as well as memorials of the person who dedicated this grotto to the worship of their rural deities. Engraved on the rock, at the entrance, is an inscription in verse, which announces that Archedemus, a native of Phæræ, in Thessaly, formed this cave by the counsel of the nymphs: other records of the same kind inform us, that it was sacred to the Graces, to Apollo, and to Pan. Two verses, inscribed on a slab of marble, speak of a garden planted here in honor of the nymphs. In another part of the cave is a figure of Archedemus himself, rudely sculptured on the rock, dressed in his shepherd's coat, and with a hammer and chisel in his hands, cutting the sides of the cave.

Plato, in early youth, was led by his parents to a grotto on mount Hymettus, that he might present an offering to Pan, the nymphs, and the pastoral Apollo, to whom it was dedicated. There is good reason to believe that this cave, which, as the above inscriptions on its walls assure us, was consecrated to those very deities, has been trodden by the feet of the great philosopher of Athens, and that his eye has rested upon the same objects that we now see in this simple pastoral temple, which has sustained but little injury from the lapse of years, while the magnificent fanes of the Athenian capital have crumbled to decay.

At Rome, there was a yearly festival celebrated in honor of Luper-cus, or the Grecian Pan, with whom he was identified. This celebra-tion took place on the 15th of February, and was called Lupercalia. The priests who officiated, and who were dedicated to the service of Pan, were called Luperci. This order of priests was the most ancient and respectable of all the sacerdotal offices. It was divided into two separate colleges, called Fabiani and Quintiliani, from Fabius and Quintilius, two of the high priests. The former were instituted in honor of Romulus, and the latter of Remus.

A goat was sacrificed to Pan, to which a dog was added, because as god of shepherds he protected the sheepfold from the devouring wolf.

The priests touched with a bloody knife the foreheads of two illustri
ous youths, who were obliged to smile during the ceremony; the blood
was then wiped off with a bit of wool dipped in milk.   After this, the
skins of the victims were cut into thongs, with which whips were made
for the youths, who ran about the streets, using them freely on all
whom they met.   Plutarch says, "The Lupercalia would seem to be a
feast of lustration, from its occurring on one of the inauspicious days
of the month of February, which name denotes it to be the month of
purifying.   The day was formerly called Februaita.   But the true
meaning of the Lupercalia is the feast of wolves.   And it seems for
that reason very ancient, as having been received from the Arcadians,
who came over with Evander.   This is the general opinion.   But the
term may be derived from Lupa, a she-wolf; for we see the Luperci
begin their course from the place where they say Romulus was
exposed.

"Butas, who in his elegies has given a fabulous account of the origin
of the Roman institutions, writes, that when Romulus had overcome
Amulius, in the transports of victory, he ran with great speed to the
place where the wolf suckled him and his brother when infants; and
that this feast is celebrated and the young noblemen run in imitation
of that action; and the touching of the forehead with a bloody knife
is a symbol of the slaughter and danger, as the wiping off the blood
with milk is in memory of their first nourishment.   But Caius Acilius
relates, that before the building of Rome, Romulus and Remus having
lost their cattle, first prayed to Faunus for success in the search of
them, and then ran out naked to seek them; therefore the Luperci ran
about in the same manner.   If this was a feast of lustration, we may
suppose that the dog was sacrificed in order to be used in purifying ·
for the Greeks in their purifications made use of dogs.   But if these
rites are observed in gratitude to the wolf that nourished and preserved Romulus, it is with propriety they kill a dog, because it is an
enemy to wolves."

According to Baronius, Pope Gelasius abolished the Lupercalia in
the year 469 of the Christian era.

Like Pan, Lupercus, or Faunus, as he was also called, was multiplied,
therefore we meet with abundant mention of Fauns.

The Syrinx, or Pan's pipes, is generally placed in the hand of Fauns
and Satyrs, but is sometimes also the accompaniment of rustics.   It is
frequently found figured upon ancient monuments.   Upon the Sarcoph·

agus* of Tyrania, preserved in the museum at Arles, is depicted a Syrinx in a case or box. It is occasionally found on the earlier Christian monuments as an emblem of our holy faith; the founder of Christianity having been regarded as the shepherd of his spiritual flock, and the Syrinx being the common musical instrument of the husbandman or shepherd.

---

* Sarcophagus is a sort of coffin or grave itself. This kind of sepulchral chest among the ancients was made of stone, marble, or porphyry. The Greeks also used hard wood, which was calculated to resist humidity. Occasionally *terra cotta*, and even metal. The form of these *sarcophagi* was ordinarily a long square, like our coffin. Sometimes the angles were rounded, giving it an elliptical shape. It was not usual for these funeral chests to narrow downwards, as, for instance, the species of bathing-tub called *labrum*. The lid of the sarcophagus varies also both in shape and ornament. Sometimes it bears the statue of the person inhumed therein, often in the posture assumed by the ancients as they took their meals. The size of the *sarcophagi* was also various. Those of the primitive Christians, destined to enclose several corpses, had often two several sets of *basi relievi*.

The workmanship on the sarcophagi of the ancients was frequently of a very high order. The figures sculptured or engraved thereon, are either those of the parties connected immediately with the history of the deceased, or the heroic, half fabulous personages of mythology. Achilles detected by Ulysses among the daughters of Lycomedes; Orestes, the parricide, pursued by the Furies; the combats of the Centaurs and Lapiths; these and others are very often treated on these monuments. Sometimes the young warrior is characterized by some hero of antiquity; and the *sarcophagus* represents the condemnation of Hyppolitos by his father Theseus; the death of Phaëthon, who could not escape his evil destiny; the death of Patroclos, announced to Achilles by Autilochus; that of Hector, announced by his father, etc., etc.

The ancients were fond of denominating death a sleep. With them Sleep and Death are brothers, and are often placed on the sides of a sarcophagus. Often, also, by an ingenious allegory, the artist represented the eternal sleep of the pale inhabitants of the *sarcophagus* by some celebrated mythological slumber; such, for instance, as the sleep of Endymion.

Again, the figures on the *sarcophagi* were moral or allegorical. The twelve labors of Hercules, so often found upon the tombs of the thirteenth and fourteenth centuries, present an ingenious allegory of the triumph of virtue over the passions. The various seasons, frequently found depicted upon them, are emblematical of the several ages of man. Occasionally, the peculiar taste or profession of the deceased is indicated, as in the three *basi relievi*, wherein the figure of a young poet is introduced, encircled by the Muses. In fact, these ancient monuments present almost every variety of decoration; in some instances bearing an obvious relation to the person entombed; in others, to subjects of a general, a political, or a religious character.

Certain sarcophagi contained merely an urn, enclosing the ashes of the deceased. This is the case with that regarded as having been appropriated to Alexander Severus, wherein was found the beautiful glass urn, called the "Portland Vase."

PARCÆ OR FATES.

"There are three Fates, three single sisters, wh.)
Rejoicing in their wind-outspreading wings,
Their heads with flour snow'd over white and new,
Sit in a vale, round which Parnassus flings
Its circling skirts."

The Parcæ were daughters of Night, or an invisible, overruling power. According to some, the daughters of Necessity, or the necessary·connection of things—by which is meant the Creator's eternal and immovable essence, to which the fable of her daughters, and their fatal spindle plainly points.

This necessary connection of things, or necessity itself, called by the Greeks Moira and Heimarmene, and by the Romans Fatum, was that mysterious power, which, with invisible sceptre, ruled over gods and men . The inexorable Parcæ were the attendants of this unknown being, and presided chiefly over the life and fate of mortal men.

They were three in number, according to the triple division of time into past, present, and future. Their ever-running thread is partly spun and wound up, partly just drawn out and twisting, and partly as yet on the distaff. Clotho holds the distaff, and is ever furnishing the present; Lachesis (allotment) spinning the thread of life, lays out the future; and Atropos (irreversion) with the fatal scissors cuts it off, severing the past; so that the grand transaction of time is not badly represented in the fable. But as Plato has nobly said, " All this is nothing but God himself, who, according to the ancient tradition, having the beginning, middle, and end of all things in his power, keeps one straight, steady course according to nature, with his inseparable adherent, Justice, who is ever ready to avenge the least deviation from his divine law."

Although the Parcæ signify that terrific power which governs as it were from the dark, whose decrees are passed as soon as conceived, and against which there is no resistance, yet, they are represented as beautiful females, spinning, and joining at the same time in the song of the Sirens. In high and unlimited power, all things are easily accomplished; and the resistance even of the mighty finds in this height its termination. To prescribe bounds to all revolutions, only the slightest touch of the fingers is requisite, and to manage the mysterious course of events is made the easiest work of a female hand. This beautiful representation of the thread of life, delicately spun and easily severed, cannot be equalled by any other. The thread does not break, but is cut off; and the cause of this lies in a superior power, which has already firmly and irrevocably disposed of what gods and men still strive to accomplish in their own way.

Ancient representations of the Parcæ by the hand of art are seldom found. Upon the gems which antiquity has left us, Lachesis, who spins the thread of life, and is sometimes called the handsome daughter of Necessity, is represented in youthful beauty. seated, and spinning, having one distaff before and another behind her, and at her feet lie a comic and tragic mask. These masks are among the happiest allusions to human life, if we behold it with all its serious and comic scenes. Unaffected by either, she cannot be diverted from her purpose; but, during their course, the tender and delicate finger of the goddess never ceases to turn the fatal thread.

Another gem shows Lachesis leaning against a pillar in a quiet posture, carelessly holding a distaff in her left hand, and playing as it were with the thread of destiny. This quiet attitude in which the sublime goddess of destiny looks down upon the far extended designs of men. is an extremely beautiful idea of the ancient artist. For while gods exert all their power, and mortals all their strength to bring their plans and views to bear, this goddess, smiling, playfully holds the thread on which depend the limits of all things, even the proudest projects of gods and men.

In vain, for instance, does Jupiter endeavor to preserve the life of his son, Sarpedon, in the battle of Troy, against the will of Fate. "Wo 's me," he exclaims, "that my son, Sarpedon, must fall under the hand of Patroclos, according to the doom of Fate." And although he would gladly rescue his son, yet his power must yield before that of the inexorable goddess. Nothing is left to his own will, but to deliver the body to his messengers, Death and sweet Sleep, who carry it to his native land, where the friends and relatives may weep over it. (Il. xvi. 434.)

In the same manner Ulysses was doomed by destiny to wander ten years over foreign seas and countries, and at last to reach home without his companions. And in the history of his wanderings it may be seen, that where circumstances appear to afford the greatest pleasure, happiness, and security, there the greatest dangers lie concealed. As. for instance, in the quiet harbor of the Lestrigons, on occasion of the song of the Sirens, and in that of Circe's magic cup.

It is the history of human life in general. However near at hand Ulysses beholds the accomplishment of his wishes, all recedes; his tears and fervent prayers are in vain, until it is the will of Destiny that he shall again find his home, and he reaches his native island— sleeping.

The worship of the Parcæ was well established in some cities in Greece, and though mankind were convinced that they were inexorable, and that it was impossible to mitigate their will, yet they wished to show a proper homage to their divine power by raising to them temples and statues. They received the same worship as the Furies, and their votaries yearly sacrificed to them black sheep; during which ceremony the priests were obliged to wear garlands and flowers.

NEMESIS.

Nemesis, like the Parcæ, was the daughter of Night. Her office was to baffle pride and haughtiness, and to punish secret vice. She presided over the distribution of retributive justice, and her vengeance. if once provoked, was sure to fall on the offender at last, however long delayed. In this fable is plainly seen the idea of retributive justice which, though slow in its course, never fails, sooner or later, to overtake the wicked, who must inevitably suffer the consequences of their own wrong-doing. As a personification of the moral reverence for law, of the natural fear of committing a guilty action, and hence of conscience, she is mentioned in Hesiod's Theogony in connection with Shame.

Having belonged with the original deities, those mysterious beings who were regarded with awe and veneration by gods as well as men, she is allowed the same rank among the modern heathen deities, and was particularly worshipped at Rhamnus in Attica, where she had a celebrated statue made by Phidias—or as others say, by one of his pupils.

The Greeks celebrated a festival in memory of their deceased friends, called Nemesia,—as the goddess Nemesis was supposed to preserve the memory and relics of the dead from insult.

The Romans, also, were particularly attentive to the worship of Nemesis, whom they solemnly invoked, and to whom they offered sacrifices before declaring war against their enemies, to prove to the world that they did not act without the most just occasion. Her statue at Rome was in the Capitol.

In a solitary scene in Attica, near the channel of Euripus, at about half a mile from the sea, and three hundred feet above it, is a rectangular terrace, of which two sides, namely, those on the north and east, are faced with massive blocks of white Pentelic marble, fitted to each other with the nicest symmetry. The earthen wall is one hundred and fifty feet in length; it rises eight feet above the soil below it, which slopes gently to the sea.

This terrace was a sacred enclosure. On it two temples formerly stood; they belonged to the city of Rhamnus, which lay below them on a circular knoll upon the sea-shore. The direction in which they were placed was from north to south; the remains of both are considerable.

Whether they ever existed contemporaneously in a perfect state, is a matter of much uncertainty. Had this been the case, the buildings, as is clear from their actual foundations, would have been almost contiguous without being parallel to each other, and would thus have presented a very irregular and unsymmetrical appearance, for which there is no reason, on account of the ample dimensions of the area around them.

Of these two fabrics, that to the west was a single cella built in *antis*, as it is called; that is, with but one portico, and that formed by the two columns, placed between two pilasters, in which the walls of the cella terminate. This temple was only thirty-five feet long, and twenty-one broad; it was constructed of polygonal masses of marble; of the four walls which formed the cella some portions are still standing. The entrance to the temple was on the south; on each side of it, under the portico supported by two columns and antæ above mentioned, was a marble throne, each having an inscription on the plinth, from which it appears that the chair on the right hand of the door was dedicated to Nemesis, and that on the left to Themis. Within the temple was a marble statue of very ancient workmanship, which represented the goddess to whom the temple was dedicated.

Adjacent to this temple, on the east, stood a second building, of the same kind, but of a much more magnificent style, and larger dimensions. It was a *peripteral hexastyle;* that is, it was surrounded on all sides by columns, having six on either end; namely, at the *pronaos* or front, on the south, and at the *posticum*, or hinder porch on the north; there were twelve columns on each flank; in both the temples these were of the Doric order. This latter temple measured seventy-five feet in length, and thirty-seven in breadth. Within it some fragments of a colossal statue are still visible.

From the testimonies of ancient authors, especially Pausanias, and from the fact that the town of Rhamnus, to which these temples belonged, was under the special patronage of the goddess Nemesis, and also from the language of an ancient inscription, still extant in the larger temple, which speaks of an honorary statue of a young Athenian there dedicated to *her*, it is clear that this latter building was consecrated to that deity. This large and splendid building was, we say, the temple of Nemesis.

The smaller fabric first noticed has generally been supposed to have been the temple of Themis; but there is no ground for this opinion except the circumstance that one of the marble chairs, noticed above as standing in its vestibule, is inscribed to her; but it should be observed, that the chair on the left of the entrance is dedicated to Themis, while that on the right was sacred to Nemesis. In addition to this, since the awkward position of the buildings with respect to each other suggests the belief that they never *both* existed in a state of integrity at the *same time*, and as it is just to conclude that the patron goddess of Rhamnus was *never* without a temple in this place, from the time when the place itself was first dedicated to her, we are inclined to believe that the older and smaller temple was also consecrated to the *same* goddess.

It appears then probable, that when this building fell into decay,— whether from lapse of time, or as is more likely from hostile violence,— and when the inhabitants of Rhamnus had advanced both in wealth and architectural skill, that then they thought fit to erect another temple of a more magnificent and spacious kind in honor of their own deity, while their respect for antiquity and their veneration for the consecrated building, in which she had been worshipped by their forefathers, caused them to retain, in its actual state, the smaller and simpler fabric which stood by its side.

The ruins of this ancient temple, if it had been laid waste by human force, were, perhaps, preserved in their dismantled condition, for a particular purpose, by the inhabitants of Rhamnus; for they were of service on the one hand, as stimulating their indignation and courage against those who had thus treated them; and, on the other, as conjuring Nemesis, the goddess of retribution, by a silent and perpetual prayer, that she would aid them in repelling and chastising those enemies who had thus violated her dignity and profaned her worship.

It is impossible to contemplate the ruins of these temples and the peculiar features of their site, without being impressed with a deep feeling of admiration for the spirit and intelligence which set apart this spot for purposes of religious devotion. Let us imagine this scene as it existed in former days. Then these buildings were standing— the larger of them, at least, in its full beauty—on an enclosed terrace. supported by long and high walls of pure marble. This was their pedestal. They were surrounded by a sacred grove of green and fragrant shrubs, among which were statues and altars.

One of these two buildings reminded the spectator of the simplicity of earlier days by its chaste and severe style; the other charmed him by the size and beauty of its structure, by its long lines of columns, its lofty pediments, the richness of its sculptural decorations, and by the brilliancy of the coloring with which they were adorned. Beneath them, at some distance, was the sea; on its shore was the city of Rhamnus, one of the strongest and most important fortresses of Attica, to which these temples belonged. The town stood on a peninsular knoll it was surrounded with lofty walls of massive stone, and was entered on the west by a gate flanked with towers; on the southern side was its port.

5

From contemplating the picture which these latter objects suggest
to the imagination—from ideal visions of the military or naval prepa-
rations which the town of Rhamnus, now lying in ruins before us, was
wont to witness in early days—from sights such as it then presented,
of seamen hastening down to its port, and invited to embark there by
a favorable gale; or of Athenian merchants unlading their ships, and
transporting their freight to warehouses on the quay ; or of travellers
entering the gate of the city, or issuing from it—we turn again to a
more quiet scene—to the view of these beautiful temples, standing
above on their lofty platform amid the silence and shadows of their
consecrated grove.

However mistaken its object, we cannot bear to condemn, nay, rather,
we cannot but fervently approve and admire, the temper of that devotion which raised these two buildings—one of grave simplicity, the
other of sumptuous splendor—in such a scene as this. We reverence
the feeling which removed them from the turmoil of the city, sequestered them by a local consecration from all buildings devoted to traffic
and to toil, and placed them in this tranquil spot, which invited the
worshipper to come here from the stir of the streets below, and to
taste the pleasure and enjoy the fruits, if not of devotion, at least of
meditation and repose ; we venerate the principle—a principle not of
Paganism, but one of a purer spirit, speaking in a pagan age—which,
in the dignified structure, and in the hallowed and peaceful precincts
of these temples at Rhamnus, seems to have conceived and realized the
idea of what we may be allowed to call an architectural sabbath. such
as a heathen could enjoy and no Christian can despise.

THE ERINNYES OR FURIES.

The Erinnyes were originally a personification of the curses pronounced upon a guilty criminal. In this sense the word Erinnys is
often used in the Homeric poems ; and the poet, conceiving them as‾
distinct beings, considered them as among the inhabitants of Erebus.
whence they were called to life and activity, when some curse is pronounced upon the guilty.

The crimes which they are represented as punishing, are, disobedience to parents, violation of the respect due to old age, violation of
the laws of hospitality, and improper conduct towards suppliants. As
ministers of the vengeance of the gods, they were stern and inexorable.

Upon earth they were employed to inflict vengeance by wars, pestilences, and dissensions, and
by the secret stings of conscience; and in hell
they punished the guilty by continual flagella-
tions and torments. Gradually they assumed
the character of goddesses who punished crime
after death, and seldom appeared on earth.

Neither Homer nor the Greek tragedians designate the Erinnyes by any particular names;
but the later poets make them three in number, viz.: Tisiphone, the avenger of murder;
Megæra, the wrathful; and Alecto, the restless;
and so great was the awe in which men stood of
these inexorable sisters, that they scarcely ventured to mention their names, or fix their eyes on
the temples dedicated to the Furies. They had
a temple in Achaia, which no one guilty of crime
could enter without being suddenly deprived of reason and made furi
ous; and whoever was conscious of having secretly perpetrated an un
lawful action, endeavored to propitiate the Furies by prayers and of
ferings.

Their temple at Athens was near the Areiopagos, and few even of
the superior deities received so much homage as the three avenging
sisters; and their priests formed a tribunal before which no one dared
to appear, until he had sworn upon the altar of the Eumenides to tell
nothing but the truth.

Their worship was almost universal; and in their sacrifices the
votaries used branches of cedar and of alder, hawthorn, saffron, and
juniper. The victims were generally turtle doves and black sheep,
with libations of wine and honey.

They were represented with snakes around their heads instead of
hair, and wearing funereal robes fastened with girdles formed of snakes
and scorpions. With one hand they grasp a dagger with whips of
serpents and scorpions; in the other is held a flaming torch; and thus
they are represented as pursuing the perpetrators of crime and wicked-
ness. The Grecian artists, however, frequently represented the Furies
as young and beautiful: sometimes with, and sometimes without serpents around their heads.

On a vase of terra cotta, from the Porcinari cabinet at Naples, rep

resented in the second volume of Sir William Hamilton's vases, they
are painted as young females, with bare arms, and having snakes twined
round their heads. In their hands they held torches. On another
vase, Orestes appears with his hands tied behind him, while below the
altar on which he is placed, is a black winged Fury, with snakes in her
hair, and others curling round her arms. Even here, however, the
expression is far from terrific. Different bas-relievos of the Romans,
representing the same subject, characterize these avenging deities by
the same attributes of youth and beauty.

The Furies were also called Eumenides; but the term Eumenides,
that is, the kindly disposed goddesses, is applied to them by a euphemism, or antiphrasis.

Helicon was consecrated to the Muses; but Cithæron was the mountain of the Erinnyes, and rang with the frantic yells of the wildest
nocturnal orgies of Bacchanalian revelry. The aspect of Cithæron is
the reverse of that of Helicon ; it is savage, cold, gloomy, and inhospitable. All the mythological traditions connected with it, partake of
the physical sternness which characterizes the mountain itself. The
dark forests of pine trees and silver firs which crown the precipitous
cliffs, and the caves which are hollowed in their craggy sides, were,
according to the songs of Greek poets, the witnesses of inhuman and
sanguinary deeds. Here Pentheus, the Theban king, was pursued by
the infuriate troop of women, led on by his mother and sisters, and
torn in pieces by their hands. Here Actæon, the son of Aristæus, and
Autonöe, the daughter of Cadmus, having on a sultry day, when he
was hunting, ascended from the Gargraphian fount in the plain below,
where Diana, when bathing, was seen by him, was mangled by his own
dogs, which were set upon him by that goddess. Here, the luckless
Œdipus was exposed by order of his father. Here a little more than
a mile to the south of the loftiest summit of the mountain, which is
upwards of four thousand feet in height, and overhangs the site of the
ancient Platæa, was the altar of the Cithæronian Jupiter, to which the
fourteen cities composing the Bœotian Confederacy brought, at the
feast of Dædalia, every sixty years, fourteen statues of oak, and burned
them upon an altar of wood, upon the summit of the mountain. Here
is a grotto formerly dedicated to the Sphragitian Nymphs who inspired
men with the frenzy known to the Greeks of old, by the name of
Nympholepsy. The whole mountain was identified with the wildest
and most painful passions which distract the human heart. It was

dedicated to tragedy, while the mountain on the western side of the valley was sacred to the genius of pastoral poetry. Cithæron and Helicon were, if we may use the comparison, the mount Ebal and the mount Gerizim of Greek geography.

THE HESPERIDES.

The Hesperides are called daughters of Night, that is to say their origin and existence are veiled in darkness. Their names were Ægle, Erytheia, and Arethusa;—and they were appointed to guard the golden apples, which were the gift of Earth to Juno on her wedding day.

The celebrated gardens of the Hesperides aboundod with fruits of the most delicious kinds, and were carefully guarded by a dreadful dragon, which never slept. By Hesiod, these gardens were placed beyond the Atlantic Ocean in the dusky horizon of the west, where they rested upon the shoulders of Atlas. By geographical writers they are placed near the ancient Berenice, now Bengazi in Cyrenaïca on the Mediterranean coast of Africa.

A modern traveller, Captain Beechy, has given us some curious information upon this point. He remarks, that some very singular pits or chasms of natural formation were discovered by him in the neighborhood of Bengazi.

" They consist of a level surface of excellent soil several hundred feet in extent, enclosed within steep and for the most part perpendicular sides of solid rock, rising sometimes to a height of sixty or seventy feet or more before they reach the level of the plain in which they are situated. The soil at the bottom of these chasms appears to have been washed down from the plain above by the heavy rains, and is frequently cultivated by the Arabs: so that a person walking over the country where they exist, comes suddenly upon a beautiful orchard or garden blooming in secret, and in the greatest luxuriance, and a considerable depth beneath his feet, and defended on all sides by walls of solid rock, so as to be at first sight apparently inaccessible.

" The effect of these secluded spots, protected as it were from the intrusion of mankind by the steepness and depth of the barriers which enclose them, is singular and pleasing in the extreme; they reminded us of some of those secluded retreats of which we read in fairy tales and legends. It was impossible to walk along the edge of these precipices looking every where for some part less abrupt than the rest by which we might descend into the gardens beneath, without calling to mind the description given by Syclax, of the far-famed gardens of the Hesperides."

It has been supposed by many, and among the rest by Gosselin and Pacho, that the Hesperian gardens of the ancients were nothing more than some of those verdant caves which stud the Libyan desert, and which from their concealed and inaccessible position, their unknown origin, and their striking contrast to the surrounding waste, might well suggest the idea of a terrestrial paradise, and become the types of the still fairer creations of poetic fable. It would really seem, however, that the first of these Elysian groves was at this extremity of Cyrenaica, and that the original idea of the legend was taken from a subterranean garden of the above description.

This celebrated retreat is stated by Syclax to have been an enclosed spot of ten stadia each way, filled with thickly planted fruit trees of various kinds, and inaccessible on all sides. It was situated at 620 stadia (fifty geographical miles) from the port of Barce ; and this agrees precisely with that of the place described by Captain Beechy from Ptolemeta.

The testimony of Pliny is also very decided in fixing the site of the Hesperides in the neighborhood of Berenice. He says :

"' Not far from the city' (Berenice) 'is the river Lethon and the sacred groves where the gardens of the Hesperides are said to be situated.'

"We do not mean," remarks Captain Beechy, "to point out any *one* of these subterranean gardens as that which is described in the passage just quoted from Syclax; for we know of no one which will correspond in point of extent to the garden which the author has mentioned. All those which we saw, were considerably less than the fifth of a mile in diameter (the measurement given by Syclax) ; and the places of this nature which would best agree with the dimensions, are now filled with water sufficiently fresh to be drinkable, and take the form of romantic little lakes.

"Scarcely any of the gardens we met with, were, however, of the same depth or extent; and we have no reason to conclude that, because we saw none which were large enough to be fixed upon for the garden of the Hesperides, that there is therefore no place of the dimensions required ; particularly, as the singular formation alluded to, continues to the feet of the Cyrenaïc chain, which is fourteen miles distant in the nearest part from Berenice."

MORS OR DEATH.

Mors, born of Night and without a father, was one of the infernal deities. By the ancients she was worshipped with great solemnity, and was represented by them, not as an actually existing power, but as an imaginary being.

"The figures of Mors or Death," says Spence, "are very uncommon, as indeed those of the evil and hurtful beings generally are. They were banished from all medals, and on seals and rings they were probably considered as bad omens, and were perhaps never used. Among the very few figures of Mors I have met with, that in the Florentine gallery is, I think, the most remarkable; it is a little figure in brass of a skeleton sitting on the ground, and resting one of its hands on a long urn. I fancy Mors was common enough in the paintings of old, because she is so frequently mentioned in a descriptive manner by the Roman poets."

The face of Mors, when they gave her any face, seems to have been of a pale, wan, dead color. The poets describe her as ravenous, treacherous, and furious, and as roving about open-mouthed and ready to swallow up all who came in her way. They give her black robes and dark wings; and often make her of a colossal stature. From the epithets *pallida* and *lucida*, pale and wan, she must have been represented with a pale face and meagre body, instead of the bare skull and skeleton of some modern painters.

The description of Death by the ancients was more frightful and dismal than that of modern artists and poets. They describe her as thundering at the doors of mortals to demand the debt they owe her. Sometimes as approaching their bedsides; and sometimes pursuing her prey; or as hovering in the air, and ready to seize it. Mors is represented, like the gladiators called *retiares*, pursuing men with a net, as catching or dragging them to their tombs; or, as surroun᠁ persons like the hunters of old, and encompassing them on ev with her toils. This way of hunting is very distinctly dᵣ Statius, and Plutarch speaks of toils twelve miles in leng an eastern custom still practised, and the author of the speaks in a similar figurative style, of being encompassed of Death.

The most picturesque description of this deity to be found in the ancient poets, is where Statius represents her by the side of a youth in the flower of his age and attended by Envy and Vengeance, or Nemesis. These terrific deities show great friendship for each other in the execution of their purpose, and Vengeance, in particular, seems, by the account, to take the net out of Death's hand to perform her office for her.

Death is sometimes represented as a skeleton, wearing a black robe, covered with stars, and having wings of an enormous length, and her fleshless arms supporting a scythe. No temples were dedicated to her, and no sacrifices offered, because Death is inexorable, inaccessible to entreaties, and unmoved by prayers and offerings.

The Greeks acknowledged no god or goddess of Death. They knew only of a genius of Death, who reversed and quenched his torch whenever he brought a mortal to his last rest. He is represented on an Etrurian bas-relief as a perfect cherub.*

SOMNUS.

Somnus, the son of Night, presided over sleep. According to some mythologists, his palace was a dark cave, where the sun never penetrates ; at the entrance are a number of poppies and somniferous herbs. Virgil places him in the entrance to the infernal shades, on account of his relation to Lethe ; but Ovid and Statius give him a place on our Earth.

The God of Sleep is represented as a child stretched on a couch in a profound slumber, holding in his hand a bunch of poppies, which serve also for a pillow. The Dreams stand by him ; and Morpheus, as his attendant, watches to prevent the disturbance of his repose. Sometimes his head rests upon a lion's skin and sometimes on a lion (as in a statue in Maffei), with one arm either a little over or under his head, and the other hanging carelessly by the side of the couch, having placed in it poppies, or a horn full of poppy juice.

is often winged ; and so like Cupid as to be frequently mistaken notwithstanding the lizard at his feet, the proper attribute of it sleeps during half the year. The lizard is not men-
poets, and may have been used by artists merely for the

sake of distinction, though the poppy seems sufficient for the purpose, except in some few pieces, where the distinguishing attributes of both are blended together. In that case, it may be intended to represent Cupids under the character of Somnus.

Poets speak often of the wings of Somnus and of their being black, as most proper for the god who chiefly rules at night. For the same reason, the figures of him are of ebony, basalt, or dark-colored marble. Such is the fine statue at Florence, which holds a horn in the hand so remissly, that the poppy juice is running out of it. Somnus is supposed to give sleep to mortals by shedding some drops from his horn, by touching them with his *virga* or rod, or by gently passing by their bedside. When he gave troubled sleep, or tumultuous dreams, he mixed the water of some infernal river with his poppy juice

Statius describes Somnus more frequently than any other poet. He represents him as standing on the highest point in the moon's course, and hovering down from thence just at midnight, with his wings spread over the Earth. He speaks of several relievos, on each of which this god was grouped with appropriate companions. In the first, he was with Voluptas, as the goddess of feasts; in the second, with Labor, represented as tired and inclined to rest; in the third, with Bacchus; and in the fourth, with the God of Love.

All these fine images are in Statius' description of the palace of Sleep. He places it in the unknown parts of Ethiopia; and Ovid in Italy, near the lake Avernus. Somnus' attendants before the gates, were Rest, Ease, Indolence, Silence, and Oblivion; and within, were a multitude of dreams in various forms and attitudes. Over these, says Ovid, presided the three chiefs who inspire great persons only with dreams. Morpheus, such as relate to men; Phobætor, such as relate to animals; and Photæsæ, such as relate to inanimate things.

MORPHEUS.

Morpheus, the God of Dreams and son of Night, can assume any shape at pleasure, presenting dreams to those who sleep. To the palace of Somnus there are said to be two gates, one of ivory and the other of horn, out of which dreams pass and repass—the false through the ivory, the true through the transparent horn.

Morpheus is sometimes represented as a man advanced in years with two large wings on his shoulders, and two small ones attached to his head. In the museum Pia Clementina, he is represented in relief on a *cippus*,* as a boy treading lightly on tip-toe; on his head are two wings; in his right hand he holds a horn, from which he appears to be pouring something; his left holds a stalk bearing three poppy heads. On a relief in the villa Borghese, the god of dreams is again represented as a boy with wings, and holding the poppy stalk, but without the horn.

MOMUS.

Momus, a son of Night, was the god of raillery and repartee; at the feasts of the gods he played the buffoon. His office was to reprove the faults of the gods, which he did in so sarcastic a manner as to put himself out of favor. He blamed Vulcan, because in the human form which he made of clay, he had not placed a window in the breast, by which whatever was done or thought there might easily be brought to light. He censured the house made by Minerva, because it was not movable, by which means a bad neighborhood might be avoided. Of the bull which Neptune made, he observed, that the blows might have been surer, if the eyes were nearer the horns. Venus herself was exposed to his satire; and when the sneering god could find no fault in the figure of the goddess, he observed as she retired, that the noise of her feet was too loud, and very improper in the goddess of beauty.

---

* Among the ancients the *cippus* was generally a small column, sometimes without a base or capital, and its greatest ornament, an inscription which preserved the memory of some event, or of some deceased person.

They were used for several purposes;—one was marking distances. These were the miliary columns, sometimes having the names of roads, serving as directing posts; and sometimes marking boundaries, with inscriptions indicating the consecrated grounds for the burial of particular families. From the form and ornaments of the last mentioned, they have been frequently mistaken for altars. They were consecrated to infernal deities, and the manes of the deceased.

Wher. the ancients marked the enclosure of a new town with the plough, they fixed *rippi* from space to space, upon which they first offered sacrifices. Afterwards towers were built in their places. *Cippi* are often represented upon medals and engraved gems, with some divinity placed near them whom they support. They generally bear some symbolical figures, and are of varied and elegant proportion.

The British Museum, in their department of antiquities, have several *cippi*, one of which appears never to have been used, a blank space being left for the name. Another has an inscription to the memory of Virla Primitiva, the wife of Lucius Virius Helius, who died at the age of eighteen years, one month, and twenty-four days. Two rams' heads are placed at the corners, from which a festoon of flowers is suspended below the tablet. At the lower corners are two Sphinges, with a head of Pan in the area between them

For these illiberal reflections upon the gods, he was driven from Heaven.

Momus is generally represented raising a mask from his face, and holding a small figure in his hand.

OHARON.

Charon, a god of Hell, and son of Erebus and Night, conducted the souls of the dead in a boat over the rivers Styx and Acheron, to the infernal regions. But he conveyed no one without their tribute, and it was a custom among the ancients in preparing the dead for burial, to place a piece of money under the tongue for Charon.

When a departed soul presented herself for a passage in his boat he first inquired whether the traveller could furnish the requisite fee ; and if it should happen that the obolus had been forgotten, the poor soul was left to wander on the gloomy shores a hundred years before being conducted over the river; and such as had not been honored with a funeral, were subjected to the same penalty.

> "A hundred years they wander on the shore,
> At length, their penance done, are wafted o'er."—*Æn.* vi.

Among the ancients, it was considered an inexpressible cruelty to deny to the dead a burial; and for this reason, all great commanders were careful, after a battle, to inter the bodies of those whose lives had been lost in their service.

No living person was received into Charon's boat, unless he could show a golden bough which he had received from the Sybil as a passport. Yet it is said that Æneas by his piety, Hercules and Theseus by their valor, and Orpheus by his music, obtained the privilege of passing to and fro in old Charon's ferry boat.

Charon is represented as an old man with a ragged garment, a long grey neglected beard, and his forehead lined with wrinkles.

NEREUS.

Nereus, the son of Pontos and Terra, was the personification of the smooth sea.

He married Doris, the daughter of Oceanos, and their children were the Nereides, or the nymphs of the sea. They are said to have been fifty in number, and their names are all mentioned; yet but few of them are introduced into the history of the gods. The greater part of them are represented as forming a splendid retinue when Thetis and Amphitrite, the principal ones, appeared on the sea.

The imagination of the ancients allowed no place to remain uninhabited, and therefore formed a multitude of creatures, and a variety of abodes, in regions which none but immortals could inhabit; and the rising of the marine deities from their crystal palaces to the surface of the waters afforded a subject for some attractive fables among the ancient poets. When on the sea shore, the Nereides resided in grottoes and caves, which were adorned with shells and shaded with vine branches.

They are represented as young and handsome virgins, sitting on dolphins, and holding Neptune's trident, or sometimes garlands of flowers. Their duty was to attend upon the more powerful deities of the sea, and to be subservient to the will of Neptune.

The Nereïdes were implored as well as the rest of the deities. Their altars were chiefly on the coasts of the sea, where the piety of mankind made them offerings of milk, oil, and honey, and often of the flesh of goats; as they had the power of ruffling or calming the waters, they were always addressed by sailors, who implored their protection, and that they would grant them a favorable voyage and a prosperous return.

Nereus was represented as an old man, with a long flowing beard, and hair of an azure color, and sometimes crowned with sea weed. The chief place of his residence was in the Ægean Sea, where he was surrounded by his daughters, who often danced around him in chorus.

He had the gift of prophecy, and informed those who consulted him of the different fates that awaited them.

When Paris carried Helen across the sea, Nereus predicted to him the consequences that would follow this elopement; and, casting his quiet looks into the future, revealed the downfall of Troy.

But the sea-god often evaded the importunities of inquirers by assuming different shapes, and totally escaping from their grasp. When Hercules was in quest of the apples of the Hesperides, he was directed by the nymphs to Nereus; finding the god asleep, he seized him. Nereus, on waking, changed himself into a variety of forms, but in vain; he was obliged to instruct Hercules how to proceed before the hero would release him.

Nereus was worshipped in all the maritime towns in Greece, and was considered as mild, upright, and never unmindful of equity and justice.

AMPHITRITE. THETIS. GALATÆA.

Amphitrite became the wife of Poseidon, and was goddess of the sea (the Mediterranean). She seldom occurs as a goddess; and in the Homeric poems, Amphitrite is merely the name of the sea. Poseidon's attachment to Scylla excited the jealousy of Amphitrite to such a degree, that she threw some magic herbs into the well in which she bathed herself, and thereby changed her rival into a monster with six heads and twelve feet.

In works of ancient art, Amphitrite was represented in a figure that resembled Venus, but was distinguished from that goddess by a net that confined her hair, and by the claws of a crab on her forehead. She was sometimes represented as riding on marine animals, and sometimes as drawn by them.

Thetis was married to the Thessalian king, Peleus.

Galatæa loved Acis, the handsome shepherd, and the monstrous Cyclop, Polyphemos, sued in vain for her favor. On a certain occasion, the monster beheld the nymph at the foot of Mt. Ætna, embracing his handsome rival. He became distracted with furious jealousy, and tearing up a rock from its roots, raised it in the air, and hurled it upon the lovers in order to bury them under its weight.

The nymph swiftly escaped into the sea, but Acis, overwhelmed by the massy stone, sprang forth from beneath it as a purling brook, the waters of which produced a meandering stream that bore his name

THAUMAS.

Astonishment at the grand spectacles of nature rises out of the sea, and with a few leading features, is personified in Thaumas, a son of Pontos.

Thaumas is the father, and the Oceanide, Electra (*Brightness*), the mother of Iris or the rainbow; that wonderful being, who, on account of the rapidity with which her feet touched the earth, while her head has not yet left the clouds, is represented as the female messenger of the immortals. She shared with Mercury the honor of conveying to the inhabitants of the earth the mandates of the superior divinities; especially of Juno, to whose service she was particularly attached, and whose person she constantly attended. She is represented with all the colors of the rainbow.

Her most serious charge was to cut the thread of life which seemed to detain the soul in the expiring body; she is thus represented by Virgil, as being sent by Juno from Olympus to release the struggling soul of Dido.

HARPIES.

Children of the same parents are the swift-winged Harpies, Aëllo, Ocypete, and Celæno; who, like raging tornadoes, rush forth from the sea and seize their prey—a horror to mortals who are unable to resist their rapacious claws. They are represented as having the faces of virgins, the bodies of vultures, and the claws of lions.

They were sent by Juno to plunder the tables of Phineus, whence they were driven to the islands called Strophades. They plundered Æneias during his voyage towards Italy, and predicted many of the calamities which attended him.

According to Damm, the term Harpya signifies properly a violent wind, carrying off any thing that is exposed to its fury; in other words, a furious whirlwind. Hence the fable of the Harpies. To the vivid imagination of the Greeks, the terrors of the storm were intimately associated with the idea of powerful and active dæmons directing its fury. The names given to the Harpies indicate ' this ; viz. Ocypete, *rapid ;* Celæno, *obscurity ;* and Aëllo, *a storm.* With Homer, the Harpies are goddesses who suddenly carry off persons unseen and unheard.

Penelope, in her prayer to Diana, represents them as goddesses of the storm and winds, who dwell in the vicinity of the Furies, on the borders of Oceanos, near the opening that leads to the world of spirits (Od. xx. 62.)

The mixed form commonly assigned to them, was the addition of a later age.

GRÆÆ.

Phorcys, and his wife Ceto, are the children of Pontos and parents of the monsters. Grææ (*Gray-maids,*) Perphredo (*horrifier*), Enyo (*shaker*), and Deino (*terrifier*), three decrepit virgins, who were grey with age from their very birth. Their abode was at the end of the earth, where reigns eternal night.

THE GORGONS.

The Gorgons, Euryale, Stheïno, and Medusa, were daughters of the same parents. Instead of hair their heads were covered with serpents. They had the faces and breasts of women, and their bodies, which terminated in the tails of serpents, were covered with scales. Their very looks had the power of turning the beholder to stone. Medusa, who was killed by Perseus, was the only one of them subject to mortality.

We find the Grææ always united with the Gorgons, whose guards they were, according to Æschylus. This poet describes them as " three long-lived maids, swan formed, having one eye and one tooth in common, and on whom the sun with his beams nor the mighty moon ever looks." Perseus, he says, intercepted the eye as they were handing it from one to the other, and having thus blinded the guard, was enabled to approach the Gorgons unperceived.

CHRYSAOR.

From the blood of Medusa, sprang Chrysaor with the golden sword, and the winged Pegasos.

Chrysaor married Callirrhöe, a daughter of Oceanos ; and they became the parents of the triple-bodied Geryon, and Echidna, who was upwards a beautiful nymph, but terminated below in a hideous coiling dragon.

With Echidna, the giant Typhœus produced the triple-headed dog Cerberos, that watched the gates of Pluto's dismal realm ;—the two-headed dog Orthrus, the Lernæan Hydra, and the fire-vomiting Chimæra. Echidna is also said to be the mother of the Nemæan Lion and the mysterious Sphinx.

CERBEROS.

Cerberos was variously described by the ancient mythologists and poets. According to Hesiod he had fifty heads, and according to others only three. He was stationed at the entrance of Hell as a watchful keeper, to prevent the living from entering the infernal regions, and the dead from escaping their confinement. It was usual for the heroes, who in their lifetime visited the dominions of Aides, to appease the barking mouth of Cerberos with a cake.

HYDRA.

The celebrated Hydra, which infested the lake of Lerna in Peloponnesus, had, according to Diodorus, a hundred heads ; according to Simonides, fifty ; and according to the more received opinion of Apollodorus, the number was nine. As soon as one of these heads was cut off, two immediately grew in its place, unless the wound was instantly touched with fire. To destroy the Hydra was one of the twelve labors of Hercules.

CHIMÆRA.

Chimæra was represented as a dreadful monster, having the head and breast of a lion, the body of a goat, and continually vomited forth fire. This fiction was probably occasioned by a lambent flame of some ignited gas issuing from a small cavity in the side of a lofty mountain of Lycia, and which is still apparent. On the summit of the mountain were lions; in the middle goats pastured; and the lower parts cf it were infested with serpents. Bellerophon, a famous hero, made this mountain habitable, and was therefore said to have killed the Chimæra

> " First dire Chimæra's conquest was enjoined;
> A mingled monster of no mortal kind:
> Behind a fiery dragon's tail was spread;
> A goat's rough body bore a lion's head;
> Her pitchy nostrils flashy flames expire;
> Her gaping throat emits eternal fire."

We are indebted to Capt. Beaufort for an accurate account of the Chimæra flame, which after the lapse of so many centuries is still unsubdued. This able navigator and antiquary, being at the same time east of Olympos, says:

" He had seen from the ship, the preceding night, a small but steady light among the hills; on mentioning the circumstance to the inhabitants, we learned that it was a *yanar* or volcanic flame, and they offered to supply us with horses and guides to examine it.

" We rode about two miles, through a fertile plain partly cultivated, and then winding up a rocky and thickly-wooded glen, we arrived at the place. In the inner corner of a ruined building, the wall is undermined so as to leave an aperture of about three feet diameter, and shaped like the mouth of an oven; from thence the flame issues, giving out an intense heat, yet producing no smoke on the wall; and though from the opening we detached some small lumps of caked soot, the walls were hardly discolored. Trees, brushwood, and weeds grow close around this little crater; a small stream trickles down the hill hard by, and the ground does not appear to feel the effects of its heat beyond the distance of a few yards. No volcanic productions whatever were perceived in the neighborhood. The guide declared that in the memory of man there had been but one hole, and that it had never

6

changed its appearance. It was never accompanied by earthquakes or noises, and it ejected neither stones, smoke, nor noxious vapors; nothing but a brilliant and perpetual flame, which no quantity of water could quench."

THE SPHINX.,

The Sphinx was a monster with the face of a woman, the breast, feet, and tail of a lion, and the wings of a bird. Juno, always hostile to the city of Dionysos, sent this monster to ravage the territory of Thebes. She had been taught riddles by the Muses, and from the Phicean Hill propounded one to the Thebans: It was this: "What is that which has one voice, is four-footed, two-footed, and at last three-footed?" The oracle told the Thebans that they would not be delivered from the Sphinx until they had solved her riddle. They often met to try their skill, and when they failed, the Sphinx carried off and devoured one of their number. At length Hæmon, son of Creön, having become her victim, his father, by public proclamation, offered his throne and the hand of his sister Iocasta to whoever should solve the riddle.

Œdipus, who was then at Thebes, hearing this, came forward and answered the Sphinx, that it was man, who when an infant creeps on all fours; when a man, goes on two feet; and when old, uses a staff, a third foot. The Sphinx then flung herself down to the earth and perished.

The Sphinx was a favorite emblem among the Egyptians, and served, according to some, as a type of the enigmatic nature of the Egyptian theology.

M. Maillet is of opinion, that the union of the head of a virgin with the body of a lion is a symbol of the retreat of the Egyptians to the high lands, when the sun is in the signs Leo and Virgo, and the Nile overflows. According to Herodotus, however, the Egyptians had also their Androsphinges, with the body of a lion and the face of a man.

At the present day there still remains, about three hundred paces east of the second pyramid, a celebrated statue of a Sphinx, cut in the solid rock. Formerly, nothing but the head, neck, and top were visible, the rest being sunk in the sand. It was, at the expense of eight or nine hundred pounds (contributed by some European gentlemen), cleared from the accumulated sand in front of it, under the superintendence of Captain Caviglia.

This monstrous production consists of a virgin head joined to the body of a quadruped. The body is principally formed out of the solid rock ; the paws are of masonry, extending forward fifty feet from the body; between the paws are several sculptured tablets, so arranged as to form a small temple, and further forward, a square altar with horns. The length of the statue from the fore-part of the neck to the tail is a hundred and twenty-five feet. The face has been disfigured by the arrows and lances of the Arabs, who are taught by their religion to hold all images of men and animals in detestation.

GIANTS. CYCLOPES. TITANS.

Earth united with Heaven produced Oceanos and the giants with fifty heads and a hundred hands—by which is meant, the personification of the great powers of nature—as their names signify : Cottos (*erup-tion*), Briareos (*hurricane*), and Gyes (*earthquake*). The Cyclopes which represented the energies of the sky ; Steropes (*lightning*), Brontes (*thunder*), and Arges (*the candent bolt*). Also the Titans and Titanides, whose names signify the milder powers of nature, or some of the planets. Titans,* Cœos (*he that begets*), Hyperion (*superior or wandering on high*), Crios (*the ruler*), Japetos (*intention*), Kronos (*time*). Titanides—Phœbe (*the shining*), Rhea (*succession*), Themis (*justice*), Theia (*order*), Tethys (*the nourisher*), Mnemosyne (*retention or memory*).

These productions became formidable to their father, who closely confined them in the grottoes of the earth and never permitted them to see the light. Earth, displeased at their fate, forged the first sickle or scythe, and giving it to Kronos, the youngest of the Titans, insti-gated him to limit the power of his father by maiming him. From the drops of blood that Earth received in her lap, arose the giants Por-phyrion, Alcyoneus, Cromedon, Encelados, and Rhœtus. What fell into the sea rendered it prolific, and from the foam arose Venus, the goddess of Love and Beauty. She was the first beautiful object that arose from the contest of power against power among the produc-tions of Earth ; and deriving her origin from the creative power of Heaven, she is the representation of all that is beautiful and attrac-tive, commanding the homage of gods as well as men.

---

* So call'd from Titaia, one of the epithets of earth.

THE NYMPHÆ.

According to Hesiod, the Nymphs were also the productions of Heaven. The Greeks divided them into various orders according to the place of their abode.

Thus, the Mountain-Nymphs (*Oreiads*) haunted the mountains. The *Napææ*, or Dale-Nymphs, the valleys; the *Leimoniades*, or Mead-Nymphs, the meadows; the *Naiades*, or Water-Nymphs, the rivers, brooks, and springs; the *Limniades*, or Lake-Nymphs, the lakes and pools. There were also the *Hamadryades*, or Tree-Nymphs, who were born and died with the trees; the *Dryades*, or Wood-Nymphs, and the *Meliades*, the Fruit-tree-Nymphs, or Flock-Nymphs, who watched over gardens, or flocks of sheep.

The charge of rearing various gods and heroes was committed to the Nymphs; for instance, they were the nurses of Dionysos, Pan, and even Jupiter himself; and they also brought up Aristæos and Æneias. They were also the attendants of the goddesses; they waited on Juno and Venus, and in huntress-attire, pursued the deer over the mountains in the company of Artemis.

In the Homeric poems, the most ancient portion of Grecian literature, we meet the various classes of Nymphs. In the Odyssey, they are the attendants of Calypso, herself a goddess and a Nymph. Of the female attendants of Circe, the powerful daughter of Helios, also designated as a goddess and a Nymph, it is said,

> "They spring from fountains and from sacred groves,
> And holy streams that flow into the sea."—Od. x. 350.

Yet these Nymphs are of divine nature; and when Jupiter, the father of the gods, calls together his council,

> "None of the streams, save Ocean, stayed away;
> Nor of the Nymphs; who dwelled in beauteous groves,
> And springs of streams, and verdant grassy shades!"—Il. xx. 7.

The good Eumæos prays to the Nymphs to speed the return of his master, reminding them of the numerous sacrifices which Odysseus has offered to them. In another part of the poem their sacred cave is thus described:

"But at the harbor's head a long-leafed olive
Grows, and near to it lies a lonely cave,
Dusky, and sacred to the Nymphs, whom men
Call Naiades. In it large craters lie,
And two-ear'd pitchers, all of stone ; and there
Bees build their combs. In it, too, are long looms
Of stone, and there the Nymphs do weave their robes,
Sea-purple, wondrous to behold. Aye-flowing
Waters are there. Two entrances it hath ;
That to the north is pervious unto men ;
That to the south more sacred is, and there
Men enter not, but 'tis the immortals' path."

One of the most interesting species of Nymphs are the Hamadryades, those personifications of the vegetable life of plants. They possessed the power to reward and punish those who prolonged or abridged
the existence of their associate-tree. In the Argonautics of Apollonius
Rhodius, Phineas thus explains to the heroes the cause of the poverty
of Peræbios :

"But he was paying the penalty laid on
His father's crime; for one time cutting trees
Alone among the hills, he spurned the prayer
Of the Hamadryas Nymph, who, weeping sore,
With earnest words besought him not to cut
The trunk of an oak tree, which, with herself
Coëval, had endured for many a year.
But, in the pride of youth, he foolishly
Cut it: and to him and his race the Nymph
Gave ever after a lot profitless."

The Scholiast gives, on this passage, the following tale from Charon
of Lampsacus :
A man named Rhœcos, happening to see an oak just ready to fall to
the ground, ordered his slaves to prop it up. The Nymph, who had
been on the point of perishing with the tree, came to him expressing
her gratitude for having saved her life, and at the same time desired
him to ask what reward he would. Rhœcos then requested permission
to be her lover, to which the Nymph acceded ; charging him at the
same time to avoid the society of other women, and told him that a bee
should be her messenger. On a time, the bee happened to come to
Rhœcos as he was playing at draughts, when he made a rude reply ;
which so incensed the Nymph that she deprived him of sight.

OCEANOS.

Oceanos, son of Heaven and Earth (*Uranos* and *Ge*, or *Calus* and *Terra*), married Tethys, in connection with whom he produced the Rivers and Fountains, and the Oceanides.

The name of Oceanos is made to signify an immense stream, which according to the rude ideas of the ancients circulated round the terra-queous plain, and from which the different seas ran out in the manner of bays. This opinion, which was also that of Eratosthenes, was preva-lent even in the time of Herodotus. This same river Oceanos was supposed to ebb and flow thrice in a single day; and the heavenly bodies were believed to descend into it at their setting, and emerge from it at their rising.

On the shield of Achilles the poet represents Oceanos as encircling the rim or extreme border of the shield, in full accordance with the popular belief of the day. But in Virgil's time, when this primitive meaning of the term was obselete, and more correct geographical views had been obtained, we find the sea (the idea probably being borrowed from the position of the Mediterranean) occupying, in the poet's descrip-tion, the centre of the shield of Æneias.

The ancients were superstitious in their worship of Oceanos, rever-encing, with great solemnity, a deity to whose care they intrusted themselves when going on a voyage. He presided over every part of the sea, and even rivers were subject to his power. According to Homer, he was father of all the gods, and on that account received frequent visits from the other deities.

Oceanos is generally represented as an old man, with a long, flowing beard, and sitting upon the waves of the sea. He often holds a pike in his hand, and ships under sail appear in the distance.

RIVERS AND FOUNTAINS.

As productions of Oceanos, the Rivers and Fountains belong to the ancient Deities; but in the later history of the gods, imagination has given them personality, and they appear as active beings. As for example, Scamander, Achelous, Peneus, Alpheios, and Inachos. This personification of the running waters has given rise to some beautiful fictions, and the head of a people whose origin is not known, is called a son of the river near the shores of which are found the dwellings of

his descendants. Æschylus introduces the Fountains as pitying Prometheus, when he was chained to the rock by Jupiter, and complaining
with him of the tyranny to which he was subjected.

The river Nile, fabled to
be the son of Oceanos, has
been personified in several
statues, but more particularly a very fine one of
black marble now in the
Vatican. He is distin-
guished by his large Cor-
nucopia, by the Sphinx
couched under him, and
by the sixteen little children playing around him.
The Cornucopia is in-
troduced with great pro-
priety, this river being
the absolute cause of the
great fertility of Lower
Egypt, which it supplies with soil as well as moisture. He was their
Jupiter Pluvius, or chief river god, and thence termed by Tibullus,
the Egyptian Jupiter. The Sphinx is supposed by some to allude to
the mystic knowledge so much cultivated in Egypt; and by others to
the retreat of the Egyptians from the Nile, in the signs Leo and
Virgo. By the sixteen children are understood the several risings of
the river every year, as far as to sixteen cubits. This piece of statuary is said to be of black marble, in allusion to the Nile's coming from
Ethiopia.

It is worthy of remark, that Virgil, in his account of Æneias' shield,
describes the Nile as of a vast size, and exhibiting in his countenance
a mingled expression of terror and concern, spreading his robe, and
inviting the defeated fleet of Cleopatra to the inmost recesses of this
stream. In the Vatican statue the water flows down from under his
robe, which conceals his urn, to denote that the head of this river was
impenetrable. In some modern statues, the head of the figure is for
the same reason quite hidden under the robe.

There are few streams so celebrated in antiquity as the Alpheios.
Its proximity to the scene of the Olympic contests, continually connects

its name with the mention of those memorable games, on the part of the ancient poets, and gives it, in particular, a conspicuous place in the verses of Pindar.

There is also a pleasing legend connected with this stream. According to the poets, Alpheios loved and pursued the Nymph Arethusa; who was only saved from him by the intervention of Diana, who for that purpose changed her into a fountain. This fountain she placed in the island of Ortygia, near the coast of Sicily. The ardent river-god, however, did not then desist, but worked a passage for himself amid the intervening ocean, and rising again in the Ortygian island, his waters were mingled with those of the fountain Arethusa.

According to another version of the same legend, it was Diana herself, and not the nymph Arethusa, whom the river-god of the Alpheus pursued ; and when this pursuit ended in the island of Ortygia, then arose the fountain Arethusa.

This account affords a clew to the true meaning of the entire fable. The goddess, it appears, had an altar at Olympia in common with the god of the Alpheus. To the same Diana water was held sacred ; and this part of her worship, having passed from the Peloponnesus into Sicily, the worship of the Alpheus accompanied it; or, in other words, a common altar for the two divinities was erected by the Syracusans in Ortygia, similar in its attendant rites and ceremonies to the altar at Olympia. In the island of Ortygia all water was considered sacred, and Diana was worshipped at the fountain of Arethusa. And from this commingling of rites arose the poetic legend, that the Alpheus had passed through the ocean to Ortygia and blended its waters with those of Arethusa ; or, in other words, its rites with those of Diana.

INACHOS.

A considerable portion of ancient history is traced back to Inachos, son of Oceanos. Inachos was a stream that watered the fields of Argolis in Peloponnesus; fiction gave it personality, and made it the author of the people who lived around its shores.

His son Phoroneus taught them the use of fire ; and having previously been dispersed in the woods, he persuaded them to unite and build themselves contiguous dwellings. Thus, Phoroneus causing his people to make the first step towards civilization, became one of the earliest and principal benefactors to mankind

Io, a daughter of Inachos, loved by Jupiter, and persecuted by Juno, was transformed into a cow, and furiously driven over the whole earth, until she found a resting-place in Egypt. There she had a temple erected, and was worshipped as a goddess (Isis). She gave a son to Jupiter, called Epaphos, from whom sprang a royal race, that after-wards reigned in Greece; founding their right of royal authority on descent from old Inachos.

Lybia, a daughter of the Egyptian king Epaphos, gave two sons to Poseidon, Belus and Agenor; the latter was king of Tyre. Cadmos, who is said to have brought the first letters into Greece, and to have founded the city of Thebes, was his son; and Europa, the mother of Minos, his daughter.

Belus, the other grandson of Epaphos, was the father of Danäos and Egyptus, the former of whom came over from Egypt to Greece, and reigned in Argos. From him Acrisius descended, the father of Danäe, and the grandfather of the heroic Perseus. Alcæus was a son of Perseus; and a grand-daughter of Alcæus, Alcmena, was the mother of Hercules.

These are the principal personages descended from the heroic family of Inachos. From the impossibility of tracing back any family of kings further than Inachos, arose the common saying of the ancient poets: " Though thou canst derive thy origin from old Inachos, thou still remainest a victim of inexorable Orcus."

IO.

Io, daughter of Inachos, was priestess of Juno at Argos, and, unhap pily for her, was beloved by Jupiter. When this god found that his conduct had excited the suspicions of Juno, he changed Io into a white cow, and declared with an oath that he had been guilty of no infidelity. The Goddess, affecting to believe him, asked the cow as a present; and, on obtaining her, set the " all-seeing Argus" to watch her. He accordingly bound her to an olive-tree in the grove of Mycenæ, and there kept guard over her. Jupiter, pitying her situation, directed Mercury to steal her away. The god of ingenious devices made the attempt; but, as a vulture always gave Argus warning of his projects, he found it impossible to succeed. Nothing then remained but open force. Mercury killed Argus with a stone, having first lulled him to sleep with his lyre, and hence obtained the appellation of Argus-slayer The vengeance of Juno, however, was not yet satiated; and she sent

a gadfly to torment Io, who fled over the whole world from its pursuit.
She swam through the Ionian Sea, which was fabled to have hence
derived its name from her. She then roamed over the plains of Illyria, ascended Mount Hæmus, and crossed the Thracian Strait, thence
named the Bosphorus; she rambled on through Scythia and the country of the Cimmerians, and, after wandering over various regions of
Europe and Asia, arrived at last on the banks of the Nile, where she
assumed her original form, and bore to Jupiter a son named Epaphos.

The legend of Io appears not to have attracted much attention from
the earlier poets. Æschylus introduces her into his "Prometheus
Bound," and he also relates her story in his "Suppliants." Her story,
however, was noticed in the Ægimius, where it was said that her father's
name was Peirea, and that her keeper, Argus, had four eyes, and that
the island of Eubœa derived its name from her.

When the Greeks first settled in Egypt, and saw the statues of Isis
with the cow's horns, they, in their usual manner, inferred that she was
their own Io, with whose name hers had a slight similarity. At Memphis they afterwards beheld the worship of the holy bull Apis, and
naturally supposing the bull-god to be the son of the cow-goddess, they
formed from him a son for their Io, whose name was the occasion of a
new legend, relative to the mode by which she was restored to her
pristine form.

The whole story of Io is an agricultural legend, and admits of an
easy explanation. Io, whether considered as the offspring of Iasos
(the favorite of Ceres), or Peiron (the "experimenter" or "tryer"), is
a type of early agriculture, progressing gradually by the aid of slow
and painful experience. Jupiter represents the firmament, the genial
source of light and life; Juno, on the other hand, is the type of the
atmosphere, with its stormy and capricious changes. Early agriculture
suffers from these changes, which impede more or less the fostering
influence of the pure firmament that lies beyond; and hence, man is
obliged to watch with incessant and sleepless care over the labors of
primitive husbandry. This ever-watchful superintendence is typified
by Argus with his countless eyes, save that in the legend he becomes
an instrument of punishment in the hands of Juno.

If we turn to the version of the fable as given in the Ægimius, the
meaning of the whole story becomes still plainer ; for here, the four
eyes of. Argus are types of the four seasons, while the name, Eubœa,
contains a direct reference to success in agriculture. Argus, continues

the legend, was slain by Mercury, and Io was then left free to wander over the whole earth. Now, as Mercury was the god of language, and the inventor of letters, what is this but saying, that when the rules and precepts of agriculture were introduced, first orally, and then in writing, mankind were released from that ever-watching care which early hus-bandry had required from them, and agriculture, now reduced to a regular system, went forth in freedom and spread itself among the nations? Again, in Egypt Io finds at last a resting-place; here she assumes her original form, and here brings forth Epaphos as the off-spring of Jupiter. What is this but saying, that agriculture was car-ried to perfection in the fertile land of the Nile, and that here it was touched by the true generative influence from on high, and brought forth in the richest abundance? Still further, the eyes of Argus, we are told, were transferred by Juno to the plumage of her favorite bird; and the peacock, it is well known, gives sure indications, by its cry, of changes about to take place in the atmosphere, and is in this respect, therefore, intimately connected with the operations of husbandry. We see, too, from this, why, since Juno is the type of the atmosphere, the peacock was considered as sacred to that goddess.

Ovid gives to Argus a hundred eyes, of which only two ever slept at the same time: he also makes Mercury to have slain him with a *harpé*, or short curved sword.

STYX.

Styx, a daughter of Oceanos and Tethys. Also a celebrated river of hell round which it flowed nine times. The waters of this subterra-nean fountain trickle in nightly gloom from a high vaulted rock, form-ing the stream over which there is no return; and by this stream the gods swear that inviolable oath, the obligation of which no power of heaven or earth can dissolve. Thus the gods on high swear by the deep where night reigns, and where, according to the ancients, are the foundations of the universe on which depend the preservation of all things.

If any of the gods were guilty of perjury, Jupiter obliged them to drink of the water of the Styx, which for a whole year lulled them to senseless stupidity; for the nine following years they were deprived of the nectar and ambrosia of the gods; after the expiration of this period of punishment they were restored to the assembly of the gods and to the enjoyment of their original privileges.

It is said that this veneration was shown to the Styx, because it received its name from the nymph Styx, who with her three daughters assisted Jupiter in the war of the gods against the Titans. One of the early Greek traditions says, that the oath by the Styx originated in the supposition that the waters of this river formed a draught that was fatal even to the gods.

According to some writers, the Styx was a small river of Nonacris in Arcadia, whose waters were so cold and poisonous as to be fatal to all who tasted them. Among others, Alexander the Great is mentioned as a victim to their poison. They even consumed iron and demolished vessels; and their wonderful properties suggested the idea that they formed a river of hell; especially when they disappeared in the earth a little below their fountain-head.

HYPERION

Hyperion and Theia unite and produce Eos (*Dawn or Aurora*), Helios, and Luna. Eos married Astræos (*Starry*), the son of the Titan Crios, and became the mother of the winds, Zephyros, Boreas, and Notos, and Eosphoros (*Dawn-bearer*), or the morning star.

Appearing in the grey twilight of morning, Aurora lifts with rosy fingers the veil of Night, sheds a radiant lustre over the earth, and disappears at the entrance of Helios.

She is represented as standing in a magnificent chariot, and sometimes drawn by winged steeds. A brilliant star sparkles upon her forehead, and while with one hand she grasps the reins, she holds in the other a lighted torch.

ANEMOI. WINDS.

In the Iliad, the winds are represented as gods, but not winged. Wings, horses, and chariots are the additions of later poets. The Winds were feasting in the dwelling of Zephyros when Iris bore to them the prayer of Achilleus, that they would inflame the pyre of Patroclos. In the Odyssey they are not directed by separate deities, but are all under the charge of Æolos.

The winds were divided into *wholesome* and *noxious*. The former were Boreas (*North*), Zephyros (*West*), and Notos (*South*). In Greece and the rest of Europe, the east wind is regarded as noxious, and those that blow from the east are described by Hesiod as of the race of Typhœus, the last and most terrible child of Earth.

Boreas was called *Clear-weather* or *Frost-producer.* He is fabled to have loved and carried off Oreithyia, the daughter of Erechtheus, king of Athens. The Athenians ascribed the destruction of the fleet of Xerxes by a storm, to the partiality of Boreas for the country of Oreithyia, and after that event, built a temple to his honor.

Zephyros is described by Homer as a strong-blowing wind, but he was afterwards regarded as gentle and soft-breathing.

HELIOS OR SOL.

Helios, or Sol, belonged likewise to the ancient deities; in which, with a few strong features, the grand objects of nature are personified; for it is the shining sun that appears in the image of Helios. His head is surrounded by rays, and he gives light both to gods and men. He sees and hears every thing, and discovers all that is kept secret.

To him were sacred those fat oxen that grazed without herdsmen in the island of Sicily, and at the sight of which he was delighted as he passed through the skies. When, therefore, the companions of Ulysses had killed several of them, the god of the sun threatened Jupiter that he would descend into Orcus and carry light to the dead unless he avenged the injury done him. Jupiter terrified by his threats, immediately dashed the ship in pieces, so that Ulysses' companions became a prey to the sea. (Il. xii. 260.)

Sometimes the god of the sun is called Titan, on account of his belonging to that family; or from his father, with whom he is sometimes confounded in ancient tales; or Hyperion, a name which signifies height or sublimity; and it is remarkable that a term of precisely the same import (*Ikare*) is applied to the same luminary by the Iroquois of North America.

Sol was an object of veneration among the ancients, and was particularly worshipped by the Persians under the name of Mithras.

HECATE.

Coïos and Phœbe unite and produce Latona and Asteria. The latter married Perses, and became the mother of Hecate; who, although of the Titan family, is highly honored by Jupiter as well as the other gods; for she belonged to that class of beings whose power was supposed to extend throughout the universe. She was considered as one of the fatal deities who distributed either victory or renown according to her pleasure, and in whose hands lies the fate of men. She reigns on earth, in the sea, and in the air; and was called Luna in heaven, Diana on the earth, and Persephone in hell. She was supposed to preside over magic and enchantment; and to her, kings and nations considered themselves indebted for their prosperity.

Hecate is undoubtedly a stranger divinity in the mythology of the Greeks. It would appear that she was one of the hurtful class of deities, transported by Hesiod into the Grecian mythology, and placed behind the more popular deities, as a being of earlier existence. Hence the remark of the bard, that Jupiter respected all the prerogatives that Hecate had enjoyed previous to his ascending the throne of his father. Indeed, the sphere which the poets assigned her, places her out of the reach of all contact with the acting divinities of the day. She is mentioned neither in the Iliad nor Odyssey, and the attributes assigned her in the more recent poem of the Argonauts, are the same with those of Persephone in Homer.

Jablonski regards Hecate as the same with the Egyptian Tithrambo. Her actions upon nature, her diversified attributes her innumerable functions, are a mixture of physical, allegorical, and philosophical traditions respecting the fusion of the elements and the generation of beings. Hecate was the night; and by an extension of this idea, the primitive night, the primary cause or parent of all things. She was the moon; and hence were connected with her all those ideas which are grouped around the moon; she is the goddess that troubles the reason of men; the goddess that presides over nocturnal ceremonies, and consequently over magic; hence her identity with Diana for the Grecian mythology, and with Isis for the Egyptian; and hence also her cosmogonical attributes assigned to Isis in Egypt.

Dogs, lambs, and honey were generally offered to Hecate, especially in highways and cross-roads—hence she obtained the name of Trivia. Expiatory sacrifices were offered to her on the thirtieth of every month, in which eggs and young dogs were the principal objects. The remains of the offerings, together with a large quantity of all sorts of comestibles, were exposed in the cross-roads, and called the supper of Hecate. The poorer classes and cynics seized upon these viands with an eagerness that passed among the ancients as a mark of extreme indigence, or the lowest degree of baseness.

The Athenians also paid particular worship to Hecate, who was deemed the patroness of families and children. From this circumstance the statues of the goddess were erected before the doors of houses. Upon every new moon a supper was provided at the expense of the wealthy, and set in the streets, where the poorest of the citizens were allowed to feast upon it, while they reported that it was devoured by Hecate This public supper was always held in a place where three ways met, in allusion to the triple nature of the goddess

There were also expiatory offerings to supplicate the goddess to remove whatever evils might impend on the head of the public.

Her statues were in general dog-headed ; and were set up at Athens and elsewhere in the market-places and cross-roads. It is probable that the dog-headed form was the ancient and mystic one of Hecate, and that under which she was worshipped in the mysteries of Samothrace, where dogs were immolated in her honor. Her mysteries were also celebrated at Ægina, and their establishment was ascribed to Orpheus. Numerous statues of the goddess were to be seen in this island, one by Myron with a single face, others with two faces, attributed to the famous Alcamenes.

Hecate was generally represented as a woman with the head of a female, a horse, or a dog ; and sometimes with three distinct bodies, having three different faces united in one neck.

ASTRÆOS. PALLAS. PERSES.

Crios and Eurybia (*Wide-strength*), a daughter of Pontos, gave birth to the Titans, Astræos (*Starry*), Pallas (*Shaker*), and Perses (*Bright*).

Pallas married Styx, the daughter of Oceanos, who gave him powerful children ; Zelos (*Zeal*), Nike (*Victory*), Kratos (*Power*), and Bia (*Strength*). In the war of the gods, Styx, by the advice of her father, went over with her children to Jupiter, and since that time the latter have their seat near the ruler of Heaven and Earth. Victory became one of the attendants of Jupiter.

IAPETOS.

Iapetos marries Clymene, Oceanos' daughter, and is the parent of the Titans, Atlas, Menœtius, Epimetheus, and Prometheus. Atlas married Pheïone, one of the Oceanides, and had twelve daughters called Atlantides. Seven of the daughters were changed into a constellation called Pleïades, and the rest into another called Hyades. Atlas was also the father of the fair nymph, Calypso, who so long detained Ulysses in her island in the distant west.

ATLAS.

The name of Atlas signifies the Endurer; and Homer calls him the *wise* or *deep thinking*, who knows all the depths of the sea, and keeps the long pillars which hold Heaven and Earth asunder.

It is hardly necessary to state, that the Atlas of Homer and Hesiod is not the personification of a mountain. In process of time, however, when the meaning of the earlier legend had become obscured or lost, Atlas, the keeper of the pillars that support the Heaven, became a mountain of Libya. It is remarkable, however, that in all the forms which the fable assumes, it is the god or man Atlas who is turned into, or gives name to the mountain. Thus, according to one mythologist, Atlas was a king of the remotest west, rich in flocks and herds, and master of the trees that bore the golden apples. An ancient prophecy delivered by Themis, had announced to him, that his precious trees would be plundered by a son of Jupiter. When therefore Perseus, on his return from slaying the Gorgon, arrived in the realms of Atlas, and seeking hospitality, announced himself to be a son of the king of the gods, the western monarch, calling to mind the prophecy, attempted to repel him from his doors. Perseus, inferior in strength, displayed the head of Medusa, and the inhospitable monarch was turned into the mountain which still bears his name.

According to another account, Atlas was a man of Libya, devoted to astronomy. Having ascended a lofty mountain, for the purpose of making observations, he fell into the sea, and both sea and mountain were named after him. His supporting the heavens was usually explained by making him an astronomer and the inventor of the sphere.

There is also another curious legend relating to Atlas, which forms part of the fables connected with the adventures of Hercules. When this hero in quest of the apples of the Hesperides, had come to the spot where Prometheus lay chained, moved by his entreaties, he shot the eagle that preyed upon his liver. Prometheus out of gratitude warned him not to go himself to take the golden apples, but to send Atlas for them, and in the mean time to support the Heaven in his stead. The hero did as desired, and at his request Atlas went to the Hesperides and obtained three apples from them; he then proposed to take them himself to Eurystheus, while Hercules remained to support the sky. At the suggestion of Prometheus, the hero feigned consent, but begged him to take hold of the heavens till he made a pad to put upon his head. Atlas threw down the apples and resumed his burden, and Hercules picked them up and went his way.

Various elucidations of the legend of Atlas have been given by the modern expounders of mythology. The best is that of Vollker. This writer, taking into consideration the meaning of his name, in connection with the position assigned him by Homer and Hesiod, and the species of knowledge ascribed to him, and also his being the father of two constellations, regards Atlas as a personification of navigation; the conquest of the sea by human skill, trade, and mercantile profit

PROMETHEUS AND EPIMETHEUS.

The origin of men in these fictions is so subordinate, that they are represented as not even owing their existence to the reigning gods, but to a descendant of the Titans. Prometheus, a son of Iapetos, is said to have formed the first man out of clay. His three brothers, Atlas, Menœtius, and Epimetheus, were, as well as himself, hated by the gods. Iapetos, their father, was at the same time with the other Titans thrown into Tartarus. His powerful son, Menœtius, on account of his dangerous strength and haughty pride, was killed by Jupiter's lightnings; upon the shoulders of Atlas, Jupiter laid the whole burden of the weight of the skies; Prometheus was by his direction fastened to a rock, where a vulture perpetually gnawed at his liver; and Epimetheus was destined to bring woe and misery upon mankind. Thus odious to the gods was the family of Iapetos, from which man took his origin, and on whom all immeasurable sufferings were afterwards heaped together, by which he was made to atone for his grudged existence.

According to ancient fable, the formation of man was accomplished in the following manner:—Prometheus took a piece of earth, a portion of clay still impregnated with divine particles, moistened it with water, and formed man after the image of the gods; so that he alone raises his look to heaven, while all other creatures bend their eyes to the ground. This representation shows that Fancy could not ascribe even to the gods, a form superior to that of man, for there is, in universal nature (and nature is Fancy's great magazine), no being deserving this preference. The beams of the sun give light, but man sees; the thunder rolls and the waves of the sea roar, but the tongue of man utters distinct and intelligible sounds; the moon and stars glitter in light

7

and beauty, but the human countenance is indicative of a superior illumination.

When Prometheus had succeeded in representing the divine form, he burned with desire to bring his work to perfection. He rose therefore to the chariot of Phœbus, in order to kindle the torch, from the fire of which he blew ethereal flames into the breasts of his creatures—thus giving them warmth and life. But the wrath of Jupiter was kindled against him, as a creator of divine formations, and he determined on the destruction of mankind. Prometheus, having sacrificed two bulls, wrapped the meat in one hide and the bones in the other, and then, in order to try Jupiter, asked him which he would prefer as an offering. Jupiter designedly chose the worse part, that he might have a plausible pretext for anger against Prometheus, and of persecuting his creatures, and immediately deprived them of fire. He durst not give vent to his hatred against Prometheus himself. His first object was, to destroy his work; but in this he did not succeed. The noble son of Earth ascended a second time to the chariot of the sun, and again brought down the ethereal spark, hiding it in the stem of a reed. But when from afar, Jupiter descried the light of fire upon the earth, he formed the design of punishing men through their own folly. He therefore requested Vulcan to make a woman of clay, which he intended sending to Prometheus for a wife; he directed him to knead earth and water till it assumed the form of a virgin, like the immortal goddesses, and then to give it human voice and strength. Jupiter also desired Minerva to endow her with artist-knowledge, Venus to give her beauty, and Mercury to inspire her with an impudent and artful disposition. When formed, she was attired by the Seasons and Graces, and each of the deities having bestowed upon her the desired gifts, she was called Pandora (All-gifted).

Jupiter then gave her a beautiful box which she was ordered to present to the man who married her; and by the commission of the god, Mercury conducted her to Prometheus. In the box was enclosed the whole train of evils that threaten mankind. Prometheus, aware of the fraud, rejected the dangerous gift, and sent Pandora away without suffering himself to be captivated by her charms.

He continued to teach men every useful art, for which the employment of fire is necessary, and which was the greatest of his benefits; but deprived them of the view into futurity, lest they should anticipate unavoidable evils. Thus, notwithstanding the efforts of Jupiter, he went on to perfect the creation and formation of mankind, although well aware that he must atone for it in a horrible manner.

Jupiter, still more enraged by the failure of his cunning attempt, and burning with the desire of revenging himself upon Prometheus, now ordered him to be fastened to a rock, on Mount Caucasus, where a vulture fed all day upon his liver, which, growing again during the night, continued to be the means of his torments.

Meanwhile, the misfortunes appointed to men came upon them, in spite of the prudence of Prometheus. The inconsiderate Epimetheus, although warned by his brother, suffered himself to be captivated by the charms of Pandora; who, after he had married her, opened the pernicious box out of which all imaginable evils spread themselves over the whole earth, inflicting misery upon mankind. Pandora, perceiving the pernicious contents of the box, immediately closed it again. But, alas! it was too late. The evils had all escaped, and nothing remained in the box but Hope; who, according to Jupiter's decree, should in due time afford some consolation to mortals. And she alone has the wonderful power of easing the labors of man, and rendering the troubles and sorrows of life less painful.

Prometheus is represented as feeling deeply the sufferings of mankind. He may be considered as the never-ceasing disquietude, the restless, never satisfied desire of mortals; for the liver upon which the vulture preys never dies, and the liver was thought by the ancients to be the seat of desire. His inventive genius introduced fire, and the arts which result from it; and man, henceforth, became a prey to care and anxiety, the love of gain and other evil passions which torment him, and which are personified in the eagle that fed on the inconsumable liver of Prometheus.

According to the fable, the pains of Prometheus lasted until a mortal by his valor and invincible courage made himself a path to immortality, and thus, as it were, reconciled Jupiter to mankind. Hercules, son of Jupiter and Alcmene, killed the vulture with his father's consent, and delivered the sufferer from his long torments. As the mortal foe of the Titans, and the unrelenting persecutor of Prometheus, Jupiter strove to ruin the race of men. But as the quiet power that is superior to its own wrath, and in concord with fate, he at last calmly beheld the rising of new generations, that by sufferings, strength, and perseverance, became assimilated to the gods themselves.

The story of Pandora's box is of a more recent date than that given by Hesiod. The elder fable is as follows : There was a chest or large box in the house of Epimetheus, which an oracle had forbidden to be opened. Pandora, full of curiosity, lifted the fatal lid, and immediately all kinds of evils issued forth, and spread themselves over the earth. The terrified female at length gained sufficient presence of mind to close the lid, and Hope thereupon was alone secured.

An attempt has been made to trace an analogy between this more ancient tradition, and the account of the fall of our first parents, as detailed by the inspired penman. Prometheus (or *Forethought*) is supposed to denote the purity and wisdom of our early progenitor, before he yielded to temptation ; Epimetheus (or *Afterthought*), to be indicative of his change of resolution, and his yielding to the arguments of Eve ; which the poet expresses by saying that Epimetheus received Pandora, after he had been cautioned by Prometheus not to do so. The curiosity of Pandora violated, it is said, the positive injunction about not opening the jar, just as our first parent, Eve, disregarded the commands of her Maker respecting the tree of knowledge. Pandora, moreover, the author of all human woes, is, as the advocates for this analogy assert, the author likewise of their chief, and in fact, only solace ; for she closed the lid of the fatal jar before Hope could escape ; and this she did, according to Hesiod, in compliance with the will of Jove. May not Hope, they ask, thus secured, be that hope and expectation of a Redeemer, which has been traditional from the earliest ages of the world ? Even so our first parents committed the fatal sin of disobedience, but from the seed of the woman who was the first to offend, was to spring one who was to be the hope and the only solace of our race.

All this is extremely ingenious ; but unfortunately, not at all borne out by the words of the poet from whom the legend is obtained. The jar contains various evils ; as long as it remains closed, man is free from their influence, for they are closely confined within their prison house. When the lid or top is raised, these evils fly forth among men, and Hope alone remains behind, the lid being shut down before she could escape. Here then we have man exposed to suffering and calamity, and no hope afforded him of a better lot, for Hope is imprisoned in the jar, and has not been allowed to come forth and exercise her influence in the world. Again, how did Hope ever find admission into the jar ? Was it placed there as a kindred evil ? It surely then could have nothing to do with the promise of a kindred Redeemer. Or was it placed in the jar to lure man to the commission of evil, by constantly exciting dissatisfaction with the present, and a hope of something better in the future ? This, however, is not hope, but discontent. Yet the poet would actually seem to have regarded Hope as no better than an evil, since, after stating that the exit of Hope from the jar was arrested by the closing of the lid, he adds, " but countless *other* woes wander among men." It is much more rational, then, to regard the whole legend as an ebullition of that spleen against the female sex occasionally exhibited by the Grecian poets. The resemblance it bears to the Scripture account is very unsatisfactory. Eve was tempted ; Pandora was not ; the former was actuated by a noble instinct, the love of knowledge ; the latter, by mere female curiosity.

It seems very strange that the ancients should have taken so little notice of this myth. There is no allusion to it in Pindar or the tragedians, excepting Sophocles, one of whose lost satiric dramas was named " Pandora, or the Hammerers." It was equally neglected by the Alexandrians, and seems to have had as little charm for the Latin poets, even Ovid passing over it in silence.

It is deserving of notice, that Hesiod and all the others agree in naming the vessel which Pandora opened a jar, and never hint at her having brought it with her to the house of Epimetheus. Yet the idea has been universal among the moderns, that she brought all the evils ·from Heaven with her shut up in a box. The only way of accounting for this is, that at the restoration of learning, the narrative in Hesiod was misunderstood.

In grateful remembrance of Prometheus, the Athenians celebrated a festival, which was emblematic of the transitory and rapid course of human life. At some distance from the city of Athens stood an altar, dedicated to Prometheus, from which the young Athenians ran a race with lighted torches. He who first gained the mark with his torch still burning, obtained the prize. If all the torches happened to be extinguished before reaching the mark, no prize was given.

Prometheus is generally represented upon ancient works of art, as an artist engaged in his professional employment, with a vase standing at his feet, and before him a human bust, on which he seems to bestow the most intense study, in order to bring it to perfection. He is also represented as sitting with a torch in his hand, over which a butterfly is hovering, to denote the animating breath by which the dead mass is enlivened.

In the vestibule of the Museum of Antiques at Paris, is a modern picture of Prometheus, where he is represented as protected by Minerva, who covers him with her Ægis, and holds the laurel wreath, the recompense of genius, while he touches with the divine flame the man of his own creation, who becomes animated, and appears astonished at his own existence. At the sight of the first mortal being, Time begins his course, the Fates draw the web of human life—and Atropos, one of them, prepares the fatal scissors destined to terminate it. Above Time, Poetry is preparing to celebrate the glory of this event, and closely united, appear Painting and Sculpture, ready to consecrate him by their works.

OGYGES. DEUCALION.

After Prometheus retreats from the theatre and transactions of the world, those who take his place in the great cause of humanity, the new fathers of mankind, by whose assistance they rise as it were from oblivion, are Deucalion, Ogyges, Cecrops, and Inachos.

During the time of Ogyges, son of Terra, a deluge occurred which is anterior to that of Deucalion. The horizon of all history is closed by this Ogygian flood, and even the wide field of fable here finds its limits.

Ogyges reigned in Bœotia, which from him is sometimes called Ogygia ; his power was also extended over Attica. It is supposed that he was of Egyptian or Phœnician extraction, but his origin as well as the age in which he lived, and the duration of his reign are so obscure and unknown, that the epithet Ogygian is often applied to any thing of dark antiquity.

The Greek legend respecting the deluge of Deucalion is as follows:— Deucalion, son of Prometheus and Clymene, was married to Pyrrha, daughter of Epimetheus and Pandora. When Jupiter designed to destroy the brazen race of men on account of their impiety, Deucalion, by the advice of his father, made himself an ark, and putting provisions into it, entered it with his wife Pyrrha. Jupiter then poured rain from Heaven, and inundated a greater part of Greece, so that the people, except a few who escaped to the lofty mountains, perished in the waves. At the same time, the floods burst through the mountains of Thessaly, and all Greece without the Isthmus, as well as the Pelopon·

nesus, was overflowed. Deucalion was carried along the sea in his ark for nine days and nights, until he reached mount Parnassus. By this time the rain had ceased; and leaving his ark, he sacrificed to Jupiter who sent Mercury desiring him to ask what he would. His request was, to have the earth replenished with men. Thereupon, by the direction of Jupiter, he and his wife threw stones behind them, and those which Deucalion threw became men, and those thrown by Pyrrha, women.

Various opinions, as may well be supposed, have been entertained by modern writers in regard to the deluge of Deucalion. We give that of Cuvier. "As to Deucalion," observes the learned French naturalist, " whether this prince be regarded as a real or fictitious personage, however little we enter into the manner in which his deluge has been introduced into the poems of the Greeks, and the various details with which it necessarily becomes enriched, we perceive that it is nothing else than a tradition of the great cataclysm, altered and placed by the Hellenes in the period which they also assigned to Deucalion ; because he was regarded as the founder of their nation ; and because his history is confounded with that of all the chiefs of the renewed nations."

Neither Homer nor Hesiod knew any thing of the deluge of Deucalion, any more than that of Ogyges. The first author whose works are extant, by whom mention is made of the former, is Pindar. He speaks of Deucalion as landing upon Parnassus, establishing himself in the city of Protogeneia (first growth or birth), and recreating his people from stones. In a word, he relates (but confining it to a single nation only) the fable afterwards generalized by Ovid, and applied to the whole human race.

The first historians who wrote after Pindar, namely, Herodotus, Thucydides, and Xenophon, make no mention of any deluge, whether of the time of Ogyges or that of Deucalion, although they speak of the latter as one of the first kings of the Hellenes. Plato, in his Timæus, says only a few words of the deluge, as well as of Deucalion and Pyrrha, in order to commence the recital of the great catastrophe, which, according to the priests of Sais, destroyed the Atlantis ; but in these few words, he speaks of the deluge in the singular number, as if it had been the only one. He places the name of Deucalion immediately after that of Phoroneus, the first of the human race, without making any mention of Ogyges. Thus with him, it is still a general event, a true universal deluge, and the only one which had happened. He regards it, therefore, as identical with that of Ogyges.

Each of the different colonies of Greece, that had preserved isolated traditions, commenced them with a particular deluge of its own, because some remembrance of the deluge common to all the nations, was preserved among each of the tribes ; and when it was afterwards attempted to reduce these various traditions to a common chronology, different events were imagined to have been recorded, from the circumstance that dates, in reality uncertain, or perhaps altogether false, although considered authentic in the countries in which they originated, were not found to agree with each other. Thus in the, same manner that the Hellenes had a deluge of Deucalion, because they regarded him as the founder of their nation, the Autocthenes of Attica had one of Ogyges, because it was with him that their history commenced. The Pelasgi of Arcadia had that, which, according to later authors, compelled Dardanus to retire towards the Hellespont. The island of Samothrace, one of those in which a succession of priests had been more anciently established, together with a regular worship and connected traditions, had also a deluge, which passed for the most ancient of all, and which was attributed to the bursting of the Bosphorus and Hellespont.

Some idea of a similar event was preserved in Asia Minor, and in Syria ; and to this the Greeks would afterwards naturally attach the name of Deucalion. Arnobius even speaks of a rock in Phrygia from which it was pretended that Deucalion and Pyrrha had taken stones ; but none of these traditions assign a very remote antiquity to this cataclysm ; and there is none which does not admit of explanation, in so far as its date and other circumstances are concerned, from the variations to which narratives that are not fixed by writing must be continually liable.

Although Deucalion is called the renewer of the destroyed family of Prometheus, yet we see that other traditions, still more ancient, are connected with the fictions respecting him, and that they confine Deucalion's new creation, or formation of men, to a part of Greece.

Amphictyon, a son of Deucalion, first established a sacred association among the several tribes of Greece, who, by means of common consultations, were so closely united together as to form one nation. This sacred institution was called after the name of its founder, the Amphictyonic council.

Hellen, Deucalion's second son, from whose name the Greeks are called Hellenes, reigned in Thessaly, and was the father of Eolus, who became the ancestor of many heroes. The most renowned among them are Meleager, Bellerophon, and Iasion. Meleager killed the Caledonian boar, Bellerophon vanquished the monster Chimæra, and Iasion won the golden fleece.

These were considered as the most ancient of men, who existed before any other, and whose origin commenced beyond any record, a circumstance which fiction expressed in these words: "They were, ere the moon was." With this people, too, the original simplicity and innocence of manners degenerated into vice and depravity to such a degree, that Jupiter continued to hurl his thunderbolts upon the land of Arcadia, till at last even Earth stretched out her arms imploring mercy.

KRONOS OR SATURN.

Kronos (*Time*) was the youngest of the Titans, and as the heavens measure out time to us, and earth is considered its beginning, he is said to be born of Uranos and Ge.

According to ancient fable, Kronos is married to Rhea (or *Succession*), and with them commence a new generation of gods, by whom the former, in future times, are to be deprived of their power. Lasting forms now gain the superiority ; yet not without a long struggle against all-devouring Chaos, and all-destroying Time, of which Saturn himself is a symbol. He creates and destroys ; therefore it is allegorically said, that he devours his own children, and even the stones, because he consumes the most durable substances

Fable says, that his mother, Earth, had predicted to him that one of his sons would deprive him of his authority, and therefore he swallowed his own children as soon as they were born. Thus the crime which he had committed against his father was revenged. For as Uranos formerly dreaded, so Kronos now dreads seditious power. And while he reigned over his brothers, the Titans, he, in the same manner as his father had done, keeps the hundred armed giants and Cyclopes imprisoned in Tartaros. He fears ruin from his own children. The new-born creatures still rise against the source of creation that threatens to swallow them up again. Even as Ge formerly groaned on account of her children's imprisonment, so Rhea now laments the cruelty of her husband—the all-destroying power that spares not his own creations. When, therefore, the time came in which she was to become

the mother of Jupiter, the future ruler of gods and men, she implored
Earth and the starry Heaven, for the preservation of her child. But
the ancient primitive deities were deprived of government, and the
only influence left them was in prophecies and counsel. The supplicated parents, therefore, advised their daughter to conceal her son as
soon as it should be born, in a fertile part of the island of Crete.

Wild, roving Fancy, now fixing herself upon a certain spot of the
earth, finds on this island, where the divine child is to be reared, her
first resting-place.

By the advice of her mother, Rhea presented a stone to Kronos,
instead of her new-born child. The stratagem was successful ; and by
means of this stone so often mentioned by the ancients, bounds were
set to destruction ; the destroying power had, for the first time, taken
death instead of life; and thus the latter gained time to rise, secretly,
as it were, to light, in order to form and unfold itself. But it is not
yet secure from the persecutions springing from the very source whence
it derives its origin. Therefore the tutors of the child, the Curetes,
whose nature as well as origin are enveloped in mysterious darkness,
make a continual noise with their shields and spears, lest Kronos
should hear the noise of the crying infant.

The education of Jupiter on the island of Crete forms one of the
most attractive fictions of the imagination.

The goat Amalthea, which was afterwards placed among the stars,
and whose horn became the symbol of plenty, suckles him with her
milk. Doves bring him nourishment; golden-colored bees carry him
honey ; and the nymphs of the wood are his nurses. The physical, as
well as intellectual powers of this future king of the gods and men,
rapidly develope themselves. The old realm of Kronos approaches its
end ;—and, in addition to Jupiter, five more of his children are saved
from destruction : viz. Vesta, Ceres, Neptune, Juno and Pluto.

United with them, Jupiter, after having delivered the Cyclopes out
of prison, and received from them the thunderbolts, declares war against
Kronos and the Titans. And now the modern gods, the descendants
of Kronos and Rhea, separate themselves from the ancient deities or
Titans, the children of Uranos and Ge.

The golden years of mortal men were placed by Fancy in those
times when Jupiter did not yet rule with his thunder ; under the reign
of Saturn, imagination collected together all that is desirable to man,
but gone to return no more.

After having been deprived of his destructive power, Saturn escaped the fate of the other Titans, and

"Fled over Adria to the Hesperian fields.

There, in the plains of Latium, surrounded by high mountains, he concealed himself, and transferred thither the golden age, that happy period, when mankind lived in a state of perfect equality and all things were in common. He is said to have arrived in a ship at the Tiber, in the dominions of Janus, and in union with him to have reigned over men with wisdom and benignity.

This fiction is extremely beautiful and attractive, because of the unexpected transition from war and destruction, to peace and the quiet exercise of justice and benevolence. While Jupiter, still in danger of being deprived of his usurped authority, is hurling thunderbolts against his foes, Saturn, far from the scene of violence, has arrived in the quiet fields of Latium, where, under his reign, those happy times pass away which are celebrated in song, as a good that is passed and gone, and now sought for in vain.

Saturn's time was the grey time of yore; he swallowed his own children, buried in oblivion the fleeting years, and left no trace of bloody wars, destroyed cities, and crushed nations, which constitute the chief subjects of history ever since men began to record the events of the world. All that happy time, when liberty and equality, justice and virtue, were still reigning, men lived like the gods in perfect security, without pains and cares, and exempt from the burdens of old age. The soil of the earth gave them fruits without laborious cultivation; unacquainted with sickness, they died away as if overtaken with sweet slumber; and when the lap of earth received their dust, the souls of the deceased, enveloped in light air, remained as genii with the survivors.

In this manner the poets portray those golden times on which imagination, wearied with the scenes of the busy world, dwells with so much delight.

Saturnalia were festivals celebrated in honor of Saturn, and were instituted long before the foundation of Rome, in commemoration of the freedom and equality that existed among the inhabitants of the earth during the golden reign of Saturn.

This festival was celebrated in December, and at first lasted but one day (the 19th); it was then extended to three, and subsequently, by

order of Caligula and Claudius, to seven. This celebration was remarkable for the liberty that universally prevailed during its continuance.
Servants were then allowed freedom with their masters; slaves were
at liberty to be unruly without fear of punishment; and until the
expiration of the festival, wore a cap on the head as a badge of freedom
and equality. Animosity ceased; no criminals were executed; nor was
war ever declared during the Saturnalia, but every thing gave way to
mirth and merriment. Schools were closed; the senate did not sit;
and friends made presents to each other. It was also the custom to
send wax tapers to friends as an expression of good feeling; for the
Romans, as a particular respect to this deity, kept torches and tapers
continually burning upon his altars.

Among the Romans, the priest always performed the sacrifices with
his head uncovered, a custom never observed before any other god.

On his statues were generally hung fetters, in commemoration of the
chains he had worn when imprisoned by Jupiter. From this circumstance, slaves who obtained their liberty, generally dedicated their
fetters to him. During the celebration of the Saturnalia, the chains
were taken from the statues, to intimate the freedom and independence
that mankind enjoyed during the golden age.

In his temple, and under his protection, the Romans placed their
treasury, and also laid up the rolls containing the names of their
people, because, in his time, no one was defrauded, and no theft was
ever committed.

Saturn is generally represented by the ancients, as an old man, bent
with age and infirmity; he holds the sickle or scythe given him by his
mother, and a serpent biting its own tail, which is an emblem of time
and the revolution of the year: sometimes, he is leaning on his sickle
and clothed in tattered garments; to these were added wings, and feet
of wool, to express his fleet and silent course. Upon ancient gems, he
is sometimes represented with a scythe in his hand, and leaning on the
prow of a ship, on the side of which rises part of an edifice and a wall.
This is probably in allusion to Saturn's having built the old city of
Saturnia, near the Tiber, on the hills where Rome was afterwards
founded. In this manner, Saturn sometimes appears as a symbol of
all-destroying time, and sometimes, as a king who once reigned in
Latium.

In the representations of the ancient deities, the imagination of the poet plays with grand images only. Its objects are the great spectacles which nature exhibits—the sky and the earth, the sea and the seditious elements, represented under the images of the Titans, the beaming sun and the shining moon ; all which objects, being endowed with personality by a few striking features, afford better materials for poetry than for plastic art.

Out of the mist which envelopes these beings the more modern divine appearances spring forth in clear light, and distinct forms. Now, we behold Jove, the mighty god of thunder, with the eagle at his feet ; Neptune, the shaker of the earth, with his trident ; the majestic Juno, accompanied with her peacock ; Apollo in eternal youth, with his silver bow ; the blue-eyed Minerva, with helmet and spear ; the chaste Diana, with her bow and arrow ; Mars, the god of war ; and Mercury, the swift messenger of the divinities ; by means of plastic art, these modern deities gain distinct forms, and their individual power and majesty thus embodied, and placed in temples and sacred groves, became to mortals an object of religious veneration and worship.

But the pristine deities were, in a certain respect, the models for the modern. Fancy merely caused the sublime objects of religious veneration that already existed, to be regenerated in a new and youthful form ; ascribing to them descent, name, and native place, in order to unite them more intimately with the ideas and fates of mortals. But in the productions of Fancy, she does not bind herself to a certain and fixed series of beings, therefore we sometimes find the same deity under different forms. For the ideas of divine, supernatural power always existed ; but in the course of time, they became so blended with stories of human life, that in the magic mirror of the dark ages of antiquity, almost all divine images are repeated as in a magnifying reflector ; in this contexture of several fables, the imagination found more ample scope ; a circumstance by which the poets of all ages did not fail to profit.

Henceforth the history of the gods is mingled with that of men. The wars among the former having ceased, there is now nothing worthy their attention but the lives and fates of mortals, with which they seem to trifle ; arbitrarily exalting the one, and depressing the other, yet at the same time assisting heroes of eminent virtue and valor, and raising them to immortality.

PART SECOND

MODERN, SUPERIOR DEITIES.

JUPITER.

MODERN, SUPERIOR DEITIES.

ZEUS AND HERA;

OR,

JUPITER AND JUNO.

Hesiod, in his Theogonia, invokes the Muses who inhabit the heavenly mansions, and whose knowledge of generation and birth he had formerly sung.

"Tell, ye celestial powers," continues the poet, "how first the gods and world were made; the rivers, and the boundless sea with its raging surge. Also, the bright, shining stars, and wide stretched heaven above, and all the gods that sprang from them, givers of good things?"

The Muses answer, "First of all existed Chaos; next in order the broad-bosomed Earth; then Love appeared, the most beautiful of immortals. From Chaos, sprang Erebus and dusky Night, and from Night and Erebus, came Ether and smiling Day.

"But first the Earth produced the starry Heavens, commensurate to herself; and the barren Sea, without mutual love. Then, conjoined with Uranos, she produced the tremendous Titans; after whom, Time, crooked in counsel, was produced, the youngest, and most dreadful of her children. The Cyclops were next engendered; Brontes, Steropes, and Arges, and besides these, three other rueful sons were born to Heaven and Earth, Cottus, Briareus, and Gyes, with fifty heads and a hundred hands; haughty, hateful, and at enmity with their father from the day of their birth—for which cause, as soon as they appeared, he hid them in the grottoes and caves of the Earth, and never permitted them to see the light. Meanwhile, Oceanos married to Tethys, the eldest of the Titans, produced the rivers and fountains, with three thousand daughters, properties and productions of moisture. Heaven's usurping son, Time, marrying the second sister, Rhea, had three female

8

children, Vesta, Ceres, and Juno, and as many males; Pluto, Neptune, and designing Jove, Father of gods and men.

" No sooner was this sovereign source of light brought forth, that is, disembarrassed of heterogeneous parts, than he seized the reins of the universe, that under him at last assumed a stable form. For associating with Metis (counsel, contrivance, thought), by her supreme direction he brought his inhuman parent's progeny to light, and settled his congenial powers, each in their respective dignity; Ceres to fructify the Earth; Juno to impregnate the air; Neptune to rule the sea; and Pluto to reign in the regions below; while Saturn's first-born, Vesta, remained unmoved, the coercive band of the immense machine.

" But in this settlement he met with cruel opposition. The Titan gods (properties of matter) combined against him, and in a long and furious war endeavored to drive him from the throne of Heaven, and reverse the recent dignities of the upstart Saturnian race. And now, the mighty frame had fallen into pristine Chaos, if, prompted by his all-wise associate, he had not first made his kindred gods partakers with himself of Nectar and Ambrosia (incense and immortality), and then released from darksome durance, the predominant igneous powers, sons of Heaven and Earth, Cottus, Briareus, and Gyes, whom he called up to light and made his allies in the war. By their irresistible strength, he at last vanquished the Titan gods, and confined them fast-bound in a prison waste and wild, as far under the Earth as Heaven is above it; a bulwark of brass, with three-fold night brooding over it, and its gates of adamant guarded by three enormous brothers, jailors of Almighty Jove."

Here are the seeds of all things, the roots of the opaque Earth, the barren sea, and the beginnings and bounds of the various orders of beings, all now shut up by the will of Jove, in the bottomless chasm, where darkness reigns and tempests howl, tremendous to the gods themselves. And Fable says, that things continued in this state until Honor and Reverence begot Majesty, who filled Heaven and Earth the day she was born; Awe and Dread sat down by her, and all three being defended by Jove's thunders from the attacks of the Titans, have ever since remained by the side of this god, who now ruies supreme, having rightly arranged all the immortals, and allotted to each their respective dignity.

But after having subdued his greatest adversaries, new dangers arose to Jupiter from his own resolutions. He married Metis, daughter of Oceanos; and it was predicted by an oracle, that she would have a son who should be endowed with his mother's strength and his father's wisdom, and rule over all the gods. To prevent this, Jupiter, with flattering allurements, drew Metis over into his own person, and soon after brought forth Minerva, who, as a full-grown virgin in complete panoply, sprang from his head.

A similar danger threatened him when he wished to marry Thetis, who, according to another oracle, would have a son who should be more powerful than his father.

In this manner these fictions represent that a mighty being always dreads a still mightier; for with the idea of unlimited power, every fiction ceases, Fancy having no farther scope. But to have a just conception of Jove, let us first recollect Zeno's definition of nature—that it is a plastic fire ever generating by rule; and then obey the most philosophical of all poets, when he bids us

> " Look up, and view the immense expanse of Heaven,
> The boundless Ether in his genial arms
> Clasping the Earth. Him call thou
> God and Jove."

We can judge of the propriety of his claim to dominion upon reading what Zeno considers one of the highest steps in the scale of creation. " Ether," says he, " or pure invisible fire, the most subtle and elastic of all bodies, seems to pervade and expand itself throughout the universe. If air is the immediate agent or instrument in the productions of nature, the pure, invisible fire is the first natural mover or spring whence the air derives its power. This mighty agent is every where at hand, ready to break forth into action, actuating and enlivening the whole visible mass, equally fitted to produce or to destroy; distinguishing the various stages of nature, keeping up the perpetual round of generation and corruption, pregnant with forms which it constantly sends forth and resorbs—so quick in its motion, so extensive in its effects, that it seems no other than the vegetative soul, or vital power of the world. This, then, is the true Zeus; the source of generation and principle of life—that heavenly, ethereal, that is, igneous nature, which spontaneously begets all things, the supposed parent of gods and men; and Fancy finding nothing in nature more pure and sublime than the Earth surrounding ether and sky, it was chosen by her as the archetype of the chief deity."

And what was his Hera? " The air," says the same author, " is the receptacle as well as source of all sublunary forms—the great mass or Chaos which imparts or receives them. The atmosphere that surrounds our earth contains a mixture of all the active, volatile parts of all vegetables, minerals, fossils, and animals. Whatever corrupts or exhales, being acted on by solar heat produces within itself all sorts of chemical productions, dispersing again their salts and spirits in new generations. The air, therefore, is an active mass of numberless different principles; the general source of corruption and generation in which the seeds of all things seem to lie latent, ready to appear and produce their kind whenever they shall light on a proper matrix. The whole atmosphere seems alive,—there is every where acid to corrode and seed to engender in this common receptacle of all vivifying principles; and here is the foundation of the marriage made by the poets between these kindred gods. And when we consider at what season of the year the air is impregnated with ethereal seed, when it is that all nature teems with life, we shall not wonder at the cuckoo's being the bird of Hera carved on the top of her sceptre at Argos, or at Zeus transforming himself into the spring's genial messenger when he first enjoyed his queen.

Truth once lighted up shines on every thing around it, and the same thread of reflection will guide us through the labyrinth of a greater mystery; for this matron goddess and patroness of marriage, became once a year a pure, unspotted virgin, upon bathing herself in a sacred fountain in the Argive territory."

As the powerful and majestic goddess, Hera typifies the quick and rapidly moving energies of the productive principle that clothes the earth in the majestic garb of loveliness and beauty—and as the repelling and unattractive wife of Zeus. she typifies the cold frowns and chilling frosts of winter. Hence the physical allegories of their jealousies and quarrels.

Hera's chief archetype was the atmosphere which encompasses the earth, adhering in conjugal union to the ether that rests upon it; and this fiction of the marriage of Zeus and Hera is a representation of Fancy according to human notions and human relations; ridiculous, indeed, unless beheld with the poetical eye of imagination, that forms her gods after the images of men, and her men after the images of the gods. And here let us not pass an unjust judgment on times of old. Antiquity is not to be viewed and explained according to the ideas and customs of modern times, any more than the plays of childhood by the earnest pursuits of maturer life, or the follies of youth by the graver wisdom of old age. While we live, as it were, in the age of reason, the ancients lived in that of imagination ; and the infinite and unlimited being to Fancy a melancholy object, she gave life and animation to things formed and limited, in order to use them as models of her own creation. Therefore, to the boundless mass which surrounds man, the sky, earth, and sea, the ancients gave form and personality. They endeavored to unite the beauty and grace of formed objects, with the strength of the unformed and shapeless ; and as in the tall and erect body of man the solidity of the oak is joined to the pliancy of the sapling, so their creative genius connected the power of the raging elements, and the majesty of the rolling thunder, with the majestic form, the eloquent lips, the frowning brows, and the speaking eye of man. And thus is formed the image of Jupiter Olympius ; that being to whose hands imagination intrusted so much power, must be in harmony with the human form ; because the capacity for thought could only be indicated in the expressive features of the human face, and the power to rule and reign could be represented only in the majestic form of man. And yet the god must be the superior ; and to such a degree rose this power of embodying high conceptions in the art of the Greeks, inspired and consecrated as it was by its subjects, that they exhibited works similar indeed, but far superior to their models : for while excluding from their productions every thing con tingent, they at the same time succeeded in uniting all that is essen tial to power, beauty, and sublimity.

In the character of their gods, the leading idea of the ancients was power ; the expression of which predominates in their most sublime formations. The mighty head of Zeus, from which wisdom was created, bends forward, meditating and directing the changes of events, and producing their revolutions. Among all the celestials, the power of him who rules the thunder is the most unlimited, being restricted only by the invincible will of Fate, or the wiles of the cunning Hera.

Zeus is most frequently represented as feeling in himself the fullness of his authority, and delighting in the consciousness of power. In the language of the most ancient poet, Zeus, threatening the other gods, thus proclaims himself :

> " League all your forces then, ye powers above,
> Join all, and try the omnipotence of Jove,
> Let down our golden, everlasting chain,
> Whose strong embrace holds heaven, earth, and main,

Strive all of mortal and immortal birth,
To drag by this the thunderer down to earth;
Ye strive in vain; if I but stretch this hand,
I heave the gods, the ocean, and the land.
I fix the chain of great Olympus' height,
And the vast world hangs trembling in my sight;
For such I reign unboun-led and above,
And such are men and gods compared to Jove."—*Il.* 8.

From this representation, it is also evident, that in the most perfect idea of Zeus, the surrounding All was comprised. As, however, in this idea every thing is exalted and ennobled, it is not strange that those heroes, whose ancestors were unknown, should be called sons of Zeus. They were the eminent children of the universe, and, consequently, the genuine sons of Jove.

Almost every nation had its Jupiter. Among the first was Jupiter Ammon, of Libya. His temple, the ruins of which are still to be seen, was in an oasis or island of verdure in the desert west of Egypt. Jupiter Serapis, worshipped in Egypt, was also very ancient Jupiter Belus, mentioned by Herodotus, was the Jupiter of the Assyrians. The Ethiopians called him Assabinus, the Gauls Taranus, and the inhabitants of the Lower Nile, Apis. The Romans considered him the protecting deity of their empire, and styled him Jupiter Capitolinus from his chief temple on the Capitoline Hill; Jupiter Tonans, or Thunderer; Jupiter Fulminans, or Fulgurator, scatterer of lightning. An ancient gem shows him quietly looking into the universe, holding the thunder in his right hand, and in his left, the imperial sceptre, with the eagle at his feet. Another represents him with the horns of a ram. This is the image of Jupiter Ammon, who was principally worshipped in Libya, where he gave oracles.

The following legend accounts for the name of Jupiter Ammon:—Bacchos being in the midst of the sands of Arabia, was seized with a thirst so burning, that he longed even for a drop of water. Jupiter then presented himself in the form of a ram, and striking the earth, caused the grateful liquid to spring forth in abundance. To commemorate the deed, Bacchos erected a temple in the deserts of Libya, giving it the name of Jupiter Ammon (*i. e., sandy*).

The curled beard and hair in the representations of Jupiter are indicative of inward power and strength—he knits his black brows;
he shakes his ambrosial locks, and Olympus trembles.

> " He whose all conscious eye the world beholds,
> The eternal Thunderer sits enthroned in gold ;
> High Heaven the footstool of his feet he makes,
> And wide beneath him all Olympus shakes,
> He speaks, and awful bends his sable brows,
> Shakes his ambrosial curls* and gives the nod,
> The stamp of Fate and sanction of a God ;
> High Heaven, with trembling, the dread signal takes,
> And all Olympus to the centre shakes."

The distinguishing characteristic in all representations of Jupiter,
whether by artists' or poets, is majesty; and every thing about him
indicates dignity and authority. His look is sometimes intended to
strike the beholder with terror, and sometimes with gratitude; and
always to command respect and veneration. This would have appeared
more strongly had some of the ancient statues of Jupiter, particularly
that of Olympus, remained until our time. The statue of Jupiter in
the Verospi palace at Rome, though one of the best we have, falls very
far short of the idea we form of him from the ancient poets. It is,
however, easily recognized as Jupiter, by the dignity of his look, the
fulness of the hair, and the venerable beard ; in his left hand he holds
the sceptre, and the fulmen in his right. The fulmen in the hand of
Jupiter was a sort of hieroglyphic, having three different meanings,
according to the three ways in which it was represented. The first is
a wreath of flame in a conical shape, like what we call the thunderbolt.
This was adapted to Jupiter, when mild and calm, and was held down
in his hand. The second is the same figure, with two transverse darts
of lightning, and sometimes with wings on each side of it, to denote
swiftness. This was given to Jupiter when he was represented as
punishing. The thundering legion among the Romans bore the winged
fulmen on their shields, which spread all over them, as appears from
the Antonine and Trajan pillars. In Buonarotti's collection at Florence, there is a figure of Jupiter holding up a three-forked bolt, as if
just ready to dart it at some guilty wretch, but with the conical ful-

---

* Ambrosia, the food of the gods, was also used for anointing the body and hair;
hence the expression " ambrosial locks."

men lying under his feet as of no use in cases of severity. The third way is a handful of flames, which Jupiter held up when inflicting some exemplary punishment.

The different characters under which Jupiter was represented by the Romans were chiefly these:

The Jupiter Capitolinus, who was esteemed the great guardian of the Romans, and who was (according to a very early and strong notion among them) to give them the empire of the world. They called him Optimus Maximus, or the best and greatest, which description is often found on medals. He was represented (as appears on a medal of Vitellius) in his chief ' temple on the Capitoline Hill, as sitting in a curule chair,* with the mildest fulmen held down in his right hand, his character being one of goodness rather than of severity ; and in his left he bears his sceptre as king or father of men. But it was neither the sceptre nor fulmen that chiefly showed the superiority of Jupiter in all his different characters, but the air of majesty which it was the aim of all artists to express in his countenance.

The mild Jupiter appears as on a gem at Florence with a mixture of dignity and ease in his face ; that kind of majesty given him by Virgil when receiving Venus with so much parental tenderness, in the first Æneid. (V., 256.)

The statues of the terrible Jupiter differed in every particular from those of the mild. These were generally of white marble, as those were of black. The mild is sitting with an air of tranquillity ; the terrible is standing and more or less disturbed ; the face of the mild is serene, the terrible is cloudy or angry ; the hair of the one is composed, the other so discomposed as to fall half-way down the forehead. But the artists were careful never to represent him with such an exhibition of passion as to destroy his majesty.

---

* A curule chair was a raised, embellished seat, made of ivory, gold, or other material. Sometimes it was placed in a chariot, in which the chief officers were carried to council. It was also a mark of distinction for dictators, prætors, censors, and ædiles, who from this circumstance were called *curules*. The pontiffs and vestal virgins had also a right to a kind of curule chair.

Representations of the form and ornaments of this honorable seat are found on many Etruscan monuments, from which people the Romans received the custom through Tarquinius Priscus. Numa had previously given the power to the flamen of Jupiter, as a mark of his dignity. At a later period of the republic, under the Emperors, the curule chair was given to foreign princes. Titus Livius relates that Eumenes, king of Pergamos, received from the Roman people a curule chair and an ivory sceptre.

The Jupiter Tonans resembled the Jupiter Terribilis, and is represented on medals and gems, as holding up the triple-forked fulmen, and
standing in a chariot drawn by four horses. The Jupiter Fulminans
and Jupiter Fulgurator appear much the same. The Fulminans may
be considered as the dispenser of lightnings which dart from the clouds;
and the other, of the Fulgetra, or lesser lightnings, which shoot along
the clouds like the Aurora Borealis.

The flint-stone was considered as the symbol of lightning, and was
often placed in the hand of Jupiter instead of the thunderbolt. In
ancient times, a flint-stone was exhibited as a symbolic representation
of the god.

The Jupiter Pluvius, or dispenser of rain, is nowhere represented, except on a medal, and
on the Trajan and Antonine pillars, where he is seated in the
clouds, holding up his right hand,
from which pours a stream of
rain and hail upon the earth,
while his fulmen is held down in
his lap. On the pillars as well
as the medals, he appears with
an elderly and sedate look ; and
with his arms extended nearly in a straight line each way. The wings
given him on the pillar, relate to the original and principal character
of this god, that of presiding over the air. His hair and beard are all
spread down by the rain which descends from him in sheets and falls
for the refreshment of the Romans. whilst their enemies are represented
as struck with lightning and lying dead before them.

There was scarcely any character of Jupiter that was more capable
of giving sublime ideas to the artists than this of Jupiter Pluvius.
For though on the medal and Antonine pillar he appears calm and
still, on the Trajan he is represented as much more agitated, and the
Roman poets (whose works are counterpart to those of the artists) not
only speak of Jupiter as descending in violent showers, but as quite
ruffled by the winds which usually attend them. Silius actually rises into
poetry when he is treating this subject, and one of the finest passages
in the Æneid relates to the same. It is where Evander is pointing
out the Capitoline Hill to Æneias, which Virgil supposes Jupiter to

have chosen for his peculiar residence, before his temple was built, or even before the building of Rome.*

From this hill he looked down upon the city and the forum, and from the Alban and sacred mounts surveyed the whole of Latium, for he was protector of the city and surrounding country. As such he was worshipped by the consuls, on entering upon their office ; and a general, returning from a campaign, had first of all to offer up his thanks to Jupiter, and in his honor the victorious celebrated their triumph.

According to the belief of the Romans, Jupiter determined the course of all earthly affairs, and revealed the future through signs in the heavens and the flight of birds; hence they are called his messengers. For the same reason, Jupiter was invoked at the beginning of every undertaking, together with Janus, who blessed the beginning itself.

Rams were sacrificed to him on the ides of every month, and the beginning of every week. It may be remarked, in general, that the first day of every period of time, both at Rome and in Latium, was sacred to Jupiter, and marked by festivals, sacrifices, and libations.

Jupiter was considered as the guardian of law and the protector of justice and virtue. He maintained the sanctity of an oath, and presided over all transactions that were based upon faithfulness and justice. Hence Fides was his companion on the capitol ; and hence a traitor to his country, and persons guilty of perjury, were thrown down the Tarpeian rock.

As Jupiter was the prince of light, the white color was sacred to him. The animals sacrificed to him were white ; his chariot was believed to be drawn by four white horses ; his priests wore white caps, and the consuls were attired in white when they offered sacrifices.

The worship offered to Zeus was the most solemn of any paid to the heathen deities ; it was greatly diversified among different nations, and the stories of his birth in a cave on the island of Crete, or at Thebes in Bœotia, or on a mountain in Arcadia, are but so many tra-

---

* In the temple of Jupiter on the Capitoline Hill, the shrines of Jupiter, Juno, and Minerva were joined together. These three were considered superior among the twelve great gods, as the rest of the twelve were over the multitude of Roman divinities. Jupiter probably signified supreme goodness, Minerva supreme wisdom, and Juno, supreme power. *Spence.*

ditions of the several places where his worship became famous and was celebrated with the greatest pomp and ceremony. The reason of its having been so in Crete, is very evident; for these states were founded by Minos and Cadmos, two Attic princes, who introduced their national rites. But the Arcadians, whose lives were devoted to war or pasturage, in a rough, mountainous country, became afterwards a rude and fierce people in comparison to their neighbors, and yet they retained more traditions respecting the birth, education, and adventures of the gods, than the more civilized tribes of the Peloponnesus. This was owing probably to their early instruction ; first by the descendants of Inachos, and then by the Danaides, in the religion and rites which each brought from their own country.

The victims most commonly offered, were a goat, a sheep, or a white bull with gilded horns ; though not unfrequently the sacrifice consisted only of flour, salt, or incense. The eagle, the oak, and the summits of mountains were sacred to him. The Dodonean Zeus was a prophetic god, and wore a wreath of oak leaves. The Olympian Zeus sometimes wears a wreath of olive.

At Olympia, every fifth year, the Olympic games were celebrated in honor of Zeus, where he was considered as the father and king of gods and men, and the supreme god of the Hellenic nation.

Many objects, says Pausanias, may a man see in Greece, and many things may he hear that are worthy of admiration, but above them all, the doings at Eleusis, and the sights at Olympia, have somewhat in them of a soul divine.

In Wordsworth's Greece we find the following account of Olympia : " In descending the slopes which fall to the south-west of Mount Erymanthus, we come in sight of a valley, about three miles in length, and one in breadth, lying from east to west below the hill on which we stand, and bounded on the south by a broad river, running over a gravelly bed, and studded with small islands. Its banks are shaded with plane-trees ; and rich fields of pasture and arable land are watered by its stream. The valley is Olympia, the hill is Mount Cronius, the river, the Alpheus. The eastern and western boundaries of the plain are formed by two other streams, both flowing into the Alpheus. Beginning at Mount Cronius, and following the western of these two brooks, formerly called the Cladeus, among the clusters of pines and olives, to the point where it falls into the Alpheus, and tracing our course eastward along the Alpheus for about a mile, till we arrive at a

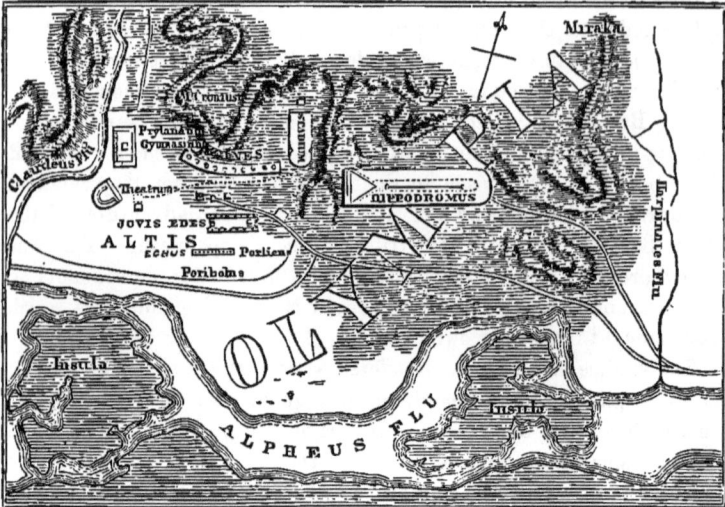

ridge which falls downward to the east, and pursuing this ridge, which runs to the north, till we come to Mount Cronius, from which it de- scends, we have made the circuit or traced the limits of the peribolus of the ancient Altis, or sacred grove of Jupiter, which was formerly the seat of the most glorious and holy objects of Olympia. On the south and east, it was bounded by a wall; on the north by the moun- tain which we have mentioned, and on the west by the Cladeus.

" Looking downward towards the river from the southern slopes of Mount Cronius, we have immediately on our right, the positions of the ancient Gymnasium and Prytaneum. Beneath us, stood the row of ten treasuries from west to east, which were raised by different Greek states, and contained statues and other offerings of great value and exquisite workmanship. Below them, on a basement of some steps, were six statues of Jupiter called Zanes, made from the fines levied upon the athletes who had transgressed the laws, by which the Olym pian contests were regulated. Further to the left, in a wood of wild olives in a declivity of Mount Cronius, and running from north to south, was the stadium. It was approached by the Hellanodicæ or judges of the course, by a secret entrance as it was called. The start- ing-place, or aphesis, was at the northern extremity, near which was the tomb of Endymion.

"Beyond the stadium and eastern limit of the Altis, still further to the left, was the Hippodrome, which stretched from west to east; its western façade was formed by a portico built by the architect Agnaptus. Passing through it, the spectator arrived at a triangular area, of which the vale coincided with the back of the portico; in each of the two sides, which were more than four hundred feet in length, was a series of stalls or barriers, in which the chariots and horses stood, parallel to each other : all looking straight towards the course. A rope was stretched in front of these barriers. At the apex of the triangle or point nearest the course, stood a bronze dolphin raised upon a style. In the middle of the triangle was an altar of unbaked brick, which was whitened at every successive Olympiad; raised above it, was a bronze eagle, stretching its wings at full length. When the proper time had arrived, the officer of the course touched the spring concealed within the altar, and the eagle began to soar aloft, an impulse being thus given to it, so that it became visible to all the spectators. At the same time the bronze dolphin fell to the ground. Then the rope was withdrawn, first from the barriers on each side nearest to the base of the triangle, so as to allow the horses in them to start; when they had arrived in a line with those in the second barriers, these latter were let out, and thus the next in order, till gradually they were all liberated, so that at the moment when the last pair were released, they were all side by side in a line drawn through the apex, parallel to the base.

"An isolated longitudinal ridge, or spine, commencing at some distance from the apex, divided the Hippodrome into two parts; around this the course lay, beginning on the right or southern side of it.

"Nearly in the centre of the Altis, or consecrated ground, stood the temple of the Olympian Jove. It was erected from the spoils taken by the Eleans, in their contests with the inhabitants of Pisa. It was a Doric edifice hypaethral and peripteral, ninety-five feet in breadth, two hundred and thirty in length, and sixty-eight to the summit of the pediment in height. The interior was divided into three compartments, by two rows of columns each in double tiers. The stone of which it was constructed was the poros of the country; its architect, Libon of Elis.

"A golden vase adorned both ends of the roof. In the centre of both the pediments was a golden statue of Victory, and under the Victory a shield of gold, having a figure of Medusa upon it   In later times,

one and twenty gilded bucklers hung upon the architrave over the
columns, the offering of Mummius after the destruction of Corinth. In
both the pediments were groups of sculpture; the eastern exhibited
the contest between Pelops and Œnomaus; this was the work of Pæo-
nius, a native of Menda in Thrace; that on the western front represented the contest of the Centaurs and Lapithæ, and was the work of
Alcamenes, a contemporary of Phidias. In the Metopes were scenes
from the history of Hercules.

"But the most glorious ornament of this magnificent fabric, and one
which, in the language of the ancient critic, added dignity to religion,
was the statue of Jupiter within the temple; it was the work of Phidias, and formed of ivory and gold. This combination, as a great
English sculptor expresses it, 'equally splendid and harmonious, in
such a colossal form, produced a dazzling glory, like electric fluid,
running over the surface of the figure, and thus giving it the appearance
of an immortal vision in the eyes of the votary.' No wonder, therefore, if it was commonly believed that Jupiter himself had lighted up
the statue, and had kindled in its aspect a blaze of divinity by a flash
of lightning from Heaven. The ivory, with which a greater part of the
figure was overlaid, had a flesh tint, which communicated to it the
appearance of a real, living, and intelligent object, while the gold, the
precious stones, and the painting with which it and its accessories were
decorated, and the stupendous size of the whole work, sixty feet in
height, produced a brilliant and astounding effect, which awed the
beholder into a belief that he was looking at the form and face of Jupiter himself. Nor let it be forgotten, that the whole work was informed by a spirit within, breathed into it from the mouth of Homer;
for it was his description of the king of gods and men, which filled the
mind of Phidias, as he himself confessed, when he executed this statue.

"This god sat upon his throne wearing a crown like an olive wreath
upon his head. In his right hand he supported a statue of Victory,
which he seemed to offer to the combatants who came hither to adore
him; it was made of ivory and gold, and bore a chaplet. In his left
hand was a staff or sceptre, inlaid with metals of every description, and
having an eagle perched upon its summit. The sandals of the deity
were of gold, as was also his robe, which was embroidered with figures
and lilies. The throne on which he sat was adorned with gold and
precious stones, with ebony and ivory, with painted figures and others
in relief. Embossed on each of the four feet of the throne were four

dancing victories, and besides them, two statues of Victory standing near each foot. In addition to this, on the two front feet were repre- sented the children of the Thebans, seized by the Sphinges; and below the Sphinges, Apollo and Diana were transfixing with their arrows the sons of Niobe.

"Between the feet were single horizontal bars; on that towards the entrance were seven figures in relief; and on the others, the contests of Hercules and his comrades with the Amazons. Each of the bars was bisected by an upright column, which, together with the feet, served to support the statue. Other decorations of a minute character were scattered near it in rich profusion.

"Such was the appearance which the Olympian Jove presented to the view when the purple embroidered veil which hung before him descend- ed to the ground, and exhibited the father of Gods and men in all the glories of which the greatest spirits of antiquity could conceive and execute the idea.

"The Olympic games were celebrated once in four years. They lasted for five days, and terminated on the full moon which preceded the summer solstice. Contrasted with the particular æras which served for the chronological arrangement of events in distinct provinces in Greece, the epoch supplied by their celebration to all the inhabitants of the Hellenic soil, deserves peculiar attention. While the succession of Priestesses of Juno at Argos—while the Ephors at Sparta, and the Archons at Athens, furnished to those states respectively the bases of their chronological systems, it was not a personage invested with a civil or sacerdotal character who gave his name merely to the single years, but to the quadrennial periods of the whole of Greece; it was he who was proclaimed victor, not in the chariot race of the Hippo- drome, but as having outrun his rivals in the stadium at Olympia. A reflection on the rapid course of Time (the great racer in the stadium of the world) might well be suggested by such a practice; but it is more remarkable, as illustrating the regard paid, by the unanimous consent of all the states of Greece, to these exercises of physical force which preserved them so long from the corruptions of luxury and effem- inacy, into which, through their growing opulence and familiarity with oriental habits, they would very soon otherwise have fallen. Olympia was the Palæstra of all Greece. The simplicity of the prizes, the an- tiquity of their institution, the sacred ceremonies with which they were connected; the glory which attached, not merely to the victor, but to his parents, his friends, and country; his canonization in the Greek calendar; the concourse of rival tribes from every quarter of the Greek continent and peninsula, to behold the contests and applaud the conqueror; the lyric songs of poets; the garlands showered upon his head by the hands of friends, of strangers, and of Greece herself; the statue erected to him in the precincts of the grove, by the side of princes, of heroes, and of gods; the very rareness of the celebration, and the glories of the season of the year at which it took place, when all the charms of summer were poured upon the earth by day and the full orb of the moon streamed upon the olive groves and the broad flood of the Alpheios by night; these were influences which, while they seemed to raise the *individual* to an elevation more than human, produced a far more noble and useful result than this—that of maintaining in the nation a *general* respect for a manly and intrepid character, and of supporting that moral dignity and independence which so long resisted the aggressions of force from without, and were proof against the contagion of weak and licentious principles within.

" Without interruption for a thousand years, the full moon, after the summer solstice every fourth year, witnessed the celebration of these games. The first Olympiad coincides with the year B. C. 776, the last with A. D. 394, or the sixteenth of the Emperor Theodosius, when the calculation by indications was adopted in its stead. According to the assertion of Polybius, Timæus, the Sicilian historian, who had flourished B. C. 300, was the first annalist who introduced the regular practice of comparing chronologically the Archons of Athens, the priestesses of Argos, and the Ephors and kings of Sparta, with the contemporary victors at Olympia. He was thus the founder of the Olympic æra as applied to history, without which no records for the general use of Greece could have existed.

" There is now no habitation on the site of Olympia. On the north of it are rocky heights crowned with wood; some pines are seen on the hills to the west; and oriental palm-trees hang over the wide gravelly bed of the river Alpheios on the south. Some few ruins of brick are scattered over the soil of what was once the Altis, or consecrated enclosure, but hardly a vestige remains even of the foundations of the temple of Olympian Jove; and all the altars and statues which once crowded its precincts have passed away like those countless multitudes who came here and departed hence in successive generations during a fifth part of the long period of time which has elapsed from the creation of the world to the present day."

The origin of the Olympic games is concealed amid the obscurity of the mystic period of Grecian history. Olympia was a sacred spot, on which stood a statue of Zeus long before the institution of the games.

The Eleans had various traditions which attributed the original foundation of the festival to various gods and heroes, at a long period prior to the Trojan war, and among these, to the Idæan Heracles, to Pelops, and to Heracles, the son of Alcmena. The Eleans further stated that after the Ætolians had possessed themselves of Elis, their whole territory was consecrated to Zeus; that the games were revived by their king Iphitos, in conjunction with Lycurgos, as a remedy for the disorders of Greece; and that Iphitos obtained the sanction of the Delphic oracle to the institution, and appointed a periodical sacred truce to enable persons to attend the games from every part of Greece, and to return to their homes in safety. This event was recorded on a disc, which was preserved by the Eleans, and on which the names of Zeus and Lycurgos were inscribed.

The territory of Elis itself was considered especially sacred during the continuance of this truce, and no armed force could enter it without incurring the guilt of sacrilege. When the Spartans on one occasion sent forces against the fortress of Phyneum and Lepreum, during the existence of the Olympic truce, they were fined by the Eleans, according to the Olympic law, two thousand minæ, being two for each Hoplite. The Eleans, however, not only pretended that their laws were inviolate during the existence of the truce, but that by the original agreement with the other states of Peloponnesus, their lands were made sacred for ever, and were never to be attacked by any hostile force; and they further stated, that the first violation of their territory was made by Pheidon of Argos. But the Eleans themselves did not abstain from arms, and it is not probable that such a privilege would have existed without imposing on them the corresponding duty of refraining from any attack upon the territory of their neighbors. The later Greeks do not appear to have admitted this claim of the Eleans, as we find many cases in which their country was made the scene of war.

The Olympic festival was probably confined at first to the Pelopon-
9

nesians, but as its celebrity extended, the other Greeks took part in it till at length it became a festival of the whole nation. No one was allowed to continue in the games, but persons of pure Hellenic blood; barbarians might be spectators, but slaves were entirely excluded. All persons who had been branded by their own states with atimia,* or had been guilty of any offence against the divine laws, were not permitted to contend. When the Hellenic race had been extended by colonies to Asia, Africa, and other parts of Europe, persons contended in the games from very distant places; and in later times, a greater number of conquerors came from the colonies, than from the mother country.

After the conquest of Greece by the Romans, the latter were allowed to take part in the games. The emperors, Tiberius and Nero, were both conquerors; and Pausanias speaks of a Roman senator who gained the victory. During the freedom of Greece, even Greeks were sometimes excluded, when they had been guilty of a crime which appeared to the Eleans to deserve this punishment. The horses of Hiero of Syracuse were excluded from the chariot race through the influence of Themistocles, because he had not taken part with the other Greeks against the Persians. All the Lacedemonians were excluded on the 90th Olympiad because they had not paid the fine for violating the Elean territory, as mentioned above; and similar cases of exclusion are mentioned by the ancient writers.

No women were allowed to be present or even to cross the Alpheus during the celebration of the games, under penalty of being huiled down the Typæan rock. Only one instance is recorded of a woman's having ventured to be present, and she, although detected, was pardoned in consideration of her father, brothers, and son having been victors in the games. An exception was made to this law in favor of

---

* *Atimia.*—The forfeiture of a man's civil rights. It was either total or partial. A man was totally deprived of his rights, both for himself and his descendants, when he was convicted of murder, theft, false-witness, partiality as arbiter, violence offered to a magistrate, etc., etc. The highest degree of atimia, excluded a person affected by it from the forum, and from all public assemblies; from the public sacrifices, and the law courts; or rendered him liable to immediate imprisonment if he was found in any one of those places. It was either temporary or perpetual, and either accompanied or not with confiscation of property. Partial *atimia* involved the forfeiture of some few rights; as, for instance, that of pleading in courts. Public debtors were suspended from their civic functions, till they had discharged their debt to the state; and people who had once become altogether *atimia*, were seldom restored to their lost privileges.

the priestess Demeter Chamyne, who sat on an altar of white marble opposite to the Hellanodicæ. It would appear from another passage of Pausanias, that virgins were allowed to be present, though married women were not; but this statement is opposed to all others on the subject, and the reading of the passage seems to be doubtful. Women were allowed, however, to send chariots to the races; and the first woman whose horse won the prize was Cynisca, the daughter of Archidamus, and sister of Agesilaus. The number of spectators at the festival was very great, and these were drawn together, not merely by the desire of seeing the games, but partly through the opportunity it afforded them of carrying on commercial transactions with persons from distant places, as is the case with the Mahomedan festivals at Mecca and Medina. Many of the persons present were also deputies sent to represent the various states of Greece; and we find that these embassies vied with one another in the number of their offerings, and splendor of their general appearance, in order to support the honor of their native cities. The most illustrious citizens of a state were frequently sent in this capacity.

This festival, celebrated every fifth year, consisted of religious ceremonies, athletic contests and races, and was under the immediate superintendence of the Olympian Zeus. The exact interval at which they recurred was one of forty-nine and fifty lunar months alternately; so that the celebration sometimes fell in the month of July and sometimes in August.

The worship of Apollo was associated with that of Zeus, and the early tradition connects Hercules with the festival. This is another proof of the Dorian origin of the games, for Apollo and Hercules were two of the principal deities of the Doric race. There were altars at Olympia to other gods, which were said to have been erected by Hercules, and at which the victors sacrificed.

The festival itself may be divided into two parts, the games or contests, and the festival rites connected with the sacrifices, with the processions, and with the public banquets in honor of the conquerors. The conquerors in the games and private individuals, as well as the theori or deputies from the various states, offered sacrifices to the different gods; but the chief sacrifices were offered by the Eleans in the name of the Elean state.

The contests consisted of various trials of strength and skill, which were increased in number from time to time. The earliest of these games was the foot race, and was the only contest during thirteen Olympiads. The space run was the length of the stadium in which the games were held, namely, about six hundred English feet

In the 14th Olympiad wrestling was introduced B. C. 708. The wrestlers were matched in pairs by lot. When there was an odd number, the person who was left by the lot without an antagonist, wrestled last of all with him who had conquered the others. The athlete who gave his antagonist three throws, gained the victory. There was another kind of wrestling in which if the combatant who fell could drag down his antagonist with him, the struggle was continued on the ground, and the one who succeeded in getting uppermost and holding the other down, gained the victory.

In the same year was introduced the Pentathlon, which consisted of five exercises, viz. leaping, running, throwing the quoit, throwing the javelin, and wrestling. In leaping, they carried weights in their hands, or on their shoulders; and their object was to leap the greatest distance without regard to height. The Discus or quoit was a heavy weight of a circular or oval shape; neither this nor the javelin was aimed at a mark; but he who threw the furthest was the victor. In order to gain a victory in the Pentathlon, it was necessary to conquer in each of the five parts. Boxing was introduced in the 23d Olympiad (B. C. 688). The boxers had their hands and arms covered with thongs of leather called *cestus,* which served to defend them as well as to annoy their antagonists. The Pancratium consisted of boxing and wrestling combined. In this exercise, and in the cestus, the vanquished combatant acknowledged his defeat by some sign; and this is supposed to be the reason why the Spartans were forbidden by the laws of Lycurgus to practise them, as it would have been esteemed a disgrace to his country, that a Spartan should confess himself defeated.

The horse races were of two kinds, the chariot race and the horse race. The chariot race, generally with four horse chariots, was introduced in the 25th Olympiad (B. C. 680). The course had two goals in the middle, at the distance probably of two stadia from each other. The chariots started from one of these goals, passed round the other, and returned along the other side of the Hippodrome. This circuit was made twelve times; and the great art of the charioteer consisted in turning as close as possible to the goals, but without running against them or against the other chariots. The places at the starting post were assigned to the chariots by lot. There was another race between chariots with two horses, and a race between chariots drawn by mules was introduced in the 70th Olympiad and abolished in the 84th. There were two sorts of races on horseback—one in which each competitor rode one horse throughout the course, and another, in which as the horse approached the goal, the rider leaped from his back and keeping hold of the bridle, finished the course on foot. In the 37th Olympiad (B. C. 632), running on foot and wrestling between boys was introduced. There were also contests in poetry and music at the Olympian festivals.

The Hellanodicæ, or judges in the Olympic games, were chosen by lot from the whole body of the Eleans. Their office probably lasted only for one festival, during which time it was their duty to see that all the laws regulating the games were observed by the competitors and others, to determine the prizes, and to give them to the conquerors. An appeal lay from their decision to the Elean Senate. Their office was considered most honorable. Their dress was a purple robe, and in the stadium a special seat was appropriated to them. Under the direction of the Hellanodicæ was a certain number of deputies, who formed a kind of police, who carried into execution the commands of the Hellanodicæ.

All persons were admitted to a contest in the Olympic games who could prove that they were free men, that they were of genuine Hellenic blood, and that their characters were free from infamy and immorality. So great was the importance attached to the second of these particulars, that the kings of Macedon were obliged to prove their Hellenic descent before gaining admittance. The equestrian contests were necessarily confined to the wealthy, who displayed in them great magnificence; but the poorest citizens could contend in the athletic contests. The owners of the chariots and horses were not obliged to contend in person; and the wealthy vied with one another in the magnificence of the chariots and horses which they sent to the games. Alcibiades sent seven chariots to one festival, a greater number than had ever been sent by a private person; three of them obtained prizes.

The Greek kings in Sicily, Macedon, and other parts of the Hellenic world, contended with one another for the prize in the equestrian contests.

The combatants underwent a long and vigorous training, the nature of which varied with the game in which they intended to engage. Ten

months before the festival they were obliged to appear at Elis, to enter
their names as competitors, stating at the same time the prize for which
they wished to contend.

This interval of ten months was spent in preparatory exercises, and
for a part of it, the last ninety days at least, they were thus engaged
in the gymnasium at Elis. When the festival arrived their names
were proclaimed in the stadium, and after proving that they were not
disqualified from taking part in the games, they were led to the altar
of Zeus, the guardian of oaths, where they swore that they had gone
through all the preparatory exercises required by the laws, and that
they would not be guilty of any fraud, nor of any attempt to interfere
with the fair course of the games. Any one detected in bribing his
adversary to yield him the victory was heavily fined. After taking
the oath they were accompanied by their relatives and friends into the
stadium, who exhorted them to acquit themselves nobly.

The only prize given to the conqueror was a garland of wild olive,
which, according to the Elean legend, was the prize originally instituted by the Idæan Heracles.* This garland was cut from a sacred
olive tree, which grew in the sacred grove of Altis, in Olympia, near
the altars of Aphrodite and the Hours. Heracles is said to have
brought it from the country of the Hyperboreans and to have placed it
himself in the Altis. The victor was originally crowned upon a tripod
covered over with bronze, but afterwards, and in the time of Pausanias,
upon a table made of ivory and gold. Palm-leaves were at the same
time placed in the hands of the victors, and their names, together with
the games in which they had conquered, were proclaimed by a sacred
herald.

A victory at Olympia, besides being the highest honor which a Greek
could obtain, conferred so much glory upon the State to which he be-

---

* In mythological story, the Idæan Heracles, according to Pausanias, was one of the
Idæan Dactyli, to whom Rhea committed the care of the infant Zeus. They were
also called Curetes. They came from Ida, a mountain of Crete, and were named Heracles, Pæeneus, Epimedes, Iasion, and Idas.

It is further related that to the Idæan Heracles is attributed the honor of having first
proposed the Olympic games, and selected as a reward the crown of olives; and the
periodical renewal of these games was appointed every fifth year to commemorate, it
is said, the number of the Dactyli. To the same Heracles, with the surname, Auxilia-
tor, an altar was erected at Olympia, by his descendant Clymenus, only fifty years
after the deluge of Deucalion, and long previous to the age of Theseus. At Megalo-
polis, in Arcadia, there was a statue of the Idæan Heracles, one cubit high.

onged, that successful candidates were frequently solicited to allow themselves to be proclaimed as citizens of States to which they did not naturally belong. The festival ended with processions and sacrifices, and with a public banquet given by the Eleans to the conquerors in the prytaneum.

Fresh honors awaited the victor on his return home. He entered his native city in triumph through a breach made in the walls for his reception; banquets were given him by his friends, at which odes were sung in honor of the victory; and his statue was then erected at his own expense, or that of his fellow-citizens, in the Altis or sacred grove of Zeus. At Athens, according to a law of Solon, the Olympic victor was rewarded with a prize of 500 drachmæ; at Sparta, the foremost place in battle was assigned him. and three instances are recorded in which altars were built, and sacrifices offered to the conquerors at the Olympic games.

It seems to be generally admitted, that the chief object of this festival was to form a bond of union for the Grecian States. Besides this, the great importance which such an institution gave to the exercises of the body, must have had an immense influence in forming the national character. Regarded as a bond of union, the Olympic festival seems to have had but little success in promoting kindly feelings between the Grecian States; perhaps the rivalry of the contest may have tended to exasperate existing quarrels; but it undoubtedly furnished a striking exhibition of the nationality of the Greeks, and the distinction between them and other races. The contingent effects of the ceremony were, perhaps, after all, the most important. During its celebration. Olympia was a centre of the commerce of all Greece, for the free interchange of opinions, and for the publication of knowledge. The concourse of people from all Greece afforded a fit audience for literary productions, and gave a motive for the composition of works worthy to be laid before them. Poetry and statuary received an impulse from the demand upon them to aid in perpetuating the victor's fame. But the most important and most difficult question connected with the subject is, whether their influence on the national character was for good or for evil. The exercises of the body on which these games conferred the greatest honor, have been condemned by some philosophers, as tending to unfit men for the active duties of citizens; while they were regarded by others as a most essential part of manly education, and as the chief cause of the bodily vigor and mental energy which marked the character of the Hellenic race.

As persons from all parts of the Hellenic world were assembled together at the Olympic games, it was the best opportunity which the artist and the writer possessed of making their works known. Before the invention of printing, the reading of an author's works to so large an assembly was one of the easiest and surest methods of publishing them ; and this was a favorite practice of the Greeks and Romans. Accordingly, we find many instances of literary works thus published at the Olympic festivals.

The Olympic games continued to be celebrated with much splendor under the Roman Emperors, by many of whom great privileges were awarded to the conquerors.

In the sixteenth year of the reign of Theodosius, A. D. 394 (Ol. 293), the Olympic festival was for ever abolished.

The description of the Olympic games will, for the most part, serve also for the other three great festivals of Greece, viz. the Isthmian, Nemean, and Pythian games.

HERA OR JUNO.

By the poets, Hera is represented as the personification of sublime beauty united with power ; and in her person is represented that high, commanding order of beauty which is superior to the delicacy of female charms and does not need them. She is called the reigning, the large-eyed, the white-armed ; epithets which tend to inspire us with admiration rather than love. It is not the soft and tender eye that graces her image ; it is greatness and majesty commanding awe and veneration ; and of all the charms which constitute the reigning queen of heaven, poetry celebrates none but the powerful arm. And indeed, Hera acts a part in nearly all the violent events in heaven and on earth.

The raging elements in which the whole train of human passions is but a copy in miniature, are personated in her ; for the violence of the elements is chiefly displayed in the lower atmosphere. Here they come in collision and interfere with each other ; here they rob, and spoil, and breathe revenge ; the rock groans in the furious sea ; and under the blast of the storm the billows howl ; here is a perpetual round of formation and destruction ;—here is the theatre of insurrection and

HERA OR JUNO.

war ; the seat of wrath, and mourning, and misery ; here must Hecuba
pull out her grey hairs, and Troy become a prey to the flames.

But above the atmosphere, in the pure ether, every thing is quiet,
permanent, and regular ;—there, the celestial globes complete their
courses undisturbed, and nothing interrupts the music of the spheres ;—
the top of high Olympos rises above the clouds into the still ether, and
thither imagination transfers the abodes of the blessed immortals, who,
exempt from care and pain, sip the sweet nectar, while charmed with
the sound of Apollo's lyre

In this manner, Fancy always unites the human form of her deities
with the heavenly archetype. The swan in the bosom of Leda, as the
blue ether surrounds the earth ; and the ether opens again to show the
ruler of Olympos with his ambrosial locks, holding the nectar cup in
his hand. Hera surrounds the globe with a transparent mist, which,
pierced by the glittering rays of the sun, produces the rainbow, the
archetype of Iris, Hera's swift messenger ; who, standing in the clouds,
announced to mankind the approach of the august queen of heaven ;
and the same Hera wanders on foot through this very mist to visit her
foster-parents at the bounds of the earth. But Fancy, not choosing
to dwell long on these objects, which she in a certain manner attempts
to explain by her personifications, rather delights to roam among the
beings to whom she has given personality ; and represents Hera as
opposing herself to the all-powerful Zeus, by whom she is suspended
from Olympos on a chain into her own dominion, the atmosphere, with
an anvil fastened to either foot. The heavenly and sublime is thus
made to suffer the disgrace of being lowered down, and all celestials
mourned at the sight ; but Fancy, the earth-born daughter, delights in
the sport.

The worship of Hera was solemn and universal in the heathen world.
Young geese and the hawk as well as the peacock were sacred to her ;
and of plants, the dittany, the poppy, and the lily. The ancients
offered on her altars a sow and a ewe lamb the first of every month.

Argos is the first place mentioned by Hera herself as among her
favored and beloved cities. Urging Zeus to consent to the downfall
of Troy, a city which she hated, together with Priam s family, because
of the decision of Paris on Mount Ida, she endeavored to carry her
point by a kind of barter ; " There are three cities," said she, " which
are dearest of all to me, Argos, Sparta, and Mycenæ ; nevertheless, I

willingly part with them, I abandon them entirely to thy will, if thou wilt consent to the downfall of Troy." (Il. iv. 50.)

The reason of this partiality to Argos, was the extraordinary venera-tion paid to her by its inhabitants. There, particular festivals were cele-brated in her honor, which from her Greek name Hera, were called Heræa. During this celebration, there were always two processions to the temple of the goddess without the city; the first was of the men in armor, and the second of the women, when her priestess, mounted on a splendid chariot, rode in triumph to the temple of the goddess to offer a hecatomb of white heifers. The goddess was here particularly venerated in the person of her high priestess; a veneration with which the touching history of Cleobis and Biton is connected. On one occa-sion, when the white heifers which were to have drawn their mother were not at hand, they, with filial devotion, yoked themselves to her chariot and drew it to the temple, forty-five stadia from the gates of Argos, lest she should be deprived of the honor of the day. Having been crowned as victors in the gymnastic contests, the two youths were welcomed on their arrival at the temple by the congregated peo-ple, who congratulated the mother on her sons, and the sons on their strength and virtue. The mother, rejoicing in her own happiness and her children's deeds, repaired to the shrine of Juno, and standing before the statue, prayed for her sons the greatest blessing which the goddess could give, and they receive. It happened that after their mother's prayer, and when they had offered their own sacrifices, that the two brothers, overcome with fatigue, reclined in the temple and fell asleep to wake no more. Their statues were erected at Delphi, by the hands of their admiring countrymen, and their lot was declared by the wise Solon to the wealthy Croesus, to be only inferior in happiness to that of the Athenian Tellus.

It is worthy of observation, that a spot so distant from the capital city itself, should have been selected for the position of the edifice con-secrated to its patron deity. Thus removed, however, as the temple of Juno was from the haunts of men, placed upon a quiet and solitary hill, visited by shepherds and their flocks, surrounded by groves of trees, watered on each side by a mountain stream, with a long ridge of lofty hills rising at its back, and with the wide Argolic plain stretch-ing itself at its feet, this sacred building inspired more of that particu-lar feeling of awe and veneration, which was specially due to the stately dignity of the wife of Jove, and the queen of the gods, than if it had stood on a less sequestered spot, or had been exposed to the daily gaze of man amid the noise of the streets, or in the crowd of the Agora of the Argolic capital itself.

The road which leads from Argos to this temple, has gained a lasting interest,—similar to that possessed by the Plain of the Pious on the sides of Mount Ætna,—from the act of filial devotion in the sons of the high priestess.

The games and contests of the Heræa took place in the stadium, near the temple, on the road to the Acropolis. A brazen shield was fixed in a place above the theatre, which was scarcely accessible to any one, and the young man who succeeded in displacing it, received a shield and a garland of myrtle as a prize.

The Argives always reckoned their year from her priesthood, as the Athenians from their Archons, and the Romans from their consuls.

Festivals were celebrated in honor of Hera in all the towns of Greece, where the worship of the divinity was introduced. At Ægina, the Heræa, or Hecatombæa, were celebrated in the same manner as those at Argos. The Heræa of Samos were derived from Argos, and were, perhaps, the most brilliant of all the festivals of this divinity. A magnificent procession consisting of maidens and married women in splendid attire and floating hair, together with men and youths in armor, went to the temple of Hera, and on arriving within the precincts, the men deposited their armor, and prayers and vows were offered to the goddess.

The Heræa of Elis were celebrated every fifth year, chiefly by maidens, conducted by sixteen matrons, who wove the sacred Peplus for the goddess. But before the commencement of these solemnities, the matrons sacrificed a pig, and purified themselves in the well of Peoria. One of the principal solemnities, was a race of the maidens in the stadium; for which purpose, they were divided into three classes according to their age; the youngest ran first, and the eldest last. The winner of the prize received a garland of olive boughs, together with part of a cow which was sacrificed to Hera. She was also allowed to dedicate her own painted likeness in the temple of the goddess. The sixteen matrons had each a female attendant, and performed two dances.

Juno, as well as Jupiter, appeared in a variety of characters. Among the Romans, the favorite one was that of Juno Matrona, dressed in a long robe; and thus their empresses were often represented. She was regarded as the protectress of married women, and was invoked by the Romans under the name of Juno Lucina.

She is generally represented by plastic art in her whole regal splendor, sitting upon a throne or on the eagle of Jupiter, holding in one hand a sceptre, and in the other a veil spangled with stars which flows round her head. Among earthly appearances, the tail of the peacock bears the strongest resemblance to the bright colors of the rainbow; therefore the chariot of Juno is represented as drawn through the air by those brilliant and majestic birds.

HESTIA OR VESTA.

Hestia was said to transfuse the earth with sacred warmth; and her archetype is the sacred flame of life, which invisibly pervades all animated beings. As an emblem of this animating and life-nourishing warmth in nature, as well as the pure flame that quickens the chaste bosom of the goddess, a perpetual fire was preserved in her temples. This fire signified that pure, unmixed, benign flame that quickens the chaste bosom of the goddess, and is so necessary to us, that human life cannot exist without it; for this latent heat being diffused through all parts of the human body, quickens, cherishes, refreshes, and preserves it; a flame really sacred and divine, moving and actuating the whole system of life, and expiring only with its last breath.

Poets say, that as it was by the assistance of Hestia, the enlivening, igneous principle, that Zeus obtained the supreme government of the universe, he allowed her to choose her own honors and privileges; being incapable of associating with any other element, she made choice of perpetual virginity, and the first share of every offering made to the other gods. Her priestesses, therefore, must be pure, unspotted virgins, and allowed the precedency at all feasts and sacrifices.

A pure feeling of gratitude led the ancients to acknowledge each benefit of nature by itself, under some significant emblem ; and it was a particularly beautiful idea to cherish and preserve, as it were, this sacred flame, which serves man so beneficently, and to devote to its service immaculate virgins as its most sacred priestesses. A particular place of refuge was appointed to that element, which is so requisite to man, where it never was employed for human necessity, but always burned for its own sake, attracting the veneration of mortals.

Among the contemplative priests of the East, Hestia passed for the latent power of fire, or the internal texture and disposition of some sorts of matter that render it combustible. while others are little affected with heat. As such, she was the wife of Uranos and mother of Kronos—the sacred, eternal fire, worshipped with the greatest reverence and most pompous ceremonies by all the eastern nations. But among the less speculative Europeans, who received the knowledge of this goddess at second hand, she was considered only as Saturn's daughter, and a national tutelary deity. Numa, the pious Sabine. priest and king, made her the guardian of the infant state, though, generally speaking, she was worshipped as a domestic deity and protectress of the family seat all over Italy, and long before in Greece.

This goddess, then, the pure, eternal Hestia, appears in a double capacity ; either as the grand, enlivening genius of the terrestrial globe, worshipped with solemn ceremonies. and honored by annual processions, under the name of Orosmades by the Persians, and that of Serapis by the Egyptians ; or, as the permanent, immovable seat of gods and men, the Earth itself ;—and by an easy transition, the native soil of a nation, or the fixed habitation of a family. Ovid, in his Fasti, hints at them both ; but Plato confines them to the latter ; when describing the movement of the universe, he says that the supreme god, the beneficent Zeus, driving a winged chariot through the heavens, marches first, directing and inspecting all things ; after whom the whole host of deities and dæmons, ranged in twelve bands, follow in order, but that Hestia alone remains at home.

The very ancient worship of Vesta spread its influence over domestic life, contributing to render it pure and happy. She was the genius of the fireside ; and every beneficial influence of the fire that tends towards physical preservation, or moral improvement, was considered as her gift. And as the surrounding all of nature itself which she animated with tender glow, was, as it were, her temple. so Vesta is said to have caused man to surround his dwelling by a covering for shelter ; teaching him to secure himself against the severe influence of the elements, and to assemble together and dwell in union with his family around the domestic hearth. For this reason, she was one of the household gods to whom the Romans daily sacrificed. Her statue was placed at the entrance of every dwelling, which was therefore sacred to Vesta, and called Vestibulum.

In the ancient Roman house, the hearth was the central part, and around it the inmates daily assembled for their common meal. Every meal thus taken was a fresh bond of union among the members of the family, and at the same time an act of worship to Vesta, combined with a sacrifice to her and the Penates. Every dwelling was therefore, in some sense, a temple of Vesta, but a public sanctuary united all the citizens of the state into one family. This sanctuary stood in the Forum, between the Capitoline and Palatine hills, and not far from the temple of the Penates.

The mysteries and worship of Vesta were first brought into Italy by Æneias from Phrygia ; where they were originally received from the East. Numa Pompilius built her a temple at Rome, into which no males were allowed to enter ; he also instituted those celebrated priestesses who bore the name of Vestals, or Vestal virgins ; and who were, as their name indicates, consecrated to Vesta. Their existence at Alba Longa is connected with the earliest Roman traditions ; for Silvia, the mother of Romulus, was a member of the sisterhood.

Their establishment in the city, in common with almost all matters connected with religion, is generally ascribed to Numa, who first appointed four ; to which Tarquin added two more. They were originally chosen by the monarchs ; but during the republic and empire, this duty was intrusted to the Pontifex Maximus.* The virgins chosen for this service were between six and ten years of age ; and if a sufficient number did not voluntarily present themselves as candidates for the office, twenty virgins were selected for a choice, and those among the number upon whom the lot fell, were obliged to become priestesses.

---

* The institution of that high order of priests called *pontifices*, was attributed to Numa. The *pontifex maximus*, chief of these priests, was interpreter of all sacred rites, or rather a superintendent of religion ; having the care, not only of public sacrifices, but even of private rites and offerings, forbidding the people to depart from stated ceremonies, and teaching them how to honor and propitiate the gods.

Plebeians, as well as Patricians, were eligible to the office, but the choice fell on those who were born of good families, and whose persons were free from blemish or deformity.

The time of their consecration to this service lasted thirty years. During the first ten years, the priestess was engaged in learning her mysterious duties; the ten following were employed in discharging them with fidelity and sanctity; and the ten last, in the instruction of those who had entered the novitiate; while thus employed, she was bound by a solemn vow of chastity; but after the time specified was completed, she was at liberty to throw aside the emblems of her office, return to the world, and even enter the marriage state. Few, however, availed themselves of these privileges; those who did so were said to have lived in sorrow and remorse; hence such a proceeding was considered ominous, and priestesses generally died as they had lived, in the service of the goddess.

The chief employment of the Vestals was, to maintain the sacred fire which burned in honor of Vesta. If it ever happened to expire, all Rome was in consternation, as it was considered a direful presage, and was made the occasion of a general mourning; and public spectacles were forbidden until the crime was expiated by a severe punishment inflicted on the offender, to whose carelessness the calamity was to be attributed. The fire was again rekindled by friction.

Another sacred charge of the Vestals was, to preserve a sacred pledge on which was supposed to depend the very existence of Rome, which, according to some authorities, was the Palladium of Troy, and others, the mysteries of the god of Samothrace. Their other ordinary duties consisted in presenting offerings to the goddess at stated times, and in sprinkling and purifying the shrine every morning with water; which, according to the institution of Numa, was to be drawn from the Egerian fount, although in later times it was considered lawful to use any water from a living spring or running stream; but not such as had passed through pipes. When used for sacrificial purposes it was mixed with salt which had been pounded in a mortar, then placed in an earthen jar, and dried in an oven.

They also assisted at all the great public, holy rites, such as the festivals of the Bona Dea, and the consecration of temples; they were invited to the public banquets; and we are told that they were present at the solemn appeal made to the gods by Cicero during the conspiracy of Catiline.

If a Vestal violated her vows of chastity, nothing could save her from a violent death. Numa ordered such to be stoned; but a more cruel torture was devised by Tarquinius Priscus, and inflicted from that time till the abolishment of the order by Theodosius the Great. When condemned by the college of Pontifices, she was stripped of her vittæ and other badges of office, scourged, attired like a corpse, placed in a close litter, and borne through the forum, attended by her weeping friends with all the ceremonies of a real funeral, to a rising ground called the Campus Sceleratus, just within the city walls, close to the Colline gate. There, a small vault was prepared under ground, containing a couch, a lamp, and a table with a little food. The Pontifex Maximus, having lifted up his hands to heaven and uttered a secret prayer, opened the litter, led forth the culprit, and placing her on the steps of the ladder which gave access to the subterranean cell, delivered her over to the common executioner and his assistants, who conducted her down, drew up the ladder, and having filled the pit with earth until it was level with the surrounding ground, left her to perish, deprived of all the tributes of respect usually paid to the departed.

The labors of the Vestals were unremitting, and the rules of the order rigidly enforced ; but as a compensation for their privations, extraordinary honors and privileges were granted them. They were maintained at the public cost, and from sums of money and land bequeathed from time to time to the corporation. From the moment of their consecration, they became, as it were, the property of the goddess alone, and were completely released from all parental authority without going through the forms of emancipation. They had a right to make a will, and to give evidence in a court of justice without taking an oath ; distinctions first conceded by a Horatian law to a certain Caia Tarratia, or Tufetia, and afterwards communicated to all belonging to the order.

From the time of the triumviri, each was preceded by a lictor when she went abroad, and so great was the deference paid them by the magistrates, as well as the people, that the consuls themselves made way for them, bowing their *fasces** as they passed. Augustus granted

---

* *Fasces* were rods bound in the form of a bundle, and containing an axe in the middle, the iron of which projected. These rods were carried by the *lictors*, or public officers, who attended the superior magistrates at Rome.

From the representations of the *fasces*, they appear to have been usually made of birch, but sometimes also of the twigs of the elm. They are said to have been derived from Vetulonia, a city of Etruria.

to them all the rights of matrons who had borne three children, and assigned them a conspicuous place in the theatre ; a privilege they had previously enjoyed at gladiatorial shows. Great weight was attached to their intercession in behalf of those who were in danger and diffi- culty, of which we have a remarkable example in the entreaties which they addressed to Sulla on behalf of Julius Cæsar, and if they chanced to meet a criminal as he was led to punishment, they had a right to de- mand his release, provided it could be proved that the encounter was accidental. Wills, even those of emperors, were committed to their charge, for when in such keeping they were considered inviolable ; and in like manner very solemn treaties, such as that of the triumvirs with Sextus Pompeius, were placed in their hands. If any one died in office, her remains were interred within the walls of the city ; an honor seldom granted by the Romans.

To offer insult to the Vestals was a capital crime, and if any one attempted to violate their chastity, he was publicly scourged to death in the Forum.

The dress of the Vestals was a *stola*,* over which was an upper vest- ment made of linen ; on the head they wore a close covering called infula, from which hung ribbons or vittæ; and in addition to this, they wore, when sacrificing, a peculiar head-dress called suffibulum, consist- ing of a piece of white cloth bordered with purple, oblong in shape, and secured by a clasp. In dress and general deportment, they were re- quired to observe the utmost simplicity and decorum ; as any fanciful ornaments in the one, or levity in the other, were always regarded with disgust and suspicion. From a passage in Pliny, we infer that their hair was cut off, probably at the period of their consecration ; whether this was repeated from time to time, does not appear ; but they are never represented with flowing locks.

Annual festivals were celebrated by the Romans, in honor of Vesta, on the 9th of June, and were called Vestalia. Banquets were then prepared before the houses, and plates of meat were sent to the Vestals to be offered up to the goddess. Mill-stones were turned by asses,

---

* A dress worn over the tunic, which came as low as the ankles or feet. It was fastened round the body by a girdle, and over the shoulder by a clasp. It usually had sleeves, but not always.

The *stola* was the characteristic dress of the Roman matrons, as the *toga* was of the men.

decked with garlands, as they were led in procession around the city; ladies followed bare-footed to the temple of the goddess, where an altar was erected to Jupiter, surnamed Pistor.

By the poets, Mercury and Vesta are made intimate friends: they are the beneficent teachers and keepers of men, in whose songs they are united, and represented as dwelling in friendly concord, and teaching the useful arts.

Whenever ancient art ventured to represent Vesta, the goddess bore a flambeau in her hand; but a mystical veil always covers her chaste form. An antique gem, preserved in a German museum, contains so complicated and mysterious a group, of which Vesta makes a component part, as to show clearly that the artist's only object was to indicate the mystery with which the goddess was covered. Pluto, or as he was likewise called, Jupiter Serapis, sitting on a throne, holds in his left hand a scythe, and with his right hand strokes the triple-headed Cerberus; on his left stands Harpocrates, the god of silence, having his finger placed upon his lips; and on his right the veiled Vesta, with the torch in her hand; Harpocrates carries a cornucopia; these are combined emblems of the innermost, concealed, mysterious part of nature, from which life and fulness continually flow.

Vesta, represented with the torch, is sometimes thought to be the ancient Vesta, who probably was the same as Terra. In the fictions of the ancients, the earlier and later deities are often confounded, and, as it were, lost in one another; and since Earth, one of the pristine deities, no longer makes a distinct appearance among the moderns, she seemed to be renewed in Vesta, as Helios in Apollo.

CYBELE.

The Greeks renewed the fiction of Terra in Cybele, and considered her as the mother of all creatures, gods as well as men. The archetype of Cybele was likewise the great productive power that gives rise to all formations. She was conceived to be the ruler of the elements and the beginning of time; the highest goddess of the heavens, as well as the queen of the lower world; and even the representative of every deity, keeping the female character, because of her ever-producing power.

Although this goddess is represented sitting in a chariot drawn by lions, and bearing a mural or tower crown upon her head, to indicate her all-subduing power, together with her sovereignty of the earth overspread with cities, yet this representation is merely an external cover for her incomprehensible formless character.

In the temple of the great mother of life, at Pessinus in Galatia, a small stone of a blackish color, and rough, irregular surface, represented the Alma Mater. It was also the idea of this mysterious being which was hidden in the Egyptian Isis, whose temple bore this inscription, " I am all that is, that was, and that will be, and no mortal has lifted my veil."

In the same degree as Cybele herself was venerated, her priests (the Corybantes) were despised and detested. Their sensuality was notorious through all antiquity; and their own goddess was said to have taken a terrible vengeance on them for having approached her person too nearly. She drove them distracted, and in their fury they scourged, lacerated, and maimed themselves. Thus they ran about in wild ecstasy, while the goddess looked triumphantly at the troop of unmanned, despicable wretches in her train. The frantic fury of the priests was not prejudicial to her veneration: the idea of her was always preserved in its original sublimity, comprehending the all-producing, all-fertilizing, and all-animating mother of nature.

Cybele is generally represented in works of art, either as sitting in a chariot drawn by lions, or as riding upon a lion, and holding a timbrel near her head as if listening to the sound.

POSEIDON OR NEPTUNE.

HOMERIC HYMN TO NEPTUNE.

Neptune, the mighty marine god, I sing,
Earth's mover, and the fruitless Ocean's king,
That Helicon and Ægean deeps dost hold.
Oh, thou Earth-shaker! thy command two-fold
The gods have sorted; making thee of horses
The awful tamer, and of naval forces
The sure preserver. Hail! Saturnian birth,
Whose graceful green hair circles all the Earth.
Bear a benignant mind, and helpful hand
Lend thou, to all subjected to thy dread command.

In the great division of the universe by Zeus, the empire of the sea
was committed to Poseidon, who rises in imperial majesty as Pontos,
Oceanos, and Nereus retreat to the shade. He was made the ruler
of the waters; his supreme command raised the stormy waves, and his
mighty trident calmed the seditious floods. Not only the ocean, rivers,
and fountains were subjected to him, but he also caused earthquakes
at his pleasure, and raised islands from the depths of the sea, by a
blow of his trident Homer represents him as rising from the depths
of the sea, and in three steps crossing the whole horizon. "The mountains and the forests," says the poet, "trembled as he walked; all the
hosts of the sea rose to hail their king, and the waves fell back in awful
respect."

As god of the sea, Poseidon was entitled to more power than
any other deity except Zeus; but though descended from the same
father as the Thunderer, Poseidon, like the element in which he reigns,
is but a subordinate power.

During the Trojan war, Iris was sent to him with a message from
Zeus, warning him to beware of measuring himself with him who sways
the thunderbolts, and to refrain from assisting the sons of Danaus.
The shaker of the earth replied with boldness, saying, "However mighty
Zeus may be, he has spoken very arrogantly. Are we not all the sons
of Kronos and Rhea?—and is not the universe divided between us?
He may terrify with such words his sons and daughters, but not me"
Iris reminded him that the elder brother is protected by the Erinnyes.
Poseidon instantly complied with the will of the Thunderer, saying,
'Thou hast spoken mildly, O goddess! It is well if a messenger knows
what is useful.' (Il. xv. 185.)

Polyphemos was deprived of his only eye by Ulysses; and this injury done to his beloved son, by mortal hands, Poseidon left not unavenged, but severely punished the daring Ulysses, by rendering vain, as long as possible, all attempts made by the unfortunate traveller to regain his home. He made him endure all dangers and hardships that can befall a seafaring man; and when, by the will of Fate, he must at last reach his native island, Poseidon avenged himself by transforming into a rock the innocent ship of the hospitable Phæacians, which had brought him thither. Thus dangerous was it, even to the favorite of Minerva, to offend the dreadful power of the resistless element

When the Muses entertained themselves in the Aönian mountain with song, and play on the lyre, in so gay a manner that all the environs participated in their joy, and Helicon itself leaped under their feet, falling into a passion, Poseidon sent up Pegasos charging him to set limits to the mirth and noisy merriment of those revellers. On arriving at the top of the mount, Pegasos had only to paw the ground, to bring all to its quiet, proper course; and from beneath his foot arose that well-known fountain, from which the poets sip their inspiration, and which from its origin is called Hippocrene.

The archetype of Poseidon is the vast sea, which being, as it were, angry at all that is prominent, strives to reduce every thing to its own level. Therefore, when, during the siege of Troy, the Greeks were building a wall around their ships, to serve as a bulwark against their enemies, Poseidon was angry; and hastening to Zeus, gave vent to the bitterness of his wrath in these words: " The renown of this wall will spread over the earth; yet my own wall, which with the assistance of Apollo I built around Troy for Laomedon, will be forgotten." To which Zeus replied, " Illustrious shaker of the earth, if another god, less powerful than thou, should care for such a work as that, I should not wonder; but thy glory already reaches as far as the sun; and thou wilt, I trust, as soon as the Greeks have departed, sink that wall into the sea, and cover the shores with sand, that no traces of its existence may remain." With such words Zeus upbraided him for his envy, as well as his regard for the works of mortal men. (Il. vii. 546.)

All that moves rapidly onward affords pleasure to the ruler of the waves. He bends over his spirited steeds, to encourage them, and the swiftly flying ship is his delight. Poets tell us, that the horse owes to him its existence, saying that he produced that animal by striking the ground with his trident. Hence he is called Hippias or Hippodromus, and is esteemed the president of the horse race. They also make him the father of the winged Pegasos, and of Arion, the noblest steed that ever bore kings or heroes. Endowed with the swiftness of the wind, he threw off his rider in one of the Grecian games, to win the prize for himself.

To the Egyptians, who hated the sea, and seldom left their own country, Poseidon was scarcely known; but with all maritime nations he was a favorite deity. As the god of ships and all marine affairs, altars were consecrated and temples erected to his honor.

The Libyans in particular held him in great veneration; esteeming him above all other gods. His most celebrated temples were at the Corinthian Isthmus, at Onchestos, Helice, and Træzene.

According to Herodotus, Neptune was originally an African or Libyan deity, and from them the Greeks derived his worship. Others have supposed that the Phœnicians first introduced him as a deity into Greece, and also a knowledge of the horse, and in that way they became associated together. It would seem, however, that there is a deeper meaning contained in this fable; the horse being sacred to Neptune and the rivers, and employed as a general symbol of the waters. Hence it may have been assumed as one of the types of fertility, and in this signification may furnish a clue to the fable of Neptune and Ceres, and also throw some light on the narration of Pausanias, where he states that the Phigalenses dedicated a statue to Ceres, having the figure of a woman in every part except the head, which was that of a horse. In one hand she held a dolphin, and in the other a dove. The ancients considered animals as the emblems of nature, and nature as containing the archetype of all divine representations; therefore in their fictions, we find the animal world closely connected with the deities they worshipped.

Some writers suppose that the Romans worshipped Neptune as Consus, the god of counsel; and as such, counsel being generally given in private, his altar was under ground, or in an obscure and private place, where sacrifices were offered to him.

The Consualia, at Rome, were festivals instituted in honor of Consus. It was during one of these festivals that Romulus carried away the Sabine women, who had assembled as spectators of the games.

The animals offered to him in sacrifice, were a black bull, rams, and a boar-pig; and the Roman soothsayers always offered to him the gall of their victims, which in taste resembles the bitterness of sea water

Neptune was generally represented sitting in a chariot made of a scollop shell, and drawn by sea horses, or dolphins, but sometimes standing, holding his trident, guiding winged horses as his chariot flies over the sea. These sea horses had the tails of fishes, with only two feet, which were the fore-feet of a horse, according to the description given in Statius:

> " Good Neptune's steeds to rest are set up here
> In the Ægean gulf; whose fore-parts harness bear;
> Their hinder parts fish shap'd."

In the grim aspect of Neptune is depicted the raging element over which he presides. He is often represented as holding in his right hand the trident, or the three-pointed sceptre, the symbol of his power, and in his left, the reins by which he guides his proud coursers, and his garment waving in the tempest. A beautiful antique gem shows him coming out of the sea, treading with the whole weight of his power upon a rock, his right hand carelessly thrown behind him, while the left shoulder bears his trident. On a common medal of Adrian, Neptune is represented standing; in his left hand he holds a dolphin, and in his right his peculiar sceptre, the trident, which he seems chiefly to use to rouse the waves, and lays it aside when he wishes to appease them; the foot rests on a part of a ship, to indicate that he presides over the inland seas, more particularly the Mediterranean, which was the great, and almost the only scene of navigation among the Romans.

Poetic, as well as plastic art, represents the king of the waters in majesty similar to Zeus; but still, the expression of power and dignity in the former always appears subordinate. It is not that quiet, eminent power which commands with the brow of the eye, clears the sky with a smile, and is seldom prompted to anger by restraint. On the contrary, with Poseidon, the expression of anger and wrath is prevailing. He chides the wind, which at the instigation of Hera had ruffled the waves without his consent; and the expressive "*Quos ego!*" (Æn. i. 133) with which he threatens and overawes them, has, even in modern times, been frequently referred to by plastic art, with the view of exhibiting his character in appropriate representation.

The Isthmian games, one of the four great national festivals of the Greeks, derived their name from the Corinthian Isthmus, where they were celebrated. At the narrowest part of the Isthmus, between the coast of the Saronic and the western foot of the Œnian hills, was the temple of Poseidon; and near it was a stadium and a theatre of white marble. The entrance to the temple was adorned with statues of the victors in the Isthmian games, and with groves of pine trees.

These games were said originally to have been instituted in honor of Melicertes, who was also called Palæmon. Their original mode of celebration, as Plutarch remarks, partook more of the character of mysteries than of a great national assembly with its various amusements, and was performed at night. Subsequent to the age of Theseus, the Isthmian games were celebrated in honor of Poseidon; this innovation is ascribed to Theseus himself, who, according to some legends, was the son of Poseidon, and who, in the institution of the games, or Isthmian solemnities, is said to have imitated Hercules, the founder of the Olympian games.

The celebration of the Isthmia was henceforth conducted by the Corinthians, but Theseus had reserved for his Athenians some honorable distinctions. Those Athenians who attended the Isthmia, sailed across the Saronic gulf in a sacred vessel, and an honorary place as large as the sail of their vessel was assigned to them during their celebration of the games. In time of war, a sacred truce was concluded, and the Athenians were invited to attend at the solemnities. The Eleans took no part in the games, and various stories were invented to account for this singular circumstance. It is a very probable conjecture of Wachsmuth, that the Isthmia, after the changes ascribed to Theseus, were merely a panegyri of the Ionians of Peloponnesus, and those of Attica; for it should be observed that Poseidon was an Ionian deity, whose worship appears to have been unknown to the Dorians.

During the reign of the Cypselids at Corinth, the celebration of the

Isthmian games was suspended for seventy years; but after this time they gradually rose to the rank of a national, Greek festival.

In the forty-ninth Olympiad, they became periodical; and were henceforth regularly celebrated every third year of every Olympiad, and with this regularity the solemnities continued to be observed by the Greeks down to a very late period. In 228 B. C., the Romans were allowed the privilege of taking part in the Isthmia, and it was at this solemnity that in 196 B. C. Flaminius proclaimed, before an innumerable assembly, the independence of Greece. After the fall of Corinth in 146 B. C. the Sicyonians were honored with the privilege of conducting the Isthmian games; but when the town of Corinth was rebuilt by Julius Cæsar, the right of conducting the solemnities was restored to the Corinthians; and their celebration was continued till Christianity became the state religion of the Roman empire.

The season of the Isthmian solemnities was, like that of all the great, national festivals, distinguished by general rejoicing and feasting. The contests and games were the same as those of Olympia; and embraced all the varieties of athletic performances, such as wrestling, the pancratium, together with horse and chariot racing. Musical and poetical contests were likewise carried on; and in the latter, women were allowed to take part, as we must infer from Plutarch, who, on the authority of Polemo, states that in the treasury of Sicyon, there was a golden book which had been presented to it by Aristomache, the poetess, after she had gained the victory at the Isthmia. At a late period of the Roman Empire, the character of the games at the Isthmia appears greatly altered; for in the letter of the Emperor Julian, above referred to, it is stated that the Corinthians purchased bears and panthers for the purpose of exhibiting their fights at the Isthmia; and it is not improbable that the custom of introducing fights of animals on this occasion commenced soon after the time of Cæsar.

The prize of a victor at the Isthmian games consisted at first of a garland of pine leaves and afterwards of a wreath of ivy; but in the end, the ivy was again superseded by a pine garland. Simple as such a reward was, a victor in these games gained the greatest distinction and honor among his countrymen; and the victory not only rendered the individual who obtained it a subject of admiration, but shed lustre over his family and the whole town or community to which he belonged.

Hence Solon established by a law that every Athenian who gained a victory at the Isthmian games, should receive from the public treasury a reward of one hundred drachmæ. His victory was generally celebrated in lofty odes, of which we still possess some beautiful speci-mens among the Odes of Pindar.

" The only vestiges of the buildings connected with the celebration of the Isthmian games which now remain, are those of the stadium in the southern part of the enclosure ; the shell of a theatre, nearly three hundred yards to the north of it, and the foundations of the sacred precinct, which contained the temple of Neptune and Palæmon. Imme-diately to the east of the enclosure are substructions of the long line of wall which stretched from the Saronic gulf on the east to the Corinth-ian on the west, and defended the Isthmus ; a little beyond, upon the western shore, are the excavations for the canal of three miles and a half, by which Nero designed to unite the waters of these two gulfs. and to make the Peloponnesus an island.

" Returning towards Corinth from this part of the coast of the Co-rinthian gulf, at a quarter of a mile from the eastern entrance of the modern town, are the remains of an ancient amphitheatre. It lies from north to south, and measures about one hundred yards from one end of its length to the other, while its breadth is half that distance. Several of the seats and viæ are still visible, hewn in the rocky soil.

" We have thus had before our eyes three objects which exercised a powerful influence upon the tastes and manners of the Corinthians of old—their Theatre, their Stadium, and their Amphitheatre. While, brought together as they are now by being almost the only survivors among the public amusements of ancient Corinth, they remind us of the spectacles once exhibited within them, they at the same time recall to our recollection, in the most forcible manner, the circumstance that the Apostle, who spent nearly two years in this city, refers, in his Epistle, which he addressed to its inhabitants, to all these three objects, or to circumstances connected with them. Familiar as they were, both to him and to them, they supplied the most vivid illustration of the expressions he used, and of the emotions he both felt and wished to in-spire. This Amphitheatre, for instance, afforded to the readers of the Epistle a specimen of what he had endured, who, for the sake of the truth, as he there tells them, had fought with beasts at Ephesus. His words again,—' We are become a theatre to the world, to angels, and to men,'—came home with double force to the minds of those who saw how the mere actors of fictitious dramas were exposed in the eye of day to the gaze and censure of innumerable spectators in this theatre upon their own shore ; and nothing could give a more vivid picture of the Christian's duty, difficulties, and reward, than the question, ' Know ye not that they who run in the stadium, run all, but one receiveth the prize ? and every one who contendeth, is temperate in all things ? they, indeed, that they may receive a corruptible crown (a pine tree or a parsley chaplet), but we an incorruptible,'—coupled with the allusion which follows, to the gymnastic and athletic exercises practised before their eyes near the same spot."

HADES OR PLUTO.

Hades was the god of Hell, of riches, and funeral obsequies. His name, Hades, or Aides, signifies the invisible or un-known ; a name indicating of itself a gloom which no mortal could penetrate. He was also called the subterranean or Sty-gian Jupiter, and plastic art represented him like imperial Jove, but with gloomy, rather than benignant features. His Latin name was Dis, signifying wealth, — so called because wealth comes from the bowels of the earth ; and because, as Cicero observes, all things pro-ceed from the earth, and return to it again under his direction.

He is sometimes represented as having on his head an ancient corn measure, the emblem of Earth's fertility. At others with a helmet, which renders the wearer invisible, and which is supposed to indicate the safety that men find in the grave ; or with his garment drawn over his head to intimate the god concealed.

Hades was much renowned among the Egyptians, who had frequent representations of funeral ceremonies. In their representations of him, a radiant crown surrounds the head, and a serpent is twined round his body, sometimes accompanied with the signs of the zodiac. According to some mythologists, Hades, as well as many other gods of the Egyptians, was originally worshipped as the sun; and Zeus, Poseidon, and Hades are considered as the symbols of one solar year, diversified according to the changes of the seasons.

Tartaros, or Erebos, was the abode of night, where, at the remotest boundary of the Earth, the sun was supposed to sink into the sea. There, too, was the mansion of Hades, beneath which, in a dark prison, the Titans bemoaned their fate. The boundary of the earth was supposed to be the Atlantic Ocean; and there, near the abode of Night, fiction also placed those blissful islands where reigns everlasting spring. There, also, in the same dusky horizon of the west, the sky rested upon the shoulders of Atlas, and there the golden fruit was guarded by the Hesperides.

In Greece, the entrance to Hades' dominions was supposed to be near the promontory of Tænarus; and farther west, in Thesprotia, two streams took their rise, which we again find in Orcus; the rivers Acheron and Cocytus. Here Theseus and Pirithoös are said to have descended to the dark abode of the shades. Still farther west, on the coast of Italy, imagination discovered another fit place for an entrance from the higher to the lower world, where a dark and spacious cavern led to a gloomy grove contiguous to the Lake Avernus, the poisonous exhalations of which were fatal to every bird that attempted to fly over it. and permitted no man to dwell within its borders. Fable says, that the residence of Pluto was so obscure and gloomy that all the goddesses refused to marry him, and he therefore determined to obtain a wife by force, and that, after a violent earthquake, he visited the island of Sicily, where he saw Persephone, the daughter of Ceres, gathering flowers in the plains of Enna, surrounded by her female attendants, and immediately carried her away in his chariot, concealing his retreat by opening a passage for himself with a blow of his trident.

As wife of Pluto, and queen of hell, Proserpina presided over the death of mankind; and according to the opinion of the ancients, no one could die if the goddess herself. or Atropos, the minister, did not cut off one of the hairs from the head. From this superstitious belief, it was customary to strew some of the hair of the deceased at the door of the house as an offering to Proserpina

The Sicilians were very exact in their worship of Proserpina; and as they believed that the fountain Cyane had risen from the earth at

the very place where Pluto had opened himself a passage, they annually sacrificed there a bull, the blood of which was suffered to flow
into the water. Her worship was universal, and she was known by
the different names of Theogamia, Libitina, Hecate, Juno Inferna,
etc., etc.

Hades is represented as sitting on a throne, surrounded by the most
gloomy darkness; his countenance severe and frowning, holding in his
hand a two-pointed sceptre, and also a key, which signifies that when
once the dead ·are received into his kingdom, the gates are locked
against them, and thence there is no regress.

> "To the shades you go a down-hill, easy way,
> But to return and re-enjoy the day,
> This is a work, a labor."—*Æn.* vi.

Hades was considered as inexorable, and for that reason no temples
were erected to him as to the rest of the superior gods. Sacrifices of
black sheep and a bull were offered to him in the night. Their blood
was not sprinkled upon altars, or received into vessels, as at other
sacrifices, but was permitted to run into the earth, as if it could penetrate the realms of the god. Among plants, the cypress and maiden-
hair were sacred to him, as well as every thing deemed inauspicious,
particularly the number two.* According to some of the ancient writers, Hades sat on a throne of sulphur, from which issued the rivers
Lethe, Cocytus, Phlegethon, and Acheron. The triple-headed dog,
Cerberos, watched at his feet; the Harpies hovered around him; Persephone sat on his left hand, and near her the Erinnyes, their heads
wreathed with snakes, while the Parcæ, each holding the symbol of
her office, completed the group. According to others, the gates to his
dominions were watched by the triple-headed dog Cerberos; and before they can be reached, four rivers must be crossed, the very names
of which fill the soul with terror. The first is Acheron, the sighing
river, a son of Earth. He was born in a cave, and having an uncon-
querable aversion to light, ran down into Orcus, where he was changed

---

* The pagans looked upon an odd number as the more perfect, and the symbol of
concord, because it cannot be divided into two equal parts, as the even number may,
and is therefore the symbol of division. This prejudice was not only the reason why
the first month was consecrated to the celestial and the second to the terrestrial deities,
but it also gave birth to many superstitious practices.

into the river which still retains his name. Styx, terrible above all, is a lake rather than a river, and has already been mentioned among the ancient deities. The third river, Cocytus, flows out of the river Styx, and the murmur of its waters, the sound of which imitates the howlings of the damned, is inexpressibly dismal; Phlegethon, the fourth river, rolls slowly along its waves of fire.

The entrance to the infernal regions, called Avernus, is described as having around it a host of dreadful forms; Disease, Old Age, Terror, Hunger, Death, War, Discord, and the Furies, the avengers of guilt, with snaky hair, and whips of scorpions. Near this dismal eavern is the road to the river Acheron, whither resort the departed spirits, in order to obtain a passage over. Charon, the aged, surly boatman, receives them into his boat, if they have been honored with funeral rites, but inexorably rejects those who have not On the other side of the river is the gate leading to the palace of Hades, the sovereign of those dreary realms, guarded by the triple-headed Cerberos, which is always on the watch.

Within this seat of horror, are first seen the souls of infants who expired as soon as born. Then those who destroyed themselves, or were put to death unjustly. Beyond them, wandering in myrtle groves, are the victims to love and despair. Then succeed the abodes of heroes. Not far from them, is seen the dread tribunal, where Minos, Æacos, and Rhadamthys administer strict justice, and pass the irrevocable sentence. Then Tartaros, the tremendous prison, surrounded by three massy walls, having three gates of solid brass, round which the flaming Phlegethon rolls its waves of fire, and Cocytus extends its stagnant marsh. Here, likewise, is the river Styx, by which the gods swear their inviolable oath; and Lethe, whose waters produced forgetfulness of past events to those who drank them. In Tartaros, according to Virgil, those were punished who had been disobedient to parents, traitors, faithless ministers, and such as had undertaken unjust or cruel wars; or had betrayed their friends for the sake of gain. According to Ovid, it was the place where the Danaïdes, Tantalos, Sisyphos, and others were punished.

The Elysian fields are represented as adorned with all the beauties of nature which can soothe and delight the mind, and was the abode of the heroic and virtuous. Hills, covered with fragrant shrubs, delightful valleys, flowery plains, shady groves, lucid streams, mild and balmy air, and gentle and unclouded sunshine, all conspire to render the Elysian fields the seat of happiness and tranquillity. It was the habitation of the blessed ; particularly of the souls of those who had lived in the golden age, before man was stained with guilt. Here the souls of the just, freed from the passions and prejudices of mortality, ranged from grove to grove, enjoying the pleasures of friendship and contemplation, until, at the command of Zeus, they drank of the waters of Lethe, and the oblivious draught caused them instantly to lose all remembrance of the past. They then returned again in human form to the earth, where, forgetful of the joys of Elysium, they patiently endured the cares and sorrows of humanity, until the close of a well-spent life again restored them to the mansions of the just.

This fiction of the Greeks and Romans is borrowed from the funeral rites of the Egyptians. Near the Egyptian towns was a certain tract of ground appropriated as a common burying-place, and Diodorus Siculus gives an exact description of the customs practised at Memphis. According to him, their burying-place was on the other side of the Lake Acherusia, on the shore of which sat a tribunal of forty three judges, who inquired into the merits of the deceased person ; and if he had been disobedient to the laws, he was refused the rites of interment. When no accuser appeared, or he who deposed against the deceased was convicted of falsehood, their lamentations for him ceased, and they commended his excellent education, his respect for religion, his equity, chastity, and other virtues. All the attendants applauded these praises, and congratulated the deceased upon being prepared to enter the eternal abode of the virtuous.

On the shore of the lake was a severe and incorruptible boatman, who, by order of the judges, and never upon any other terms, received the deceased into his boat. The kings of Egypt were treated with the same rigor, and never admitted into the boat without the permission of the judges. The other side of the lake to which they were conveyed, was a plain embellished with meadows, brooks, and groves. This place was called Elizout, or the Elysian fields—that is, a habitation of repose or of joy. At the entrance of the abode was the figure of a dog, with three pair of jaws, called Cerberos. This symbol was expressive of their affection for the departed ; the dog being, of all animals, the emblem of attachment. To the figure of the dog they gave three heads or throats, to express the three cries made over the friend's grave, according to the custom which granted that honor to none but good

men. Therefore, the placing this figure over the head of a newly
buried person, signified his having been honored with the lamentations
of his family, and the cries which friends never fail to utter over the
graves of those whom they have loved and valued for their good qualities.

These practices among the Egyptians were instructions addressed to
the people, who were given to understand by such ceremonies and symbols, that death was followed by an account which must be given before
an inflexible tribunal ; but that what was so dreadful to the wicked,
was to the good only a passage to a state of happiness and bliss.

The whole fiction of Pluto, or Hades, alludes to the grave, whose
narrow bounds imagination enlarged into a world of shades. The kingdom of Hades is therefore represented as a desolate empire, and his
palace a narrow mansion.   There is the same allusion to decay in the
·old and leaky boat of Charon, which only creeps, as it were, across the
rivers, taking up much slime in its crevices.   The dead themselves are
represented like a world of dreams ; the empty shades appearing and
disappearing in a moment, yet sensible of what they had formerly been,
and of what they had possessed ; and still strive to accomplish those
pursuits in which they had been engaged when living in the upper
world, like a man who works and fatigues himself during a dream without attaining his object.

When Ulysses, by the command of Circe, went down into the lower
world, the souls of all the departed whom he had known during his
life-time assembled round the ditch into which he shed the blood of
his victims.   His mother presented herself to him ; but when he wished
to embrace her, the empty shade retreated, telling him, that after the
body was destroyed, the souls evaded every touch, like a dream.   The
shade of Agamemnon stretched forth its arms towards his friend and
counsellor, but had not the power to embrace him.   Ulysses also addressed the shade of Achilles, congratulating him on the renown he
had enjoyed while living, and for his being now esteemed among the
dead.   To which Achilles replied, that were it possible, he would
return to life and serve as a poor day-laborer for scanty wages, rather
than reign in his present abode over all the departed.   The shade of
Heracles too appeared to Ulysses, although he himself had his seat
among the celestials.

" The character of the Homeric Inferno is very simple. Two rivers,
11

a rock, some tall poplars and barren willows, were all its scenery. Very different indeed from subsequent representations of the same regions. This rocky glen, through which the Acheron tumbles over steep and dark cliffs, into the Paramythian plain ; what a contrast does it present to those later, and especially Roman representations of the subterranean world, in which a splendid vestibule leads through massive walls, and a peristyle of adamant into lengthening corridors, and thence into groves of myrtle and fragrant laurels—into the Inferno, in short, of an age and nation which introduced a Baian luxury even into its dreariest abodes, and dressed up the gloomy mansion of Pluto with the pomp of a palace of the Cæsars.

" Very different, too, the principles which suggested these later descriptions, from the melancholy language in which the Achilles of Homer declares upon this spot that he had rather cultivate those swampy fields as a day-laborer, than enjoy the honors of a royal state among the dead ; and very different the influence of this diversity of belief on the character of the respective nations by which it was entertained !

" Three or four cottages, a ruined church, and a paltry fortress, are all the artificial adjuncts of this spot. They stand on the verge of the plain, on the right bank of the Acheron. The place is called Aia Glyky. Above them, to the north-east, rise the lofty mountains of Suli, one crowning the other, and some bearing on their summits those proud castles which nothing but famine and avarice could storm. The Acheron falls from these hills through a deep and rocky gorge ; leaving these cottages to the right, it expands into a turbid and eddying stream, and then winds quietly through a flat, marshy country (in which it forms the Acherusian lake and unites itself with the Cocytus), into the Ionian Sea.

" The port of Glyky, into which the Acheron discharges itself, seems to have communicated its name to this place. Its adoption may also have been suggested by a desire to merge all the former sadness of the spot in such an agreeable euphemism. The feeling which in other cases appeased the most awful deities, and beguiled the most painful diseases, by the charm of a name, might also hope to sweeten the river of woe ; the name, too, it is evident, was conferred at a time when Christianity gave an additional reason for the choice, as well as another meaning to it when made. The ruined church at Aia Glyky stands on the site of an ancient temple. The fragments of eight or nine granite columns of the former structure still remain. We are inclined to believe that this was the oracular shrine, where the spirits of the dead were consulted. It was natural to inquire of the departed in the place where they were supposed to have passed into another state of being. The banks of the Acheron, therefore, were the private resort of necromancy. There was also high authority for this practice. Homer no sooner places here the sons of his seers and Heroes, than he begins to consult them on the spot. We see no willows at present, such as are placed by him on the banks of the Acheron. There are, indeed, few trees of any kind in the plain, and none of any size; a few oriental plane-trees, some low tamarisks by the water's edge, two or three wild fig-trees, and some bright-leaved pomegranates—a somewhat melancholy group, but not inappropriate. A plucked fruit of the latter tree, bursting with the crimson grains which give it its name, and placed as it was in ancient times, in the hands of a sculptured figure of a deceased person reclining on a sarcophagus containing his ashes, served as a pleasing symbol to express the assurance that though his life was now plucked from its stem, yet that it was not gathered too early, but ripely teeming with many seeds of rich fruit. The price of a few grains of the same tree gained also a queen for the nether world."

In a painting discovered about the end of the last century, in an old burial-place of the Massonian family, Hades and Persephone are represented sitting on thrones, whilst Hermes is introducing the ghost of a young woman, who seems intimidated at the stern look of Hades. Behind, stands her mother, waiting to conduct her to some grove in Elysium. Hades holds a sceptre in his hand and has a veil over his head.

DEMETER OR CERES.

Of the three august daughters of Kronos and Rhea, Hera alone is the reigning queen of Heaven: while Hestia and Demeter exercise their beneficent influence upon the earth; the one impregnating it with sacred, fertilizing warmth, and the other calling forth the nourishing ear of corn.

Demeter, the mother of Persephone, was evidently a goddess of the earth, whom some ancient system married to Zeus, the god of the Heavens. In Homer, she is but slightly mentioned, and she does not appear among the deities of Olympus. She seems to have been early distinguished from the goddess called Earth, and to have been regarded as the protectress of the growing corn, and of agriculture in general.

Demeter was the happy mother of Persephone; to whom, however, the sweet light of day was granted but a short time; youth and beauty in her soon becoming a prey of inexorable Orcus.

Persephone, sang the Homerid, was in the Nysian plain with the ocean-nymphs gathering flowers. She plucked the rose, the violet, the crocus, the hyacinth, when she beheld a Narcissus of surprising beauty, an object of amazement to "all immortal gods and mortal men," for one hundred flowers grew from one root,

> "And with its fragrant smell wide heaven above
> And all earth laugh'd, and the sea's briny flood."

Unconscious of danger, the maiden stretched forth her hand to seize the wondrous flower, when, suddenly, the wide earth gaped; Aïdoneus in his golden chariot rose, and catching the terrified goddess, carried her off in it, shrieking to her father for aid, unheard and unseen by gods or mortals, save only by Hecate, the daughter of Persæos, who heard her as she sat in her cave, and by king Helios, whose eye nothing on earth escapes.

So long as Persephone beheld the earth and the starry heaven, the fishy sea, and beams of the sun, so long she hoped to see her mother and the tribes of the gods; and the tops of the mountains and the depths of the sea resounded with her voice. At length her mother heard; she tore her head attire with grief, cast a dark robe around her, and like a bird hurried over moist and dry. Of all she inquired tidings of her lost daughter; but neither gods, nor men, nor birds could give her intelligence. Nine days she wandered over the earth with flaming torches in her hand; she tasted not of nectar nor ambrosia, and never once entered the bath. On the tenth morning Hecate met her; but she could not tell who had carried away Persephone. Together they proceeded to Helios; they stand at the head of his horses, and Demeter entreats that he will say who is the ravisher. The god of the Sun gives the required information, telling her that it was Aïdoneus, who, by the permission of her sire, had carried Persephone away to be his queen; he then exhorts the goddess to patience, by dwelling on the rank and dignity of the ravisher.

Helios urges on his steeds; the goddess, incensed at the conduct of Zeus, abandoned the society of the gods, and came and dwelt among men. But she now was heedless of her person and no one recognized her. Under the guise of an old woman—" such," says the poet, " as are the nurses of law-dispensing king's children, and house-keepers, in resounding houses," she came to Eleusis and sat down by a well, beneath the shade of an olive. The three beautiful daughters of Keleos, a prince of that place, coming to the well to draw water, and seeing the goddess, inquired who she was, and why she did not go into the town. Demeter told them that her name was Dos, and that she had been carried off by the pirates from Crete, but that when they got on shore at Thoricos, she had contrived to make her escape, and wandered thither. She entreats them to tell her where she is ; and wishing them young husbands and as many children as they may desire, begs that they will endeavor to procure her a service in a respectable family.

The princess Callidice tells the goddess the names of the five princes, who with her father governed Eleusis, each of whose wives would, she was sure, be most happy to receive into her family a person who looked so god-like : but she prays her not to be precipitate, but to wait till she had consulted her mother, Metaneira, who had a young son in the cradle, of whom, if the stranger could have the nursing, she would obtain a large recompense.

The goddess bowed her thanks, and the princesses took up their pitchers and went home. As soon as they had related their adventure to their mother, she agreed to hire the nurse at large wages :

> And they as fawns or heifers in spring-time
> Bound on the mead when satiate with food;
> So they, the folds fast-holding of their robes
> Lovely, along the hollow cartway ran;
> Their locks upon their shoulders flying wide,
> Like unto yellow flowers.

The goddess rose and accompanied them. As she entered the house a divine splendor shone all around. Metaneira, filled with awe, offered the goddess her own seat, which, however, she declined. Iambe, the serving-maid, then prepared one for her, where she sat in silence, thinking of her " deep-bosomed" daughter, till Iambe, by her tricks, contrived to make her smile and even laugh. Metaneira offered her a cup of wine, which she declined, and would only drink the *kykeon*, or mixture of flour and water. She undertook the task of rearing the babe, who was named Demophoön, and beneath her care " he throve like a god." He ate no food ; but Demeter breathed on him as he lay in her bosom, and anointed him with ambrosia, and every night she hid him " like a

torch within the strength of fire," unknown to his parents, who mar-
velled at his growth.

It was the design of Demeter to make him immortal; but the curiosity and folly of Metaneira deprived him of the intended gift. She
watched one night, and seeing what the nurse was about, shrieked with
affright and horror. The goddess threw the infant on the ground,
declaring what he had lost by the inconsiderateness of his mother, but
announcing that he would be great and honored, since he had " sat in
her lap, and slept in her arms." She then tells who she is, and directs
that the people of Eleusis should raise an altar and temple to her without the town on the hill Callichoros.

> Thus having said, the goddess changed her size
> And form, old age off-flinging, and around
> Beauty respired; from her fragrant robes
> A lovely scent was scattered, and afar
> Shone light emitted from her skin divine:
> And yellow locks upon her shoulders waved;
> While, as from lightning, all the house was filled
> With splendor.

She left the house, and the maidens waking at the noise found their
infant brother lying on the ground. They took him up, and kindling
a fire, prepared to wash him; but he cried bitterly, finding himself in
the hands of such unskilful nurses.

In the morning the wonders of the night were narrated to Keleos,
who laid the matter before the people, and the temple was speedily
raised. The mourning goddess took up her abode in it, but a dismal
year came upon mankind; and the earth yielded no produce. In vain
the oxen drew the curved ploughs in the fields; in vain was the seed
of barley cast in the ground; " well-garlanded Demeter" would suffer
no increase. The whole race of man ran the risk of perishing, and the
dwellers of Olympos of losing gifts and sacrifices, had not Zeus discovered the danger and thought on a remedy.

He despatches " gold-winged Iris" to Eleusis to invite Demeter back
to Olympos, but the dissatisfied goddess will not comply with the call.
All the other gods are sent on the same errand, and to as little purpose. Gifts and honors are proffered in vain; she will not ascend to
Olympos, or suffer the earth to bring forth, until she shall have seen
her daughter.

Finding there was no other remedy, Zeus sends " gold-rodded Argos-slayer" to Erebos, to endeavor to prevail on Hades to suffer Persephone to see the light. Hermes obeyed, quickly reached the "secret places of earth," and found the king at home seated on a couch with his wife, who was mourning for her mother. On making known to Aïdoneus the wish of Zeus, "the King of the Subterraneans smiled with his brows" and yielded compliance. He kindly addressed Persephone, granting her permission to return to her mother. The goddess instantly sprang up with joy, and heedlessly swallowed a pomegranate which Hades presented to her.

> Then many-ruling Aïdoneus yoked
> His steeds immortal to the golden car:
> She mounts the chariot, and beside her mounts
> Strong Argos-slayer, holding in his hands
> The reins and whip : forth from the house he rushed,
> And not unwillingly the coursers flew.
> Quickly the long road they have gone; not sea,
> Nor streams of water, nor the grassy dales,
> Nor hills retard the immortal coursers' speed,
> But o'er them going, they cut the air profound.

Hermes conducted his fair charge safe to Eleusis : Demeter, on seeing her, "rushed to her like a Mænas on the wood shaded hill," and Persephone sprang from the car "like a bird," and kissed her mother's hands and head.

When their joy had a little subsided, Demeter anxiously inquired if her daughter had tasted any thing while below; for if she had not, she would be free to spend her whole time with her mother; whereas, if but one morsel had passed her lips, nothing could save her from spending one third of the year with her husband; and the other two she could pass with her and the gods :

> And when in spring-time with sweet smelling flowers
> Of various kinds the earth doth bloom, thou'lt come
> From gloomy darkness back—a mighty joy
> To gods and mortal men.

Persephone ingenuously confesses the swallowing of the grain of pomegranate, and then relates to her mother the story of her adventures. They pass the day in delightful converse :

> And joy they mutually received and gave.

"Bright-veiled Hecate" arrives to congratulate Persephone, and henceforward becomes her attendant. Zeus sends Rhea to invite them back to Heaven. Demeter now complies,

> And instant, from the deep-soiled cornfields fruit
> Sent up; with leaves and flowers the whole wide earth
> Was laden.

She taught " Triptolemus, horse-lashing Diocles, the strength of Eumolpos, and Keleos the leader of the people," the mode of perform- ing her sacred rites. The goddess then returned to Olympos. " But some," cries the Homerid,

> But come, thou goddess who dost keep the land
> Of odorous Eleusis, and round-flowed
> Paros, and rocky Anthron, Deo queen,
> Mistress, bright-giver, season-bringer, come;
> Thyself and child, Persephoneia fair,
> Grant freely, for my song, the means of life.
> But I will think of thee and other songs.

Throughout the whole of this attractive fiction, may be traced the idea of the mysterious development of the grain hidden in the lap of the earth, and of the inward, secret-life of nature. There is no other object found in nature, in which to appearance life and death border so closely together, as in the grain of seed buried in the earth, never again to re-appear to the eye of man ; but, at the moment when life seems entirely extinct, a fuller and richer existence begins anew. De- meter, who is said first to have bestowed the blessing of grain upon mortal man, is in the chain of divine beings, that one, who, through the medium of her person, carries the blessed influence of the sky down to the dark dominions of Hades. Hades, who is called the sub- terranean or Stygian Jupiter, is married to the beautiful daughter of Jupiter Olympius, and in this manner the opposite ideas of life and death being united in the person of Persephone, she connects with a mysterious band the high and the deep—Olympos and Orcus.

Upon ancient marble coffins, the ravishment of Persephone is often met with ; and in the mysterious festivals which were celebrated in honor of Demeter and her daughter, it seems as if the close connection of the terrible and beautiful had been intended to fill the minds of the initiated with astonishment and awe ; and at last, all that appeared opposite and contrary in the beginning, melted away, and was lost in harmony and beauty.

Demeter is represented as one of the most placid and meek among the heathen deities; yet she made Erisicthon, who violated one of her groves, sensible of her power by afflicting him with perpetual hunger. At another time, during her search for her daughter, she entered a cottage to slake her burning thirst. and was scoffed at by a rude boy, because of her eagerness in drinking.

Indignant at the ignominy, she bespattered the offender with water, by which he was immediately transformed into a spotted lizard, and in this shape, bore witness to the power of the formidable goddess.

Demeter is commonly represented as holding a sickle in her right hand, and in her left, the torch which she lighted at Mount Ætna. At her feet are coiled the dragons which drew her chariot; a wreath of wheaten ears confines her golden tresses, and a cornucopia is generally placed near her, to indicate the plenty produced by agriculture. She is also represented with a garland of corn upon her head; in one hand holding a poppy, and in the other a lighted torch. Again she appears as a countrywoman, on the back of an ox, carrying a basket on her left arm, and holding a hoe; and sometimes riding in a chariot drawn by winged horses. In the Vatican, are some fine antique statues of this goddess; one of them is nearly nine feet high, and was for nearly three centuries the principal ornament of the theatre of Pompey at Rome. Another of these is smaller, not above three feet six inches high.

The Romans paid great adoration to Ceres, and her festivals were celebrated yearly by the Roman matrons, during eight days in the month of April. These matrons abstained for several days from wine, and every carnal enjoyment; and at the festivals, bore lighted torches in commemoration of the goddess; and whoever attended them without a previous initiation, was punished with death. These festivals were called Cerealia, and were the same as the Thesmophoria of the Greeks.

Sicily was supposed to be the favorite retreat of Ceres, and Diodorus says that she and her daughter first made their appearance to mankind in Sicily, which Pluto received as a nuptial dowry from Jupiter. The Sicilians made a yearly sacrifice to Ceres, every man according to his ability; and the fountain of Cyane, through which Pluto opened himself a passage when conveying away Proserpina, was publicly honored with an offering of bulls, and the blood of the victims was shed in the

waters of the fountain.   Besides these, other ceremonies were observed
in honor of the goddess who had so peculiarly favored the island.   The
commemoration of Proserpina's disappearance was celebrated about the
beginning of harvest, and the search of Ceres, about the time that the
corn is sown in the earth.   The latter festivals continued six successive
days.

Attica, which has been so eminently distinguished by the goddess,
greatly remembered her favors in the celebration of the Eleusinian
mysteries.

This great festival was celebrated every fourth year by the Celeans
and Philiasians, as also by the Lacedemonians, Parrhasians, and Cretans; but more particularly by the Atticans at Eleusis, where it was
introduced by Eumolpos B. C. 1356, and was the most celebrated of
all the religious ceremonies of Greece.

Each of the gods had, besides the public and open, a secret worship
paid to him, to which none were admitted who had not previously been
through the preparatory ceremonies of initiation.   This secret worship
was termed *the mysteries*, and was the most sacred part of the pagan
religion.

The first original mysteries of which we have any account, were
those of Osiris or Isis in Egypt, from whence they were derived
by the Greeks.   They were observed in various places, and always with
the same object, viz. to inculcate the doctrine of a future state of rewards and punishments; but those celebrated at Athens in honor of
Ceres, were termed, by way of eminence, *The Mysteries;* and were so
superstitiously observed, that if any one ever revealed them, it was
supposed he would be followed by divine vengeance.

In cultivating the doctrine of a future life, it was taught that the
initiated would be happier after death than other mortals; that while
the souls of the profane stuck fast to mire and filth, and remained in
darkness, the souls of the initiated wing their way to the islands of
bliss and the habitations of the gods.   But lest it should be mistaken
that any other means than a virtuous life should entitle men to future
happiness, the restoration of the soul to its original purity was openly
proclaimed as the object of the mysteries.   " It was the end and design
of initiation," says Plato, " to restore the soul to that state from whence
it fell, as from its entire native seat of perfection."   They contrived
that every thing should tend to show the necessity of virtue, as appears

from Epictetus. " Thus the mysteries became useful ; thus we see the true spirit of them, when we begin to apprehend that every thing therein was instituted by the ancients for the amendment of life." Porphyry gives us some of those moral precepts which were enforced in the mysteries; as to honor parents, to offer up fruits to the gods, and to forbear cruelty to animals. It was required that the aspirant to the mysteries should be of a pure and unblemished character, and free even from the suspicion of any notorious crime; and to ascertain the truth on these requisitions, he was severely interrogated by the priests, or hierophantes, who impressed him with the same sense of his obligation to conceal nothing, as is now done at the Roman confessional.

During the celebration of the mysteries, the greatest purity and elevation of mind was enjoined upon the votaries. " When you sacrifice or pray," says Epictetus to Arrian, " go with a prepared purity of mind, and with dispositions so previously disposed, as are required of you when you approach the ancient rites and mysteries." And Proclus tells us, that " the mysteries and the initiation drew the souls of men from a material, sensual, and merely human life, and joined them in communion with the gods." Nor was a less degree of purity required of the initiated for their future conduct. They were obliged by solemn engagements to commence a new life of strict piety and virtue, which was done by a severe course of penance. According to Gregory Nazianzen, no one could be initiated into the mysteries of Mithras, until he had undergone all sorts of mortifying trials, and approved himself holy and impassible. Under this discipline and these promises, the initiated were esteemed the only happy men ; and the advantages conferred by the ceremonies of initiation, both here and hereafter, made its subjects an object of universal regard. Persons of all ages and sexes were initiated, and it was considered so serious a crime to neglect that part of the religion, that the accusation of it contributed' to the death of Socrates.

The chief minister who officiated at these festivals was called a hierophantes or mystagogos, the revealer of sacred things. He was a citizen of Athens, and held his office during life ; though, among the Celeans and Philiasians, it was limited to the period of four years. The priest was obliged to devote himself wholly to the deities, and his life must be chaste and single. The Hierophant had three attendants ; the first was a torch bearer, and was permitted to marry ; the second was a sacred Herald ; and the third administered at the altar. Besides these, there were other inferior officers, who took particular care to see that every thing was done according to custom. The first was one of the archons, whose duty was to offer prayers and sacrifices, and to see that there was no indecency or irregularity during the celebration. Four others were elected by the people called curators, or Epimeletes; one from the sacred family of the Eumolpids;* another was one of the Ceryces, and the rest from among the citizens. This celebration, sacred to Ceres and Proserpina, lasted for nine successive days from the 10th to the 20th of September. These days were consecrated to the ceremonies of preparation and purification, the particulars of which were founded upon the story of Ceres' adventures in search of Proserpina. The singing of sacred hymns, in honor of the goddess, always formed a part of the service.

The first day of celebration was called the assembly, as the worshippers then met together; the second day they were commanded to purify themselves by bathing in the sea;—on the third day sacrifices were offered; chiefly a mullet, and also barley from the field of Eleusis. These oblations were considered so sacred, that the priests were not permitted to partake of them, as at other sacrifices. On the fourth day they made a solemn procession, while on every side the people shouted, Hail, Ceres! Women followed carrying baskets, in which were sesamum, carded wool, grains of salt, a serpent, pomegranates, etc., etc. The night of the fifth day they ran about with torches; the sixth day the statue of Inachus, holding a torch, was carried in solemn procession from Ceranicus to Eleusis; the statue, as well as those who accompanied it, was crowned with myrtle, and nothing was heard but singing and noisy merriment. The way through which they issued from the city was called the Sacred Way; on the bridge over the Cephissus they derided those that passed by; and after passing this

---

* The Eumolpids were the priests of Demeter, at the celebration of her mysteries. All causes relating to impiety or profanation were referred to their judgment; and the decision, though occasionally severe, was generally considered impartial. They were descended from Eumolpos, a king of Thrace, who was made priest of Demeter by Erectheus, king of Athens; and, after this appointment, became so powerful that he maintained a war against Erectheus, which proved fatal to both. Peace was re-established among their descendants, on condition that the priesthood should for ever remain in the family of Eumolpos, and the regal power in the house of Erectheus.

The priesthood continued in the family of Eumolpos 1200 years; and this is still more remarkable, as he who was once appointed to the holy office, was obliged to remain in perpetual celibacy.

bridge, they entered Eleusis, by a place called the mystical entrance. On the seventh day were sports in which the victors were rewarded with a measure of barley, as that grain was first sown in Eleusis. On the eighth day the mysteries were celebrated a second time, when those who had not been initiated were admitted by a repetition of the lesser mysteries. The ninth and last day of the festival, two vessels were filled with wine, one of which was placed towards the east, and the other towards the west; after the repetition of some mystical words, they were both thrown down, and the wine being spilt on the ground, was offered as an oblation to the goddess.

The road from Athens to Eleusis on which the procession passed, was in some respects the most remarkable in Greece. Year by year, in the autumnal season, on the sixth day of the Eleusinian mysteries, the figure of Bacchus—not the Theban deity, but the youthful son of Ceres, and the giver of the vine to man—crowned with a chaplet of myrtle, and holding a torch in his hand, was carried in procession; he was followed over hill and plain by thousands of worshippers, clad in festal attire, and wearing garlands of the same leaves as those which were woven round the head of the object of their devotion, and chanting his praise in strains of solemn and harmonious adoration.

The stone pavement of the ancient road which this procession fol-lowed, still remains entire in some parts of the plain near the sea-coast; on its surface the tracks of the wheels which passed over it in former days are still visible. They remind us of the slow trains of Eleusinian cars in which the women of Athens went along it from their own city to that of Eleusis.

But not merely the women of Athens—the mothers of Miltiades and Cimon, of Themistocles and of Pericles—nor only the youth and men of the city have passed over this paved way, to visit and participate in this most august ceremony of the heathen world; for these stones have also been trodden by the feet of her poets, her statesmen, and her phi-losophers, all tending to the same place, and on the same errand; and again, not merely by them, but also by Kings and Princes, by Satraps of Asia and by Monarchs of Egypt, by Consuls and Prætors of Rome, by her wise, and eloquent, and learned men—by her Augustus Cæsars, her Ciceroes, her Horaces, and her Virgils—going on their way to Eleusis to pay their homage to the awful deities of that place, and to receive, as they believed, by initiation into the mysteries of their worship, both a clearer knowledge of the most abstruse and perplexing questions which could be presented to the intellectual contemplation of man, and also a fuller assurance of their own personal felicity both in the present and future world.

To this road a remarkable contrast is presented in character, scenery, and circumstances, by that of the capital of Italy, which bore the same name as this which leads from Athens to Eleusis. The sacred way of Rome, we mean to say, affords a remarkable parallel to the sacred way of Athens. These two roads, it is worthy of observation, are, as it were, the representations of the peculiar character, genius, and influence of the people to which they respectively belong. Each of them exhibits to the eye and mind of the traveller along them, the very objects which would be selected as the most appropriate characteristics of the pursuits and tastes, the qualifications and achievements, by which each of the two nations in question was peculiarly distinguished.

The via sacra of Rome starts from the Colosseum ; it passes under arches of triumph ; it traverses the Roman forum, and terminates in the Capitol. Thus it begins its course with pointing to the scene of the gladiatorial shows which afforded a savage pleasure to assembled thousands of the imperial city in that vast amphitheatre, that *splendid disgrace* of Rome. By the triumphal arches which span it, it refers to the military conquests which gained for Rome the title of mistress of the world ; it speaks of the cars of the conqueror, of the captives in chains which passed over it, of the triumphal processions of victorious armies which moved along it, laden with spoil and decorated with trophies, some from the most distant regions of the earth. Again, the Rostra and Senate House of the Forum through which it passes, supply a memorial of the grave and dignified eloquence and wisdom which controlled the people and guided the Senate of Rome ; of that eloquence and wisdom which governed provinces, and ratified peace, and made laws, and returned answers to foreign kings and nations ; and lastly, from the summit of the Capitol, whither all these triumphal processions tended, as to the goal and limit of their course, to offer prayers and spoils and thanks after their victories to the Capitoline Jove, it seems, as it were, audibly to declare that the consummation of the hopes and aspirations of Rome was military glory ; that conquest and empire were *her* mysteries ; that they were the temple to which she marched along her Sacred Way ; that this was the initiation by which she raised herself above the nations of the earth ;—this the Apotheosis by which she became a partaker of the immortal dignity of her own deities.

But the Sacred Way which led from Athens to Eleusis was of a very different character. It issued from the western and principal gate of the Athenian city into the most beautiful of her suburbs; here in the Ceranicus, as it was called, were the monuments of her great men, monuments decorated with the ornaments of poetry and sculpture; and among them the orations were spoken over the graves of those who had fallen in their country's cause, which made their fate an object to their survivors and friends rather of congratulation than of grief. It then pursued its course through the olive groves of Plato, and the Academy; it crossed the stream of the Cephissus; it mounted the hill of the Ægaleös; it passed by the temples of Apollo and Venus, and descended into the Sacred Plain; it ran through a long avenue of tombs of priests, and poets, and philosophers; it coasted the bay of Eleusis, which, girt as it is on all sides (with the exception of two narrow channels) by majestic mountains, presents the appearance of a beautiful lake; and at length, as the termination of its course, it arrived at the foot of the ample hill of Eleusis, crowned with marble porticoes and spacious courts, and with the stupendous pile of the temple of Ceres, celebrated as the work of the most skilful architects, and venerable for its sanctity and its mysteries, which claimed for Eleusis the title of the religious capital of Greece.

In its course it had passed within sight of Colonos on the right and Salamis on the left, one the birthplace of Sophocles, and the other that of Euripides; and it was ended at Eleusis, which was the native city of Æschylus.

Thus did the Sacred Way, in its commencement, its career, and its conclusion, make an appeal to those peculiar objects both of nature and of art which obtained for Athens a moral, intellectual, and religious supremacy over the nations of the world, of greater exten; and permanence than that military sway which was exercised over them by the invincible arm of Rome.

Of the temple of Ceres at Eleusis, few vestiges now remain. It stood on an elevated platform at the eastern extremity of the rock on which the city was built. It was approached by a portico, similar to that at the western side of the Acropolis at Athens. Thus these two

Propylæa, which were both the work of Pericles, looked towards each other.

The entrance through this vestibule led to another of smaller dimen-sions, which opened into a vast enclosure, in which the temple itself stood, which was the largest in Greece. It was faced on the south by a portico of twelve columns, and the interior of the cella was divided by four rows of pillars parallel to each other and to the portico, and on which the roof of the fabric was supported.

Æschylus was summoned before the religious tribunal at Athens, on a charge of having divulged, in one of his dramas, the secrets which were revealed to the initiated in this place; and the traveller Pausa-nias was forbidden in a dream to communicate the information he re-ceived here with respect to the mystical signification of some of the objects of adoration at Eleusis; nor are the expressions of Horace on the same subject an insignificant indication of the awe with which men shrank from the sacrilege, of which he who made such a revelation was supposed to be guilty. It would, therefore, be a vain and presump-tuous enterprise to attempt to describe, at this time, what they who alone could tell were least willing to express.

But some of the *external* circumstances which attended the celebra-tion of the Eleusinian mysteries are not involved in the same obscurity. We are still enabled, while standing within the sacred enclosure, and on the marble pavement of the temple of Ceres, to revive in our minds some of the scenes which gave to this place, in ancient times, a solem-nity and a splendor, the impression of which was never erased from the memory of those who had once felt its effects.

The fifth day of the sacred festival was distinguished by a magnifi-cent procession of the initiated, who were clad in purple robes, and bore on their heads crowns of myrtle; the priests led the way into the interior of the temple through the southern portico, which has been described. The worshippers followed in pairs, each bearing a torch, and in solemn silence. But the evening of the tenth day of this august pageant was the most remarkable. It brought with it the consumma-tion of the mystic ceremonies. On it, the initiated were admitted for the first time to a full enjoyment of the privileges which the mysteries conferred. Having gone through the previous rites of fasting and purification, they were clad in the sacred fawn skin, and led at even-tide into the vestibule of the temple. The doors of the building itself were as yet closed. Then the profane were commanded by the priests with a loud voice to retire. The worshippers remained alone. Presently strange sounds were heard; dreadful apparitions, as of dying men, were seen; lightnings flashed through the thick darkness in which they were enveloped, and thunders rolled around them; light and gloom succeeded each other with rapid interchange. After these preliminaries, at length the doors of the temple were thrown open. Its interior shone with one blaze of light. The votaries were then led to the feet of the statue of the goddess, who was clad in the most gorgeous attire; in her presence their temples were encircled by the priests with the sacred wreath of myrtle, which was intended to direct their thoughts to the myrtle groves of the blessed in those happy isles to which they would be carried after death; their eyes were dazzled with the most vivid and beautiful colors, and their ears charmed with the most melodious sounds, both rendered more enchanting by their contrast with those fearful and ghastly objects which just before had been offered to their senses. They were now admitted to behold visions of the creation of the universe, to see the workings of the divine agency by which the machine of the world was regulated and controlled, to contemplate the state of society which prevailed upon the earth before the visit of Ceres to Attica, and to witness the introduction of agriculture, of sound laws, and of gentle manners, which followed the steps of that goddess; to recognize the immortality of the soul, as typified by the concealment of corn sown in the earth, by its revival in the green blade, and by its full ripeness in the golden harvest; or, as the same idea was otherwise expressed, by the abduction of Proserpina, the daughter of Ceres, to the region of darkness, in order that she might pass six months beneath the earth, and then arise again to spend an equal time in the realms of light and joy. Above all, they were invited to view the spectacle of that happy state in which they themselves, the initiated, were to exist hereafter. These revelations contained the greatest happiness to which man could aspire in this life, and assured him of such a bliss as nothing could exceed or diminish in the next.

Besides the various rites and ceremonies described above, several others are mentioned, but it is not known to which day they belonged; the Eleusinian games, which Mersius assigns to the seventh day, are said to have been the most ancient in Greece. In these contests, the prize of the victors consisted of ears of barley. It was considered the greatest profanation of the Eleusinia, for any to come as a supplicant to the temple with an olive branch, and whoever did so, was put to

death without trial, or fined one thousand drachmæ. At other festivals, as well as at Eleusis, no man could be seized or arrested foɪ any
offence during the celebration. The garments in which the votaries
were initiated, were held sacred, and considered as efficacious in avert
ing evils, charms, and incantations.

The Eleusinian mysteries lasted about eighteen hundred years ; long
surviving the independence of Greece. Attempts to suppress them
were made by the Emperor Valentinian, but he met with strong opposition ; and they were finally abolished by Theodosius the Great.

Respecting the nature and end of these mysteries, various opinions
have been entertained by modern scholars. The following are some
of the results of inquiries made by the learned and judicious Lobeck.

In the very early ages of Greece and Italy, and probably of most
countries, the inhabitants of the various independent districts into
which they were divided. had very little communication with each
other ; and a stranger was regarded as little better than an enemy.
Each state had its favorite deities, under whose special protection it
was supposed to be. and each deity was propitiated by sacrifices and
ceremonies which were different in different places. It is further to be
recollected, that the Greeks believed their gods to be very little superior
in moral qualities to themselves. and they feared that if promises of
more splendid and abundant sacrifices and offerings were made to them
they might not be able to resist the temptation. As the best mode of
escaping the calamity of being deserted by their patrons, they adopted
the expedient of concealing their names. and excluding strangers from
their worship. Private families in like manner excluded their fellow
citizens from their family sacrifices ; and in those states where ancient
aërolites and the like were preserved as ancient Palladia, the sight of
them was restricted to the magistrates and the principal persons in the
state.

The worship of Ceres and Proserpina was the national and secret
religion of the Eleusinians. from which the Athenians were of course
excluded, as well as the other Greeks ; but when Eleusis was conquered, and the two states coalesced, the Athenians became participa-
tors in the worship of these deities. Gradually, with the advance of
knowledge, and the decline of superstition and national illiberality,
admission to witness the solemn rites celebrated each year at Eleusis,
was extended to all Greeks of either sex and of every rank provided

they came at the proper time, had committed no inexpiable offence, had performed the requisite previous ceremonies, and were introduced by an Athenian citizen. These mysteries, as they were termed, were performed with some splendor at the expense of the state, and under the superintendence of the magistrates; hence it follows, as a necessary consequence, that the rites could have contained nothing that was grossly immoral.

The ancient writers are full of the praises of the Eleusinian mysteries, of the advantage of being initiated, and the favor of the gods in life, and the cheerful hopes in death which resulted in consequence. Hence occasion has been taken to assert, that a system of religion little inferior to pure Christianity was taught in them. But these hopes, and this tranquillity of mind, and favor of Heaven, are easily accounted for without having recourse to so absurd a supposition. Every act performed in obedience to the will of Heaven, is believed to draw down its favor on the performer. The Mussulman makes his pilgrimage to the Kaäba at Mecca; the Catholic to Loretto, Compostella, or elsewhere; and each is persuaded that, by having done so, he has secured the divine favor. So the Greek, who was initiated at Eleusis (the mysteries of which place, owing to the fame in which Athens stood, and the splendor and magnificence with which they were performed, eclipsed all others), retained ever after, a lively sense of the happiness which he enjoyed when admitted to view the interior of the illuminated temple, and the sacred relics which it contained; when to his excited imagination the very gods themselves seemed to descend from their Olympian abodes, amid the solemn hymns of the officiating priests. Hence there naturally arose a persuasion, that the benign regards of the gods were bent upon him through life; and as man can never divest himself of the belief of his continued existence after death, he cherishes a vivid hope of enjoying bliss in the life to come.

It was evidently the principle already stated, of seeking to discover the causes of remarkable appearances, which gave origin to most of the ideas respecting the recondite sense of the actions and ceremonies which took place in the Eleusinian mysteries. The stranger, dazzled and awed by his own conception of the sacredness and importance of all he beheld, conceived that nothing there could be without some mysterious meaning. What this might be, he inquired of the officiating ministers; who, as various passages in Pausanias and Herodotus show, were seldom without a legend, or sacred account. as it was called, to explain the dress or ceremony, which perhaps owed its true origin to the caprice or sportive humor of a ruder period. · Or, if the initiated person himself was endowed with inventive power, he explained the appearances according to the general system of philosophy which he had embraced. It was thus that Porphyry conceived the Hierophant to represent the Platonic Demiurgus, or creator of the world; the torch-bearer, the sun; the altar-man, the moon; the Herald, Hermes; and the other ministers, the inferior stars.

These fancies of priests and philosophers have been formed by mod ern writers into a complete system; and St. Croix in particular describes the Eleusinian mysteries with as much minuteness as if he himself had been actually initiated.

It is to be observed in conclusion, with respect to the charges of impiety and immorality brought against the Eleusinian mysteries by the fathers of the church, that this arose from their confounding them with the Bacchic, Isiac, Mithraic, and other private mysteries, mostly imported from Asia, and which were undoubtedly liable to the imputation. It must always be remembered, that the Eleusinia were public, and celebrated by the state.

PHŒBOS-APOLLO.

The Grecian Apollo is one of those divine representations that are completely finished to the finest strokes and features. Fancy, adorning him with the charms of eternal youth, calls him the far-shooting god, who bends the silver bow; and the father of poetry, who plays on the golden harp. But since Apollo cannot fulfil the various tasks of being on earth the divine patron and teacher of poesy and music—of delighting the gods on Olympos with his lyre and song, and at the same time driving the chariot of the sun, the imagination of the poets seems to have blended the two persons of Helios and Apollo merely for the sake of unity, while in fact they recognized two different beings; the one going up and down the sky as the shining sun, the other wandering on the earth, a new born, immortal youth, with golden locks, charming the hearts of gods and men with play and song.

The chief archetype of Apollo is the sun's rays, in eternal and youthful splendor. It assumes human form, and with it, rises to perfect beauty, in which the very expression of destructive power melts away in the harmony of the youthful features. As in the rays of the sun, that are both beneficent and destructive, fertilizing and producing decay, creation and destruction are united, so the divine form of which those rays are the archetype, unites in itself both terror and mildness. For the god of beauty and youth, who delights in lyre and song, carries at the same time the quiver upon his shoulder, draws the silver bow, and in wrath sends his arrows among men to cause by their means contagious sickness ; or he kills them with his soft weapons.

The twins of Latona, Apollo and Diana, are the twin deities of death, who divide the human race between them. Apollo takes man for his aim, and Diana, woman ; and thus they kill with mild arrow, those who are overcome with old age ;—like the leaves of verdant trees, that keep themselves in a state of sempiternal bloom and fresh color, merely by successively falling to decay, or like those sacred doves of Jupiter, which, flying by the dangerous Scylla, always lose one of their company, which is instantly replaced by the father of the gods, lest the number be impaired. Thus one generation of men imperceptibly makes room for another ; and whoever falls asleep overpowered by age and infirmity, is said, in the language of poetry, to have been killed by a soothing weapon, either from the hand of Apollo or Diana.

That this was the way of thinking among the ancients, appears from the manner in which they express themselves. " The small, happy island where I was born," relates the swineherd Eumæos to Ulysses, " is situated beneath a healthy and benevolent sky ; there men are not swept away by odious sickness; but when old age comes over them, Diana or Apollo appears with silver bow, and kills them with arrows that give no pain." (Od. xv. 402.) And when Ulysses, in the lower world, asks the shade of his mother in what manner she had died, he receives the answer, " Not Diana's soft arrow has killed me, nor has sickness taken me away ; but the longing after thee, my son, and my grief for thy fate, deprived me of sweet life." (Od. xi. 196.

Neither Apollo nor Diana, however, has always this pleasing and beneficent appearance. From time to time, the god of the silver bow is seen angry at the inhabitants of the earth ; and then he walks forth like a black cloud, or the dark night itself, and the quiver rings on his back as he moves on with hasty anger. " Then he sends his arrows into the camp of the Greeks, there to produce contagious sickness, which sweeps away man by man, and suffers not the flames of the funeral piles to be extinguished." (Il. i. 44.) And in the same manner the wrath of Diana brings destruction upon Actæon and the children of Niobe.

Still, serenity, benevolence, and loveliness constitute the chief character of Apollo; and he whose arrow wounds, heals again. Not only is he venerated under the name of the Healing, but he is also the father and teacher of Æsculapius, who is acquainted with the means of soothing every pain, and knows a medicine for every sickness, and who, by his art, can save even from death itself.

With reference to this turn of character, an ancient poet, endeavoring to fill the mind with serenity and joy, suggests the following consolation : " If thou art afflicted now, and mourning, it will not always be thus; for not always does Apollo bend his bow; soon will he awaken again the silent Muse to play and song." (Horace, Lib. ii. Od. x)

In all these fictions, the image of Helios is to be recognized : it is the animating sunbeam which awakens the heart to gaiety and song. It is also the all-seeing, the all-discovering sunbeam, that assumed a form in the prophesying Apollo, as well as in Apollo the herdsman ; for those flocks that graze without herdsmen and shepherds, are, as fiction asserts, watched by the all-seeing sun. Yet, all these grand features are embodied in the more tender form of that Apollo whose parents were Jupiter and Latona. He is the shepherd of king Admetus' flocks; he inspires the divining Pythia ; he leads the choruses of the Muses.

Fable says that on the isle of Delos he awoke to life ; and soon after his birth, the divine power that dwelt in him speedily developed itself. The august goddesses, Themis, Rhea, Dione, and Aphrodite, were present at his birth, and wrapped him in soft habiliments. Thetis gave him nectar and ambrosia ; and when he had tasted the divine food, his swathing bands no longer confined him ; the divine boy stood on his feet, and even his tongue was loosed. " The golden lyre," cried he, " shall be my joy ; the carved bow my pleasure ; and in oracles will I reveal the events of futurity." And when he had thus spoken, now a blooming youth, he walked forth majestically over mountains and islands. He came to Pytho, with its craggy summits, and there arose, as swift as thought, into the assembly of the celestials. There then at once reigned lyre and song ; the Graces tenderly embracing their friends and companions, the Horæ, joined with them in the Olympian dance ; while the Muses, with harmonious voice, sang the joy of the blessed immortals ; the grief of mortal men, who know no means of escaping old age and death.

When Apollo afterwards descended from the Olympian seat, he

killed, on the very spot from which his oracles were to spread over the earth, the dragon Python, and the beams of the sun caused the slain monster to decay. There, in the deep, rocky valley of Parnassus, stood the famous temple of Apollo, and over the cleft of a cavern, the tripod was placed on which the priestess sat, through whose mouth the god revealed the future.

The tradition of the birth of Apollo on the floating island of Delos, is taken from the Egyptian mythology, which asserts that the son of Vulcan, supposed to be Orus, was saved by his mother Isis from the persecution of Typhon, and intrusted to the care of Latona, in the island of Chemnis. The ancient origin of the god is clearly shown, even in his very name; and a very striking analogy exists between the Apollo of the Greeks and the Crishna of the Hindoos. Both are inventors of the flute; Crishna is deceived by the nymph Tulasi, as Apollo is by Daphne; and the two maidens are each changed into trees, of which the Tulasi is sacred to Crishna, and the Bay tree to Apollo. The victory of Crishna over the serpent Calya-naga, on the borders of Yamuna, recalls to mind that of Apollo over the serpent Python; and it is worthy of remark, that the vanquished reptiles respectively participate in the homage that is rendered to the victors.

It appears that the ancient Egyptians, after having ascertained the great benefit of the inundation, changed the name of their evil genius, the water monster, from Ob to Python, which had reference to the deadly effects of the miasmata, arising from the steam of the mud which the deluge had left upon the earth; and in this, he is plainly making an allusion to Typhon, which, by a simple transposition, is the same name. In making Python spring from the slime of the deluge, does not the poet intend to point out the noxious vapors that rise in Egypt after the Nile has subsided? And when he says that Apollo slew him with his arrows, does he not conceal, under this emblem, the victory of Orus over Typhon, or, at least, the triumphs of the sunbeams over the vapors of the Nile? Python, says Bailey, is derived from Putho to putrify, and the serpent Python being slain by Apollo, is thus interpreted: by Python is understood the ruin of the waters; Apollo slew this serpent with his arrows; that is, the beams of the sun dispersed the noxious vapors, which destroyed man like a devouring serpent.

A very strong affinity. exists between the religious systems of Egypt and Greece. We find the same animal, the wolf, which, by its oblique course, typified the path of the star of day, consecrated to the sun, both at Licopolis and Delphi.   This emblem transfers to the Greek tradi- tions, the fables relative to the combats of Osiris.   The Egyptian comes to the aid of his son Horus under the figure of a wolf; and Latona, the mother of Apollo, disguises herself in the same form when she quits the Hyperborean region to take refuge in Delos.

In the festival of the Daphnephoria, celebrated every ninth year, in honor of Apollo, it is impossible not to see an astronomical character. It took its name from the laurel, or bay tree, which the finest youths of the city carried in solemn procession, and which was adorned with flowers and branches of olives.   To an olive tree, decorated in its turn with branches of laurel and flowers intertwined, and the lowest part covered with a veil of purple, were suspended brazen globes of different sizes, types of the sun and planets, and ornamented with purple gar lands, the number of which (three hundred and sixty-five) was the symbol of the solar year.   On the altar, too, burned a flame, the agita- tion, color, and crackling of which served to reveal the future; a species of divination peculiar to the sacerdotal order, and which prevailed also at Olympia in Elis, the centre of most of the sacerdotal usages of the day.

At the head of the procession walked a youth, whose father and mother must be living.   This youth was, according to Pausanias, chosen priest of Apollo every year, and called Bay-Bearer.   He was always strong, of a handsome figure, and selected from the most dis- tinguished families of Thebes.   Immediately before this youthful priest, walked his nearest kinsman, who bore the adorned olive wood.   The priest followed, bearing in his hand a bay-branch; his hair dishevelled and floating, wearing a golden crown, and a magnificent robe, which reached down to his feet, and a kind of shoe which was introduced by Iphicrates; behind the priest followed a choir of maidens, with boughs in their hands, and singing hymns.   In this manner the procession went to the temple of Apollo Ismenius.   It would seem from Pausanias, that all the boys of the town wore laurel garlands on this occasion, and that it was customary for the sons of wealthy parents to dedicate to the god brazen tripods; a considerable number of which were seen by Pausanias himself.   Among them was one which was said to have been dedicated by Amphitryon at the time when Hercules was Daphnepho- ros   This last circumstance shows that the Daphnephoria, whatever changes may have been subsequently introduced, was a very ancient festival.

There was a great similarity between this festival and a solemn rite observed by the Delphians, who every ninth year sent a sacred boy to Tempe. This boy went on the sacred road and returned home as Bay-Bearer, amid the joyful songs and choruses of maidens. This solemnity was observed in commemoration of the purification of Apollo at the altar in Tempe, whither he fled after killing the Python.

The Athenians seem likewise to have celebrated a festival of the same nature; but the only mention we have of it is in Proclus, who says that the Athenians honored the seventh day as sacred to Apollo; that they carried bay-boughs, and the basket containing what appertained to the sacrifice, adorned with garlands, and sang hymns.

As soon, however, as this Apollo, whether his origin is to be traced to the banks of the Nile or the plains of India, assumes a marked station in the Grecian mythology, the national spirit labors to disengage him from his astronomical attributes. Henceforward every mysterious or scientific idea disappears from the Daphnephoria: they now become only commemorations of the passion of the god for a young female, who turns a deaf ear to his suit.

The god Helios now discharges all the functions of the sun; who, in his quality of son of Uranos and Ge, is placed among the cosmogonical personifications; he has no part to play in the fables of the poets, and is only twice named in Homer—once as the father of Circe, and again, as revealing to Vulcan the infidelity of his spouse. He has no priests, no worship, and no solemn festival is celebrated in his praise. Thereby freed from every attribute of an abstract nature, Apollo appears in the halls of Olympos, participates in the celestial banquets, interferes with the quarrels of Earth, becomes the tutelary deity of the Trojans, the protector of Paris and Æneias, the slave of Admetos, and the lover of Daphne. So true is it, that all these changes in the character of this divinity were effected by the transmuting power of the Grecian spirit, that we see Apollo preserve in the mysteries which form so many deposits of the sacerdotal traditions, the astronomical attributes of which the public worship has deprived him : and at a later period, we find the new Platonists endeavoring to restore to him these same attributes, when they wished to form an allegorical system of religious science and philosophy out of the absurdities of Polytheism.

But in the popular religion, instead of being the god from whom emanate fecundity and increase, he is a simple shepherd, conducting the herds of another.   Instead of dying and rising again to life, he is ever young.   Instead of scorching the earth and its inhabitants with his devouring rays, he darts his fearful arrows from his quiver of gold. Instead of announcing the future in the mysterious language of the planets, he prophecies in his own name.   Nor does he any longer direct the harmony of the spheres by the notes of his mystic lyre; he has now an instrument invented by Mercury and perfected by himself. The dances of the stars, too, cease to be conducted by him, for he now moves at the head of the nine Muses (the nine strings of the divine cithara), the divinities, who each preside over one of the liberal arts. The god of the sun also became the god of music by a natural allusion to the movements of the planets, and the mysterious harmony of the spheres ; and the hawk, the universal type of the divine essence, among the Egyptians, is with the Greeks the sacred bird of Apollo.

The worship of Apollo was universal, and his power acknowledged in every country ; but more particularly in Egypt, Greece, and Italy, where temples and statues were erected to his honor.   His most famous temple was at Delphi ; his statue, which stood upon mount Action, was particularly famous.   It was seen from a great distance at sea, and was a mark to mariners in navigating that dangerous coast.   Before the battle of Actium, Augustus addressed himself to it for victory. He had a famous colossus at Rhodes which was one of the seven wonders of the world.*

This statue, which Moratori reckons among the fables of antiquity, was raised by the Rhodians in honor of Apollo, who, according to Solinus, seemed to delight in Rhodes more than in any other part of the earth, because there is never any day so dark or clouded but that the sun appears to the inhabitants of that island.   Besides, they say that it was the birth-place of his favorite daughter, Rhodia, and that he sent down upon it showers of gold, and on her birth-day caused roses to open and spread.

This colossus, or brazen statue of the sun, was placed across the mouth of the harbor ; and its legs stretched to such a distance, that a

---

* The following enumeration is generally given of the Seven Wonders of the World : The Colossus of Rhodes, the Temple of Diana at Ephesus, the statue of Jupiter Olympius, the gardens of Babylon supported on pillars, the Walls of Babylon, the Pyramids of Egypt, and the tomb of Mausoleus.

large ship under sail might easily pass between them. It was seventy cubits high, or a hundred English feet; its fingers were as long as ordinary statues; and few men could with both arms grasp one of its thumbs. Scarcely sixty years had elapsed before this work of art was thrown down by an earthquake, which broke it off at the knees, where it remained till the conquest of Rhodes by the Saracens (A. D. 684), when it was beaten to pieces, and sold to a Jew merchant, who loaded nine hundred camels with its spoils.

Apollo is generally represented with long hair, and the Romans were fond of imitating his figure; therefore, their youth were remarkable for fine hair, which was not cut short until the age of seventeen or eighteen. He is always represented in the perfection of united manly strength and beauty; holding in his hand either a bow or a lyre, and his head generally surrounded with rays of light.

Upon an antique gem, which in its kind is considered a masterpiece of Grecian art, Apollo is represented in the act of tuning his lyre over the head of Pythia, who bears the sacrificial cup in her hand, as if inspiring the priestess with those heavenly harmonics, which revealed to her the time to come Another representation, also upon a gem, shows him leaning against an Attic pillar, with the bow in his left hand, and the lyre at his feet. In this image one may behold the god, who from the glittering bow shoots mortal arrows, but who likewise mingles with the choruses of the Muses, and by the healing art reno-vates the wounded body.

Among the poetical fictions of the ancients, that of Apollo is one of the most sublime and lovely, because it dissolves the idea of a destruc-tive power in that of youth and beauty; thus harmoniously combining two ideas entirely opposite. It seems owing to this circumstance, too, that plastic art in the most beautiful representation of Apollo, which, as a sacred bequest of antiquity, was spared by all-destroying time, had attained to a degree of perfection comprising all that is truly beautiful, the sight of which fills the soul with admiration, because of the harmo-nious multiplicity it expresses. The Apollo Belvidere is esteemed the most excellent and sublime of all the ancient productions. It was found about twelve leagues from Rome, in the ruins of ancient Antium, and purchased by Pope Julius II. when a cardinal; he removed it to the Belvidere of the Vatican from whence it takes its name.

Apollo Musagetes is another celebrated statue which takes its name from his occupation as Musagetes or conductor of the songs of the

APOLLO MUSAGETES.

Muses. It is of Pentelic marble, about five feet eight inches high, dressed in a long, loose tunic fastened round the waist by a girdle; the chlamys (or scarf) is fastened on the shoulders, and falls down the back in graceful folds. He appears listening attentively, and is accom·panying the songs on the greater lyre. Visconti, who was formerly conservator of the statues in the Napoleon Museum, in which this statue was placed, thinks that this dress is that of the Citharides, or players on the lyre; and that it is an antique copy of the Apollo Citharides of Timarchides, which was formerly in the portico of Octavia at Rome with the nine Muses of Philiscus. This statue was found at Tivoli in 1774, in the ruins of the country-house of Cassius, called the Piancella di Cassio. The head bound with laurels has been broken off, but is the original; the right hand and part of the lyre are restorations.

The statues and busts of this god are always distinguished by the beauty of the face, and he is represented in all the antique statues with an air of supreme divinity. He is handsomer than Mercury, and not so effeminate as Bacchus, who is his rival in beauty. His features are extremely fine, and his limbs exactly proportioned, with as much soft-ness as is consistent with strength. The ancient sculptors always represent him as young and beardless, and his long and beautiful hair, according to the poets, fell in natural, easy ringlets down his shoulders, and sometimes over his breast.

The animals and birds consecrated to Apollo were the wolf and hawk, as symbols of his piercing eye; the crow and raven, from their supposed faculty of presiding over the future; the cock, which announces the dawn, and foretells the rising of the sun; the swan, because from Apollo it is supposed to have a faculty of divination, and fore-seeing happiness in death, dies singing; the grasshopper, from its tuneful powers, and hence the custom among the Athenians of fasten-ing golden grasshoppers in their hair in honor of Apollo.

As the natural enemies of the flocks over which he presided, wolves and hawks were offered in sacrifice to him; also bullocks and lambs. The olive tree was sacred to him, as its fruits cannot ripen without his influence; and the laurel, always flourishing, ever young, and condu-cing to divination, furnished the leaves with which he was often crowned.

The first discovery of the oracle at Delphi is said to have been oc-casioned by some goats, who were feeding on Mount Parnassos, near a deep and large cavern with a narrow mouth. These goats were observed by a goatherd (called by Plutarch, Ceretas) to leap and frisk strangely, and as they approached the cavern, to utter unusual sounds; his curiosity excited him to examine it, when he found himself seized with a like fit of madness, skipping. dancing, and foretelling things to come.

At the news of this discovery, multitudes flocked thither ; and the place was soon covered with a kind of chapel. originally made of laurel boughs, but finally converted into a temple of great magnitude and splendor. Such indeed was its reputation, and so great the multitude that came from all parts to consult the oracle, that the riches brought into the temple and city became comparable to that of the Persian kings.

At first, the whole mystery requisite for obtaining the prophetic gift, was, to approach the cavern and inhale the vapor issuing therefrom ; but at length, several enthusiasts having in the excess of their frenzy cast themselves headlong into the chasm, it was thought expedient, by way of prevention, to place over the hole whence the vapor issued, a machine which they called a tripod, because it stood upon three feet. Upon this a woman was seated, when she imbibed the vapor without danger, as the tripod stood firmly upon the rock. This priestess was named Pythia, the Greek etymology of which word is to *inquire*.

The Pythia, before placing herself upon the tripod, bathed in the waters of the fountain Castalis, at the foot of Parnassos, and also crowned herself with the leaves of a laurel tree that grew near the place. While seated upon the tripod she was closely surrounded by the priests of the temple. The sanctuary itself was entirely covered with bay-branches ; in addition to this, the burning incense overclouded every thing as if with mysterious night, which no profane curiosity ventured to investigate.

The priestess was originally a virgin ; but the institution was changed when Echecrates, a Thessalian, had offered violence to one of them, and none but women above the age of fifty were permitted to enter upon that sacred office. They always appeared dressed in the garments of virgins to intimate their purity and modesty, and they were solemnly bound to observe the strictest laws of temperance and chastity, that neither fantastical dresses nor lascivious behavior might bring the religion or sanctity of the place into contempt.

There was originally but one Pythia, besides subordinate priests;

afterwards two were chosen, and sometimes more.   The most celebrated
priestess was Phemonoë, supposed to be the first that gave oracles at
Delphi.   They were said to have been agitated by strange and ghastly
contortions on ascending the tripod, which resulted no doubt from the
anguish of convulsed and shattered nerves.   At times they attempted
to escape from the priests, who detained them by force.   At length,
yielding to the impulse of the god, they gave forth some unconnected
words, which were put into wretched verse by the poets who attended,
giving occasion to the raillery, that Apollo, though prince of the Muses,
was the worst of poets.   This oracle, like all others, was obscure and
ambiguous, and not inaccessible to the temptation of corruption.

The oracle could be consulted only on certain days; and excepting
on these, the priestess was forbidden on 'pain of death to enter the
sanctuary of Apollo.   Alexander, before his expedition into Asia, came
to Delphi on one of those forbidden days, and entreated Pythia to
mount the tripod, which she steadily refused to do.   The impetuous
prince, not brooking opposition, drew her by force from her cell; on
their way to the temple, she exclaimed, " My son, thou art invincible !"
As soon as these words were pronounced, Alexander declared himself
satisfied, and would have no other oracle.   It was always required that
those who consulted the oracle should make large presents to Apollo :
and hence arose the opulence, splendor, and magnificence of the temple
at Delphi.*

The Pythian games celebrated in honor of Apollo near the temple
at Delphi, were, according to the most received opinion, first instituted
by Apollo himself, in commemoration of his victory over the serpent
Python.   They were originally celebrated once in nine years, and afterwards every fifth year.   According to some authors the gods were

---

* It is related in one of the Grecian legends, that the tripod on which the priestess
of Apollo sat was lost in the sea, and afterwards taken up in the nets of some fishermen,
who contended among themselves which should have it.   The Pythian goddess being
applied to, gave answer that it should be sent to the wisest man of Greece.   It was
then carried to Thales of Miletos, who sent it to Bias as a person wiser than himself;
Bias referred it to another, who referred it to a fourth person.   After it had been sent
to all the wise men, it was again returned to Thales, who dedicated it to Apollo at
Delphi.

The seven wise men of Greece were Thales of Miletos, Solon of Athens, Chilon of
Lacedæmon, Pittacus of Mytilene, Bias of Priene, Cleobulus of Lindi, and Periander
of Corinth.

among the combatants, and the first prizes won by Pollux in boxing, Castor in the horse race, Hercules in the Pancratium, Zetes in fighting with armor, Telamon in wrestling, and Peleus in throwing the quoit. These illustrious conquerors are said to have been rewarded by Apollo himself, who was present with crowns and laurels. Others say, that it was merely a musical contest, in which he who best sang the praises of Apollo obtained the prize, which was presents of gold or silver, and afterwards changed to a garland of the palm tree. The songs which were sung were called the Pythian, and were divided into five parts, containing a representation of the victory of Apollo over the serpent Python. A dance was also introduced ; and in the 48th Olympiad, the Amphictyons, who presided over the games, increased the number of musical instruments by the addition of the flute ; but as that instrument was more particularly used in funeral songs and lamentations, it was soon rejected as unfit for merriment, and the festivals which represented the triumph of Apollo over the conquered serpent.

In speaking of the city of Delphi, poets commonly use the appellation of Pytho ; but Herodotus, and historians in general, prefer that of Delphi, and are silent as to the other. Though not so ancient as Dodona, it is evident that the fame of the Delphic shrine was established at a very early period, both from the mention made of it by Homer, and the accounts supplied by Pausanias and Strabo. The Homeric hymn to Apollo informs us, that when the Pythian god was establishing his oracle at Delphi, he beheld on the sea a merchant ship from Crete ; this he directs to Crissa, and appoints the foreigners the servants of his newly established sanctuary, near which they settled. When this story (which we would not affirm to be historically true) is stripped of the language of poetry, it can only mean that a Cretan colony founded the temple and oracle at Delphi. Strabo reports that this oracle was at first only consulted by the neighboring states; but that after its fame became more widely spread, foreign princes and nations eagerly sought responses from the sacred tripod, and loaded the altar of the god with rich presents and costly offerings.*

Pausanias states, that the most ancient temple of Apollo at Delphi was formed with branches of laurel ; and that the branches were cut from the tree that was at Tempe. The form of the temple resembled a cottage. After mentioning a second and a third, the one raised, as

---

* For a full account of oracles see Appendix.

the Delphians said, by bees, from wax and wings, and sent by Apollo to the Hyperboreans, and the other built of brass, he adds, that to this succeeded a fourth and more stately edifice of stone. Here were deposited the numerous presents of Gygos and Midas, Alyattes and Crœsus, as well as those of the Sybarites, Spinatæ, and Siceliots; each prince and nation having their separate chapel or treasury for the reception of those offerings, with an inscription attesting the name of the donor, and the occasion of the gift.

This temple, having been accidentally destroyed by fire in the first year of the 58th Olympiad, or 548 B. C., the Amphictyons undertook the building of another for the sum of three hundred talents, of which the Delphians were to pay one-fourth. The remainder is said to have been obtained by contributions from the different cities and nations. Amasis, king of Egypt, furnished a thousand talents of Alumina. The Alcmæonidæ, a wealthy Athenian family, undertook the contract, and agreed to construct the edifice of Porine stone, but afterwards liberally substituted Parian marble for the front; a circumstance which is said to have added much to their influence at Delphi.

The vast riches accumulated in this temple, led Xerxes, after having forced the pass of Thermopylæ, to detach a portion of his army into Phocis, with a view of securing Delphi and its treasures, which, as Herodotus affirms, were better known to him than the treasures of his own palace; the enterprise failed, however, owing, as it was reported by the Delphians, to the manifest interposition of their deity, who terrified the barbarians, and hurled destruction on their scattered bands.

Many years subsequent to this event, the temple fell into the hands of the Phocians, headed by Philomelus, who scrupled not to appropri-• ate its riches to the payment of his troops in the war he was then waging against Thebes. The Phocians are said to have plundered the temple of the enormous amount of ten thousand talents, nearly ten million six hundred thousand dollars. At a still later period, Delphi became exposed to a formidable attack from a large body of Gauls, headed by their king Brennus. These barbarians, having forced the defiles of Mount Œta, possessed themselves of the temple and ransacked its treasures. The booty which they obtained on this occasion must have been immense; this they must have succeeded in removing to their own territory, since we are told that on the capture of Tolosa, a city of Gaul, by the Roman general Cæpio, a great part of the Delphic

13

spoils was found there. Pausanias, however, relates that the Gauls met with great disasters in their attempt on Delphi, and were totally discomfited through the miraculous intervention of the god.

Strabo assures us that in his time the temple was greatly impover ished ; all the offerings of any value having been successively removed. The Emperor Nero, according to Pausanias, carried off five hundred statues of bronze at one time. Constantine the Great, however, proved a more fatal enemy to Delphi, than either Sylla or Nero. He removed the sacred tripods to adorn the Hippodrome of his new city, where, together with the Apollo, the statues of the Heliconian Muses, and a celebrated statue of Pan, they were extant when Sozomen wrote his history. Among these tripods was the famous one which the Greeks, after the battle of Platæa, found in the camp of Mardonius. The brazen column which supported this tripod is still to be seen at Constantinople.

The site of Delphi has been well described as a natural theatre, sloping in a semi-circular declivity from the foot of Parnassus. At the highest point of this theatre stood the temple of Apollo. Its form may still be recognized on the coins and sculptured marbles that belong to the ancient history of Delphi. An interesting record of the ornaments with which it was decorated is preserved in the Ion of Euripides. On the place once occupied by its foundation, not a vestige of its structure remains. In its shrine was the elliptical stone which was regarded as the centre of the earth. Here was the oracular chasm, whence the prophetic vapor issued, which determined the fate of kingdoms and of empires.

To the west of the temple was the stadium, of which the outline is still visible. To the east of it was the glen through which fell a cascade fed by the snows of Parnassus, and which descended into a basin hewn in the rock, which was also supplied by a perennial stream of clear and salubrious water. This was the poetic fountain of Castalia. It still flows on while the temple of Apollo, and the Council Hall of the Amphictyons, the Treasure-house of Crœsus, and the three thousand statues that crowded the buildings and streets of Delphi, even in the time of Pliny, have all vanished as though they had never been. The spring is now dedicated to St. John, in whose honor a small chapel has been erected over its source. It falls down the declivity on which Delphi stood, into the river Pleistus, which flows along the valley at the foot of the city. It passes, in a westerly direction, through groves of olives, by the side of the Delphian Hippodrome, and at the base of the lofty crags where stood the Crissa of Homer, which preserves, in its modern name of Crissa, and in the huge polygonal walls of its Acropolis, the memorials of its ancient greatness. It then receives a tributary stream coming from the north, and flowing beneath the city of Amphissa. Their united waters glide through a wide and beautiful plain, known and reverenced with a feeling of religious awe in ancient times as the hallowed plain of Cirrha, till they fall into the gulf of Corinth in the Crissean Bay, which is at the distance of five miles from the site of Delphi, of which city it was formerly the harbor.

Of the beauty of this scene, and of the peculiar features which distinguish it, no better or more accurate description can be given than that which is contained in the following lines of Milton, to whose imagination, when he composed them, a landscape presented itself similar to that which the traveller beholds from the ruins of the citadel of Crissa.

> "It was a mountain at whose verdant feet
> A spacious plain, outstretch'd in circuit wide,
> Lay pleasant; from his side two rivers flow'd,
> The one winding, the other straight, and left between,
> Fair champaign with less rivers intervein'd,
> Then meeting, join'd their tribute to the sea.
> Fertile of corn the glebe, of oil and wine;
> With herds the pasture thronged, with flocks the hills;
> Huge cities and high tower'd, that well might seem
> The seats of mightiest monarchs."

ARTEMIS OR DIANA.

ARTEMIS, the daughter of Zeus and Leto, or Latona, and twin sister of Apollo, was the goddess of chastity, of the chase and the woods. As a celestial deity, she was Luna or the moon; as a terrestrial goddess, Artemis or Dictyna; and in the infernal regions, Hecate, or Persephone. She was supposed to enlighten heaven by her rays, to restrain wild animals by her bow and dart on earth, and to keep in awe the multitude of ghosts in the regions below.

Her father, Zeus, at her earnest entreaties, granted her the sempiternal state of a virgin; she then took up her bow and arrows, kindled her flambeau at Zeus' lightning, and accompanied by her nymphs went forth through the dark forests and woody mountains. Bending her silver bow, she sends forth the fatal shafts on every side; the tops of the mountains tremble, and the forests resound with the panting of the wounded deer.

Yet, even in the tumult of the chase, the goddess does not forget her divine brother, whom, of all immortals, she loves most. After having enjoyed herself in the sylvan sport in which she delighted—speeding over the hills, followed by a train of nymphs, in pursuit of the flying game, she unbends her bow, hastens to Delphi, the residence of the shining Apollo, suspends there her weapon, and leads the choruses of the Muses and Graces, who chant forth the praises of the heavenly Leto because she was the mother of such children.

Diana shines brightest as the sister of Phœbos-Apollo, who sheds upon her his own·glorious splendor. United with him, she with terrible arrows kills the children of Niobe; in union with him, she directs her soothing weapons against the families of men, who, like withering leaves, are to make room for generations to come. She is said to have prepared herself for this, by trying her arrows first on trees, then on animals, and lastly on a lawless city, annoying its inhabitants with pernicious shafts that carried sickness and plagues along with them.

The archetype of Diana is the shining moon; who, cold and chaste, scatters her modest, silver light over mountain-tops and forest glades. The chasteness of Diana is a fearful trait in her character, as witnessed in the fate of Actæon, the hunter, who surprised her when bathing. He fell a victim to her offended, virgin modesty, for she immediately changed him into a stag, and suffered his own dogs to devour him.

Another example of her severity is afforded in that unfortunate priestess of hers who profaned her sanctuary by receiving into it the youth whom she loved. The offended goddess punished the whole country with plagues and pestilence, until the guilty couple were sacrificed upon her altar. Virgins making the vow of chastity devoted themselves to Diana, who, with dreadful punishments avenged the violation of this vow. Whenever therefore, one of the virgins who by sacred promises had become a devoted priestess of Diana, changing her resolution, wished to marry, she trembled at the thought of the vengeance of her goddess, and endeavored to reconcile her by supplications and sacrifices

During the Trojan war, Diana ventured to challenge the stronger Juno; but she had reason to repent of her forward boldness when made to feel the powerful arm of Jupiter's spouse. " The deer of the mountain thou canst kill, but not fight against those who are stronger than thou." Thus saying, Juno, with her left hand laid hold of both Diana's, took off with her right the quiver from the shoulder of the poor prisoner, and struck her with it on either cheek, so that the arrows were scattered upon the ground. Like a timid dove escaped from the claws of a hawk, so fled Diana, weeping, and leaving her quiver, which, together with the scattered shafts, were taken up and restored to her by Latona. (Il. xi. 480.)

Although these divine persons act in the manner of human beings, the fiction itself, if viewed as a whole, is not destitute of beauty. The same dreadful quiver from which deadly arrows spread over the race of mortals, is an easy toy in the hands of the august Juno, who uses it as an instrument wherewith to chastise the forward insolence of the less powerful Diana ; and the latter, whose blushing cheeks feel the blows of that quiver inflicted by a stronger hand, accoutred with which she is accustomed to walk forth in majestic pride, affords a striking picture of female power deeply humbled.

The wiser Apollo, when challenged by Neptune, on the same occasion, returns his antagonist this answer : " Why should I fight with thee for the sake of miserable mortals, who, like the leaves of trees, last but a short time, and then wither away ? Let us refrain from fighting, and let them carry on the war among themselves." (Il. xi. 461.)

Diana was supposed to be the same as the Isis of the Egyptians, whose worship was introduced into Greece, with that of Osiris, under the name of Apollo. In the previous article we have spoken of the change produced by Grecian ideas on the attributes and worship of that Deity, and a change no less remarkable took place in that of Diana. At Delos she is evidently a cosmogonical power ; for there she is the mother of Eros, who, in the Theogonies, is always taken for the creative force. With the Scythians, she is a ferocious goddess, of a frightful form, and eager after the blood of men. As such she first appeared to the Spartans ; since, at the very sight of her, they were seized with fright bordering on delirium. In Colchis, she has so little of the Grecian character as to defend the golden fleece against the attempts of the Argonauts. Her hounds guard the seven doors of the enclosure which contains the precious treasure, and her voice issues commands to monsters that recall the fictions of India. At Ephesus, the slightest inspection of her figure betrays the sacerdotal imprint

But how different a being is she in the Grecian mythology! And yet, on a closer inspection, we shall find that even here none of her attributes are completely lost. Diana is the goddess of the chase ; and Isis, accompanied by her faithful hounds and the dog-headed Anubis, searched for the body of her husband ; and the companions of Isis become the pack of Diana. Diana guides in the heavens the silvery globe that dissipates the obscurity of the night, and her bow is adorned with the splendors of the crescent; Isis is also the moon, and the crescent appears among the ornaments of the goddess at Ephesus. Diana is the cause of the infirmities of women, strikes them with delirium, and sometimes with death ; Isis was once the Tithrambo of Egypt, or the moon viewed with reference to its unhealthy influence.

In the same manner, Diana becomes Hecate, slain by Hercules and resuscitated by Phorcys. And yet, so great is the repugnance of the Greeks to admit any thing into their religious system which may have a reference to science, that as they separate Apollo and Helios, so they make two distinct deities of Diana and Selene ; and thus render the goddess of the chase more free, more independent, and possessed of more individuality.

A chaste virgin, she defies the power of love, and punishes with severity the errors of her attendant nymphs. This notion of virginity, prevalent even in the worship of the savage nations, is an idea natural to man, and which sacerdotal influence seeks to record and prolong. With the Greeks, however, over whom none of this influence was exercised, such an attribute becomes an object of secondary importance, and is considered the effect of caprice, or of the modesty of a young female ; and the poets at one time throw doubts on its reality, and at another upon its duration. Yet, virgin as she is, Diana presides over the birth of children, a combination in which no one can mistake the union of the power which destroys with that which creates. We see, then, how incoherent are the traces of sacerdotal ideas, which survive this strange metamorphosis. The Hertha of Scythia, the Bendis of Thrace, the Isis of Egypt, the Diana of Ephesus, that motionless, enigmatical, and fettered mummy, become, beneath Grecian skies, a young and active huntress, who, in her course as rapid as the winds, pursues on the mountain tops the timid inhabitants of the woods.

Diana is always represented as taller by the head than her attend-

ARTEMIS OR DIANA.

ants; her face somewhat manly, her legs bare, well shaped and strong,
her feet sometimes bare, and sometimes covered with the cothurnus*
or buskin of the ancient hunters. By poets and artists, she is represented as armed with bow and arrows, and has threescore nymphs in
her train. She is also represented with a quiver and attended by
dogs, and sometimes drawn in a chariot by two white stags or her
nymphs. Again, she appears with wings, holding a lion with one hand
and a panther in the other; or in a chariot drawn by two horses, one
white and one black.

The representations of this goddess are generally known by the
crescent on her head, by the dogs which attend her, and by her
hunting habit. Isis, Diana, and the Bull Apis, are decorated with the
crescent, which announced the commencement of a new moon. The
dogs and buskins more particularly mark the goddess of the chase, as
the crescent was often used by the ancients as an ornament to the
female head—an example of which may be seen on a bust of Marciana,
in the villa Pamfili. On many medals of queens, the bust is supported by a crescent, allusive of their relative situations to their husbands, who, as kings, were as the sun, while they were as the moon.
It is also an emblem of the eternity of an empire, and found on the
medals of many cities, particularly Byzantium, from whence it is supposed to have been borrowed by the Ottomans.

Upon one of those antique gems which have reached our own times,
Diana is represented with her garments tucked up, leaning in an easy
posture against a pillar, her quiver and her bow suspended from her
shoulder; and, as the being who clears up the shades of night, she
holds a flambeau in her hand which she is about to extinguish; behind
her a mountain is seen, illustrative of her being the goddess who ranges the woody tops, and follows the track of the deer.

The Diana Triformis, also called Hecate, and Trivia by Ovid, Horace, and Virgil, when her statues stood where three roads met, is rep-

---

* *Cothurnus* was a kind of boot or buskin worn by the hunters, and also by actors of
tragedy, when they represented the characters of gods or heroes. They differed from
the *sandal*, which was a mere sole tied about the toes and ancles with thongs and straps
of leather, while the *cothurnus* covered the foot and leg as high as the calf, and was
ornamented with gold, gems, and ivory. The Melpomene of the Vatican is accoutred
with *cothurni*, and both Virgil and Cicero mention them as forming a part of the costume of hunters and tragedians.

resented by these poets as having three heads, and sometimes
with three bodies. She was
frequently invoked in enchant-
ments, as being the infernal Diana, and then appears more
like a Fury than a celestial
goddess.

As the celestial Diana, she
is described by Statius as of
majestic stature; and, in the
council of the gods, appears
with the bow and quiver on her
shoulders. Cicero describes a
statue answering to this description, that once belonged to
Scipio Africanus.

In antique sculpture, Diana
is frequently represented as descending with her head veiled
to a shepherd who is sleeping. This fable might have originated from
an eclipse of the moon; if so, her veil would be the most significant
and characteristic part of her costume. The ancients represented death
under the symbol of the sleeping Endymion, and upon marble coffins,
enclosing the ashes of youths who had fallen early into the tomb, Diana is to be seen descending from on high to the lips of the happy
slumberer

The inhabitants of Taurica were particularly attached to the worship
of this goddess, and cruelly offered on her altars all strangers who
were shipwrecked on their coasts. In Asia her temple was served by
a priest who had always murdered his predecessor, and the Lacedæmo-
nians yearly offered her victims till the age of Lycurgos, who changed
this barbarous custom to that of flagellation.

Her most famous temple was that at Ephesus. There the statue of
the goddess was regarded with peculiar veneration ; and was believed
by the vulgar to have fallen from the skies. It was never changed,
though the temple had been more than once restored. This rude object of primeval worship was a block of wood, said by some to be of

beech or elm—by others, cedar, ebony, or vine, and attesting its very great antiquity by the fashion in which it was formed. It was carved in the similitude of Diana, not as the elegant huntress, but as an Egyptian hieroglyphic, which we call the goddess of nature, with many breasts ; and the lower part formed into a Hermean statue, grotesquely ornamented, and discovering the two feet beneath. It was gorgeously apparelled, and the vest richly embroidered with emblems and symbolical devices ; to prevent its tottering, a bar of metal, probably of gold, was placed under each hand. Except while service was performed in the temple, this image was concealed by a veil or curtain drawn up from the floor to the ceiling, and was preserved till the later ages in a shrine, on the embellishment of which mines of wealth were consumed. The priests of the temple were eligible only from the superior ranks, and enjoyed a great revenue, with privileges, the eventual abuse of which induced Augustus to restrain them.

It may easily be imagined that many stories of the power and inter position of Diana were currently believed at Ephesus. A people who were convinced that the self-manifestations of their deity were real, could not easily be turned to a religion which did not pretend to a similar or equal intercourse with its divinity ; and this is perhaps the true reason why, in the early ages of antiquity, a belief of the supernatural interposition of the Panagia, or Virgin Mary, and saints appearing in daily or nightly visions, was encouraged and inculcated. It helped by its currency to procure and confirm the credulous votary ; to prevent or refute the cavils of the heathen ; to exalt the new religion, and to deprive the established of its ideal superiority. The address of the town clerk to the Ephesians, " Ye men of Ephesus. what man is there that knoweth not how the city of the Ephesians is a worshipper of the great goddess Diana, and of the image that fell down from Jupiter ?" is curiously illustrated by an inscription found by Chandler, near the aqueduct, commencing as follows :—" Inasmuch as it is notorious, that not only among the Ephesians, but also every where among the Greek nations, temples are consecrated to her, and sacred portions, etc."

The reputation and riches of their goddess made the Ephesians desirous of providing for her a magnificent temple. The fortunate discovery of marble in Mount Prion gave them new vigor, and the cities of Asia (so general was the esteem of the goddess) contributed largely ; Crœsus was at the expense of many of the columns. The spot chosen for it was a marsh, as being most likely to preserve the structure free from gaps and uninjured by earthquakes. The foundation was made with charcoal rammed, and with fleeces; and the edifice was exalted on a base of ten steps.

The architects were Ctesiphon of Crete, and his son Metegenes, who lived 541 B. C. Their plan was continued by Demetrius, a priest of Diana; but the whole work was completed by Daphnis of Miletos, a citizen of Ephesus, the building having occupied two hundred and twenty years. It was the first specimen of the Ionic style in which the fluted column and capital with volutes were introduced. The whole length of the temple was four hundred and twenty-five feet, and the breadth two hundred and twenty, with one hundred and twenty-seven columns of the Ionic order, and of Parian marble, each of a single shaft, and sixty feet high. Of these columns, thirty-six were carved, and one of them, perhaps as a model, by Scopas. The temple had a double row of columns, fifteen on either side, and Vitruvius has not determined whether it had a roof; probably over the cell only. The folding-doors or gates had been kept four years in glue, and were of cypress wood, and highly polished, which had been treasured up for four generations. These were found by Mautianas as fresh and beautiful four hundred years afterwards, as when new. The ceiling was of cedar, and the steps for ascending the roof (of the cell?) of a single stem of a vine, which witnessed the durable nature of that wood.

The dimensions of this temple excite ideas of magnificence and uncommon grandeur, from mere massiveness; but the notices we collect of its internal ornaments increase our admiration. It was the repository in which the great artists of antiquity dedicated their most perfect works to posterity. Praxiteles and his son Cephisodorus adorned the shrine; Scopas contributed a statue of Hecate; Tymarete, the daughter of Mycon (the first female artist upon record), furnished a picture of the goddess, the most ancient in Ephesus; and Parrhasius and Apelles employed their skill in embellishing the walls. The excellence of these performances may be supposed to have been proportionate to their prices; a picture, by the latter artist, of Alexander grasping a thunderbolt, was added to the collection at the expense of twenty talents of gold.

This description, however, applies to the temple as it was rebuilt after it was partially burned (perhaps the roof of timber only) by Herostratos, who chose that method to ensure to himself an immortal name, on the very night that Alexander the Great was born. Twenty years

after, that magnificent prince, during his expedition against Persia,
offered to appropriate his spoils to the restoration of it, if the Ephesians
would consent to allow him the sole honor, and would place his name
on the temple. They declined the proposal, with the flattering remark,
that it was not right for one deity to erect a temple to another. National vanity, however, was the real ground of their refusal.

The extreme sanctity of the temple inspired universal awe and reverence ; and it was for many ages a repository of foreign and domestic
treasure. There, property, whether public or private, was secure amid
all revolutions. The conduct of Xerxes was an example to subsequent
conquerors, and the impiety of sacrilege was not extended to the Ephesian goddess. But Nero deviated from this rule, and removed many
costly offerings and images, and an immense quantity of silver and
gold. It was again plundered by the Goths from beyond the Danube,
in the time of Gallienus, a party under Raspa crossing the Hellespont,
and ravaging the country until they were compelled to retreat, when
they carried off a prodigious booty. The destruction of so illustrious
an edifice deserved to have been carefully recorded by contemporary
historians, but we may conjecture that it followed the triumph of
Christianity. The Ephesian reformers, when authorized by imperial
edicts, rejoiced in the opportunity of insulting Diana, and deemed it
piety to abolish the very ruin of her habitation.

When under the auspices of Constantine and Theodosius churches
were erected, the pagan temples were despoiled of their ornaments, or
accommodated to other worship. The immense dome of Santa Sophia
now rises from the columns of green jasper which were originally placed
in the temple of Diana ; they were taken down and removed to Constantinople by order of Justinian ; two pillars in the great church at
Pisa were also transported from hence.

Another celebrated temple of Artemis was that of Scythia Taurica
whence Orestes and Pylades, at the command of Apollo, brought away
the statue of the goddess, and Iphigenia, the sister of Orestes. who
was detained as a priestess by Thoas, the king and high priest.

ARES OR MARS.

Ares, the son of Zeus and Hera, and the god of war, presided over gladiators, and whatever exercises and amusements were manly and warlike.

From his name the hill at Athens, the assembling place of that court of judicature so renowned for its justice, was called Areiopagos; and also the hill of Ares, because he was said to have been tried there for the murder of Hallirrothios, son of Poseidon.

Ares is generally represented in the figure of a man, armed with a helmet, pike, and shield, or in a chariot drawn by furious horses, called by the poets Flight and Terror. Sometimes Discord precedes him in tattered garments, while Clamor and Anger follow behind.

His companion, Bellona, daughter of Phorcys and Keto, was called Enyo by the Greeks. She was anciently called Duelliona, and according to some was the sister of Ares, or to others, his daughter, or wife, and was often confounded with Athena, the goddess of war. She prepared the chariot of Ares for battle, drove the horses, and also appeared in battles with dishevelled hair, a torch in her left hand, and the right armed with a whip which she used to animate the combatants.

Thus we see that to the dreadful and terrible, even to destructive war, the imagination of the ancients ascribed personality. Thus they tempered the idea of that wild, impetuous power that rages like a tempest through the host engaged in the bloody strife, that breaks helmets, dashes weapons to pieces, and crushes chariots; that throws alike to the ground the valiant and the faint-hearted in the whirling storm of the battle, triumphing over its wasting destruction. The human form in which this terrible appearance was embodied by imagination, and associated in the assembly of the gods, presented a model to the warrior, the majesty of which he partly appropriated to himself by bold and valorous deeds.

That the human form of Ares should be dissolved from time to time in the idea of the fighting army itself, lies in the nature of poetical representations. Thus, when in a combat before Troy, he was wounded by the valiant Diomedes, aided by Athena, he roared, as the poet tells us, like ten thousand men, so that on hearing the voice of the brazen god of war, terror seized both Greeks and Trojans. Enveloped in clouds, he immediately ascended to Olympos, appearing to Diomedes as the nightly gloom that precedes a tempest. On arriving at the abode of the immortal gods, he complained to Zeus of the audacity of men. But Zeus reproved him with angry words: "Trouble me not with thy complaints, inconstant! Thou art to me the most odious of all the gods that dwell in Olympos; for thou knowest no other pleasure than strife, war, and contest. In thee dwells the whole character of thy mother, and hadst thou been the son of another god, and not my own, thou wouldst long ago have lain deeper than the sons of Uranos." (Il. v. 850.)

The inconstancy of Mars, with which he is reproached, not only by his father, but also by Minerva, who calls him a deserter, that now sides with one enemy now with another, implies the idea of war itself, represented by poetry as something that exists, as it were, for its own sake, not caring if the bustle and tumult of the battle are continued, who are the conquered, and who the conquerors.

Although the violent and inconstant Mars was often reproved and upbraided by Jupiter and Minerva, the more gentle and meek deities, and for this very reason the more powerful, he still held his seat among the celestials; and on earth, temples and altars were erected to his honor. Indeed, by his youthful impetuosity, he even contrived to win the love of the tender Venus, who, unmindful of her duty towards her husband, maintained a secret intercourse with the god of war. From this disguised connection between the tender and the violent, Harmonia was produced; who afterwards became the wife of Cadmos, the founder of Thebes.

In the same manner as Venus binds the impetuous god of war by her tenderness, Minerva restrains his violence by her wisdom For when on a certain occasion, the threatening injunction of Jupiter prohibited the gods from taking any part in the contests between the Greeks and Trojans, and Mars had been apprised that in one of their fights, Ascalaphus was slain, immediately commanded his servants, Fear and Terror, to put his horses to his chariot; then taking up his glittering arms he thus addressed the inhabitants of Olympos: "Be not angry with me, celestials, because I go to avenge the death of my son Ascalaphus; my paternal heart will not suffer me to remain tranquil, even though Jupiter should hurl his lightnings upon me." Minerva sprang from her seat, and pulling his brazen spear out of his hand, tore the helmet from his head, and the shield from his shoulder. "Madman," she cried, "thou wilt bring ruin upon us all, if Jove's wrath be excited to the utmost! Refrain from thy anger, for many lie slain who

were stronger than thy son, and many stronger than he will yet fall.
Who can save mortals from death?" Thus spoke the goddess of wisdom
and brought the furious Mars back to his seat.   (Il. xv. 115.)

In all these human representations of the gods, who does not perceive the display of great images and sublime ideas, which give beauty
and dignity to the fictions themselves? Wild destruction, tender sublimity, high charms of beauty, and guiding wisdom, are variously mingled and concealed, under the guise of human forms.

Mars, according to his profession as a warrior, is represented in
complete armor, bearing shield and spear.   An antique gem preserved
in one of the German Museums, shows him as descending from the
cloud-capt Olympos, supporting himself by his right hand upon the
cliffs of mountains, and carrying on his left arm a buckler and spear.

Among the ancients, the worship of Mars was not very universal;
his temples in Greece were not numerous, but in Rome he received
the most unbounded honors.   The warlike Romans were proud of paying homage to a deity, whom they esteemed the patron of their city,
and the father of the first of their monarchs.   His most celebrated
temple at Rome was built by Augustus, after the battle of Philippi,
and dedicated to Mars Ultor, or the Avenger.   Among the Romans it
was usual for the consul, before entering on an expedition, to visit the
temple of Mars, where he offered his prayers, and in a solemn manner,
shook the spear which was in the hand of the statue of the god, at the
same time exclaiming, "Mars, Vigila! God of War, watch over the
welfare and safety of the city."

His priests among the Romans were called Salii; they were first
instituted by Numa, and their chief office was, to guard the sacred
ancile, which was supposed to have fallen from heaven.   The oracle
was consulted respecting it, and declared that the empire of the world
was destined for the city that should preserve that shield.   Numa
Pompilius, second king of Rome, caused several to be made so exactly
like it, that it was almost impossible to distinguish the original.   The
form was oval.

His altars were frequently stained with the blood of the horse and
the wolf—the former for his warlike spirit, and the latter for his
ferocity; the dog was consecrated to him for his vigilance in the pursuit of his prey; the raven because he follows the march of armies;
and the magpie and vulture for their greediness and voracity.   The
Scythians generally offered him asses, and the people of Caria, dogs.

The weed called dog grass was sacred to him, because it is supposed to grow in places which are fit for fields of battle, or where the ground has been stained by the effusion of human blood.

The Romans paid great adoration to Bellona; but she was held in still greater veneration by the Cappadocians, where she had above three thousand priests.

Her temple at Rome, in which the senators gave audience to foreign ambassadors, and to generals returned from war, was without the city, in the Porta Carmentalis. At the gate was a small column, called the column of war, against which a spear was thrown whenever war was declared against an enemy.

The priests of the goddess were called Bellonarii; they consecrated themselves by making large incisions, particularly in the thigh, and receiving the blood in their hands to offer as a sacrifice to the goddess. Lactantius described them as cutting themselves most furiously in her worship; and Tertullian adds, that having collected the blood that flows from these gashes, they pledged the neophytes who were initiated into their mysteries, and then, in their wild enthusiasm, predicted bloodshed and wars, the defeat of enemies, and the besieging of towns.

ATHENA OR MINERVA.

When the blue-eyed Athena sprang forth from the immortal head of Zeus, Olympos shook and trembled; and the charioteer of the sun stopped his snorting steeds, until the new-born goddess took off her radiant armor.

Athena was immediately admitted to the assembly of the gods, and had great power awarded to her. She could prolong the life of men. bestow the gift of prophecy, and indeed was the only divinity whose authority and consequence were equal to those of her father.

Not being the offspring of a mother, her bosom was as cold as the steel with which it was covered. Her nature approached to manly greatness; tenderness and female affection dwelt not in her heart. By this disposition, equally adapted to quiet, unprejudiced musing on art and science, and to undaunted participation in warlike occupations. her two-fold character, as Goddess of Wisdom and as Heroine, is at once explained and justified; for in a female, the want of tender feelings is always connected with a desire of destruction, which constantly gains strength. It is the tender-hearted, affectionate Aphrodite, who, merely out of love to Adonis, and not on her own account, pursues with him the roes and fawns of the forest; but the colder Artemis delights in chase and destruction itself, only forgetting it for a moment, when, with secret fondness, she steals a look at the slumbering Endymion.

Athena, the cold and chaste virgin, being destitute of every feeling of tenderness and languishing passion, finds her pleasure, like the stern god of battle, in warlike tumult, and delights in the sight of destroyed cities. There is, however, this difference; she at the same time patronising the peaceful arts, does not share with him the impetuosity and violence of character by which he is distinguished. Repulsive coldness is the chief feature that characterizes her, and renders her equally capable of being the directress of just wars, and of practising the laborious task of weaving; of inventing useful arts, and guiding the wrathful minds of heroes. When Achilles was about to draw his sword against Agamemnon, his king and chief, the blue-eyed goddess suddenly stood behind him with terrible look, invisible to every one but himself, seized his yellow hair, and assuaged the wrath of the young hero with prudent advice. He withdrew his mighty fist from the silver handle, and the sword dropped back into its scabbard. Thus Pallas-Athene, even in the midst of war, appears as a mediator and peace-maker; nor is she by any means to be confounded with Bellona, who, with terrific countenance, and dishevelled hair, brandishes a bloody whip in her right hand, while the other shakes the heavy lance, and drives the chariot of the God of War. Bellona is a subordinate being, who, even by her appearance and deportment, betrays her inferior standing. In her wild aspect, no quiet look discloses the divine spark of inward wisdom or inventive genius. Her glaring eye darts rage and fury; her figure is not graced with that majestic air, in which the just ruler of battles and the august guide of heroes is to be recognized; her headlong impetuosity, her cruel desire of murder and devastation, discovers the worthy companion of Discord, as well as the ferocious driver of Ares' snorting coursers.

In the divine person of Athena, warlike disposition was tempered partly by her female sex; yet more so by those faculties which rendered her the benefactress of mankind in bestowing upon them the peaceful arts. For the same goddess who delighted in the din of battle and the shouts of fighting heroes, taught mankind the art of weav-

14

ing, of building ships, and of pressing oil from olives. When she was engaged in the contest with Poseidon as to the right of giving a name to the capital of Cecropia, than which none more advanced in the arts and sciences has ever adorned the earth, it was agreed in the council of the gods, that the honor of naming it should belong to whichever of the claimants should bestow the most useful present upon its inhabitants. Poseidon, upon this, struck the ground with his trident, and immediately a horse issued from the earth. Minerva produced the olive, and obtained the victory by the unanimous voice of the gods, who observed that the olive, as the emblem of peace, is far preferable to the horse, the symbol of war and bloodshed. The victorious deity called the capital Athenæ, and became the tutelar goddess of the place.

The opposition of apparently quite different and incongruous features in the character of Minerva, is by no means prejudicial to the beauty of her fictitious person. On the contrary, fiction becomes thereby, as it were, a sublimer language, which summons together a number of dispersed ideas into tuneful harmony; as is the case in the representation of Apollo. It is true, that such diversified ideas are seldom united in the microcosm of the thinking mind; yet a single glance into the immense world of nature, must convince us that their prototypes are connected in sisterly union, all apparent differences and contradictions of creation and destruction being dissolved, and life and death combined in the most perfect and beautiful harmony.

Nor can it be justly asserted, that the unity and harmony of the whole in Minerva's character is distorted by the seeming contradiction of its single features. They all refer to the cold, reflecting wisdom, which, guarded by the want of feeling, and a sort of forbidding callousness, never hears the voice of passion. The petrifying head of Medusa threatens from the shield that covers Minerva's breast; and over her head hovers the gloomy, melancholy bird of night. She is the faithful friend of the enduring, persevering, cold, and cunning Ulysses, as well as the admonisher, who recalls the enraged heroes to presence of mind.

The deep sense which lies concealed in all the fictions of the ancients, betrays itself also in the power of Minerva, being represented as superior to that of Mars. The warlike spirit that keeps possession of itself, that looks with quiet eye over the field of battle, and at the same time sufficiently comprehensive to attend to the arts and sciences of peace, gets advantage of the impetuous one who is always ready to fight. When, during the war with Troy, the gods themselves had engaged in the combats, either to aid the Greeks or assist the Trojans, and had challenged each other, the turbulent god of war, rushing on the more tender Pallas, furiously thrust his spear against her shield; but, against that, even Jupiter's lightnings are of no avail. The goddess, however, falling back a little, takes up in her strong hand an immense field stone, and hurls it upon the forehead of Mars, so that he is precipitated to the Earth, covering with his body seven acres of ground.

Notwithstanding the strong, manly features, with which the picture of Minerva is drawn by poetry, she still continues a woman, who shares the foibles common to her sex. She is said to have invented the flute; but seeing in a fountain the distortion of her face while playing on this instrument, she threw it away, to the great misfortune of Marsyas, who found it, and challenged Apollo to a trial of skill in music. Like Juno she was jealous, too, and like her, could not rest until Troy stood in flames and Priam's race was destroyed, because Paris had denied her as well as Juno the prize of beauty, awarding it to the soft charms of Venus. The actions of Minerva are numerous, as well as the kindnesses by which she endeared herself to man. She and Neptune disputed as to which would give a name to the city of Cecropia. Fabulous as the narratives of that period confessedly are, and prone as the inhabitants of Attica were to enhance their national glory, by adorning its annals with fictitious embellishments, yet it is not difficult to trace some footsteps of truth in those legendary records which they have handed down to us, of the most distant ages of their own history.

The earliest monarch of this country whose name is preserved, was Cecrops. Backward, beyond him, historical tradition did not go. He was therefore an Autochthon or Indigenous—the offspring of the earth. In his days, it is said, the gods began to choose favorite spots among the dwellings of men for their own residence; or, as the expression seems to mean, particular deities were worshipped with especial homage in particular cities. It was at this time, then, that Minerva and Neptune strove for the possession of Attica. The question was to be determined by the natural principle of priority of occupation. Cecrops, the king of the country at that period, was called upon to arbitrate between them in the controversy. It was asserted by Neptune, that he had appropriated the territory to himself, by planting his trident on the rock of the Acropolis at Athens, before the land had been claimed by Minerva. He pointed to it, there standing erect, and to the salt spring which had then issued, and was flowing from the fissure of the cliff which had opened for the reception of the trident.

On the other hand, Minerva alleged that she had taken possession of the country at a still earlier period than had been done by the rival deity. She appealed, in support of her claim, to the Olive, which had sprung at her command from the soil, and which was growing near the fountain produced by the hand of Neptune from the same place.

Cecrops was required to attest the truth of her assertion. He had been witness to the act; and he therefore decided in favor of Minerva, who then became the tutelary deity of Athens.

It is not difficult to perceive that, in this tradition, a record is preserved of the rivalry (which may be considered the natural production of the soil, the form and the situation of Attica itself) between the two classes of its population—the one devoted to maritime pursuits, and aiming at commercial eminence—the other contented with its own domestic resources, and preferring the tranquil occupations of agricultural and pastoral life, which were typified by the emblematical symbol of peace. The victory of Minerva which it commemorates, is a true and significant expression of the condition of this country, and of the habits of its people, from the days of Cecrops to those of Themistocles.

Athena was invoked by all artists, particularly such as worked in wool, embroidery, painting, and sculpture, and it was considered the duty of every member of society to invoke the assistance of a deity who presided over industry, taste, and wisdom. Her worship was universal, and she had magnificent temples in Egypt, Phœnicia, and all parts of Greece, Italy, Gaul, and Sicily.

The Panathenæa, the greatest of the Athenian festivals, was celebrated in honor of Athena as the guardian deity of the city of Athens. It is said to have been instituted by Erichthonios, and to have been called originally Athenæa; but in the time of Theseus, it obtained the name of Panathenæa, in consequence of his uniting into one state the different independent communities into which Attica had been previously divided.

There were two Athenian festivals which had the name of Panathenæa; one called the Great and the other the Less. The former was celebrated once in every five years, with great magnificence, and attracted spectators from all parts of Greece. The latter was celebrated every year in the Piræus. In both the Panathenæa there were gymnastic contests, among which the torch race seems to have been very popular. In the time of Socrates a torch race on horseback was introduced at the Less Panathenæa. At the Great Panathenæa there was also a musical contest, and a recitation of the Homeric poems by rhapsodists; in these contests the victors were rewarded with vessels of sacred oil. The most celebrated part of the grand Panathenaic festival, was the solemn procession of the Peplos, or sacred robe of Athena. This Peplos was covered with embroidery, the work of maidens belonging to the noblest families of Athens, representing the battles of the Gods and the Giants, especially the exploits of Zeus and Athena, and also the achievements of the heroes in the Attic mythology; hence, Aristophanes speaks of men worthy of this land and the Peplos.*

At the celebration of the festival, the Peplos was brought down from the Acropolis where it was wrought, suspended like a sail upon a ship, and then drawn through the principal parts of the city to the Parthenon, and there placed before the statue of the goddess within. The old men carried olive branches, the young men wore armor, and the young women carried baskets on their heads, and were called Canephores.† On this occasion, the sacrifices were very numerous, and during the supremacy of Athens, every subject state was obliged to furnish an ox for the festival. It was made a season of joy, and even

---

* "Minerva (or Science) sprang from the head of Jove, contrived the texture of the universe, and to her, crowded with curious representations, is carried the robe, its emblem, in solemn procession from the town to her temple in the citadel." This idea gives much significance to the sacred Peplos.

† *Canephores.*—When a sacrifice was to be offered, the round cake, the chaplet of flowers, the knife used to slay the victim, and sometimes the frankincense were deposited in a flat, circular basket, called calathus, which was frequently carried to the altar on the head of a virgin. This practice was observed more especially at Athens. When the sacrifice was offered by a private citizen, either his daughter or some unmarried female of his family officiated as Canephoros; but in the Panathenæa, the Dionysia, and other public festivals, two virgins of the first Athenian families were appointed for the purpose.

That the office was accounted highly honorable, appears from the fact, that the resentment of Harmodius, which instigated him to kill Hipparchus, arose from the insult offered by the latter in fɪ rbidding his sister to walk as Canephoros in the Panathenaic procession.

In architecture, Canephores have sometimes been erroneously called Caryatides; the former are properly used only by the side of an altar, and were never applied by the Greeks in this manner to columns.

prisoners were liberated that they might take part in the general re-joicing.

The Minerva of the Romans corresponded in some measure with the Pallas-Athene of the Greeks. She was the patroness of arts and indus-try, and the mental powers were considered as under her peculiar care. She was the deity of schools: her statue was always placed in them, and the five days of the festival called Quinquatria, celebrated in the month of March, were holidays to the scholars. At their expiration, they presented their master with a gift called Minerval. According to Varro, Minerva was also the protecting goddess of olive grounds; but it may be doubted whether this was not a transference of one of the attributes of Pallas-Athene.

The festivals of Minerva were named Minervalia, or Quinquatria. They were two in number; the former, called the Greater, were cele-brated in March, the time when, according to the Tuscan discipline, Minerva cast her lightnings. It was named Quinquatrus as being on the fifth day after the Ides; the ignorance of the Romans made them extend the festival to five days; it was followed by the Tubilustrum. The Lesser was in the Ides of June, and was celebrated by the flute players. As both the trumpet and flute came to the Romans from Etruria, this proves Minerva to have been introduced there from that country. Therefore, no derivation of her name can be given, as it does not seem to be a translation.

Athena is represented as a beauty of the severer kind, and without the grace and delicacy which for instance distinguished Aphrodite. Dig-nity, and a becoming air, firmness and composure, with regular features, and a certain masculine sternness, form the peculiar characteristics of her face and figure. Hence the heads of her are so like Alexander the Great, that they have been occasionally mistaken for his. Her dress and attributes are adapted to her character. She has a helmet upon her head, and a plume nodding formidably in the air. In her right hand she holds a spear, and in her left grasps a shield with the head of the dying Medusa upon it. The same figure, with all its terrors and beauties, is also on her breast-plate; and sometimes she is represented with serpents about her shoulders. An owl, the bird sacred to her, is sometimes seen hovering over her helmet.

It was common among the Romans to transfer the distinguishing attribute of their divinities to the statues of their emperors. This kind

of flattery was in no point carried so far by the ancients, as
in the Gorgon's head on Athena's breast-plate, as the emperors were fond of this badge
of strength and wisdom. There
might be found a series of Roman Emperors, from Augustus
to Gallienus, with this attribute on their breast-plates,
except, perhaps, two or three
of whom scarce any figures remain. The strongest for the
dying cast of the eyes, is on the
bust of Nero at Florence, and
answers to Virgil's fine description. (Æn. iii. v. 438.)

In most of her statues,
Athena is represented as seated, and sometimes holds in her
hand a distaff instead of a
spear. When she was depict-
ed as the goddess of the liberal arts, she was arrayed in a variegated
veil. Sometimes her helmet was covered with the figure of a cock,
which, on account of its great courage, was appropriated to the deity of
war. Some of her statues represented her helmet with a sphinx in the
middle, supported on either side by griffins ;* and on some medals a
chariot drawn by four horses; and in others a dragon or serpent appears with winding spires at the tops of her helmet.

---

* *Griffin*—A fabulous animal, said to be generated between the Lion and the
Eagle. It is described as having the head and paws of the lion, the ears of the
horse, the wings of the eagle, and a crest formed like the dorsal fins of a fish. According to Ælian, in the fourth book of his History of Animals, this creature derived its
origin from India. Its back was covered with black feathers, its breast with red, and
its wings with white. Ctesias, Herodotus, and other writers, also give similar descriptions of the Griffin.

According to a tradition of the Bactrians, the gold mines of the country were guarded by Griffins. The Griffin is also one of the attributes of Apollo; and according to
Philostratus, in his life of Apollonius, the Indians figured the sun in a quadriga drawn
by Griffins.

The shield or corselet with the Gorgon's head is supposed by some to represent the full-orbed moon ; by others it is regarded as the emblem of divine wisdom.

It was customary among the Egyptians and other Armorians to place upon the architrave of their temples some emblem of their tutelary deity.   Among others, the serpent was considered a most salutary one, of which they made use to signify superior skill, wisdom, or knowledge. A beautiful female countenance, with an assemblage of serpents, was made to denote divine wisdom.

These devices upon temples were often regarded as talismans, and were supposed to have a hidden and salutary influence by which the temple was preserved.   In the temple of Minerva at Tegea (where she was worshipped from the earliest times), was some sculpture of Medusa, which was said to have been given by the goddess herself for the preservation of the city.   It was probably from this opinion that the Athenians had the head of Medusa represented upon the walls of their Acropolis, and it was made the badge of many cities, as we find from various coins.

Pallas-Athene is in Homer, and in the general, popular system, the g-ddess of wisdom and skill.   In war she is opposed to Ares, the wild war-god, as the patroness and teacher of just and scientific warfare. Therefore she is on the side of the Greeks, and he on that of the Trojans.   But on the shield of Achilleus, where the people of the besieged town were represented as going forth to lie in ambush, they are led by Ares and Athena together ; possibly to denote the union and skill required for that service   Every prudent chief was supposed to be under the patronage of Athena ; therefore, Odysseus (or Ulysses) was her special favorite, whom she relieved from all perils, and whose son Telemachos she also took under her protection, assuming a human form to be his guide and director.   In like manner Cadmos, Heracles, Perseus, and other heroes, were favored by this goddess.

As the patroness of arts and industry in general, Pallas-Athene was regarded as the inspirer and teacher of all able artists.   Thus she taught Epios to form the wooden horse, by means of which Troy was taken ; and she also superintended the building of the ship Argo. She was expert in female accomplishments, having woven her own robe and that of Hera, which last she is said to have embroidered very richly. When Pandora was made for the ruin of man, she was attired by Pal·

las-Athene; and wherí Iason was setting forth in quest of the golden fleece, she gave him a mantle wrought by herself. She is said to have taught this art to mortal females, who had won her affection.

By the Homerid, Athena and Hephæstos are united as the civilizers and benefactors of mankind by means of the arts which they taught them, and we find them in intimate union in the mythic systems of Attica.

Homer thus describes Pallas-Athene, as arraying herself in the armor of Zeus, when preparing to accompany Hera to the plain where the Greeks and Trojans were engaged in conflict:

> "But Athenæe, child of Zeus supreme,
> The ægis holder, on her father's floor
> Let fall the peplos various, which she
> Herself had wrought, and labored with her hands.
> The tunic then of cloud-collecting Zeus
> She on her put, and clad herself in arms
> For tearful war; and round her shoulders cast
> The fringed ægis dire, which all about
> Was compassed with fear. In it was strife,
> In it was strength, and in it chill Pursuit;
> In it the Gorgon head, the portent dire—
> Dire and terrific, the great prodigy
> Of ægis-holding Zeus. Upon her head
> She placed the four-coned helmet formed of gold,
> Fitting the footmen of a hundred towns.
> The flaming car she mounted, seized the spear,
> Great, heavy, solid, wherewith the strong-sized
> Maiden the ranks of heroes vanquisheth,
> With whom she is wroth."

The ægis or shield of Zeus and Athena was supposed to have been made originally of the skin of a goat, and afterwards by Hephæstos of brass, and rendered terrible by a Gorgon's head being sculptured upon it. Lactantius says, that it was made of the skin of the goat which suckled Jupiter, and that he first used it against the Titans. Ægis is also used for the pieces of goat-skin with which the warriors covered their breasts and shoulders as a guard against the weapons of their enemies. A variety of ancient monuments attest the antiquity of this practice.

Homer gives to the ægis of Zeus the power of being both offensive and defensive, as all his deities, with whatever circumstances they are

endued in common with mortals, are made to possess some peculiar and supernatural power. The blood which issues from their wounds is *ichor;* their drink is *nectar;* and their food is *ambrosia.* This poet always personifies the effects which the arms of his gods and heroes, and the charms of his gods and goddesses, have over mortals; placing in the girdle of Aphrodite the most attractive charms of love, which influence in secret the hearts of the wisest. He who on the buckler of Agamemnon has placed Fear and Terror, naturally added to the ægis of Zeus, Force and Discord; and to add more honor to the arms of this most powerful god, he places the head of the terrible Gorgon with its intertwined serpents in the middle of his breast-plate. These are the arms which gave to Jupiter the name of *Ægiochus,* the holder of the Ægis.

The ægis of Athena, with which she descended into the camp of the Greeks, to excite them to battle and dissuade them from the disgraceful intentions they had conceived of abandoning Troy and returning home, is described by Homer, as precious, indestructible, and eternal, fringed with a border composed of a hundred tufts of gold, each valued at a hundred oxen.*

The ferocious custom of cutting off the heads of their enemies, or scalping them, as practised by barbarous nations, and which is undoubtedly the origin of the ægis, is sometimes found even among the Greeks; as in the Iliad we find Diomedes cutting off the head of Dolon. Among ancient nations, the head or scalp of an enemy was carried as a mark of triumph on their shields; and in later times they imitated it in metal for the centre and ornament of their bucklers. On one of the vases in Sir W. Hamilton's collection, now in the British Museum, is represented a large buckler, bearing in the middle a human head which has nothing in common with the Gorgon. In more modern times, a head was placed on the cuirass. Homer, in describing the ægis, does not mention its being covered with scales, but only a skin, in the middle of which is a Gorgon's head encircled with snakes. The scales appear to be a posterior addition, and give an idea of greater resistance. Virgil has not omitted the scales in describing the ægis forged by the Cyclops in the depths of Ætna.

As Athena typifies the mind or wisdom of Zeus, there is a peculiar

---

* Theseus gave to his money the impression of an ox. Hence the expression, worth ten or a hundred oxen.

propriety in her wielding the same ægis with her great parent. But this armor was not peculiar to Zeus and Athena, although generally appropriated to them by the poets. In the fifteenth book of the Iliad, Apollo marches at the head of the Greeks, conducting to combat the people who followed the mighty, terrific, shagged, dazzling ægis which the artist Hephæstos had given to Zeus. In the temple of Zeus at Olympia, there was a statue of Victory which had a golden buckler, on which were the ægis and Gorgon, probably because victory proceeded from Jupiter; and Rome, for a similar reason, namely, being under the special protection of Jupiter and Minerva, was personified on a beautiful medallion, as a female warrior armed with the ægis.

The ægis at length descended from deities to heroes, warriors and emperors. On a fine cameo, in the royal library at Paris, Ulysses is covered with the ægis, as a symbol of the protection of Minerva. This allegory of the protection which the gods offered to men, became a species of amulet; and above all, the Gorgon, or Medusa's head, was conceived by the ancients to have the virtue of averting witchcraft, or enchantment; for which reason the Roman emperors, without bearing what is more properly the ægis, have a Gorgon's head sculptured in the middle of their breasts on the *lorica* or brigantine. The only in-stance generally known, of the ægis being fixed on the arm, is on an intaglio in the cabinet of the Emperor of Russia, representing Jupiter Axur, or the Beardless. Jupiter is generally represented with the ægis on the left shoulder, as in the beautiful cameo of the royal cabinet at Paris, which represents Jupiter Ægiochus. The ægis on the knees, as in the figure of Tiberius, on the grand cameo of the same cabinet, indicates peace and repose to the world.

The Palladium, a celebrated statue of the goddess Pallas-Athene, was about three cubits high, and represented her as in a sitting pos-ture, holding a pike in her right hand and a distaff and spindle in her left.

The Palladium is said to have fallen from heaven near the tent of Ilus, at the time when that prince was employed in building the cita-del of Ilion or Troy; and Apollo, by an oracle, declared that the city should never be taken whilst the Palladium was contained within its walls. Hence, the assailants of Troy became exceedingly anxious to get possession of this treasure; and Ulysses, accompanied by Diomedes, undertook to purloin it. Having entered the citadel at night by stealth, they stole the Palladium away; the consequence of which act was the fall of Troy. The goddess, however, did not fail to testify her wrath at this ungallant action, for the Palladium appeared to receive life and motion at the period of its capture. In allusion to this, Virgil makes Sinon say:

> "Scarce to the camp the sacred image came,
> When from her eyes she flashed a living flame;
> A briny sweat bedew'd her limbs around,
> And thrice she sprang indignant from the ground;
> Thrice was she seen in martial rage to wield
> Her ponderous spear, and shake her blazing shield."
>
> (*Æn.* ii. 228.)

It is averred, that anciently, there existed a statue of Pallas at Rome, which was said to be the veritable, heaven-descended Palladium above spoken of; that it was brought into Italy by Æneas, deposited in the temple of Vesta, and secured as well as possible from capture by the construction of others precisely similar to it. It was regarded as the fated pledge of the continuance of their empire; and not even the Pontifex Maximus was allowed to behold it. Hence, on ancient gems, we sometimes see Vesta represented with the Palladium.

Herodian relates, that when in the reign of Commodus, the temple of Vesta was consumed, the Palladium was for the first time exposed to public view, the Vestal virgins having conveyed it through the Via Sacra to the palace of the emperor. This was the only instance of its having been disturbed since the time when Metellus, the Pontifex, rescued it from the flames on a similar occasion. On the reign of Elagabalus, however, that emperor, with daring impiety, caused the sacred statue to be brought into his bedchamber.

In order to account for the Romans having the Palladium among them, it was pretended that Diomedes restored it to Æneas in obedience to the will of Heaven when the latter had reached Italy; and that Æneas being engaged in a sacrifice at the time, an individual named Nautes received the image, and hence the Nautian, not the Julian family, performed the rites of Minerva.

This story deserves to be classed with another which states that the Ilienses were never deprived by the Greeks of the statue of Minerva; but concealed it in a cavern until the period of the Mithridatic war, when it was discovered and sent to Rome by Fimbria.

From all that has been said, it would appear that the ancient cities in general were accustomed to have tutelary images, which they held peculiarly sacred, and with which their safety was thought to be intimately connected; and as Minerva was in an especial sense the protectress of cities, it was but natural that many places should contend for the honor of having the true image of that goddess contained within its walls.

Carrying off the Palladium, has, from ancient times, been a favorite subject among artists. Among the most considerable of those works of sculpture which were framed on it, however, one only remains still in existence—a basso-relievo of marble, preserved in the Spada Palace. Pliny makes mention of an artist of the name of Pytheas, who, upon a vase, depicted in relievo Ulysses and Diomedes stealing the Palladium. A great number of engraved gems present the same story at different points of it, and may be said to form a mythic circle of the raising of the Palladium.

The Parthenon, or chief temple of Athena, the virgin goddess, and patroness of Athens, stood on the summit of the Acropolis. This celebrated structure is now reduced to the last stages of ruin and decay; little remains of what formerly constituted one of the most elegant, if not the most spacious monuments of heathen superstition, but this little is venerable for its age and history; and highly interesting for the evidences which it still affords of Grecian skill in architecture. Its beautiful proportions are, indeed, now lost in the surrounding mass of miserable huts; its glittering whiteness dimmed by the corroding hand of time, and its towering columns shattered and cast down by the merciless engines of modern warfare; but yet, while a vestige is to be found of such excellence, it will not cease to be inestimable to the scientific traveller, and the philosophical inquirer into the state of society in former ages.

The original Hecatompedon, so called on account of its being a hundred feet square, was a very ancient edifice dedicated to Athena, and probably not remarkable for its decorations. It was burnt by the Persian troops when they gained possession of the Acropolis in the year B. C. 480, under Xerxes. On the site which had been already rendered sacred to the tutelary deity, Pericles erected the magnificent edifice denominated the Parthenon, and spared no expense in bringing to perfection the immortal work, which employed the united talents of the first sculptors and architects whom the world has ever seen—of

Phidias, Ictinus, and Callicrates. The new temple occupied more than double the space of its predecessor, being two hundred and twenty-seven feet in length, and one hundred and one in width. It stood on a pavement elevated by three steps, and was surrounded by forty-six columns of the Doric order, eight in front of each portico, and seventeen on either flank, reckoning those of the angles twice. The porticoes were both surmounted by pediments filled with statues; those in the eastern end or entrance representing, according to Pausanias, the mythological story of the nativity of Athena, and those in the hinder or western pediments, being figures of the deities present at the contest of Athena and Poseidon for the honor of naming and patronising the newly-built city. The Metopes were executed in high relief, and each displayed a distinct group of a Centaur and Lapitha. About twelve feet within the outer range of columns of each portico, was another row of less diameter, the frieze of which was continued round the walls of the cella, or inclosed area of the temple; this frieze exhibited in low relief and continued succession, an amazing number and variety of figures forming the Panathenaic procession. The interior of the dwelling was divided into the cella and opisthodomus. In the middle of the cella was an oblong space, sunk a little more than an inch below the level of the opisthodomus. At the eastern end of the shrine was erected the famous idol mentioned in the life of Phidias, and thus described by Pausanias: " The image itself is of ivory and gold; on the middle of her crest is placed the figure of a sphinx. It is erect, and covered· with a garment down to the feet. There is a head of Medusa wrought in ivory on her breast, and a Victory four cubits high. In her hand she holds a spear, at her feet lies her shield, and at the bottom of the spear is a dragon, which dragon may be Ericthonius. On the base is carved the nativity of Pandora."

The open space between the front wall of the cella and the hinder columns, about twelve feet in depth, was called the pronaos, and that corresponding to it at the other extremity, the posticum, elevated two steps above the portico; from thence there was another step of an inch only in height, into the opisthodomus. The roof is supposed to have been of wood, overlaid with marble slabs, in a regular form imitating tiles, the joinings of which were covered with narrow pieces of marble, so fitted in as to preserve the interstices from the weather, and terminated at the eaves by an upright ornament.

Such was the Parthenon under its heathen masters; there is no precise mention made of the date of its transformation into a Christian church; but it was probably despoiled of its remaining treasures by the ruthless Alaric. It retained its idol down to the time of the Roman emperors Valentinian and Valens, B. C. 364; and Attica, in common with other states of Greece, suffered about forty years afterwards from the predatory incursions of the Gothic king. The building, however, was not destroyed, and having passed from a Christian to a Moham- medan place of worship, was found by Sir G. Wheeler in 1676, almost entire except the roof, which had been constructed of a more modern fashion, to suit the religious purposes to which the Greek Christians had applied the edifice. "When the Christians," said Wheeler, "con- secrated it to serve God in, they let in the light at the east end; which is all that it yet hath. And not only that, but made a semicircle for the holy place, according to their rites; which the Turks have not yet much altered. This was separated from the rest by jasper pillars; two of which on each side yet remain. Within this chancel is a canopy, sustained by four porphyry pillars, with beautiful white marble chap- ters of the Corinthian order. But the holy table under it is removed Beyond the canopy are seats two or three degrees, one above another, in a semicircle; where the Bishop's presbyters used to sit in time of communion, upon certain solemn days." * * * "On both sides, and towards the door is a kind of gallery, made with two rows of pillars, twenty-two below and twenty-three above. The odd pillar is over the arch of entrance, which was left for the passage. It being now turned into a mosque, the niche of the Turk's devotion is made in the corner on the side of the altar, at the right hand, by which is their place of prayer; and on the other side a pulpit to read their law in, as is usual in all mosques. The Turks, according to their measure of wit, have washed over the beautiful white marble within with lime. At one side of the sacred choir, there are four presses made in the wall, and shut up with doors of marble. They say no one dares open them, and that one undertaking to do it, immediately died the first he opened; and that the plague soon after followed in the town."

About eleven years after this account was given, the Venetians besieged the citadel of Athens under the command of General Kö- ningsberg, and threw a shell from the hill of the Museum, which unfor tunately fell on the devoted Parthenon, set fire to the powder which the Turks had made therein, and thus the roof was entirely destroyed; nineteen pillars were overthrown, and the whole building almost reduced to ruins. The eastern pediment was nearly demolished; and the Venetian general being afterwards desirous of carrying off the statue of Athena which adorned the western, had it removed; thereby assisting in the defacement of the place without any good result to himself, for the group fell to the ground and was shattered to pieces.

Since this period, every man of taste must have deplored the demolition of this noble structure, and the enlightened travellers who have visited the spot, have successively published engravings of its remains. But not content with these artistical labors and publications, more recent travellers have borne away with them the actual spoils of the Parthenon. The foremost of these was Lord Elgin, who about the year 1800, removed a variety of the matchless friezes, statues, etc., which were purchased of him by Parliament, on the part of the nation, and now form the most valuable and interesting portion of the British Museum. This act, at the time, called forth severe animadversions, though it is now well known that there was imminent danger of those relics of art being totally destroyed by the wanton barbarism of the Turks and others.

Wordsworth gives the following animated description of this splendid edifice in the days of its glory, which, at the risk of some repetition, we quote entire : Existing, in imagination, in the age of Pericles and his immediate successors, we now contemplate this city as it then exhibited itself to the eye. First, we direct our attention to the central work of the Acropolis. And let us here suppose ourselves as joining at this period that splendid procession of minstrels, priests, and victims, of horsemen and of chariots, which ascended to that place at the quinquennial solemnity of the great Panathenæa. Aloft, above the heads of the train, the sacred Peplos, raised and stretched like a sail upon a mast, waves in the air : it is variegated with an embroidered tissue of battles of giants and of gods : it will be carried to the temple of the Minerva-Polias in the citadel, whose statue it is intended to adorn. In the bright season of summer, on the twenty-eighth day of the Athenian month Hecatombæon, let us mount with this procession to the western slope of the Acropolis. Towards the termination of its course, we are brought in face of a colossal fabric of white marble, which crowns the brow of the steep, and stretches itself from north to south across the whole western front of the citadel, which is about one hundred and twenty-seven feet in breadth.

The centre of this fabric consists of a portico sixty feet broad, and formed of six fluted columns of the Doric order, raised upon four steps, and intersected by a road passing through the midst of the columns, which are thirty feet in height, and support a noble pediment. From this portico two wings project about thirty feet to the west, each having three columns on the side nearest the portico in the centre.

The architectural mouldings of the fabric glitter in the sun with brilliant tints of red and blue; in the centre, the coffers of its soffits are spangled with stars, and the antæ of the wings are fringed with an azure embroidery of ivy leaf.

We pass along the avenue lying between two central columns of the portico, and through a corridor leading from it, and formed by three Ionic columns on each hand, and are brought in front of five doors of bronze; the central one, which is the loftiest and broadest, being immediately before us.

The structure which we are describing is the Propylæa or Vestibule of the Athenian citadel. It is built of Pentelic marble. In the year B. C. 437 it was commenced, and was completed by the architect Mnesicles in five years from that time. Its termination, therefore, coincides very nearly with the commencement of the Peloponnesian war.

After a short pause, in order to contemplate the objects around us, to explore the gallery, adorned with the paintings of Polygerotus, in the left wing of the Propylæa, and to visit the temple of Victory on our right, which possesses four Ionic columns on its western and four at its eastern end, thus being approached by its two façades, and whose frieze is sculptured with figures of Persians and of Greeks fighting on the plain of Marathon, we return to the marble corridor of the Propylæa.

We will now imagine that the great bronze doors, of which we have spoken as standing at the termination of this gallery, are thrown back upon their hinges, to admit the riders and charioteers, and all that long and magnificent array, of the Panathenaic procession, which stretches back from this spot to the area of the Agora at the western foot of the Citadel. We behold through this vista the interior of the Athenian Acropolis. We pass under the gateway before us, and enter its precincts, surrounded on all sides by massive walls: we tread the soil on which the greatest men of the ancient world have walked; and behold a building ever admired and imitated, and never equalled in

15

beauty. We stand on the platform which is at once the Temple, the Fortress, and the Museum of Athens.

To speak, in the first instance, and very briefly, of minor objects here presented to our notice, which it is impossible to specify in detail We behold before and around us almost a city of statues, raised upon marble pedestals, the works of noble sculptors—Phidias and Polycletus, of Alcamenes, and Praxiteles, and Myron—and commemorating the virtues of benefactors of Athens, or representing the objects of her worship: we see innumerable altars dedicated to heroes and to gods: we perceive large slabs of white marble inscribed with the records of Athenian history, with civil contracts and articles of peace, with the memorials of honors awarded to patriotic citizens or munificent strangers.

Proceeding a little further, we have, on our left, raised on a high base, a huge statue of bronze, the labor of Phidias. It is seventy feet in height, and looks towards the west, upon the Areiopagos, the Agora. and the Pnyx, and far away over the Ægean Sea. It is armed with a long spear and oval shield, and bears a helmet on its head; the point of the lance, and the crest of the casque, appearing above the loftiest building of the Acropolis, are visible to the sailor who approaches Athens from Sunium.

This is Minerva-Promachus, the champion of Athens, who, looking down from her lofty eminence in the citadel, seems by her attitude and accoutrements to promise protection to the city beneath her, and to bid defiance to its enemies.

Passing onward to the right, we arrive in front of the great marble Temple, which stands on the most elevated ground of the Acropolis. We see eight Doric columns of huge dimensions elevated on a platform, ascended by three steps at its western front. It has the same number on the east, and seventeen on each side. At either end, above the eight columns, is a lofty pediment, extending to a length of eighty feet, and furnished with nearly twenty figures of superhuman size. The group which we see before us, at the western end, represents the contest of Minerva with Neptune for the soil of Athens ; the other, above the eastern front, exhibits the birth of the Athenian goddess.

Beneath the cornice which ranges on all sides of the Temple, is the frieze, divided into compartments by an alternating series of triglyphs and metopes, the latter of which are ninety-two in number—fourteen on either front, and thirty-two on either flank: they are a little more than four feet square, and are occupied by one or more figures in high relief; they represent the actions of the goddess to whom the Temple is dedicated, and of the Heroes, especially those who were natives of Athens, who fought under her protection, and conquered by her assistance. They are the works of Phidias and his scholars; and, together with the pediments at the two fronts, may be regarded as offering a history in sculpture of the most remarkable sub-jects contained in the mythology of Athens.

Attached to the Temple, beneath each of the metopes on the eastern front, hang round shields covered with gold ; below them are inscribed the names of those who dedicated them as offerings to Minerva, in testimony of their gratitude for the victories they had won ; the spoils of which they shared with her, as she partook in the labors which achieved them.

The members of the building above specified are enriched with a profusion of vivid colors, which throw around the fabric a joyful and festive beauty, admirably harmonizing with the brightness and trans-parency of the atmosphere which encircles it.   The cornice of the ped-iments is decorated with painted ovoli and arrows; colored mæanders twine along its amulets and beads, and honeysuckle ornaments wind beneath them : the pediments themselves are studded with disks of various hues; the triglyphs of the frieze are streaked with tints which terminate in plate-bandes and guttæ of azure dye; gilded festoons hang on the architrave below them.   It would, therefore, be a very erroneous idea to regard this Temple which we are describing merely as the best school of architecture in the world.   It is also the noblest Museum of Sculpture and the richest Gallery of Painting.

We ascend by three steps which lead to the door of the Temple at the posticum or west end, and stand beneath the roof of the peristyle. Here, before the end of the cella, and also at the pronaos or eastern front, is a range of six columns, standing upon a level raised above that of the peristyle by two steps.   The cella itself is entered by one door at the west, and another at the east : it is divided into two apartments of unequal size, by a wall running from north to south ; of which the western, or smaller chamber, is called the Opisthodomus, and serves as the treasury of Athens ; the eastern is the Temple properly so called ; it contains the colossal statue of Minerva, the work of Phidias, com-posed of ivory and gold, and is peculiarly termed from that circumstance, the Parthenon, or residence of the Virgin Goddess, a name by which the whole building is frequently described.

At the summit of the exterior walls of the cella, and extending along the sides of it, is a frieze in low relief, representing the Panathenaic procession ; it is moving from west to east, and may be imagined to have just entered the Acropolis, by the gate of the Propylæ, to have advanced to the south-west angle of the Temple, and then to have divided itself into two lines, one of which proceeds first along the western end and then round the north-west corner and along the northern flank of the building ; the other by the southern flank, so that when they arrive at the eastern front they face each other. Here they are separated by twelve *seated* figures, of size superior to the rest, and of whom six face the north and six the south. They form a striking contrast, by their sedate attitudes, to the rapidity of the procession, composed of cars and horsemen chasing each other in quick succession, and increasing in speed as they approach the eastern front of the temple. The twelve figures which have been mentioned are Deities. To appear in their presence was the object of the Panathenaic procession, and by the juxta-position of their dignified calmness as the goal of its eager rapidity, the train itself seems, as it were, to pass insensibly from the restlessness of earth to the tranquillity of heaven.

Such, then, is the Parthenon of Athens ; the work of Ictinus and Callistratus, adorned with sculptures from the hand of Phidias and his scholars, completed under the administration of Pericles, in the year B. C. 439.

The Peplos, borne in the Panathenaic solemnity, is destined to adorn the statue of Minerva-Polias, which stands in the beautiful and singular Temple to the north of the Parthenon. The direction of this fabric is from east to west, its cella is seventy-three feet long, and thirty-seven broad, and, like that of the Parthenon, is divided into two apartments ; but these two chambers, unlike those of that temple, are dedicated not to one, but to two different deities. This structure, when considered as a whole, is called the Erectheum, from the ancient king of Attica who was buried within it. Its eastern division is consecrated to Minerva-Polias ; the western to Pandrosos : the eastern is faced by an Ionic hexastyle portico, and the level of the floor is eight feet higher than that of the rest of the building. At the north-west angle is another portico which consists of six Ionic columns—of which four are in front, namely, to the north, and one on each side—and leads into the

western chamber. A third portico, at the south-west angle of the Temple, conducting also into the western chamber, is formed not of columns,
but of Caryatides, or rather, as they should be described, of Athenian
virgins dressed in the Panathenaic costume. They are six in number; four of them standing in front towards the south, and one on
each side : they are raised on a podium or dwarf wall, about four feet
high from the ground.*

The western wall of the cella is pierced by three windows, the aper-
tures of which are narrower at the top than they are at the bottom,
and by their interposition four Ionic columns *engaged* in the wall are
separated from each other. A frieze of grey Eleusinian stone, to which
sculptured figures are attached by metal cramps, surrounds the cella.

This Temple has succeeded in name and site to one of the most
ancient sanctuaries of Athens. On this account it bears the title of
the ancient Temple of Minerva. The present building dates its commencement from the age of Pericles, although in all probability on account of the death of that statesman, and the expense incurred by
Athens in the Peloponnesian war, and a fire which injured the fabric
in the year B. C. 406, it was not completed till about thirty years after
his decease.

Four different objects of great national interest, contained within
the walls of the Erectheum, give it a sanctity and an importance unequalled by that of any other temple in Athens. In its eastern chamber
is the ancient statue of Minerva-Polias, made of olive-wood, which fell
down from heaven. This was the Minerva who had contended with
Neptune for the possession of the Athenian soil: she was the original
protectress of the Acropolis and of Athens; to her the embroidered
Peplos at the festival of the Panathenæa was dedicated ; it was to this,
her Temple, that Orestes came as a suppliant from Delphi, when he

---

* *Caryatides.*—Figures in long drapery used to support entablatures. Their origin,
according to Vitruvius, was this :—The inhabitants of Carya, a city of Peloponnesus,
made a league with the barbarians in the Persian war against the other people of Greece ;
but the Persians being conquered, the Carytes were afterwards besieged, their city taken
and reduced to ashes, the men put to the sword, and the women carried away to slavery.

To perpetuate the memory of this victory, the conquerors caused public edifices to be
erected, in which, as a mark of servility and degradation, the figures of the captives, in
their matronal robes and ornaments, were used instead of columns in the servile office
of supporting the entablatures ; thus transmitting to posterity their infamy and their
punishment. The most genuine specimen of these statues was in the Pandroscium at
Athens. One of these figures is now in the British Museum.

fled from the Eumenides; before her statue burns the golden lamp both night and day, which is fed with oil only once a year: the sacred serpent, the guardian of the Acropolis, dwells here: here is the silver-footed throne on which Xerxes sat when he viewed the battle of Salamis—here the sword of Mardonius, the Persian general at Platæa.

In the western chamber, that of Pandrosos, is the salt spring which Neptune fetched from the ground in his contest with Minerva: upon the rock there is the impression of the trident with which he struck it; there, too, is the sacred olive which Minerva produced from the soil to support her claim to its possession. From this tree all the olive trees of Attica are said to have sprung: and thus the most valuable produce of the Athenian territory is protected and consecrated by its alliance with this sacred plant, which is under the immediate care of the tutelary goddess of Athens.

HEPHÆSTOS OR VULCAN.

Hephæstos, the Olympian artist, is in Homer the son of Zeus and Hera. According to Hesiod, he is the son of Hera alone, who in this wished not to be outdone by Zeus, who had produced Athena from his own brain.

Hephæstos is the god of fire, especially as a power of a physical nature, that manifests itself in volcanic districts, and as the indispensable means in arts and manufactures. Hence fire is called the breath of Hephæstos, and the name of the god is used by the Greek and Roman poets as synonymous with it. As a flame arises from a little spark, so the god of fire was delicate and weakly from his birth, for which reason he was so disliked by his mother, that she flung him from Olympos. He was received by Thetis and Eurynome, and dwelt with them for nine years in a grotto, surrounded by Oceanos, and there made for them a variety of ornaments.

According to later writers, Hephæstos was educated with the rest of the gods in heaven, and was expelled from Olympos by Zeus. Hera raised a storm, which drove Heracles out of his course at sea; Zeus then tied her hands and feet together, and suspended her between heaven and earth. Hephæstos attempted to free his mother, and, for this act, was kicked down from heaven by Zeus. The island of Lemnos is said to have received the god;

> " His hand was known
> In heaven by many a tower'd structure high.

> Nor was his name unheard or unadorn'd
> In ancient Greece. And in Ausonian land
> Men call'd him Mulciber; and how he fell
> From heaven they fabled; thrown by angry Jove
> Sheer o'er the crystal battlements. From morn
> To noon he fell, from noon to dewy eve,
> A summer's day; and with the setting sun,
> Dropp'd from the zenith like a falling star,
> On Lemnos, th' Ægean isle. Thus they relate."

In this island, where earthquakes and eruptions of volcanoes were frequently experienced, and also in the smoking of Ætna, in Sicily, from whose bowels the fire which found no vent often produced a subterranean thundering, imagination has discovered suitable places for the work-shops of Hephæstos, in which the mighty hammers of the Cyclopes resounded.

On Olympos, he is said also to have had his own palace, imperishable and shining like stars. It contained his work-shop, with the anvil, and twenty bellows which worked spontaneously at his bidding, and there he made his beautiful and marvellous works. All the habitations of the gods were of his workmanship, as were their chariots and arms. He made armor for Achilleus and other mortal heroes. The fatal collar of Harmonia was the work of his hands. The brass-footed, brass-throated, fire-breathing bulls of Æetes, the king of Colchis, were the gift of Hephæstos; and he made for Alcinoös, king of the Phæacians, the gold and silver dogs which guarded his house. For himself he formed the golden maidens, who waited on him, and whom he endowed with reason and speech. He gave to Minos, king of Crete, the brazen man Talos, who each day compassed his island three times, to guard it from the invasion of strangers. The brazen cup in which the sun-god and his horses and chariot are carried round the earth every night, was also the work of this god.

The first work of Hephæstos is said to have been a throne of gold, which he presented to his mother, to avenge himself for her want of affection towards him—upon which Hera was no sooner seated than she found herself unable to move. The gods attempted to set her at liberty by breaking the chains with which she was confined; but to no purpose, as Hephæstos alone had the power to unloose them

It is worthy of remark that the only instances we meet of Hephæstos working in any other substance than metal are in Hesiod where, at the command of Zeus, he forms Pandora of earth and water, and where he uses gypsum and ivory in the formation of the shield which he makes for Heracles. That framed by him for Achilleus, in the Iliad, is all of metal.

He was celebrated by the ancient poets for his ingenious works. By their imagination, painful and wearisome labor, in a work-shop filled with steam and smoke, joined to the idea of sublime art, that works there indefatigably with productive genius, was wrought up into this divine being, whose entire strength was concentrated in the mighty arm that managed the weighty hammer upon the anvil, while the lamed feet were enfeebled and tottering.

He was hurled from heaven, for smoke and black steam, together with half-smothered flame, do not agree with pure ether; they are in contradiction to the idea of serenity, beauty, and divine dignity. Nevertheless, Fancy contrived to usher even this personage into the splendid theatre of high, divine Olympos, securing to him a place among the celestials, by bestowing upon him the comical part on the heavenly stage. The gods raise peals of laughter when they behold Hephæstos in the place of Ganymedes, making the round in the assembly of the immortals, reaching them the nectar cup, and jesting himself at his own bodily defects.

Yet the bold imagination of the ancients, which we cannot help admiring, found means on the other hand to shroud again this comical character in divine power and sublimity, by connecting with it a dignity superior to every thing human. Her grand picture of the supernatural world, far from being degraded by a figure like that of Hephæstos, becomes, on the contrary, more variously shaded, and gains new charms. The halting son of Hera, on account of his deformity, was thrown from Olympos, and after his re-admission into the community of the gods, ministered the nectar cup in the place of the graceful Ganymedes in so awkward a manner, as to excite the shouting mirth of the immortals. The same Hephæstos is the inimitable artist, with whose assistance even they themselves cannot dispense.

At his work-shop, the limping feet are not prejudicial to him; he needs only his arms. And with strong arm, indeed, manages he the stithy! Air and fire are at his command. At his nod the bellows blow and kindle the flames, producing a greater or gentler heat, according to his wants. Every one of his ideas is instantaneously carried into effect with divine genius, and from beneath his skilful hands, the work springs forth majestically. It is also an easy matter

to him to infuse life and motion into his creations. He for-
ges twenty tripods rolling upon wheels, which, at his command, enter the assembly of
the gods, and return to him
again. He formed for himself
female servants of gold, that
support him when he is walking. When he leaves his stithy,
he arrays himself in royal attire
and bears a sceptre.

Though a deformed cripple,
he has the most beautiful being that dwells on Olympos for
his wife. Thus plastic art, although in its appearance poor
and uncomely, is, in the representation of Hephæstos, mar-
ried to beauty itself. By this marriage between Aphrodite and the
god of fire, the comical turn of his character gains the highest charm;
the conjugal unanimity of the divine couple being disturbed by
the jealousy of Hephæstos. The story of the artificial net, which
the offended husband contrived to throw over Ares and Aphrodite,
while he called together all the celestials to show them the disgraceful
spectacle, and to complain of his misfortune, is, in ancient poetry, a
source of amusement, both among gods and men.

Especially in the person of Hephæstos do we find that endeavor to
unite opposite and seemingly contradictory features into one character,
which is peculiar to the fictions of the ancients. With regard to what
is external, he, the ugliest of all the celestials, is married to the love-
liest being that Fancy ever created; in his character, the ridiculous is
united with dignity; and in his body, feebleness is connected with
strength; the strong and skilful arm compensating for the limping
feet. We are by no means to consider this apparent inconsistency in
the poetical productions of the ancients as a defect, originating, perhaps, in the heedless play of humor; on the contrary, we are rather to
admire the ingenuity and boldness of Imagination who shrinks not
from seeming difficulties, and succeeds in adjusting the variety of ma·

terials, collected together for the picture of her celestial world, into so happy and concordant a composition.

The fiction of Hephæstos also shows us the high estimation in which the ancients held the art of working metals; it is, of all the arts, the peculiar business of a god.

Although Hephæstos first appears in a clear and distinct form among the modern gods, yet his person may be faintly recognized through the clouds in which the ancient deities are shrouded. The Curetes, or Corybantes, were, according to an old tradition, his descendants. He was likewise one of the most ancient Egyptian deities, or perhaps the most ancient of them. The Curetes made a noise with their weapons, which, as tradition relates, were of iron. The Cyclopes, before the reign of Zeus, had prepared thunder and lightning in the caverns of the earth; and Earth herself had already forged the sickle with which Saturn was maimed. According to another tradition, the Cabiri, a kind of mysterious beings, who, in the remotest times of antiquity, were venerated in Egypt and Samothrace, were sons or descendants of Hephæstos. His person itself, however, is always hidden in darkness.

That mythology represents the fine arts as assisting each other, is a fine and significant intimation. When Prometheus was occupied in forming his men, both Athena and Hephæstos lent him their aid; and when the latter was afterwards, at the command of Zeus, obliged to fasten the father of mankind to the fatal rock, he, not daring to resist the will of the thunderer, complied with it, amid tears and lamentations.

Vulcan, the male artist among the celestials, had a desire to marry Minerva, the female one; but she withstood his entreaties as well as threats. His son Erichthonios, the earth-born, is said, however, to have been always a favorite with Minerva. She appointed him king of her beloved city of Athens, where the desire of hiding his mis-shapen feet, both of which were those of a dragon,* led him to the invention of the covered four-wheel carriage.

The God of Fire, represented by Homer, on occasion of Thetis coming to his dwelling to see him and his wife, and to order at the same

---

* It is worthy of observation, that, in the mythological fictions of the ancients, to almost every being sprung from the earth, or related to it, dragon form, or dragon feet are ascribed.

time a new suit of armor for her son Achilles, is entirely human. No sooner had he heard of the august Thetis, the old friend of his house, than, in order to appear with decency in the presence of the goddess, he before leaving his work-shop, washed his face, breast, neck and hands, with a wet sponge, lest his visitor should be offended at beholding him covered with dust, to which his occupation necessarily exposed him.

In the Trojan war, Vulcan, at the command of his mother, opposed himself with his flames to the river god, Scamander, who, with swelling floods, pursued Achilles, and a terrible fight took place between the two elements. Vulcan, after having scorched the shores of the river, and consumed the slain bodies that were lying there, turned his high flaring flames, with their hissing tongues, against the rising waters, so as to burn their lotus, as well as their reeds and rushes, to make the water boil, and strike the fishes with anguish and terror. Then the afflicted river god besought Juno to have mercy on him, and she bade Vulcan cease tormenting the suppliant: " Have done! It is not meet that an immortal god should be thus distressed for the sake of mortal men." (Il. xxi. 379.)

The worship of Vulcan was well established, particularly in Egypt, at Athens, and at Rome. In the sacrifices that were offered to him, it was usual to burn the whole victim, and not to reserve a part as in immolations to other gods. A calf and a boar-pig were the principal victims offered.

Vulcan was sometimes represented as lame and deformed, holding a hammer in the air, ready to strike ; while with the other hand he turns, with his pincers, a thunderbolt upon his anvil. He appears in some monuments with a long beard, dishevelled hair, his figure partially covered, and a small, round cap on his head, and holding in his hand the pincers and hammer. The Egyptians represented him under the figure of a monkey.

Upon antique gems, he is commonly represented as an artist, occupied in his work-shop with forging arrows for Cupid.

APHRODITE OR VENUS.

Aphrodite, the perfection of creation, the Goddess of Love and Beauty, who presided over the propagation of every species of being, was, according to Homer, the daughter of Zeus and the blooming Dione, the youngest of the Titan sisters.

Besides the numberless local divinities of this name, the first mythologists acknowledged two original powers—the eldest a child of Uranos and last production of Heaven, and therefore of the Titan race, who bore her part in the productions of the universe; and the youngest, the daughter of Zeus and Dione—the power arising from the vivifying, ethereal spirit, acting upon the plenitude of matter. According to Orpheus, the former brought forth the world and all it contains. " All things are of thee," says he ; " thou cementest the universe, thou swayest the three-fold Fátes; thou generatest whatever is in the heavens above, or the teeming earth below, or in the unfathomed depths of the sea." Euripides makes Aphrodite the daughter of Kronos and Eunomia (*Time and Good Order*).

The Grecian Aphrodite arose from the foam of the sea, was received by the Horæ, who dressed her in divine attire, placed a golden crown upon her head, and adorned her neck, arms, and ears with golden ornaments. Zeus gave her the Graces for companions, Cupids attended upon her, and her chariot was drawn by doves. Every stroke in this picture breathes tenderness ; yet, the son of the goddess is armed with bow and arrows, indicating the power of his heavenly mother, the all-subduing deity.

The dominion of Aphrodite over the heart was assisted and supported by a famous girdle, called *zone* by the Greeks, and *cestus* by the Latins. This mysterious cincture gave beauty and grace to the wearer, even when deformed, and possessed the power of inspiring love. When Hera wished to inspire Zeus with this affection, she borrowed the magic girdle from Aphrodite.

In this lovely goddess, those charms of grace and beauty are venerated which allude to matrimonial union ; but as the beneficent impulse of love, if not carefully guarded by reason and morality, may prove pernicious, bringing destruction on individuals, as well as war and mischief upon whole nations, the Goddess of Love is represented as a dreadful being.

Having promised Paris the fairest wife on earth, because he ad-

judged the prize of beauty to her in preference to all the other goddesses, she incited him to deprive Menelaos, king of Sparta, of his
lawful spouse, the god-like Helena—at the same time instilling into the
bosom of this woman inconstancy and unfaithfulness. Thus the goddess kept her word, not caring for the misery and ruin in which it
might result; and at all times, and in every danger, she proves a zeal-
ous friend to Paris. During the siege of Troy, the offended Menelaos
was about to kill Paris in single combat, when Aphrodite suddenly
covered him with mighty darkness, and led him safely to his perfumed
closet.

Should this deity unite in herself the cold wisdom of Athena, or the
awful earnestness of Themis, then indeed she would be incapable of
the injustice of gratifying the wishes of one favorite at the expense of
a whole city ; nay, of a whole country, laid waste on his account. But
then she would likewise cease to be exclusively the goddess of Love,
or a product of Fancy; in whose person is represented the influence
of the passion, indifferent to the consequences ; not caring whether it
leaves the traces of bloody wars, or ages exhibiting the bliss of peace,
together with generations rejoicing in their own existence.

In the productions of Fancy, it is the very want of completeness, the
very appearance of defect, in the features of the person represented, by
which alone imagination is enabled to create and people a whole world
with supernatural beings, each distinguished by its own characteristics.
The august Hera is destitute of placid loveliness, and is obliged to borrow the girdle of Aphrodite ; the mighty god of war is deficient in reflection and prudence, and his impetuosity is restrained by Athena.

Aphrodite is possessed of the highest charms imaginable; but
Athena, destitute of female delicacy, is far superior to her in power.
In one of the battles fought before Troy, in which the gods themselves
at last challenged each other, Aphrodite being on the side of the Tro-
jans, received from the strong hand of Athena (who assisted the
Greeks) such a blow as made her knees sink under her.

" Would to Heaven," exclaimed Athena, triumphantly, "that all
the Trojans might equal the heroism and valor of Aphrodite !" (Il. xii.
428.) And at another time, Aphrodite, when wounded in her snow-
white hand by the cold Diomedes, came to Olympos, complaining to
her mother Dione of the daring of mortal men. Athena railed at her
in terms like these: " Aphrodite, forsooth, was persuading a hand-
somely dressed Grecian lady to follow along with her beloved Trojans ,

and, in caressing the fondling, she scratched her delicate hand with the golden clasp which fastened the robe of her favorite." Then the father of the gods and men smiled, and said, " Warlike work, my love, is not thy business; it is thy sweet care to prepare the joys of the wedding feast; the care of war's wild tumult leave to Ares and Athena." (Il. v. 42.)

Thus the imagination of the ancients sportively trifles with the deities whom she created after the image of man, yet always choosing such natural prototypes as are both grand and sublime.

The worship of Aphrodite was universally established. Statues and temples were erected to her in every kingdom; and the ancients delighted in paying homage to a divinity by whose influence alone mankind was supposed to exist. She was chiefly worshipped at Cythera and Cyprus; and fable says, that it was to the shores of the latter island that the waves of the sea gently carried the Goddess of Love as she arose from its foam. On this charming island, whole cities, together with groves, temples, and altars, were consecrated to Aphrodite. Her favorite residence, however, was Paphos, where offerings and vows were presented in her temple, from every quarter of the earth. And from the veneration with which all nations here rendered homage to the Goddess of Beauty, she was called queen of Paphos. From two other places on Cyprus, Amathus and Idaliou, she received the poetical appellations, Idalia and Amathusia; and from the island itself, she had the name of Cypria.

From the remotest countries pilgrims came to Cnidos, there also to pay homage to the love-inspiring goddess, whom skilful art had endowed with human form, and thus rendered her visible to the eyes of men. There, the image of Aphrodite stood in an open temple, unveiled to the view of mortals. It was the Aphrodite of Praxiteles, a worthy object of admiration.

The most ancient temple of Aphrodite in Greece, stood on the island of Cythera; and the idea of the goddess herself was so intimately connected with the place of her residence, that both names became one, and in poetical language, the Goddess of Love was called Cytheræa.

In the more ancient temples of this goddess in Cyprus, she was represented under the form of a rude conical stone; but the Grecian sculptors and painters, Praxiteles and Apelles, vied with each other in forming her image the ideal of female beauty and attraction. She appears sometimes rising out of the sea and wringing her locks; sometimes drawn in a conch by Tritons, or riding on some marine animal; and sometimes drawn in a car by doves. The Venus de Medici remains to us a noble specimen of ancient art, and perception of the beautiful.

Venus is frequently represented as the genius of indolence, lying in a languishing posture, and generally attended by Cupids who execute her orders. Possibly, some of these figures were originally meant for the goddess Desidia. Thus Venus appears in one of the finest colored pictures left us by the ancients. It is in the Barberini palace at Rome. The air of the head may be compared to the Venus of Cnidos, and the coloring with Titian's. Venus is described by Statius as in this pic ture. On an ancient sepulchral lamp she is still more indolent; as not only herself, but the Cupids attending her are all sleeping. As this was in a sepulchre, it probably related to some lady of distinction who was buried there with her children.

By the poets of the third age, Venus is represented as the goddess of jealousy, or the furious Venus. Flaccus and Statius, in their ac- count of the women of Lemnos killing their husbands at the instigation of Venus, described her as a Fury in black robes armed with a torch and a sword, and also with serpents, the attributes of the Furies.

The birds sacred to Aphrodite were swans, doves, and sparrows Horace places her in a chariot drawn by swans, and Sappho gives her sparrows. In one of the odes ascribed to Anacreon, a dove announces herself as a present from the goddess to the bard. The bird called Iynx or Fritillus, of which so much use was made in amatory magic, was also sacred to this goddess ; as was likewise the swallow, the herald of Spring, the season of love. Her favorite plants were the rose and the myrtle.

The husband assigned to this goddess is the lame artist Hephæstos ; and she is fabled to have loved Anchises, the father of Æneias.

Adonis, son of Cyniras and Myrrha, was famed for his beauty, and became a favorite of Venus. The tender goddess. not able to live with- out him, partly laid aside her softness for his sake, following him to the chase of the deer. She accompanied him like his faithful genius, warn- ing him to spare his precious life, whenever his daring spirit instigated him to pursue the tracks of fierce and dangerous beasts. But, disre- garding the entreaties and warnings of the goddess, he soon ran to destruction. Meeting with a fierce boar, he hurled his dart at him ;

but, not being mortally wounded, the beast plunged his white tusks into the side of the handsome youth. He sank, the blood gushing in abundance from his wound, and when Aphrodite sought her beloved Adonis, she found him in the agony of death.

In vain did she endeavor to recall him to life, and with bitter complaints accused the cruelty of his fate. Distracted, the goddess ran barefoot through the woods and lawns ; her delicate skin was pierced by thorns ; and her blood, dropping upon the rose, changed it from white to red. By degrees, her despair changed to softer mourning ; she sprinkled with nectar the ground that received the blood of her beloved Adonis, and gave him a kind of immortality by raising from it the flower Anemone, which, by its soon withering, expresses the brief period of life allotted to the beautiful son of Myrrha.

A festival in honor of Adonis was annually celebrated at Byblos by the Phœnician women during two days ; the first of which was spent in grief and lamentation at his death, and the second in joy and triumph at the fabled resurrection of Adonis from the dead. During this festival the priests of Babylon shaved their heads, in imitation of the priests of Isis in Egypt.

In Greece, whither these rites were transplanted, the festival was prolonged to eight days. It is uncertain when the Adoneia was first celebrated in that country ; but we find Plato alluding to the gardens of Adonis, as pots and boxes of flowers used in them were called, and the ill fortune of the Athenian expedition to Sicily was in part ascribed to the circumstance of the fleet having sailed during that festival.

In Greece it was celebrated in the same manner as in Phœnicia. On the first day the citizens put themselves in mourning, and coffins were placed at every door; the statues of Venus and Adonis were borne in procession, with the gardens of Adonis. At the conclusion of the ceremony, they were thrown into the sea or some river, where they soon perished, and thus became emblems of the premature death of Adonis, who, like a young plant, was cut off in the flower of life.

This tale of Adonis is evidently an Eastern myth. His own name and those of his parents refer to that part of the world. He appears to be the same with the Thammuz mentioned by the prophet Ezekiel ch. viii., v. 14),

> Whose annual wound in Lebanon allured
> The Syrian damsels to lament his fate,
> While smooth Adonis from his native rock

Ran purple to the sea, supposed with blood
Of Thammuz yearly wounded;

and to be a Phœnician personification of the sun, who, during a part of the year is absent, with the goddess of the under world, and during the remainder with Astarte the queen of Heaven. The legend says, that Aphrodite committed Adonis to the care of Persephone, who afterwards refused to part with him ; the matter being referred to Zeus, he decreed that Adonis should have one-third of the year to himself, be another third with Aphrodite, and the remaining third with Persephone.

Adonis was an oriental title of the sun signifying Lord ; and the loss of this mighty lord was lamented in all countries where the Assyrian and the Phœnician traditions were received ; and his return to impregnate the world with his genial vigor, was welcomed with the highest demonstrations of joy. The boar supposed to have killed him, was the emblem of winter ; during which, the productive powers of nature being suspended, Aphrodite, who went hand in hand with spring, was said to lament the loss of Adonis until he was again restored to life ; hence the Syrian and Argive women annually mourned his death, and celebrated his renovation to life. The mysteries of Adonis and Aphrodite, at Byblos in Syria, were held in similar estimation with those of Demeter and Dionysos at Eleusis, and of Isis and Osiris in Egypt.

There is none of the Olympians of whom the foreign origin is so probable as that of Aphrodite. She is generally regarded as being the same with the Astarte of the Phœnicians. There can be little doubt of the identification of Astarte with the Grecian Aphrodite, for the tale of Adonis sufficiently proves it ; and that this took place at a very early period, is evinced by Homer's so frequently giving Aphrodite the name of Cypris. Still we look on Aphrodite to be, as her name seems to denote, an originally Grecian deity ; at first, probably, merely cosmogonic, but gradually adopted into the system of the Olympians, and endowed with some of the attributes of Hera (who was also identified with Astarte), and thus became the patroness of marriage. It was probably on account of her being esteemed the same with Astarte, the moon goddess and queen of Heaven, that Aphrodite was so frequently styled the heavenly (Urania) It is very important to observe that she was so named at her temple in Cithera, which was regarded as the

16

holiest and most ancient of her fanes in Greece. Her antique wooden statue in this temple was armed; as it was also in Corinth and Sparta. In this last city, she was styled Urania, and her worship there was eminently Asiatic in character.

HERMES OR MERCURY.

While Hera was sleeping, Zeus went to see Maia, the graceful daughter of Atlas, in a shady cave; and to this secret visit Hermes is said to have owed his existence. Being born in the morning, he at noon played on the lute invented by himself, and in the evening he stole Apollo's oxen.

The lute was invented by him in the following manner. Secretly leaving his cradle at noon, on the first day of his life, and stepping over the threshold, he met a tortoise, whose shell appeared to him a fit instrument for giving musical tones when furnished with strings. " Now thou art dumb," said he, " but after thy death, thy song will be heard." Thus addressing the animal, he immediately killed it, and furnished the shell with seven concordant strings, which he touched with a small stick. As soon as he had tuned the newly-invented instrument with skilful ear, he could not forbear singing to it, and chanted forth the praise of every thing that met his eye, even the tripods and vessels in his mother's house; till at last, his song, passing into a higher strain, found a worthier subject, in the love of Zeus and Maia, his divine parents.

When evening came on, and the sun had descended into the ocean, Hermes found himself upon the Pierian mountains, where the herds of the immortal gods were feeding. From these he stole fifty oxen belonging to Apollo, and devising many a crafty trick to avoid detection, as he drove them onward through valleys and over mountains, he would have escaped discovery but for an old man, who, digging in the field, saw the boy with the oxen, and afterwards betrayed him to Apollo. On the shores of the river Alpheus, Hermes killed two of the stolen oxen, making a sacrifice of them to himself. Having done this, he carefully extinguished the fire, hid the ashes in the ground, and threw the remainder of the killed animals into the river, together with the shoes he had made of twigs and put upon the feet of the oxen, in order to conceal their tracks, or render them undiscernible. All this he performed by moonlight. Before the break of day he gently stole back into his mother's dwelling, and lay down again in his cradle, pulling the clothes around him, and holding the lute, his dearest plaything, in his hand.

Apollo, angry at the theft committed on his oxen, appeared to call Hermes to account, and to recover his property. The thief feigned a deep sleep, having the lute lying under his arm. Apollo threatened to precipitate him into Tartaros, if he would not immediately point out the place where the oxen were hidden. Then the cunning boy, twinkling his eyes, answered him, " How cruelly, son of Leto, dost thou address a little boy who was not born until yesterday, and who cares for things very different from driving oxen ; who is longing for sweet slumber and his mother's breast, and whose feet are too tender and feeble to tread long and rough paths. Nay, I will swear by Zeus, my father's head, that neither I myself have stolen the oxen, nor do I know who committed the deed."

Upon this, it was agreed between them, that both should appear before the father of the gods on Olympos, that he might reconcile their difference. Apollo stated his complaint, while Hermes stood by in his swathing-clothes, in order to refute the charge by the appearance of his tender age. " Have I then indeed," said he, " the appearance of a strong man, able to drive away oxen ? Certainly, father, thou shalt hear nothing but the truth from me. Whilst the oxen were stolen, I was lying in sweet slumber, and did not pass the threshold of my mother's dwelling. Thou knowest thyself, too, that I am innocent ; yet I am ready to protest my innocence with a solemn oath, and I shall one day reward the cruel word of that false one. But thou, father, be the protector of the younger." Thus spoke Hermes, with twinkling eyes, and Zeus smiled at the boy because he was prudent enough to deny so finely the charge brought against him. But at the same time he commanded him to tell where the oxen were hidden, and when Hermes obeyed the injunction, accompanying Apollo to the hiding-place, a reconciliation took place between them, of which the invented lute was the pledge.

For when the sweet sound of the instrument had touched the ear of the god of harmony, he was enraptured ; and caressing the inventor, " Truly," said he, " this invention is worth fifty oxen." Upon this, Hermes made him a present of the lute, and Apollo became transported with joy, at the thought of possessing so inestimate a treasure. In order, however, to secure it to himself, he requested Hermes to swear by the Styx never to steal the sweetly-sounding lute from its present possessor. In return for his lute, Apollo gave him the golden wand, which had the power of settling all differences; and these two, now closely united, ascended hand in hand to Olympos. It was art that wove the band that united them, and Zeus rejoiced in the concord

Hermes became afterwards the messenger of the immortals. He is the swift, the rapidly moving power among the celestials, who, as if firmly established in their own majesty, send the fleet, inventive idea from heaven to earth, re-admitting it into their divine council as soon as its task is accomplished.

His archetype is speech. Speech, the tender breath of air must, as it were, steal into the effective connection of things, in order to make up by thought and prudence for the deficiency of power and strength. The word of speech is winged, because it is only to be heard when accompanied by the swift breath of the lungs, and flies like a bird let loose, that cannot be recalled. For this reason, the beautiful expression of the ancients, " The word wants its wings."

According to a poetical representation, a golden chain hangs down from his mouth, reaching from Olympos to the listening ears of the dwellers on the earth, who, in this manner, are persuaded by the irresistible charms of the sweet melody that flows from his lips.

Irresistible also is his art to settle differences, to reconcile enemies— in short, to dissolve all dissonant objects in harmonious union. Once, in his boyhood, he found two serpents in his way engaged in furious strife; he struck between them with his golden wand, and behold! the reptiles instantly forget their fury, and twine themselves in gentle coil round the wand, at the top of which their heads meet in eternal concord. There is no emblem to be found more expressive of reconciliation and peace. as well as harmonious connection of what is opposed and contending, than this wand surrounded with coiling serpents, which, in the hand of the divine herald, thenceforward constituted a token of his authority.

Nothing is more charming and attractive in the fictions of the ancients, than their description of the rapid development of divine power in these supernatural beings—a power, which. as if having existed long ago, and being only new born in a particular form, does not suffer itself to be long restrained by swathing-clothes and cradle.

In this light, airy representation, the imagination of the ancients embodied the ideas of quick, inventive faculty, and cunning activity.

which displayed itself alike in deceptive persuasion, and easily accomplished sportive theft, at which even the pilfered himself, hearing the adventurous roguishness, was forced to smile. Jocularity and cunning being here clothed with divinity and immortality, present a new figure in the great picture of the divine assembly; fitter, upon the whole, to charm our eyes by its variety of composition and splendid colors, than to improve our hearts by its moral exhibitions.

In the human breast, the voice of an invisible, supernatural power speaks intelligibly, bidding man lift up his eyes from the earth to a higher world. The ancients, too, heard this voice; but misapprehending it, they formed to themselves a supernatural world, after the pattern which nature and human life presented to them. Therefore, nothing appeared to them mean or unholy, that rose from the general, uncreating influence of nature, and contained, although noxious in itself, the germ of beauty or utility.

Fancy assigns to her divine beings no bounds with regard to actions; on the contrary, she gives to the inward impulse the fullest scope; suffering them to stray even to the extreme limits of mischief, because in her fictions the great contrasts, together with the huge masses of light and shade, which otherwise we perceive merely as scattered and single, are concentrated in a small compass, and because every one of her beings comprises, as it were, in its own person, the substance of all things considered from some sublime point of view.

In this respect, the fiction of Hermes is one of the most beautiful and comprehensive. He is the swift herald of the immortals; the god of speech; the tutelary genius of the roads; in him the winged word is renewed when repeated from his lips, in delivering the commands of the gods; with his golden wand he leads the dead to the world of shadows; he is likewise the author of all prudent and cunning designs, plots, and artifices; the patron of thieves, the teacher of men in the art of wrestling, or of conquering strength by agility, and the president over trade and gain.

As messenger of Zeus, he was intrusted with all his secrets; and as the ambassador and plenipotentiary of the Gods, was concerned in all alliances and treaties. In the wars of the giants, he showed himself brave, spirited, and active. He delivered Ares from his long confinement which he suffered from the superior powers of the Aloeids; he purified the Danaïdes from the murder of their husbands; he tied Ixion to his wheel in the infernal regions; he destroyed the hundred-eyed

Argos; he sold Heracles to Omphale, queen of Lydia; he conducted
Priamos to the tent of Achilleus to redeem the body of his son Hector ;
and he carried the infant Dionysos to the nymphs of Nysa. He gave
many proofs of his thievish propensity, and increased his fame by
robbing Poseidon of his trident, Aphrodite of her girdle, Ares of his
sword, Zeus of his sceptre, and Hephæstos of his mechanical instruments.

In the war of gods, Hermes is opposed to Leto, but declines the combat on the plea of the impolicy of making an enemy of one of the con-
sorts of Zeus ; at the same time, courtier-like, telling her that if she
pleases, she may boast of having vanquished him by main strength.
When the corse of Hector was exposed by Achilleus, the gods, pitying
the fate of the hero, urged Hermes to *steal* it away. On king Priamos' setting forth to ransom the body of his son, Zeus desires Hermes
to accompany him, reminding him of his fondness for associating with
mankind. The god obeys his sire ; puts on his immortal, golden sandals, which bear him over the water and the extensive earth like the
blasts of the wind ; and takes " his rod, with which he lays asleep the
eyes of what men he will, and wakes again the sleepers." He accompanies the aged monarch in the form of a Grecian youth, telling him that
he is the son of a wealthy man named Polyctor (*much possessing*).

In the Odyssey, Hermes takes the place of Iris, who does not appear
at all in this poem, and becomes the messenger of Zeus. He still retains his character of friend to man, and comes unsent to point out to
Odysseus the herb *Moly*, which will enable him to escape the enchant-
ments of Circe. Eumæos, the swineherd, makes an offering to Hermes
and the nymphs. At the commencement of the spurious twenty-fourth
book, Hermes appears in his character of conveyer of souls to the realms
of Hades.

Mythologists are pretty well agreed in recognizing a telluric power
in the Hermes of the Pelasgian system. The simplest derivation of
his name is from a Greek word, signifying *earth*, and by the name of
his mother, Maia, is probably meant Mother Earth.

He seems to have been the deity of productiveness in general ; but
he came gradually to be regarded as presiding more particularly over
flocks and herds. From this last view some of his Hellenic attributes
may be simply deduced. Thus the god of shepherds was naturally regarded as the inventor of music ; the lyre is ascribed to Hermes, as the
pipes are to Pan, music having always been a recreation of shepherds

in the warm regions of the south. In like manner, as the shepherd lads amuse themselves with wrestling and other feats of strength and activity, their tutelar god easily became the president of the *palæstra.* So also trade, having consisted chiefly in the exchange of cattle, Hermes, the herdsman's god, was held to be the god of commerce ; and the skill and eloquence employed in commercial dealings, made him to be the god of eloquence, artifice, and ingenuity, and even of cheating. As herdsmen are the best guides in the country, it may be thence that Hermes was thought to protect wayfarers, and thence to be a protector in general. For this cause it may have been, that godsends or treasure-trove were ascribed to him.

The rural deity, when thus become active, sly and eloquent, was well adapted for the office which was assigned him of agent and messenger of the gods, to whom we also find him officiating as cup-bearer. As a being whose operations extended into the interior of the earth, Hermes would seem to have been in some points of view identified with Hades. In Pindar, this latter deity himself performs the office generally assigned to Hermes, that of conducting the departed to Erebos. Possibly it may have been on this account, that Solon directed the Athenians to swear by Zeus, Poseidon, and Hermes.

The Grecian spirit completely modified the Egyptian Hermes, to produce the Hermes or Mercury of the Grecian mythology ; where he is quite a different being. In Egypt he presides over the sciences, writing, medicine, and astronomy, and composes many divine works, containing the elements of these several departments of knowledge ; in Greece he is the god of shepherds and merchandise. The interpreter of the gods in Egypt, he becomes in Greece only their messenger ; and it is by virtue of this latter title that he preserves his wings, which were among the Egyptians merely an astronomical symbol.

The god is usually represented with a *chlamys*, his *petasus* or winged cap, and his *talaria* or winged sandals, and the *caduceus* or wand presented to him by Apollo, which had the power of settling all differences, of putting any one to sleep, and of waking them again, and also of bringing souls out of Hell. The petasus and talaria were gifts from Zeus.

The ancient statues of Hermes were merely wooden posts with a rude head and pointed beard carved on them. They were what is termed ithyphallic, and were set up on the roads and foot-paths, also in the fields and gardens. From this representation he became with the Romans the god *Terminus ;* but when they were made acquainted with the twelve great deities of the Athenians, they adopted the Grecian Hermes under the name of *Mercurius.* In honor of this deity, the Romans celebrated an annual festival in a temple near the Circus Maximus, when sacrifices and prayers were offered to him.

An ancient gem exhibits the following accurate representation of Mercury : As god of the roads, he stands before an altar, over which rises an antique milestone, which he touches with his wand. Upon the altar lies a staff, as an intimation of travellers dedicating their walking staves to Mercury, after having accomplished a journey. As a sign of the safety of the roads, an olive branch is entwined around the stone. The god bears on his head the winged cap; as he is standing, the winged sandals are not fastened to his feet.

The Council of Jupiter, the supreme divinity, was composed of six gods, namely, Jupiter, Neptune, Mercury, Apollo, Mars, and Vulcan ; and six goddesses : Juno, Ceres, Vesta, Minerva, Diana, and Venus. To this assembly no other deities were admitted.

As soon as fiction descends from Heaven to Earth, divine beings become more numerous. Imagination discovers life in fountains, groves, and hills ;—and according to her pleasure, ascribes to this life corporeal form. In this manner all nature becomes sacred : deity fills the whole, and the whole is deity, revealed only in various forms. The ancients not only deified the virtues, but distempers, storms, and passions, and worshipped them that they might be saved from all harm.

This practice of personifying natural and moral qualities, seems to have been coëval with Grecian poetry and religion. It was not, however, by any means peculiar to Greece ; it will probably be found wherever poetry exists. But it was only in ancient Greece and Italy, that these personifications were made objects of worship, and regarded as having a real and personal existence.

The Genii or Dæmons were not considered as equal to the gods, but as superior to mortals. The four natures, Gods, Genii, Heroes and Men were first distinguished by Hesiod.

PART THIRD.

GENII AND INFERIOR DEITIES.

GENII AND INFERIOR DEITIES.

According to the ideas of the ancients, man was intimately connected with the Deity by means of the genii or tutelary beings. The highest divinity is multiplied, as it were, in those beings, who, like guardian angels, lead by the hand every individual mortal through life, from the hour of his birth to that of his death. In this sense it was. that man swore by his Jupiter. and woman by her Juno, speaking of their own genius, or tutelary deity.

On their birthdays, the ancients presented offerings of wine, incense, and garlands of flowers, to their respective genii, who were represented in the form of handsome youths, having their heads crowned with flowers. Thus man, following the dictates of his heart, venerated something higher and more divine than he could find in his own limited individuality, and brought to "this great unknown of himself" offerings as a god; thus compensating by veneration for the indistinct knowledge of his divine origin.

It was customary among the Romans to implore persons by their genius, as the orientals do by their souls; and in Latin writers it is not always easy to distinguish a man's genius from himself. The distinct worship of the Genii continued down to the demise of paganism. for we find it noticed in the Theodosian code.

The worship of the Genius was a remarkable part of the religion of the Romans; they having derived it from the Tuscans, in whose system it formed a prominent feature. The word Genius is evidently a Latin translation of a Tuscan term, signifying *Generator*, and the Genius was therefore viewed as a deity who had the power of producing. In the Tuscan system he was the son of the gods. and the parent of men ; according to the ancient Italian doctrine, all souls proceeded from Jupiter, and returned to him after death ; therefore the Genius Jovialis was viewed as the great agent in giving life, and uniting the soul to the body.

When Ceres and Pallas bless the growth and animals of the fields, and thereby the house, so cares the Genius Jovialis for the continuance and bloom of the family itself. Through him is Jupiter an eternal, inexhaustible giver of life to the changing generation of man.

The Genii of the Romans are frequently confounded with the Manes, Lares and Penates ; and they have indeed one great feature in common, viz., that of protecting mortals. There is, however, this essential difference ; the genii are the powers that produce life, and accompany man through it as his second or spiritual self, and the other powers have no influence till life, the work of the genii, has commenced. Neither were they confined to man, but every living thing, animal as well as man, and also every place, had its genius, or protecting spirit.

Horace, in speaking of the Genius, calls him " changeable of countenance, white and black ;" and in the well-known appearance of his evil genius to Brutus, the spirit was black, which would seem to intimate that a man had two Genii, a good and an evil one.

This does not appear to have been the Italian belief, though perhaps such a notion prevailed in Greece; for the philosopher Empedocles said, that two Moiræ receive us at our birth, and obtain authority over us.

The whole body of the Roman people also had its genius, who is often represented on the coins of Hadrian and Trajan. He was worshipped on sad, as well as on joyous occasions, as for instance at the beginning of the second year of the Hannibalian war.

When a local genius made himself visible, he appeared in the form of a serpent, that is, the symbol of renovation, or of new life. In works of art, the genii are usually represented as winged beings ; and on Roman monuments, a genius generally appears as a youth dressed in a toga, with a patera or cornucopia in his hand, and having his head covered. The genius of a place is represented in the form of a serpent eating fruit placed before him.

The Greeks called their genii, dæmons, and appear to have believed in them from the earliest times, though they are not mentioned by Homer. Hesiod speaks of them as being thirty thousand in number, and says that they dwelt on earth. invisible to mortals, as the ministers of

Zeus and the guardians of man and justice. He also considers them as the souls of righteous men who lived in the golden age. Upon this idea the Greek philosophers developed a complete theory of dæmons. Thus we read in Plato, that dæmons are assigned to men at the moment of their birth, accompany them through life, and after death, conduct their souls to Hades * Pindar also speaks of the spirit that watches over the fate of man from the hour of his birth, which appears to be the same as the genius of the Romans—the protecting spirit, analogous to the guardian angels invoked by the church of Rome.

Dæmons are further described as the ministers and companions of the gods, who bear the prayers of men to them, and the gifts of the gods to men, and accordingly float in immense numbers in the space between heaven and earth. Dæmons who were exclusively the ministers of the gods, seem to have constituted a distinct class. The Corybantes, Dactyls, and Cabeiri, are called the ministering dæmons of the great gods; Gigon, Tychon, and Ortharges, are the dæmons of Aphrodite; and Hadreus the dæmon of Demeter.

The Penates, or guardians of private families, who are also derived from the Etruscans, appear to have formed an especial class of deities among the Romans. The *dii penates* are those who are worshipped in the interior of the house. They were gods from whom blessings, cherishing, and prosperity were expected, as the name declares. There is no reason to suppose that the Penates were a class of gods distinctly divided from the others; but different gods and dæmons of different orders are honored in different houses. Therefore the great uncertainty and variety in the assertions of the ancients as to who the Penates were.

According to the Etruscans, they were divided into four classes: Penates of Jupiter, Penates of Neptune, those of the nether gods, and those of mortal men. They considered the dæmons who add to the possessions of families, as in part the souls of the dead, in part beings of the earth and lower world, of the water and the heavens; the fourth class comprised the Genii.

Among the various deities called Lares, are human souls, as among the Penates. Certain rites are described by which human souls are

---

* Hades anciently signified the grave, or place of the dead in general. All therefore that die, must go to Hades.

changed to gods called animals, because they arise from souls. These are Penates and way-gods. These rites are the same as those consecrated to the deities of the nether world, which were principally Etruscan; only the name, and perhaps certain usages, were borrowed from Greece by which souls were redeemed and conjured out of the lower world, and thereby became gods. This is the doctrine of the genii. A genius is present at birth ;—his power operates in the life of the mortal whom the gods favor, and also after death ; and of the dead he becomes again the genius. Yet, these elevated and deified souls do not become gods of every sort, but first Penates. The old Latins called the soul of man, as soon as it had left the body, *Lemur* ; and a Lemur, who retained an interest in posterity, and ruled the house with mild and peaceful disposition, *Lar Familiaris*. Those who, for a punishment, wandered about as powerless forms, empty bugbears to the good, and the torment of the bad. were *Larvæ*. But when the destiny of the man is uncertain, the term *Manes dii* is employed, and to the Manes was assigned a subterranean place of abode. There can be little doubt that Jupiter and Juno were worshipped as Penates. Vesta, also, is reckoned among them ; for each hearth, being the symbol of domestic union, had its Vesta. The public Penates of the city of Rome had a chapel near the centre of the city, in a place called *Sub Velia* ; the private had their place at the domestic hearth, which, as well as the table, was sacred to them. Every meal taken in the house resembled a sacrifice to the Penates.

After every absence from the hearth, the Penates were saluted like the living inhabitants of the house. Whoever went abroad, prayed to the Penates and Lares for a happy return ; and when he came back, he hung up his armor and staff by the side of their images. No event, whether sad or joyful, occurred in the family, without offering prayers to the Lares and Penates.

The Lares or domestic deities, were generally two in number, who had their abodes on the domestic hearth. They were represented as youths with hats on their heads, travelling staves in their hands, and dogs at their sides. Lamps, the symbol of vigilance, were consecrated to them ; they were crowned with flowerets, and received offerings of food, which was prepared upon the hearth. Again, they are dressed in short habits, to show their readiness to serve, and hold a kind of cornucopia as a signal of hospitality and good house-keeping. Being witness of domestic happiness or misfortune, they hallowed the every-day occurrences of life by their presence, rendering every house, as it were, a sacred temple.

There are various classes of Lares, such as Lares *Urbani,* to preside over the cities; *Familiares,* over houses; *Rustici,* over the country; *Marini,* over the sea; *Viales,* over the roads, etc.

If we regard the nature of Lares and Penates, we shall readily perceive why the former have a higher rank assigned them in the hierarchy of the genii than the latter. The Penates were originally gods — the powers of nature personified—powers whose wonderful and mysterious action produces and upholds whatever is necessary to life, as well as to the common good and prosperity of families and individuals; in fine, whatever the human species cannot bestow upon itself.

The case is quite different with the Lares; they were originally human beings, who had lived upon earth, and who, becoming pure spirits after death, loved still to hover round the dwellings they had formerly inhabited, watching over their safety, and guarding them from evil. Having lived as mortals, they were familiar with the dangers that surround man, and knew what assistance was required by those whose situation in every respect was once their own. They were therefore supposed to avert danger from without, while the Penates, residing in the interior of the dwelling, pour forth benefits upon its inmates with bountiful hands.

The place in which the Lares were worshipped was called the Lararium—a sort of domestic chapel in the Atrium, where were also to be seen the images and busts of the family ancestors. In the sacrifices offered to them, the first-fruits of every year, with wine and incense, were brought to their altars; and their images were adorned with chaplets and garlands. The rich had often two Lararia, one large and one small; and also "Masters of the Lares" and "Decurios of the

17

Lares ;" namely, slaves specially charged with the care of these domestic chapels and images of their divinities. The common altar, on
which sacrifices were offered to the Lares, was the domestic hearth ;
and in all family repasts, the first thing done was to cast a portion of
the viands into the fire that burned on the hearth in honor of the Lares

Certain public festivals were also celebrated in honor of the Lares,
called Lararia and Compitalia. The period for their celebration fell
in the month of December, a little after the Saturnalia. On this occasion the Lares were worshipped as propitious deities ; therefore these
festivities were gay and joyful. The Compitalia, dedicated to the *Lares Compitales*, were celebrated in the open air : the day of their celebration was not fixed. They were introduced at Rome by Servius
Tullius, who left to the Senate the care of determining the period when
they should be held.

In early times, children were immolated to the goddess Mania, who,
according to some, was the mother of the Lares, in order to propitiate her
favor for the protection of the family. This barbarous rite was subsequently abolished, and little balls of wool were hung up at the gates of
dwellings, instead of human offerings. After the expulsion of the
Tarquins, Junius Brutus introduced a new form of sacrifice, by virtue
of which, heads of garlics and poppies were offered up in place of human heads, in accordance with the oracle of Apollo. During these
festivals, every family brought a cake for an offering ; slaves enjoyed a
perfect equality with their masters, as on the Saturnalia ; and slaves,
instead of freemen, assisted the priests in the sacrifices offered on this
occasion to the tutelary genii of the ways.

In case of death in a family, a sacrifice of sheep was offered to the
family Lares. In the form of marriage, called *coëmtio*, the bride
always threw a piece of money upon the hearth to the Lares of her
family, and deposited another in the neighboring cross-road, in order
to obtain admission, as it were, into the dwelling of her husband.
Young persons, after their fifteenth year, consecrated to the Lares the
bulla* which they had worn from infancy. Soldiers, when their time

---

* The *bulla* was made of metal, and so called from its resemblance in form to a bubble
floating upon the water. It was suspended round the neck of a child as a token of
paternal affection, and a sign of high birth; as it was given to infants, it sometimes
served to recognize a lost child. Probably it contained amulets.

Instead of the *bulla* of gold, the children of inferior rank wore one made of leather.

of service was ended, dedicated to these powerful genii the arms with which they had fought the battles of their country. Captives and slaves, restored to freedom, consecrated to the Lares the fetters from which they had just been freed. Before undertaking a journey, or after a successful return, homage was paid to these deities, when their protection was implored, or thanks were rendered for their guardian care. The new master of a house crowned the Lares, in order to render them propitious; a custom which was most universal, and perpetuated to the latest times.

As regards the forms under which the Lares were represented, it may be observed that it differed slightly from that of the Penates. Thus, on the coins of the Cæsian family, they are represented as two young men, seated, their heads covered with helmets, and holding spears in their hands, while a dog watches at their feet. Sometimes the heads of the Lares are represented as covered with the skin of a dog, and sometimes it forms their mantle. At other times, we find the Lares resembling naked children, with the bulla hanging from the neck, and always accompanied by the attribute of the dog.

NYMPHÆ OR NYMPHS.

The imagination of the ancients, fond of connecting something divine with objects that are strong and lasting, and that outlive the generations of men, as the firmly-rooted mountain, the overflowing spring, and the solid oak, attributed to hills and fountains, to forests, and even to single trees, immortal souls; for in this light may those beings be considered, who, under the name of Nymphs, were thought to animate them.

The Oread roams on the mountains, pursuing with her sisters, in the retinue of Diana, the track of the deer; and, like the unyielding deity whom she follows, closes her heart to every tender affection.

At the lonely hour of noon, the Naiad sat with her water pitcher at her spring, sending forth from it the warbling brooks. Although less cruel than their mountain-sisters, the caresses of the Naiades proved dangerous. They embraced handsome Hylas, the favorite of Hercules, when he was sent for water, and drew him down into the fountain.

The sacred gloom of the forest was the abode of the Dryades, while the Hamadryad lived within her own single tree, with which she was born, and with which she died. Whoever therefore spared a tree laid the Nymph who dwelt in it under an obligation for life.

The Auræ, or Sylphs, Nymphs of the air, a species of sportive, happy beings, and well-wishers to mankind, were winged and represented as flying.

In this manner inanimate nature itself became to man an object of sympathetic benevolence.

In the Homeric Hymn to Aphrodite, we find the following descrip tion of the Nymphs. Aphrodite, as the mother of Æneias, in allusion to his birth, says to Anchises.

> But him, when first he sees the sun's clear light,
> The nymphs shall rear, the mountain-haunting nymphs,
> Deep bosom'd, who on this mountain great
> And holy dwell, who neither goddesses
> Nor women are. Their life is long; they eat
> Ambrosial food; and with the deathless, frame
> The beauteous dance. With them in the recess
> Of lovely caves, well-spying Argos-slayer
> And the Sileni mix in love. Straight pines
> Or oaks high-headed, sprung with them upon
> The earth, men feeding, soon as they are born;
> Trees fair and flourishing; on the high hills,
> Lofty they stand; the Deathless, sacred grove
> Men call them, and with iron never cut.
> But when the Fate of death is drawing near,
> First wither on the earth the beauteous trees,
> The bark around them wastes, the branches fall,
> And the nymph's soul. at the same moment leaves
> The sun's fair light.

SILENOS.

According to the Homerid, Hermes and the Silens mingle in love with the Nymphs in pleasing caverns, and Pindar calls Silenos the Naiad's husband. Socrates, on account of his wisdom, his baldness, and his flat nose, compared himself to the Silens born of the divine Naiades. Others said that Silenos was a son of Earth, and sprung from the blood, drops of Uranos: Marsyas is also called a Silen.

Like the sea-gods, Silenos was noted for wisdom; and it would therefore appear that a Silen was simply a river-god; and the name probably comes from the Greek verb, signifying *to*

roll, expressive of the motion of the streams. The connection between Silenos, Bacchos, and the Naiades, thus becomes easy of explanation, all being deities relating to moisture.

Silenos was represented as old, bald, and flat-nosed, riding on a broadbacked ass, usually intoxicated, and carrying his can (*cantharus*), or tottering along, supported by his staff of fennel (*ferula*).

PRIAPOS.

Priapos, the emblem of fecundity, and fabled to have been the son of Bacchos and Aphrodite, was introduced late into the Grecian mythology. He was a rural deity, worshipped by the people of Lampsacus, a city on the Hellespont famous for its vineyards.

Priapos was not, as is supposed from the employment usually assigned him by the Romans after they adopted his worship—merely the god of gardens, but of fruitfulness in general.

"This god," says Pausanias, "is honored elsewhere by those who keep sheep and goats, or stocks of bees; but the Lampsacenes, regarded him more than any of the gods, calling him the son of Dionysos and Aphrodite." In Theocritus the shepherds placed his statue with those of the nymphs at a shady fountain, and a shepherd prays to him, promising sacrifices if he will free him from love ; and, by Virgil, bees are placed under his care. Fishermen also made offerings to him as the deity presiding over fisheries; and in the Anthology, Priapos (*of-the-Heaven*) is introduced, giving a pleasing description of the spring, and inviting the mariners to put to sea. The Priaps are enumerated by Moschus among the rural gods :

> And Satyrs wailed and sable-cloaked Priaps;
> And Pans sighed after the sweet melody.

Like the other rural gods, Priapos is of a ruddy complexion. His cloak is filled with all kinds of fruit; he has a scythe in his hand, and usually a horn of plenty. Sometimes his statue was placed in gardens, crowned with a wreath of herbs and bearing a crooked knife in his hand.

SATYRS.

The forest, with its shades and deep recesses, is the scene also of those wanton beings, called Satyrs, whose human shape is disfigured by the horns and feet of a goat. They are, as it were, the middle link, which in nature's great chain connects the brute creation with the human world.

In these beings the slender feet of a goat is in a burlesque manner joined to a human form; and a similar contrast exhibits youthful wantonness and careless levity, blended with the higher spirit that dwells within them. Although mortal, they are superior to the cares and sorrows of mortal life.

Belief in the existence of these beings, as well as others of the same kind, must necessarily have been perpetuated from the idea that no one was permitted to behold a nymph or a satyr unpunished. Thus, instead of endeavoring to ascertain the truth or falsehood of their existence, every one shunned the sight of them, avoiding such places as they were reported to have chosen for their haunts. It was the inspired poet alone, who, amid lonely rocks, beheld in the train of Bacchos, nymphs and satyrs, listening to the instruction of the god, and goat-footed satyrs with erect and pointed ears. In the Greek mythology they were inseparably connected with the worship of Bacchos, and represent the luxuriant, vital powers of nature.

In the Satyrs, art has attempted to represent human form bordering as nearly as possible on brutal shape. A Satyr, exhibited upon an antique gem, as he is contending with a he-goat, and pushing him, is scarcely distinguished from that animal, except by his body and arms; the goat form being extended even to the face, which, although human, betrays the nature of the brute.

These comic Nymphs, Genii, and Cupids produce an agreeable contrast in the train of Bacchos; and it would seem as if they were a necessary part of those groups, and of the divine formations in general; fiction being as it were completed by those beings, half divine and half brute

FAUNS.

The Fauns differ from the Satyrs; at least, according to the tech nical language of modern times. They are represented entirely in human form, but with erect and pointed ears, and the tail of a goat. Yet without these external marks, a Faun is easily recognized by his rough, ignoble features, which indicate the character attributed to him. Still there are some ancient monuments, which exhibit Fauns of admirable beauty, in whose features that half-brutish, sensual temper is but slightly indicated.

Both the form and character of the Faun offered to the ancient artists an inexhaustible source of representations; and the chisel, as well as the pencil, is frequently employed in exhibiting the ridiculous being, either as he dances, or as he sits occupied in wreathing garlands; or playing with his goats, or rocking his little one upon his knees; and in many other different attitudes. Much waste of time and art is often displayed in the representation of the Fauns and their various occupations. To the most attractive monuments of antique art in this style, belong the following: an old Faun dancing his little one upon his foot; another turning the wheel of a well to draw water for a nymph, who in the mean time holds his thyrse; two Fauns sitting opposite each other, one occupied in taking a thorn from the other's foot; another allowing a young Faun to drink out of a wine pitcher.

All these different exhibitions show that ease is the chief feature in the character of these fictitious beings. Thus they are distinguished from mortals, and made to resemble the gods, according to the words of an ancient bard: "On mortal man the celestials heaped much trouble and pain, but they themselves are free from cares."

The peasants sacrificed lambs and kids to the Fauns with great solemnity.

SYLVANUS

Sylvanus was a deity who presided over the woods and the fruits they produced, and was worshipped by the nations of Latium. He was represented like Pan, except that he bears a branch of cypress in his hand, which intimates night in the forest, and alludes also to the joyless and melancholy nature of his abode, which rendered him an object of terror to peasants and shepherds.

There is an antique gem preserved in one of the German museums.

generally known under the name of the seal ring of Michael Angelo,
which is one of the finest specimens of lithotomy ever made; exhibiting in a moderate compass all the above-mentioned inferior deities;
Nymphs, Cupids, Satyrs, and Fauns, united in one beautiful group.
Two vines wedded to two elm trees, form by their tendrils a bower,
over which two Cupids, hovering on their wings, spread a cover of
cloth.   Three female figures are carrying baskets on their heads filled
with grapes,•while the others are seated and attending to a little child.
With this group of sitting figures a Faun is associated, who, cowering
on his knees, is pouring wine from a pitcher into a vessel, which was
brought by a boy from behind him, while a Satyr, who stands beside
the Faun, is winding a horn.   The Cupid on one elm is reaching down
into a basket of fruits, which is carried on one of the heads of the
females, while that on the other is presented by a nymph with a cup
of wine.   In the midst of the whole group, the noble form of a man
appears holding a horse by the bridle.   The whole relates probably to
the education of Bacchos, which was committed to the nymphs.

THEMIS.

Zeus, when Lord of all, united with Themis, which signifies possibility or aptitude arising from the necessary connection of things, or
the laws of their existence.   In action, Themis is the source of law,
and her predictions of truth.

Themis, as goddess of justice, still maintains her place among the
modern deities.   In this character, presiding over the distribution of
justice, she is represented as a noble and majestic woman, having her
eyes covered with a fillet, holding a balance in one hand, and a sword
in the other.   She is said to have succeeded her mother Earth in the
possession of the Delphic oracle, and to have voluntarily resigned it to
her sister Phœbe, who gave it as a natal gift to Phœbos-Apollo.

By some mythologists, Themis is considered merely as an epithet
of earth; and others consider her as the oldest purely allegorical personification of a virtue.

The ancient poets also mention her daughter Astræa, who descended
from Heaven to be the tutelary deity of mortals, distributing justice,
settling differences, teaching the principles of integrity, and inculcating
an abhorrence of injustice and crime.   Pitying the unfortunate race
of Prometheus, she dwelt with them for a long time; but when she
found that, notwithstanding her endeavors, justice was overthrown by

the misdeeds of men, and all reverence for what is holy banished from their lives, she left them in disgust and fled back to Heaven.

HORÆ.

Having become the wife of Zeus, Themis produced the three amiable guides and guardians of life, the Horæ, whose names are Eunomia (*order*), Dike (*punishment*), Irene (*peace*). Their office was to promote unanimity by the exercise of equity and justice. They likewise stand around the throne of Zeus, and their regular occupation is to open and shut the gates of Heaven, and yoke the steeds to the chariot of the Sun.

Under the name of the Horæ, the ancient fictions comprise, in the first place, the Genii of justice, children of Zeus and Themis; and then the Seasons; which, by a just partition of their benefits, as it were, preserve in continual succession the equipoise of nature.

The dancing Horæ, following each other in measured steps, are an emblem of fleeting time; and, as friends and companions of the Graces, often mingle with them in a common choir.

Winkleman's monuments contain a representation of the three Horæ, taken from an antique marble. One of them, crowned with palm leaves, and standing before an altar, bearing fruit in her hands, signifies Autumn; another, before whose feet a flower has sprung up, is an emblem of Spring; and near the third, on a pile of stones like an altar, a little fire appears, intimating Winter. Under the serene and mild sky of Greece, Summer and Autumn vary but little in temperature as well as products, therefore, one emblem is sufficient for both; the Athenians usually represented but two seasons, Thallo and Carpo, blossom and fruit, the whole year being divided by them into spring and autumn.

By poets and artists the seasons are all personified. They are frequently seen together on relievi, medals, and gems. On a medal of Commodus, they appear moving over a celestial globe, which lies by the goddess Tellus. The artists have also followed the poets in repre senting the four ages of life by depicting Ver (*spring*), as infantile and tender; Æstas (*summer*), as young and sprightly; Autumnus (*autumn*), mature and manly; and Hyems (*winter*), as old and decrepid.

Again Ver is a youth decorated with a coronet of flowers, or a basket of flowers in his hand; Æstas is crowned with corn or holds a sickle in his hand; Autumnr is usually distinguished by his crown of different fruits; and Hyems by his crown of reeds, the birds in his hand, or the beast at his feet; and also by his warm clothing.

EROS OR CUPID.

Eros or Cupid is unnoticed by Homer. In the Theogony he is one of the first beings, and produced without parents. In the Orphic poems he was the son of Kronos. Sappho made him the offspring of Heaven and Earth, while Simonides assigned him Aphrodite and Ares for parents. In Olen's hymn to Eileithyia, that goddess was termed the mother of Love; and Alcæus said, that well-sandalled Iris bore Love to gold-locked Zephyros.

Thespiæ in Bœotia was the place in which Eros was most worshipped. The Thespians celebrated games in his honor on Mount Helicon. The oldest image of the god in their city was of plain stone; but Praxiteles afterwards made for them one of Pentelican marble of rare beauty. Eros also had altars at Athens and elsewhere.

The God of Love was usually represented as a plump-cheeked, rosy boy, with light hair floating on his shoulders. He is always winged and armed with bow and arrows.

Under the appellation of Eros and Anteros, Love, and Love requited, ancient art represents two Cupids contending for the possession of a palm branch, to signify zeal in mutual love. The two Cupids, with the dolphin at the foot of Venus de Medici, are supposed to be these, and are now called by the antiquarians of Florence, Eros and Anteros.

The Platonic philosopher, Porphyrius, tells the following pretty legend: Aphrodite, complaining to Themis that her son Eros continued always a child, was told by her that the cause was from his being solitary, and that if he had a brother he would grow apace. Anteros was soon afterwards born, and Eros found his wings enlarge, and his person and strength greatly increase. But this was only when Anteros was near; for if he was at a distance, Eros found himself shrink to his original dimensions.

The divine person of Eros is multiplied by the ancients. Those little Cupids or Genii of Love, who every where appear in ancient fictions, are, as it were, sparks of this being. Poetry is inexhaustible in beautiful emblematic representations of the all-conquering god. Thus we find him as breaking the thunderbolts of Zeus; or as arrayed in the lion skin of Heracles, and armed with his club; or as stepping on the helmet of Ares, whose shield and spear are lying at his feet;

or, finally, as riding on a lion, taming the beast by the strains of his lyre ;—a beautiful emblem of the combined power of love and music. Ancient gems and pictures show us the Cupids in a variety of occupations. . One of these monuments exhibits a Cupid sitting on an elm tree, to which the vine is wedded, and gathering grapes, while two others wait under the tree for a gift from their brother. They are also found hunting, fishing, and managing the oar on the water, as well as directing the chariot by land ; and even busied with mechanical employments.

CHARITES OR GRACES.

In the Graces are multiplied the eminently dazzling charms of the powerful Goddess of Love. The three sisters descended from heaven, for the benefit of mortal men—instilling into their bosoms the lovely feeling of gratitude and mutual benevolence, and gracing their persons with the precious gift of pleasing.

The Graces were children of Zeus and Eurynome, the beautiful daughter of Oceanos; and their names were Aglaïa (*Splendor*), Thalia (*Pleasure*), and Euphrosyne (*Joy*).* Temples and altars were every where erected to their honor ; every age and every profession solicited their favor ; arts and sciences paid homage to them ; their altars were never without fragrant incense ; and at every joyful repast, their names were mentioned with veneration.

Associated in friendly union with Love and the Muses, they had often a temple in common with the former, and still oftener with the latter. In Olympos they surrounded the throne of Jupiter. In heaven, as well as on earth, their dominion was acknowledged, and their influence, without which beauty itself is but a dead picture, was respected and honored. In the dancing attitudes of the three graceful sisters, are expressed the charms of personal dignity, of elegant movement, and of attitude and countenance by which beauty gains the soul of man ; and walking hand in hand as loving sisters, they indicate also every tender emotion of a heart overflowing with affection, friendship, and benevolence.

The happy influence which the religious veneration of these lovely and significant beings exercised on the ideas and feelings of the an-

---

* Of the three Graces, the Spartans originally worshipped but one, Aglaïa, under the name of Phænna (*Brightness*). Rejecting Joy and Pleasure, they adopted Cletha (*Sound*) as a substitute.

cients, is to be recognized in the whole life of the Greeks, as well as their works of art and science.   The favor of the Graces was no where to be dispensed with ; and in order to intimate that, to make even the most extravagant formations of fancy agreeable, grace must be conceal-ed, hollow statues of Satyrs were formed, within which were found little figures of the Graces.

Homer makes Juno promise the youngest of the Graces to the God of Sleep, if he would seal the eyes of Almighty Jove for a little time. A single reflection upon the effect of late hours and undue watching, will show the propriety of the union.   It is this unnatural habit that pales the rosy lip, disarms the sparkling look, and robs a beauty of her native grace.

By the ancient artists and poets, the Graces are represented as three beautiful sisters linked together; and Horace represented the Graces and Nymphs as dancing together, with Venus at their head.   Canova's Graces, in the Duke of Bedford's fine gallery of sculptures at Woburn Abbey, are eminently beautiful and replete with grace.

CAMENÆ OR MUSES.

Mnemosyne, the personification of memory as the source and reposi-tory of every art and science, belongs to the ancient deities; for she is the daughter of Heaven and Earth; and as mankind are indebted to memory for their progress in science, Mnemosyne is said to be the parent of the Muses, who divided among themselves that treasure of wisdom which their venerable mother alone possessed.

The Muses, as well as the Horæ and Graces, all of them daughters of Zeus, originally presided over the stars and the seasons; but the later Greeks took away these functions, giving them only such as were of a poetic character.   An ancient bard thus sings the praises of the nine sisters :   " They pour on the lips of man, whom they favor, the dew of soft persuasion ; they bestow on him wisdom, that he may be a judge and umpire among his people, and give him renown among na-tions ; and the poet who wanders on the mountain tops and in the lowly dales, is inspired by them with divine strains, which dispel sor-row and grief from the breast of every mortal."

Their appropriate employments are music, song, and dance; but playful fiction has given to each of the sisters a particular vocation. Calliope was the muse of eloquence and heroic poetry (to her the an-cients gave precedence) ; Clio, of history ; Erato, of amorous poetry ;

Euterpe, of music ; Melpomene, of tragedy ; Polyhymnia, of eloquence and imitation : Terpsichore, of dancing ; Thalia, of comic and lyric poetry ; and Urania, of astronomy. On a sarcophagus, in the Capitoline Gallery at Rome, there is a relievo in which the nine muses are represented ; by the help of this, together with Ausonius' description of them (Idyl. 20), an attempt has been made to distinguish one muse from another. Herodotus has annexed their names to the nine books of his history ; and from their arrangement, as well as from the relievos, it would appear that their order is quite arbitrary. In the relievo above mentioned, they are placed and distinguished in the following manner : Clio is first, and distinguished by the roll in her hand, or sometimes with the longer, bolder pipe. Her office was to celebrate the actions of departed heroes ; though Statius makes her descend to lower functions, from the old notion that every thing penned in hexameters was an epic poem.

Thalia was the Muse of comedy and pastorals, and is distinguished by the comic mask in her hand, and her pastoral crook.

Terpsichore has nothing to distinguish her ; Ausonius gives her the cithara (or lyre), and sometimes she is represented in a dancing attitude. On the medals of the Pomponian family, three Muses have stringed instruments in their hands, and are supposed to represent Terpsichore, Erato, and Polyhymnia.

Euterpe presided over music and performed on two pipes at once, as in the remarks before Terence's plays. By these pipes she is distinguished, though sometimes she holds the fistula (or pipe), and is so described by Ausonius.

Erato, who presided over amorous poetry, is represented at times as pensive, and again full of gaiety; both which characters, though directly opposite, suit with the ever-varying moods of lovers, and are appropriate to their patroness. Ovid invokes Erato in his Art of Love, and likewise in his Fasti for April, which among the Romans was con-sidered as peculiarly the lover's month. But Virgil, in his Æneid, appears with less propriety to invoke her before a field of battle; un-less, indeed, it was that a woman was the occasion of the war. Calliope is called by Ovid the chief of the Muses, and by Horace, Regina, as skilful on all instruments. The tablets in the hand mark her distin-guishing character, which was to note down the worthy actions of men.

Polyhymnia is designated by a stringed instrument, perhaps what the Romans call *barbiton*, for which we have no name.

Urania presided over astronomy, and is distinguished by the celes-tial globe and the radius. In statues, the globe is sometimes placed in her hand, and sometimes on a column before her. Melpomene, the Muse of tragedy, was supposed to preside over melancholy subjects of all kinds. She is distinguished by the mask on her head.

In the Homeric poems, the Muses are the goddesses of song and poetry, and live on Olympos. There they sing the festive songs at the repasts of the immortals. At the funeral of Patroclus they sing lamentations.

The Muses were sometimes represented as dancing in chorus, to in-timate the near and indissoluble connection that exists between the liberal arts and sciences; but more generally appeared differently attired, and with symbols of their respective characters.

Their worship was universally established, particularly in the en-lightened parts of Greece, Thessaly, and Italy. Sacrifices were not offered to them, but no poet ever commenced his task without address-ing a solemn invocation to the Muses who preside over verse.

The sacred retreats of these divine sisters, from whose lips flowed the stream of song and sweet eloquence, were the celebrated mountains Parnassus, Pindus, and Helicon.

Mount Helicon is to Bœotia what Parnassus is to Phocis. The principal cities of that country are grouped about its sides; as the Phocian towns are connected with those of their own mountain; and as the mountain of Phocis could show upon its summit the Corycian Cave, which was dedicated to the Parnassian Nymphs, so upon the heights of the Bœotian hills were the favorite haunts of its own deities. Here flourished the grove of the Muses, whose statues stood beneath the shady recesses of these mountain glades; here flowed the sacred spring of Aganippe, round which the Muses danced; here was the clear source of Hippocrene, in which they bathed. The whole mountain was celebrated for its fresh rills, and cool groves, and flowery slopes; and while the legends connected with the other mountains of Greece were sometimes of a terrific and often of a stern and savage character, those which are produced, as it were, by the soil and scenery of Helicon, partook of the softness and amenity which distinguish the natural character of the mountain from which they sprang. Helicon had no Œdipus nor Pentheus.

Plutarch, in his treatise of Rivers and Mountains, cites from Hermesianax, the historian of Cyprus, the following legend, descriptive of the character of the two principal mountains which belong to the chain which encircles Bœotia: "Helicon and Cithæron were two brothers; but very different from each other in temper and character. The former was mild and courteous, and dutiful to his parents. Cithæron, on the other hand, was covetous and avaricious. He wished to obtain all the property of the family for himself. To gain this object he destroyed his father, and afterwards threw his brother by treachery down a precipice; but he himself, also, was carried over the cliff at the same time from the thrust with which he impelled his brother. After their death, by the will of the gods, these two brothers were changed into the two mountains which bore their names. Cithæron, by reason of his impiety, became the abode of the Furies; the Muses, on account of his gentle and affectionate disposition, chose Helicon as their favorite haunt."

The natural features of these two mountains are, as might be expected, in harmony with this mythological narrative. The dales and slopes of Helicon are clothed with groves of olives, walnut, and almond trees; clusters of ilex and arbutus deck its higher plains; and the oleander and myrtle fringe the banks of the numerous rills which gush from its soil, and stream in shining cascades down its declivities into the plain between it and the Copiac Lake.

One of the heights of Helicon is the Libethrian hill, where stood, in ancient times, a consecrated grove intersected by two fountains; beneath its shade were the statues of the goddesses, to whom it was ded-icated. Here, also, was the hallowed grotto of the Libethrian Nymphs. The site is now occupied by a monastery, about three miles to the south-west of Mazi, the modern village which stands very nearly upon the site of the ancient Haliartus.

On Helicon, according to ancient belief, no noxious herb was found. Here, also, the first Narcissus bloomed. The ground is luxuriantly decked with flowers, which diffuse around a delightful fragrance. It resounds with the industrious murmur of bees, and with the music of pastoral flutes, and the noise of waterfalls. Two of the sources which rise from its soil have acquired a celebrity unequalled by that of vast rivers. Not far from the site of the village of Ascra, the residence of Hesiod, which is five miles to the south of Haliartus, rises the spring of Aganippe ; the river of Permessus takes its rise at the same spot. Still further to the south is the fountain of Hippocrene, which springs from the soil above the valley of Marandali, shaded by pine trees planes, and hazels. Near this fountain Pausanias saw a very ancient copy of the Works and Days of the Bard of Ascra, written upon lead, which the inhabitants of Helicon, who showed it, maintained to be the only genuine production of that author.

At a monastery of St. Nicholas, a little to the north-east of Marandali, was recently found an inscription containing a catalogue of the victors in the Musea or Games in honor of the Muses, which proves that the grove consecrated to them, in which these games were celebrated, stood near the spot.

Pausanias enumerates the works of art existing in the place at the time in which he visited it, namely, in the age of the Antonines. Here, at that period, were the statues of the nine Muses, sculptured by three different artists : here stood a group consisting of Apollo, Mercury and Bacchos, contending for the lyre ; near them was an erect figure of Bacchos, one of the finest works of Myron ; here was a portrait of Eupheme, the nurse of the Muses. The statues of great poets adorned the same place ; here stood the ancient minstrel Linus ; near him was Thamyris, already blind, striking a broken lyre ; Arion riding his dolphin ; Hesiod with his harp upon his knees ; Orpheus surrounded with animals, attracted by the melody of his song, at that time stood under the shade of these trees ; but they have all now disappeared ; while the trees wave, the flowers bloom, and the streams flow as they did of yore.

Among the celestials, Apollo is most intimately associated with the Muses. He presides over the sister choir, when on Mount Parnassus they take their golden harps;

> "And with preamble sweet,
> Of charming symphony, they introduce
> Their sacred songs, and waken raptures high.
> No voice exempt; no voice but well could join
> Melodious part."

From thus presiding over and leading the choir of the Muses, he is represented by the plastic art of the ancients, clothed in a long, flowing robe; which, in olden times, was the festive attire of the bards.

Heracles also, under the name of Musagetes, was venerated by the ancients as a leader of the Muses. This fact will not surprise us, if we consider that, according to various writers, and principally Plato in his Republic, the science of harmony, together with wisdom and bodily strength, was the most desirable for a Greek; and therefore music, philosophy, and regular corporeal exercises, went hand in hand in the course of his education, in order to gain its three great ends, viz., to cultivate the heart, to unfold the mind, and to strengthen and direct the soul. Philosophy there was none in the days of Hercules; but in his person, music could be combined with strength, as both were found united in the person of Achilles.

The Muses were once challenged by the Sirens to a contest in singing; the former easily obtained the victory, and punished the arrogance of their rivals by plucking the feathers from their wings and wearing them on their own heads as a sign of superiority.

Upon an ancient monument, a Siren is represented from her waist upward as a beautiful maiden, and downward like a bird. On her shoulders are wings, and in her hand

she carries two flutes. She turns a mournful countenance towards a Muse, who, standing behind her, triumphantly holds in one hand the wing of the Siren, while with the other she plucks out the largest feathers.

Presumption and arrogance in the use of talents were always severely punished in ancient fictions. The Satyr Marsyas was flayed by Apollo for having ventured on a contest with that god, thinking to surpass the harp with his flute; and Thamyris, the Thracian bard, who, vain of his talents, both in music and poetry, presumed to challenge the daughters of Mnemosyne ; for which they punished him with blindness, and the loss of his lyre, or, in other words, his poetical ability.

The following explanation is given of the fable of Marsyas : " A strain of poetry stretched beyond its due limits turns to a strain of madness ; the soft voice of native music, which, when the mind is in its natural state, breathes nothing but harmony and love, if raised to an unnatural pitch, racks the laboring, unburdened breast, and breaks loose in rage and foaming ecstasy. Wild looks, amazing postures, and soul-rending sounds, commonly ushered the furious, dithyrambic song ; and when heightened by wine and processional worship, were as so many steps that led to the tortured bacchanal state, of tossing and roaring.

" In this condition, the beautiful order, the divine harmony of the breast is defaced ; the delicate economy of the passions reversed ; dissonance and torture rack the distorted soul, and wretched Marsyas, the rival of music (the disorderly din of the passions, the wild shout of joy, or the piercing yell of grief), is inevitably seized, first whipped by Minerva, the goddess of wisdom, and next hung upon a tree and flayed alive by Apollo. It was not long, however, before Apollo repented of his cruelty ; the passions soon subside ; the mind retires by degrees to its natural, harmonious state, and the strings of his lyre, which, in the bitterness of remorse, he had thrown away, were gathered up by the Muses (the mild powers of measure and invention), who, that they might not be again obnoxious to the like disaster, added the middle string, the chord that makes music sedate ; that prevents the elastic leaps, the irregular bounds, the dissonance and disproportion that set the passions in an uproar, and pour madness and misery into the human soul.

" We have but little conception of the ancient power over the heart-melting art. To a delicate ear, the sound can hardly be formed that does not bear a relation to some passion, or some inward sentiment,

and this fable, though so apposite and expressive, is a beautiful specimen of ancient mythology but little understood."

HEBE.

Hebe, the goddess of youth, was daughter of Zeus and Hera. She was employed
by her mother to prepare her chariot, and
harness her peacocks, whenever requisite,
and was cup-bearer to all the gods.

Fable says, that Zeus dismissed her from
this office, declaring her to be unworthy of
it, because, on one occasion, when handing
nectar to the gods, she, by a fall, violated
that gracefulness which must accompany
every motion and gesture of the attendants
at the table of Olympos.

She was superseded by Ganymedes (*Joy-promoter*), a son of Tros, and
a great-grandson of Dardanos, the founder of Troy. The poets say, "he
was the handsomest of mortal men;" and on account of his beauty,
the gods took him from the earth, that in Olympos he might reach
the nectar cup to Jove; henceforth partaking of the constant society
of the immortals. In the shape of his eagle, the Thunderer carried
away his favorite from the top of Mount Ida, softly bearing him in his
crooked talons from earth upward to the sky. In this charming fiction, consoling Fancy veiled the loss of the youth, who, in the prime of
life and beauty, could scarcely be thought mortal; and therefore his
vanishing from the earth was explained as a removal to the seat of the
celestials.

The fictions respecting the favorites of the gods, gain a peculiar charm
by a kind of dim and melancholy twilight in which they are veiled.
Whenever youth and beauty became the prey of death, some deity was
said to have removed her favorite from the earth. In this manner,
mourning was mingled with joy; and lamentations for the departed
were mitigated. These fictions, therefore, are most frequently represented upon ancient marble coffins.

When Heracles was translated to the skies, and raised to the rank
of a god, Hebe was given to him in marriage—a beautiful fiction, by
which the venerated sun-god was united to immortal youth.

Hebe, the personification of youth, had the power of restoring gods and men to youth, and, at the instance of her husband, performed that kind office to his friend Iolaos. She was worshipped at Sicyon under the name of Dia, and at Rome under the name of Juventas. Hebe is represented as a young virgin, crowned with flowers, and arrayed in a variegated garment. Sometimes she holds the nectar cup ; at others, the eagle stands by her side, which she is in the act of caressing.

PROTEUS.

Proteus, a sea-deity, was considered by some as a son of Oceanos and Tethys; by others, as a son of Poseidon and Phœnice.

Homer introduces him in the fourth book of the Odyssey, styling him a Sea-elder, and gives him the power of foretelling the future. He also calls him Egyptian, or servant of Neptune, and says that his office was to keep the seals, or sea-calves, belonging to the Ruler of the waves.

Proteus could assume any form at pleasure, changing himself into fire or water, plant or animal, which rendered him difficult of access ; and sometimes, when consulted, evaded an answer by a sudden metamorphosis. To those only who held him fast with vigorous arms, did he appear in his real character, and by his spirit of divination reveal to them the truth.

By some he is supposed to represent the various forms and shapes assumed by primitive matter, the substance itself ever remaining the same. Others, who would deduce all fable from history, suppose that he represents the various ensigns used by the kings of Egypt.

Plato, laughing, makes him an emblem of the quackish sophists ; Lucian, of the players; Eustathius, of flatterers; Cassiodorus, of traitors ; and St. Austin makes him the emblem of truth, which perhaps is the best explanation ; for, with this view of it, the allegory of Proteus is of deep philosophical import. The constant versatility of the human heart, now impelled by some praiseworthy emotion, and now by some evil impulse, its fluctuations of thought, of passion, and of purpose, is aptly represented by the ever-changing nature which is the peculiar characteristic of Proteus.

The changeable character of Proteus was more easily managed by the poets (who could describe him in all his various shapes, with the transition from one to another), than by the artists, who could exhibit him only in his own form, or in some one alone of all his transmutations. Of all the poets, Virgil has described him the most fully. He gives the character of his person and the description of his cave, with his sea-herds about him. He represents him as tending them on shore; as plunging himself into the sea; and as riding over its sur-face. He marks out, briefly indeed, but in a picturesque manner, the whole series of this changeable deity's transmutations.

JANUS.

The worship of Janus must be ascribed to the Etruscans, by whom he was regarded as the inspector of Heaven, and therefore of all trans-actions. An image of the god with four faces came from Valerii to Rome, which is supposed to have reference to the four regions of Heaven.

In Italy he was usually represented with two faces, one before and one behind, and hence called Bifrons and Biceps. Sometimes he is represented with four faces, and then called Quadrifrons. There was an ancient statue of this deity in the Forum, said to be as old as the time of Numa, of which the fingers were so formed that those of one hand represented three hundred (CCC), those of the other fifty-five (LV), the number of the days of the ancient lunar year. All this is explicable on the supposition of Janus being the sun, the author of the year, with its seasons, months, and days.

Janus was invoked at the commencement of most actions ; even in the worship of the other gods the votary began by offering wine and incense to Janus. The first month in the year was named from him ; and under the title of Matutinus he was regarded as the opener of the day. Hence he had charge of the gates of Heaven, and hence, too, all gates, *Januæ*, were called after him, and supposed to be under his care. Hence, perhaps, it was, that he was represented with a staff and key, and that he was named the Opener (*Patulcius*), and the Shutter (*Clu-sius*).

The Janus Geminus, or Janus Quirinus, was the celebrated gate (not temple) which stood on the way leading from the Palatine Quir-inal, and which was to be open in time of war, and shut in time of peace. To understand this much mistaken subject (for nothing is more common than to speak of opening or shutting the *temple* of Janus). we must go back to the early days of Rome.

The original Rome lay on and about the Palatine, while a Sabine colony had settled on the Quirinal, whose town was probably the origi-nal Quires or Cures, and the gate of Rome on that side was naturally

named the Quirine Gate—Janus Quirinus. Further, the Roman gates
were always double, that is, consisting of two arches, by one of which
people went in, while they passed out by the other ; hence this was
called a Janus Geminus. The relation of this gate to war and peace,
seems not so much a tradition of ancient usage, as a fiction of the times
when Rome was engaged in ceaseless warfare, which certainly was not
her condition in the early days of the republic.

The temples of Janus Quadrifrons were built with four equal sides,
each side containing a door and three windows. The doors were emblematic of the four seasons, and the windows of the three months
belonging to each.

The origin of Janus may be traced back to the mythology of India.
Janus, with his wife and sister Camasane, half fish and half human
being, as sometimes represented, can only be explained by a comparison with the avatars, the descents or incarnations of the Hindu deities.
Viewed in another way, the name Janus or Djanus assimilates itself
very closely to that of Diana. These two appellations resolve themselves into the simple form Dia, or the goddess by way of excellence ;
and this Dia belongs in common to the religions of Samothrace and
Attica. She is the Pelasgic Ceres, frequently found under this denomination in the songs of the Fratres Arvales.

While the Jupiter of Dodona was penetrating into Italy and Latium,
with his spouse Dione (the same as Juno), Dia-Diana and Janus arrived.
by another route, in Etruria, from the borders of Pontus and the isle
of Samothrace. From this view of the subject it would appear that
Jupiter and Janus were originally distinct from each other, but subsequently more or less amalgamated. The system of Dodona and that
of Samothrace, the Latin system and that of the Etrurians, based on
ideas mutually analogous, united, but did not become completely
blended with each other.

On the soil of Italy, Janus appears at one time as a king of ancient
days, at another as a hero who had rendered his name conspicuous by
great labors and by religious institutions ; at another again as a god
of nature. At first he is called the Heavens on the Etrurian doctrine.
He is the year personified, and his symbols contain an allusion either
to the number of months or to that of the days of the year. The
month of January, called after him, formed, from the time of Numa,
the commencement of the religious year of the Romans. On the first
day of this month, an offering consisting of wines and fruits was pre-

sented to Janus, and called the Janual. On this same day the image of the god was crowned with laurel, the consul ascended in solemn procession to the capitol, and friends made presents to one another.

By virtue of his title, God of Nature, Janus is represented as holding a key: he holds this as a god who presides over gates and openings. He opens the course of the year in the heavens; and every gate upon earth, even to those of private dwellings, is supposed to be under his superintending care. This attribute, indeed, is given him in a sense of a more or less elevated nature. It designates him at one time as the genius who presides over the productions of the year, and dispenses them to mortals; who holds the key of fertilizing sources, of refreshing streams. At another time it typifies him as the master and sovereign of nature in general; the guardian of the universe, of the heaven, earth, and sea. As holder of the key, Janus took the name of Clusius; as charged with the care of the world, he is styled Curiatius.

Thus, under these and similar points of view, Janus reveals himself to us as exactly similar to the gods of the year in the Egyptian, Persian, and Phœnician mythologies. Like Osiris, Sem Heracles, Dschemschid, and others, he represents the year personified in its development through the twelve signs of the zodiac, with its exaltation and its fall, and with all the plenitude of its gifts. And, as the career of the year is also that of the souls which traverse in their migrations the constellations of the zodiac, Janus, as well as the other great gods of nature, becomes the guide of souls. Similar in every respect to Osiris-Serapis, like him, he is called the *Sun;* and the gate of the east, as well as that of the west, becomes at once his peculiar care. Janus also assimilates himself to the Persian Mithras, and becomes the mediator between mortals and immortals. He bears the prayers of men to the feet of the great deities.

His representation of two faces has various explanations. Similar figures with a double face are found on medals of Etruria, Syracuse, and Athens. Cecrops, for example, was so represented; and in every case, it is rational to suppose that it was purely allegorical. It recalls to mind the figures, no less strange and significant, of the Hindu divinities: Janus with four faces is identical in appearance with the Brahma of India.

As the gods who preside over nature and the year, in the oriental systems, raise themselves to the higher offices of gods of time, eternity, and infinity, so it seems to have been with the western Janus. He is called the inspector of time, and Time itself: in a cosmogonical sense, he passes for Chaos. Under these two points of view, he is distinct from Jupiter, the supreme ruler, and the universal regulator of things, inasmuch as Janus had especially under his control the beginning and the end. In the higher doctrine, however, all distinction between the two disappears. As *Clusius*, or bearer of the key, Janus was the monarch of the universe, and Greece had no divinity that could be at all compared with him.

In the solemn ceremonies and religious songs of the old Romans, he figured as inaugurator, and even bore the name. At the festivals of the great gods, he had the first sacrifices offered to him. He was also called the Father, and the Salii invoked him in their hymns to the god of gods. This god of gods they named Janes or Eanus, while they assumed the name of Janes or Eani, in accordance with the ancient usage which so often assimilated the priests to their divinities.

As Janus presided over the beginning of every year, the people offered sacrifices to him on the first day of the year. The priests offered sacrifices on twelve altars, as to the beginner of twelve months, and prayed to him at the commencement of every day. The sacrifices offered consisted of cakes, barley, incense and wine.

On new-year's day, which was the principal festival of the god, people took care that all they thought, said, and did, was pure and favorable, since every thing was considered as ominous for the occurrences of the whole year. Hence the people wore festive garments, abstained from cursing and quarreling, saluted all they met with kind words, exchanged presents, and performed some part of what they intended to do in the course of the year.

The presents consisted of sweet-meats, such as gilt dates, figs, honey cakes, and copper coins showing on one side the double head of Janus, and on the other a ship.

ASCLEPIOS OR ÆSCULAPIUS.

The first beginning of medical science was likewise considered by the ancients as something divine, and its possessor and practiser as worthy of veneration. He who first applied medical art was looked upon, even after his death, as a beneficent human being, to whom the sick would not address their prayers in vain.

Æsculapius was the son of Apollo and Coronis, the daughter of a Thessalian king. By his father he was committed to the care of the wise Centaur, Cheiron, who taught him Botany, together with the secret efficacy of plants. By means of this information, Æsculapius became the benefactor of mankind, applying the various remedies that he had learned to the diseases which afflict mankind.

And so successful was he in the practice of the art, that fiction speaks of him as having awakened the dead. Pluto, the ever-destroying power, considering this an encroachment on his rights, complained before the throne of Jupiter, of the awaker from the dead as a daring criminal. Jupiter then punished the second great benefactor of mankind, as he had done the first (Prometheus), by hurling lightnings upon his innocent head. He who had assuaged the pains of men, and healed their diseases, thus became himself a victim of his beneficent art.

After his death, groves, temples, and altars were consecrated to him; but Epidaurus, in Greece, was the principal seat of honor. His sons.

Machaon and Podaleirios, were heroes and leaders in the Trojan war, and, at the same time, renowned for their skill in medical art.

The snake, as an emblem of recovery and health, was sacred to Asclepios, probably because of its renewing itself, as it were, by casting its skin. Hence the god of medicine always carries a staff, around which is twined a snake. The figure of a little boy is sometimes found with that of Asclepios, wearing a bonnet on his head, and entirely muffled in a cloak. His name is Telesphoros; and his infant form, together with his usual covering, seems to allude, in a certain manner, to his convalescence, as well as the mysterious art of his master.

Of his four daughters, Hygeia, Ægle, Panacea, and Iaso, Hygeia was the most celebrated. To her, divine honors were paid; and her occupation, like that of her father, was the preservation of health. This benefit she distributes among mortals as a mild gift, whenever she descends from the higher regions to earth. She is represented with a snake eating out of a flat cup which she holds in her hand.

The temples of Asclepios were regarded as sanctuaries which none of the profane could approach without repeated purifications; and the statue of Hygeia at Ægrium, in Achaia, could only be viewed by the priests. The temple at Tithorea was surrounded by a hedge in the vicinity of which no edifice could be erected. This hedge was forty stadia from the building itself.

The worship rendered to Asclepios had for its object the diversion of the sick, by the ceremonies of which they were the witnesses.

COMUS.

Comus, the god of gay humor and merry jests, the genius of life's cheerful enjoyment, was considered by the ancients as worthy of a place among divine beings. He presided at banquets, and in general at all social feasts.

In allusion to his midnight revelries, he is represented with heavy head, and drowsy mien, bearing in his hand a half-extinguished torch.

HYMEN OR HYMENÆUS

Hymen, the god of marriage, is represented as wearing a wreath of roses round his head, and carrying in one hand the nuptial torch, and in the other holding a veil. At every nuptial feast hymns were chanted to his honor, and his presence hallowed the sacred union, as well as the joys of the wedding feast.

The names originally designated the bridal song, which was subsequently personified.

PLUTUS.

Plutus, the personification of wealth, is represented as son of Jason and Ceres. By many mythologists he has been confounded with Pluto, though plainly distinguished from him as being the god of riches. He was reared by the goddess of peace, and on that account, Pax was represented at Athens as holding the god of wealth in her lap. The ancients represented him as blind, and as bestowing his favors indiscriminately on the good and bad. He appears as an actor in the comedy of Aristophanes, called after his name, and also bears a part in the Timon of Lucian.

The popular belief among the ancients assigned him a place in the subterranean regions of Spain, a country famed for its precious metals. Phædrus relates, in one of his fables, that when Hercules was received into Heaven, and was saluting the gods who thronged around with their congratulations, he turned aside when Plutus drew near, assigning to Jupiter as a reason when he inquired into the cause of this strange conduct, that he hated Plutus, because he was a friend to the bad, and moreover corrupted both good and bad with his gifts.

LIBERTAS.

Liberty was a goddess of ancient Rome, to whom a temple was consecrated on the Aventine Hill by T. Gracchus, and improved and adorned with many admirable statues and brazen columns by Pollio, and in which was also a gallery for the deposit of the public acts of the state.

This goddess was commonly represented in the figure of a woman in white robes, holding a rod in one hand, and a cap in the other. The cap, according to Valerius Maximus and other ancient writers, was a badge of liberty used on all occasions. It, as well as the rod or wand, referred to the custom of the Romans giving slaves their freedom. In the performance of that ceremony, the rod was held by the magistrate, and the cap by the slave, even for some period previous. Sometimes a cat is found placed at the feet of the deity, this animal being ver fond of liberty, and impatient when confined.

The statues of Liberty were numerous among the ancients, as was also the personification on medals. Of the former kind, that in the Aventine temple, before alluded to, was a conspicuous instance. It had the head crowned, and a sceptre in one hand, while the other held the cap. The emblems of liberty are more particularly met with upon the medals of Galba, and the reason appears to be, that, on the death of that infamous hero, the citizens were full of hope that the republic would be restored, and were seen running in all directions through the streets, decorated with the cap of liberty.

One of Galba's coins presents the figure of this goddess in an attitude somewhat uncommon. She is represented as standing between two ears of corn, lifting up her hands towards Heaven. This is typical of an exhortation to the people to give themselves to the cultivation of agriculture, since the execrable tyrant was dead. who had desolated the face of the country.

TERMINUS.

Terminus was worshipped at Rome, as the guardian of landmarks. His statue was a rude stone or post set in the ground to distinguish boundaries.

When Tarquinius Priscus wished to build a temple to Jupiter on the Tarpeian rock, it was necessary to remove the altars of the deities who already occupied the summit. The assent of each deity was sought by the augurs, and Terminus alone refused to go. His altar, therefore. always stood in the temple.

He was represented with a human form without feet or arms, to in timate that he never moved.

There was an annual festival observed at Rome, in the month of February, in honor of Terminus, called Terminalia.

It was then usual for peasants to assemble near the principal landmarks which separated their fields, and after they had crowned them with garlands and flowers, they made libations of milk and wine, and sacrificed a young pig. This festival was originally established by Numa. Shedding the blood of victims was at first forbidden, but in after times the landmarks were plentifully sprinkled with it.

His worship is said to have been instituted by Numa, who ordered that every one
should mark the boundaries of his landed
property by stones consecrated to Jupiter,
and at which sacrifices were to be offered at
the festival of the Terminalia. These sacred boundaries existed not only in regard
to private property, but also in regard to
the state itself, the boundary of which was
not to be transgressed by any foreign foe.
In later times the latter must have fallen
into oblivion, while the Termini of private
property retained their sacred character,
even in the days of Dionysius, who states
that sacrifices of cakes and meal still continued.

The god Terminus, himself, appears to
have been no other than Jupiter, in the
capacity of protector of boundaries. As
has been previously stated, Mercury became with the Romans the god Terminus.

PALES.

Pales, a Roman divinity of flocks and shepherds, is described by
some as a male divinity, and by others as a female. Hence some
modern writers have inferred that Pales was a combination of both
sexes ; but this is altogether foreign to the religion of the Romans.
Some of the rites performed at the Palilia, the festival of Pales, would
seem to indicate that the divinity was of a female character ; but there
are other reasons for believing that Pales was a male divinity.

The name seems to be connected with Palatinus, the centre of all
the earliest legends of Rome, and the god himself was with the Romans the embodiment of the same idea as the Pan among the Greeks.

The festival called Palilia was celebrated on the twenty-first of April,
and was regarded as the day on which Rome was founded. The shepherds, on the Palilia, lustrated their flocks by burning sulphur, and
making fires of olive, pine, and other substances. Milk, with cakes
made of millet, was the sacrifice offered to Pales Prayers were made

to him to avert disease from the cattle, and to bless them with fecundity and abundance of food. Fires of straw were kindled in a row,
and the rustics leaped thrice through them : the blood of a horse, the
ashes of a calf, and bean stalks, were used for purification.

FLORA.

Flora, the goddess of flowers, is represented as a young and handsome female, whose head is crowned with a chaplet, and whose robe is
decorated with garlands of flowers. She was supposed to be the wife
of the handsome god Zephyrus.

Flora was an ancient Italian deity, being one of those said to have
been worshipped by Tatius. Her festival, celebrated at the end of
April and beginning of May, was termed Floralia.

VERTUMNUS OR VORTUMNUS.

Vertumnus was a very distinguished Etruscan god, whom the old
Volscinian settlers at Rome established as their chief deity.

The changeable form given him by the poets relates to much of life
and the fruits of the year. He is represented of various appearance,
perhaps from the fulness and changeableness of the gifts of the seasons.
Etruscan art represents him like Bacchus. The garden growth of the
spring, and the crops of summer, are under his protection ; he especially presides over autumn and its blessings. Wine and fruit are
considered as his peculiar gifts.

The Vertumnalia were celebrated by the whole people on the twenty-
third of August. Ceres and Pomona were combined with Vertumnus ;
and though in Rome a demi-god, in Etruria he was doubtless the great
and mighty god of the seasons.

POMONA.

Pomona, the wife of Vertumnus, was a Roman goddess, who presided
over fruit trees. Her worship was of long standing at Rome, where
there was a Flamen Pomonalis, who sacrificed to her every year for
the preservation of the fruit.

The story of Pomona and Vertumnus is prettily told by Ovid. This
Hamadryad lived in the time of Procrus, king of Alba. She was devoted to the culture of gardens, to which she confined herself, shunning

all society with the male deities. Vertumnus, among others, was enamored of her, and under various shapes tried to win her hand; sometimes he appeared as a reaper, sometimes as a haymaker, and again as
a ploughman or a vine-dresser: he also became a soldier and a fisherman, but to as little purpose. At length, under the guise of an old
woman, he won the confidence of the goddess; and by enlarging on
the evils of a single life, and the blessings of a wedded state, by launch-
ing out into the praises of Vertumnus, and relating a tale of the punishment of female cruelty to a lover, he sought to move the heart of
Pomona; and then, resuming his real form, he obtained the hand of
the no longer reluctant nymph.

Vertumnus was connected with the transformation of plants, and
their progress from blossom to fruit; hence the story of his having
assumed various forms to gain the love of Pomona, and at last, that of
a blooming youth.

Pomona is represented as in the prime of youth and beauty, decorated with the blossoms of fruit trees, and at the same time bearing a
branch in her hands loaded with fruits

FERONIA.

Feronia was an inferior goddess, or guardian deity of woods and
groves, and was worshipped with great solemnity both by the Sabines
and Latins, but more particularly the former.

It is related that when a grove near Mount Soracte, in Etruria, which
was sacred to her, took fire, the inhabitants of the adjacent country
hastened to rescue the statue from the flames; but the goddess inter-
posed, and immediately restored the grove to its former verdure.

She had also a temple, grove, and fount, near Anxur, and in this
temple manumitted slaves went through certain formalities to complete
their freedom; such as cutting off and consecrating their hair, and
placing upon the head a pileus, or cap.

Flowers and first-fruits were the offerings made to Feronia.

VICTORIA.

Victory attended the conquests of all countries and all heroes. In
Italy and Greece she had temples and statues. At Rome, Sylla instituted festivals in her honor; and in the temple of Jupiter, on the Cap-

itoline Hill, a golden statue of the goddess was placed, weighing three hundred and twenty pounds. A thunderbolt having fallen upon the statue and broken its wings, Pompey restored the courage of the people, who were depressed by the circumstance, by crying, " Romans ! The gods have broken the wings of Victory ; henceforth she can never escape from us."

Victory is generally represented with wings, and almost in the attitude of flying, with her robe as carried back by the wind. As the reward of conquerors, she holds in her hand a crown of laurel, which, with the palm branch and a trophy, were her general attributes. Her wings and robe are described as white. She is sometimes seen hovering between two fighting armies, as doubtful which to choose; and sometimes standing fixed to the army she is resolved to favor.

On the medals of Roman families which had their name from her, she is represented as drawn by two horses. A picture at Rome exhibits her as ascending to Heaven in a chariot drawn by four horses, as she appears on the Antonine pillar carrying up the hero. The trophy was a proper mark for her at Rome, as there was one or more before the door of every officer who had gained any advantage over his enemies.

FORTUNA.

Fortune, that unseen power, supposed to exercise such arbitrary dominion over human affairs, was also deified, and she had her temples and altars in Greece. By Hesiod and by one of the Homerids, she is classed among the Ocean nymphs. Pindar speaks of her as the child of Zeus Eleutherios ; elsewhere he says that she is one of the Destinies. Alcman calls her the sister of Law and Persuasion, and daughter of Forethought.

From her hands were supposed to be received riches and poverty, blessings and pains, pleasures and misfortunes. She was deified by the Romans, and in Bœotia she had a statue, represented as holding Plutus in her arms, to intimate that Fortune is the source whence wealth and honors flow. She is represented blindfold, and her hand resting on a wheel to intimate her inconstancy.

Fortune was also thought to direct the events of human life. But Juvenal speaks of her as blind, Horace as inconstant and delighting in mischief, and Statius as unjust. Cybele, on an antique gem, turns her head away from Fortune, and in the attitude of rejecting. She is represented by Ovid as standing on a wheel, but more generally with wings, and a wheel by her side. Sometimes with a wheel only, to show that she presided over the expeditions of the emperors and their happy return. She is then called on the medals *Fortuna redux*. Her usual attributes are the cornucopia, as the giver of riches, and the rudder in her hand often rested on a globe as the directress of all worldly affairs.

The inconsistent character of this goddess caused several distinctions. The Romans had a good and bad, a constant and inconstant Fortune According to Horace, the *bona Fortuna* is dressed in a rich habit; and the *mala Fortuna* in a poor one. *Fortuna manens*, or the constant Fortune, is without wings, and sitting in a stately posture. She has a horse as an animal of swiftness, which she holds by the bridle. Inconstant Fortune is winged, as ready to fly away. Horace speaks of both as deserving the favor of one, and as being above the power of the other.

The Fortune worshipped at Antium seems to have been of the most exalted character among the Romans. In a solemn procession to her honor, alluded to by Horace, the statue of Necessity was carried before her, and after her, those of Hope and Fidelity.

FORTITUDO.

Fortitude, a deification of courage and bravery, was one of the moral deities of the Romans, whose worship is enjoined in the laws of the twelve tables.

Upon a common medal of Hadrian, Fortitude is represented with an erect air, resting on a spear with one hand, and holding a sword in the other. She has a globe under her feet, to show that the Romans were to conquer the world. From their military disposition, they gave Fortitude the name of Virtue, or *the virtue*, by way of excellence ; by which they understood not only military courage, but a firmness of mind and love of action ; a steady readiness to do good, and a patient endurance of all evil. Cicero speaks of Virtus and Fortitudo as the same, and of both as including a love of action.

VERITAS.

Truth is said to be the parent of Justice and Virtue. The great Apelles has represented her, in his painting of Calumny, under the appearance of a modest female. In her hand is placed a round mirror.

Ancient poets say that she was for a long time hidden from the world at the bottom of a well ; but on one occasion leaving its quiet,

19

she was so frightened at the reception she met with, that she returned immediately to her hiding-place. According to Democritus, this is intended to intimate the difficulty with which she is discovered.

VIRTUS.

Virtue, daughter of Truth, and the Roman personification of manly valor, is represented clothed in white, as an emblem of purity; sometimes holding a sceptre, at others crowned with laurel. In some instances she is represented with wings, and placed upon a block of marble, to intimate her immovable firmness.

Virtus is spoken of personally, both in verse and prose. She had several temples at Rome containing representations of her, and her figure is common on the medals of the Emperors.

Mr. Spence thinks her figure more common than is imagined, and that in the Admiranda, what Bartoli takes to be the genius of Rome, is this goddess; as where she is giving the globe to M. Aurelius, guiding the chariot of Titus, and conducting Adrian home. On these she is habited like an Amazon. She is sometimes in a coat of mail, or a short vest, with her legs bare like the Roman soldiers. She has a manly face and air, and generally grasps a sword or a spear. Her dress shows her readiness for action, and her look a firmness not to be conquered by difficulties and dangers.

HONOS.

The personification of honor was worshipped as a virtue at Rome, and her first temple was erected by Scipio Africanus, and another afterwards was built by Claudius Marcellus. An augur having warned Marcellus that these two divinities would not dwell in the circumference of the same temple, he built two distinct edifices; but to arrive at the temple of Honor it was necessary to pass through that of Virtue.

The emblems of this goddess are, the crown of laurel, the lance, and the horn of plenty; though she is sometimes represented with the olive branch of peace instead of arms, which she gives as the reward of bravery. We find her personified on several medals of Galba and Vitellius.

PAX.

Peace, the daughter of Jupiter and Themis, wears a crown of laurel; in her hand is a branch of the olive tree, and by her side the statue of Plutus, to intimate that peace gives rise to prosperity and opulence.

Venus and the Graces were her companions, and an altar was erected to her at Athens; but at Rome, where the goddess of war was peculiarly honored, several altars were dedicated to Peace. One of the most magnificent was raised by Vespasian, after the war of Judea, and contained all the treasures taken from the temple at Jerusalem, consisting of a splendid library, busts, statues, and pictures, as well as a large collection of natural curiosities.

This temple was consumed in the reign of Commodus, previous to which it was customary for men of learning to assemble there, and even to deposit their most valuable writings as a place of safety; and consequently the loss which occurred when it was consumed, could scarcely be estimated.

FIDELITAS.

Fidelity, the goddess of honesty, was one of the moral deities of the Romans, who presided over the virtues of men, and the conduct of human life. This deity was one of those to whose honor the Romans were enjoined, in the laws of the twelve tables, to erect altars.

She was represented with an erect and open air, and clad in a thin, transparent dress. The poets called her blameless and incorruptible, and the companion and sister of Justice. They also at times represent her as grey-headed and very old, but not so in her figures as found on antique medals.

Two hands joined together are the emblems of faith given and received, and she is represented as offering her hand; and sometimes as two hands conjoined, as on medals of Marcus Antoninus, Vespasian, Titus, and others. Again she is portrayed as holding in one hand a patera, and in the other a horn of plenty, a caduceus, an eagle, or some other symbol. The inscriptions on these antique medals are generally *fides publica, fides senatus, fides Romanorum, fides exercitus,* etc., etc.

Her priests were dressed in white during her public ceremonies; but no victims were sacrificed upon her altar, because she was deemed inflexible, and unyielding to prayers, however urgent.

FELICITAS.

Felicity was a symbolical moral deity of the Greeks and Romans. She was the goddess of happiness, prosperity, or blissfulness, and a personification of one of those moral beings by whose aid the ancients supposed mortals obtained a place in the heavens, and to whose honor the Romans were enjoined, in the laws of the twelve tables, to erect altars.

There is scarcely a virtue or a blessing of life, but what is represented on the medals of the emperors; and this minor divinity is represented by the ancient artists and poets, with the caduceus of Mercury in one hand, and the cornucopia in the other, as emblems of peace and prosperity, the two chief ingredients of happiness. In the hymn to Mercury, attributed to Homer, Apollo designates the caduceus as the sceptre of felicity and riches. Horace speaks of her under the name of Faustitas, and hints that she prefers dwelling in the country to residing in cities.

According to Pliny, Lucullus, on his return from the war with Mithridates, proposed to erect a statue to Felicity from the chisel of Arcesilaus, but both died before its completion. Julius Cæsar also intended to erect a temple in honor of this divine protectress in the square of his palace in front of the Caria Hostilia, but it was finished by Lepidus. There were also other temples to her honor in Rome, one of which (that erected by Claudius) was reduced to ashes in a conflagration.

AMICITIA.

Friendship, the Greeks represented clothed in a clasped garment, her head bare, her dress open near the heart, holding in the left hand an elm, around which a vine is clinging, filled with clusters of grapes.

At Rome she was represented as a young maiden with a white robe, her bosom partially covered, her head adorned with myrtle and pomegranate flowers intermixed. On the border of her tunic was written "Death and Life"—on her front, "Summer and Winter." Her side was open and the heart visible, bearing these words, "Far and near."

In Homer we meet a number of moral qualities, to which he gives personality. Terror and Fear, the children of Ares, and Strife, his sister, in connection with him, rouse the Trojans to battle. Strife is said to be small at first, but at last to raise her head to Heaven. By Zeus she is sent forth amidst the Achæans, bearing the signal of war; and standing on the ship of Odysseus in the centre of the fleet, shouts so as to be heard at either extremity. When Ares hears of the death of his son Ascalaphos, Terror and Fear are commanded to yoke the steeds to his car for war.

Prayers, says Homer, are the daughters of great Zeus, lame and wrinkled, with squinting eyes. (*Il.* ix. 502.) They follow Ate (*Mischief*), and tend those whom she has injured ; but Ate is strong and firm-footed, and gets far before them, afflicting men, whom they afterwards heal. Elsewhere he relates that Ate is the daughter of Zeus, who *injures* all ; that her feet are tender, and that she therefore does not walk on the ground, but on the heads of men. Having con spired with Hera to deceive her father, he took her by the hair and flung her to earth, with an oath that she should never return to Olympos.

The Theogony of Hesiod contains a number of these personified qualities ; they also occur in the subsequent poets. Thus Æschylus introduces on the stage Strength and Force. Sophocles, by a very beautiful and correct figure, terms Fame " the child of golden Hope ;" and to this personification the Athenians erected an altar, as they did also to Shame, Impetuosity, and Mercy.

The more stern Spartans erected temples to Fear, Death, and Laugh- ter. But in the deification of the moral qualities, the Italian religion far exceeded that of Greece.

" From having a different creed of our own, and always encountering the Heathen Mythology in a poetical, fabulous shape, we are apt to have a false idea of the religious feelings of the ancients. We are in the habit of supposing that they regarded their fables in the same po- etical light as ourselves ; that they could not possibly put faith in Ju- piter, Neptune, and Pluto ; in the sacrifice of innocent turtle doves. the libation of wine, and the notions about Tartarus and Ixion.

" The greatest pleasure arising to a modern imagination from the ancient mythology, is a mingled sense of the old popular belief, and of the philosophical refinements upon it. We take Apollo, and Mercury. and Venus, as shapes that existed in popular credulity ; as the greater fairies of the ancient world ; and we regard them at the same time as personifications of all that is beautiful and genial in the forms and ten- dencies of creation. But the result, coming as it does, too, through avenues of beautiful poetry, both ancient and modern, is so entirely cheerful, that we are apt to think it wanted gravity to more believing eyes. Every forest, to the mind's eye of a Greek, was haunted with superior intelligences. Every stream had its presiding nymph, who was thanked for her draught of water. Every house had its protecting god, which had blessed the inmate's ancestors, and would bless him also if he cultivated the social affections; for the same word which ex-pressed piety towards the gods, expressed love towards relations and friends. If in all this there was nothing but the worship of a more graceful humanity, there may be worships much worse as well as better.

" Imagine the feelings with which an ancient believer must have gone by the oracular oaks of Dodona, or the calm groves of the Eumenides, or the fountain where Proserpina vanished under ground with Pluto ; or the laurelled mountain, Parnassus, on the side of which was the tem-ple of Delphi, where Apollo was supposed to be present in person. Imagine Plutarch, a devout, and yet a liberal believer, when he went to study theology and philosophy at Delphi : with what feelings must he not have passed along the woody paths of the hill, approaching nearer every instant to the presence of divinity, and not sure that a glance of light through the trees was not the lustre of the god himself going by ! This is mere poetry to us, and very fine it is ; but to him it was po-etry, and religion, and beauty, and gravity, and hushing awe, and a path as from one world to another."

Leigh Hunt.

"Oh ! ye delicious fables, where the wave
 And wood were peopled ; and the air, with things
So lovely—why, ah ! why has science grave
 Scatter'd afar your secret imaginings ?
Why sear'd the delicate flowers that genius gave,
 And dash'd the diamond drops from Fancy's wings ?
Alas ! the spirit languishes, and lies
At mercy of life's dull realities.

No more, by well or bubbling fountain clear,
 The Naiad dries her tresses in the sun,
Nor longer may we in the branches hear
 The Dryad talk, nor see the Oread run
Along the mountains, nor the Nereid steer
 Her way among the waves when day is done.
Shadows nor shapes remain"——

Barry Cornwall.

PART FOURTH.

DEMI-GODS AND HEROES.

DEMI-GODS AND HEROES.

In the assembly of the gods, Jupiter is represented as ruling supreme. He frowns, and Olympus trembles; he smiles, and the sky brightens. But heaven is not his only theatre of action; enveloping his deity in illusive forms, he descends to earth to propagate his power in a race of heroes.

From his seat on high, he descends to Danaë in the form of a golden shower, and the valiant Perseus springs forth; who, with powerful arm, subdues monsters.

In the form of Amphitryon he appears to Alcmena, and makes her the mother of Hercules.

With the majestic neck of a swan, he clings to Leda for protection, and she becomes the mother of the magnanimous Pollux, and the god-like Helena, the most beautiful woman that earth ever produced.

In the strength of a mettled bull, he invites the virgin Europa to mount his back, and carries her through the floods of the sea to the shores of Crete, where she brings forth Minos, the wise and powerful law-giver of nations.

In these fictions all nature is deified; even animals are considered as sacred beings. Thus nothing mean or abject lies in the idea of representing the supreme divinity in any form that is offered by all-comprising nature. As the wind stirs up the quiet sea, so the jealousy of Juno brings life into these fictions of imagination; and this jealousy is not destitute of sublimity, for, being endowed with divine power, it checks even the boasted omnipotence of the Thunderer.

That an opposing, jealous, yet eminent power strives to check the highest authority, is likewise entirely appropriate to the genius of these fables ; according to which, the beautiful and strong, in developing itself, must struggle against opposition and difficulties, and sustain many trials and dangers before its value is acknowledged and approved.

The demi-gods were also called Semones, as being descended from a mortal and an immortal. The deified mortals, or peculiar gods of any country, were called Indigetes.

In the poems of Homer, the heroes are described merely as warriors who had distinguished themselves by extraordinary strength, courage, and prudence ; these qualities being essential to those who were charged either with the government of the people, or the conduct of the wars. The poets, posterior to Homer, placed the heroes in an intermediate rank between gods and men ; therefore they were called demigods, and temples were erected, and sacrifices offered to them. Their time is called the *Heroic*, and in the period to which the achievements of the heroes are attributed, much fable is mingled with true history.

The heroic times of the ancients is the period when they passed from the savage to the civilized state. That of the Greeks is the most celebrated ; perhaps from its history having been handed down to us by the most distinguished poets. Those times commenced with the establishment of the kingdom of Sicyon (an ancient city of Greece), about 2164 B. C., and were closed after the siege of Troy, 1245 ; but the greatest events are embraced in the six last centuries of that period.

PERSEUS.

The history of Perseus belongs to the earliest period of the heroic age, and is therefore the most involved in clouds and fable.

To trace the earthly descent of this hero, it is necessary to go back to old Inachos, whose daughter, Io, gave Zeus a son in Egypt, named Epaphos. Libya, the regal daughter of Epaphos, became the mother of Belos and Agenor, the sons of Neptune. Belos was the father of Danäos and Ægyptos.

Danäos came from Ægyptos over to Greece, to assert and maintain his claims to the kingdom of Argos, against Gelanor, who at that time actually reigned over the country. The claims of the former rested upon his descent from Inachos ; those of the latter, on the right of possession. The people were called upon to decide to whom the royal crown belonged ; while they were yet wavering, a wolf rushed into a

herd of cows and destroyed the bull that defended them. This unexpected accident was considered as a sign from the gods, that the
stranger was destined to reign, instead of the native. Accordingly,
Danäos ascended the throne; and to him the Argives are said to be
indebted for the knowledge of digging wells and the building of ships.

Danäos, according to the legend, had fifty daughters, and Ægyptos
as many sons. The latter came over to Greece, each of them intending
to marry a daughter of Danäos. But Danäos had received warning
from an oracle, that one of his sons-in-law would deprive him of his
royal authority; and, anxious to retain his throne, he commanded each
of his daughters to kill her husband on the first night of their marriage. This cruel order was obeyed by all of them except Hypermnestra, who, notwithstanding the danger that threatened her own life in
consequence, suffered Lynceus, her beloved husband, to fly. But he
afterwards returned; for Danäos became reconciled to his daughter,
and Perseus and Hercules, the god-like heroes, are descendants of
Lynceus and Hypermnestra. Endless labor was the punishment inflicted on the Danaïdes for this crime. They were condemned to pour
water incessantly into a vessel full of holes, and to see every moment
that their labor is vain.

Atlas, a son of Lynceus, reigned over Argos after the death of his
father, and left two sons, Prœtos and Acrisios, who at different times
contested with each other for the royal authority.

Acrisios in his turn feared destruction from his descendants. It
had been predicted to him that he should be killed by one of his grand-
sons. He therefore shut up his only daughter, Danaë, in a brazen
tower, that he might thwart the prediction of the oracle. But his
precaution was rendered ineffectual by Jupiter, who, descending in a
golden shower through an opening in the roof of the building, made
her the mother of Perseus.

When Perseus was born, his grand-father committed both mother and
child to the sea, in a crazy bark. The benevolent goddess of the deep,
tenderly taking up the divine boy, together with his mother, in the lap
of the waters, brought the bark to a haven on the shores of the small
island of Seriphos, in the Ægean sea. Here they were found by Dictys,
a fisherman, and carried by him to Polydectes, king of the island, who
kindly received both mother and child, and superintended the education

of young Per-
seus, intrusting
him to the care of
the priests of Mi-
nerva's temple.

His rising ge-
nius and manly
courage, howev-
er, soon displeas-
ed Polydectes;
and the monarch,
who wished to
get Danaë into
his power, feared
the resentment
of her son. Yet
Polydectes re-
solved to remove
every obstacle,
and invited his
friends to a sump-
tuous entertain-
ment, requiring
all who came to
present him with a beautiful horse. Perseus was included, knowing
that it was not in his power to furnish the requisite gift. But Perseus,
who wished not to appear inferior to the other guests in magnificence,
told the king, that as he could not bring him a horse, he would bring
the head of Medusa, the only one of the Gorgons who was subject to
mortality. This offer was particularly agreeable to Polydectes, as it
would remove Perseus from Seriphos ; and as his undertaking seemed
impossible, the attempt might perhaps end in his ruin.

The innocence of Perseus was protected by the gods. Pluto lent
him a helmet which had the power of rendering the wearer invisible;
Minerva gave him her buckler, which was as resplendent as glass ; and
from Mercury he received wings and the talaria, with a short dagger
made of diamonds, and called *harpe*. With these arms Perseus commenced his expedition, and traversed the air, conducted by the goddess
Minerva.

He first went to the Grææ, the sisters of the Gorgons, and with the aid of Pluto's helmet, which made him invisible, stole from them the eye and tooth which they shared in common, and refused to return them until he was informed of the residence of their sisters. When he had received every necessary information, he flew to the habitation of the Gorgons, and found the monsters asleep. He knew that, by fixing his eyes upon them, he should be instantly changed to stone, he therefore looked continually upon his shield, which reflected all objects as clearly as the best mirror. He approached them, his courage supported by the goddess Minerva, and with one blow struck off the head of Medusa. The noise awoke the two immortal sisters, but Pluto's helmet rendered Perseus invisible, and the attempts of the Gorgons to revenge their sister's death proved fruitless. The conqueror made his way through the air, and from the blood which dropped from the head of Medusa -prang those innumerable serpents which have ever since infested the sandy deserts of Libya.

Minerva was the chief instigator to this bloody deed; having resolved on the destruction of Medusa, because, in company with Neptune, the monster had profaned her sanctuary. But when Perseus had brought down the deadly stroke, Stheino and Euryale sighed and groaned so loud at the view of their slain sister, and the hissing of the snakes upon their heads echoed so mournfully to their groaning, that Minerva, moved at the terrible concert, invented a flute with which she endeav· ored to revive these mournful sounds, by imitating their different strains. Thus, even in the midst of sanguinary and terrible destruction, the goddess of Art shines forth.

Chrysaor also, with his golden sword, sprang from these drops of blood, as well as the horse Pegasos, which immediately flew through the air, and stopped on mount Helicon, where he became the favorite of the Muses. Meantime, Perseus had continued his journey across the deserts of Libya ; but the approach of night obliged him to alight in the territories of Atlas, king of Mauritania. He went to the monarch's palace, where he hoped to meet with a kind reception, by announcing himself as the son of Jupiter. But in this he was disappointed ; for Atlas recollected that, according to the prediction of an ancient oracle, his gardens were to be robbed of their fruit by one of the sons of Jupiter ; he therefore not only refused Perseus the hospitality he demanded, but even assailed his person with violence. Perseus, finding himself inferior to his powerful enemy, showed him the head of Medusa and Atlas was instantly changed into a large mountain, which bore the same, name in the deserts of Africa.

On the morrow Perseus continued his flight, and passing the territories of Libya, he fixed his eyes upon the Ethiopian coast, where he be held a maiden fastened with chains to a rock, and a monster rising out of the sea ready to devour her; while her parents stood on the shore wringing their hands in despair. Perseus rushed down upon the monster at the very moment it was seizing its prey, struck the deadly blow, and delivered the fair maiden. It was Andromeda, who, to atone for a crime of which she was guiltless, was to have become the victim of divine anger. Cassiopeia, mother of Andromeda, and wife of Cepheus, had dared to compare the beauty of her daughter with that of the powerful daughters of Nereus, and in consequence, the whole country was laid waste with plagues, which, according to the oracle of Jupiter Ammon, were not to cease until Andromeda, swallowed up by a sea-monster, should, by her death, expiate the crime of her mother.

The parents of Andromeda having been witnesses of their daughter's rescue, readily complied with the wish of her deliverer. and gave her to Perseus in marriage. Phineus, however, brother of Cepheus, to whom Andromeda had been betrothed, accompanied by an armed body, appeared at the wedding feast, and furiously assailed the bridegroom, who would have been overpowered but for the head of Medusa. Warning his friends of the dangerous power of the Gorgon's head, they turned away their eyes; but on showing it to his adversaries, they in a moment became petrified statues, each in the posture and attitude in which he then stood.

After having accomplished these exploits, Perseus conducted his bride to Seriphos, where he again saw his mother and Polydectes. But alas! he was here compelled to turn the petrifying head against his foster-father and benefactor. Polydectes, fearing him and his mighty arm, made an attempt upon his life; but was punished for his cowardly suspicion by being transformed into a rock. Dyctis had protected his mother during his absence; and Perseus, sensible of his merits and humanity, placed him upon the throne of Seriphos

He afterwards restored to Mercury his talaria, harpe, and wings; to Pluto his helmet; and to Minerva her shield; but as he was more particularly indebted to the Goddess of Wisdom for her assistance and protection, he placed the Gorgon's head on her Ægis.

When Perseus heard that his grandfather Acrisios, had been de prived of his throne by his brother Prœtos, far from seeking revenge for the cruelty with which he and his mother had formerly been treated by Acrisios, he magnanimously hastened to Argolis with the design of replacing his grandfather in possession of his kingdom. He vanquished and killed Prœtos, and after having restored to Acrisios the royal crown, he was recognized by him with joy and gratitude as his beloved grandson, his friend and benefactor. But Fate, who trifles with the hopes of mortals, had not recalled her former threat, and a tragic end was lurking beneath the seducing appearance. Perseus, knowing how much Acrisios was delighted with his skill in every bodily exercise, was one day resolved to give him a splendid proof of his dexterity; but alas! the fatal quoit, as if directed by an evil dæmon, missing its aim, struck the head of Acrisios, and he fell lifeless to the ground.

In consequence of this unfortunate accident, Perseus passed his future days in melancholy sadness, calling himself a parricide notwithstanding his innocence of the fatal event. His residence at Argos became insupportable to him, and therefore he induced the son of Prœtos to exchange territories. But finding nothing at Tyrins, the capital of his new dominion, to obliterate from his memory the event which distracted him, he built the new city of Mycenæ.

One of the children of Perseus and Andromeda was Alcæus, the father of Amphitryon, who was married to Alcmena, Electryon's daughter, and the mother of Heracles. Another son of Perseus, whose name was Sthenelos, was the father of Eurystheus, who ruled over Mycenæ, and whom Heracles was compelled to serve.

Perseus himself, as well as the chief persons connected with his history, Andromeda, Cassiopeia, and others, were, according to fiction, transposed among the constellations of the sky, where their names are immortalized. In this sense, the heroes of old were really raised to heaven, and a monument most durable and shining was erected to their names.

Creutzer regards the Perseus of the Greeks as a modification of Mithras, the Sun-god of the Persians; but his genealogy, as transmitted by the mythographers, would appear to give him still more relation to Egypt than to Asia. Descended from the ancient Inachos, the father of Phoroneus and Io, we see his family divide itself into two branches. From Phoroneus sprang Sparton, Apis-Serapis, and the Argive

Niobe. The union of Zeus and Io produced Epaphos, Belos, Danaös, and omitting some intermediate names, Acrisios, Danaë, and the heroic Perseus. If we examine closely the import of the names that form this completely mythic genealogy, we shall discover an evident allusion to Mithriac ideas and symbols. For example, *Sparton* has reference to the sowing of seed ; *Apis*, become *Serapis*, is the god bull upon or under the earth ; *Io* is the lowing heifer wandering over the whole earth, and at last held captive ; *Epaphos*, another and Grecianized name of Apis, is the sacred bull, the representative of all the bulls of Egypt ; *Belos* is the sun-king both in Asia and Egypt.

In the person of Perseus all these scattered rays seem concentrated. The name of his mother, Danaë, would seem to have reference to the earth in a dry and arid state. Zeus descending in a shower of gold, impregnating and rendering her the mother of Perseus, is Mithras or the golden sun fertilizing the earth.

Perseus, coming forth from the court of the king of shades (Polydectes, the all-recipient), proceeds, under the protection of the goddess Minerva, holding in his hand the *harpe*, symbol of fertility, to combat in the west the impure and sterile Gorgons ; after this, returning to the East, he delivers Andromeda from the sea-monster, and becomes the parent of a hero of light, another Perses resembling his sire. Having returned victorious to Argolis, he builds, by the aid of the Cyclopes (subterranean workmen whom he leads in his train), a city, Mycenæ, the name of which, according to different traditions, had reference either to the lowings of Io, or to the Gorgons mourning for the fate of their sister. Others derive the appellation from the scabbard of the hero's sword which fell upon the spot; and others again, from a mushroom torn up by Perseus when suffering from thirst, and which yielded a refreshing supply of water in the place it had occupied.

In all these there is more or less of mystic meaning, the leading idea being still that of the earth ; just as in the legend which makes Perseus to have killed Acrisios (the "confused," "dark," or "gloomy" one), in the discus by which the blow was given, there is an evident allusion to the orb of the sun.

By closely comparing the principal features of these legends with the essential symbols presented by the Mithriac bas-reliefs, there appears, both in the myths and in the sculptures of Mycenæ, a wonderful accordance with these symbols. The Argive fables tell of a heifer— a heifer lowing and distracted with pain. An allusion to the sword plunged into the bosom of the earth (represented by the heifer and by the Mithriac bull),* is preserved in the legend of the scabbard that fell to the earth, and gave a name to the city of which it presaged the founding. The shower of gold, the mushroom, the never-ending stream of water, of which this last is the pledge, are emblems of the solar emanations, the signs of terrestrial fertility, and all Mithriac ideas. The Gorgons have reference to the moon regarded as a dark body; they typify the natural impurity of the planet, which the energies of the sun (Mithras Perseus, armed with his golden sword) are to remove, and give purity in its stead. Here, then, at the very foundation of the mythus, we find ideas of purification. Perseus, as well as Heracles, who descends from him, are purifiers. They purify the stains of evil by force and by the shedding of blood; they are just murderers; and the wings given in preference to Perseus, enter into this general conception. Both assuming an aspect more and more moral, end with being intermingled in human history; and thus, according to one tradition, Perseus put to death the sensual and voluptuous Sardanapalos.

This brings us to consider the numerous points of approximation acknowledged to exist, even by the ancients themselves. between the Greek hero, Perseus, and various countries of antiquity, such as Asia Minor, Colchis, Assyria, and Persia. At Tarsus in Cilicia, of which city both Perseus and Sardanapalos passed as the founders, the first was worshipped as a god, and very probably the second also. The name of Perseus (or Perses) is found in the solar genealogies of Colchis. Perses, the son of Perseus and Andromeda, was, according to Hellanicus, the author of civilization in the district of Persia, called Artea. Herodotus also was acquainted with the traditions which, emanating originally from Persia itself, claimed Perseus for Assyria. Finally, in the place of Perseus, it is Achæmenes (Djemschid) whom the ancient expounders of Plato make to have sprung from Perseus and Andromeda.

We have here, under the form of a Greek genealogy, the fundamental

---

* Mithras is generally represented in sculpture as a young man, his head surmounted by a Phrygian bonnet, and in the attitude of supporting his knee upon a bull that lies on the ground. With one hand he holds a horn of the animal, and with the other plunges a dagger into its neck. Mithras here represents the generative Sun, in the full bloom of youth and power, while the bull indicates the earth, containing in its bosom the seeds, or germs of things, that the sun-god causes to come forth in abundant flood from the wound inflicted by his dagger of gold.—*Creutzer* idea of the worship of Mithras; the beam of fire which the sun forces into the bosom of the earth, produces a solar hero, who, in his turn, becomes the parent of one connected with agriculture. Djemschid-Perses, the chief and model of the dynasty of the Achæmenides, was the first to open the soil of Persia with the same golden sword, wielded by Perseus and Mithras, and which is nothing but an emblem of the penetrating and fertilizing rays of the luminary of day.

If Perseus, however, seems, by his father, or his primitive type, to have reference to Asia, on the mother's side he is connected with Egypt, the native country of Danaös and the Danaïdes. At Chemnis he had a temple and statue; and as Tarsus, where he was also worshipped, received its name from the impress made by the fertilizing foot of Pegasos, or Bellerophon, who followed in the track of the high deeds achieved by Perseus in Lower Asia, so the Chemnites pretended that Egypt was indebted for its fertility to the gigantic sandal left by the demi god upon earth at the periods of his frequent visitations. They alone of the Egyptians celebrated games in honor of the warlike hero of the Sun; this conqueror in his celestial career, this worthy precursor of Hercules, his grandson.

If we connect what has been here said, with the traces of Mithriac worship in Ethiopia and Egypt, as well as in Persia and Greece, we shall be tempted to conjecture, that these two branches of a very early religion, the fundamental idea of which was the contest incessantly carried on by the pure and fertilizing principle of light against darkness and sterility, unite in one trunk at the very centre of the East.

Müller regards the Mythus of Perseus and the Gorgon as one of the darkest legendary cycles of Grecian mythology, and difficult of explanation, because as yet we know nothing of the character of the worship of the ancient Athena.

He speaks of Perseus as a dæmonic being in close union with the ancient Argive Pallas, as a goddess who blesses the land with fruitfulness. His dæmonic nature being proved, not only by his wonderful achievements, but also by the divine worship which he received in Seriphos and Argive Tarsus.

The dry, sealed-up soil in the land of Pallas thirsts for rain, and Zeus, the father of life, descends into its bosom in a beautifying, bounteous, therefore golden shower, in the same manner as the cloud which embraces Hera, is called in Homer, a golden one, from which glittering dew-drops fall. From this golden shower springs Perseus, and destroys the dreadful Gorgon, through whom the moon-beams become baleful, turning the soil to stone. Pallas, the benign goddess, the kindly nurse of seeds and plants, is thereby delivered of her antitype, and restored to full power. Then spring up the clear and living fountains of which the horse is the symbol; but more particularly Pegasos, who was born at the fountain of Oceanos, was caught beside fountains, with his hoof struck out fountains, in his name also, a horse of fountains. Polydectes' demand of horses, and then the procuring of one by Perseus, are also a remnant of the symbolic legends.

Müller also remarks, that the mythus is thoroughly symbolical; and as to its age, some idea may be formed from the fact that even in the time of Homer it had become ordinary, heroic fable. The symbolic character gives it a peculiar representability, and attracted elder art. which, as yet, was able to represent but little by expression and characteristic portraiture. Hence a Gorgoneian, as a work of the Cyclopes at Argos, and the Gorgonea, as impressions on very old Attic and Etruscan coins.

The ancients represented the Gorgons as winged, and with a broad, flat face, and a long tongue protruding from an enormous mouth, which opened from ear to ear. Later artists banished this hideous mask from their compositions, and represented Medusa as the unhappy beauty who attracted the love of Neptune, giving her a melancholy air, expressive of her regret at finding serpents mingled with her beautiful locks. But few serpents are represented, and so placed as to destroy all deformity; sometimes brought under the chin, and again forming a necklace. The wings, gracefully paced upon the head, add to the beauty of the composition.

THE MEDUSA,

AS COPIED FROM AN ANTIQUE GEM.*

Fated sister of "the three,"
Mortal, though a deity;
Superhuman beauty thine,
Demon goddess—power divine!'
Thou a human death didst bear,
Thou a mortal life didst share;
Yet thy soul, supremely free,
Shrank not from its destiny:
And the life-drops from thy head
On Libyan sands, by Perseus shed,
Sprang a scourging race from thee—
Fell types of artful mystery.
Thou wast the victim of dire rage,
Minerva's vengeance to assuage;
And thy locks, like molten gold,
Sheltering love in every fold;
Transformed into the serpents' lair,
That writhe and hiss thy keen despair.

Fatal Beauty! thou dost seem
The phantom of some fearful dream·
Extremes of horror and of love
Alternate o'er our senses move,
As wrapt and spell-bound, we survey
The horrid coils which round thee play;
And mark thy wild, enduring smile,
Lit by no mortal fire the while.
Formed to attract all eyes to thee,
And yet their withering blight to be;
Thy power mysterious to congeal,
And from life's blood its warmth to steal—
To petrify the mortal clay
In its first glance of wild dismay!
Is a dread gift to one like thee,
Cursed with a hateful destiny.

Oh! couldst thou unto mortals give
Thy strength to suffer—grace to live;
Or teach them curses to defy,
By resignation's heaven-ward eye;
Oh! couldst thou ope thy mission's seal
And thy mysterious self reveal;

---

* Since these beautiful lines have appeared so differently worded in "The Female
Poets of America," I feel obliged to state that this is a correct copy as furnished by the
author.   M. A. D.

Tell to the wondering what thou art—
Hast thou a *human, feeling heart?*
Know'st thou that worse than scorpion's sting,
The misery stern remorse can bring?
The arid desert of the soul,
Sear'd 'neath its scorching dark control?
If with thine other throes of pain
Thou feel'st too this, nor dost complain,
Just is thy place 'mongst gods to be,
Their Ægis and dread mystery.—*Mrs. A. R. St. John.*

BELLEROPHONTES OR BELLEROPHON.

Bellerophon was a son of Glaucus; and his adventures form a pleasing episode in the Iliad, where they are related to Diomedes by Bellerophon's grandson.

The same Prœtus by whom Acrisios was deprived of his kingdom. and who was at last vanquished and slain by Perseus, urged on by a false suspicion, gave to Bellerophontes the first occasion for his heroic feats. He was a grandson of Sisyphos, the founder of Corinth, who was a descendant of Deucalion, and the son of Æolus, from whom the Æolic race of heroes spread through many royal families of Greece.

Having committed a murder, Bellerophon was forced to flee from Corinth, and he came to Prœtus, who at that time was reigning in Argos. with whom he found an asylum. The gods had endowed the hero with manly vigor and beauty; and Antæa, the wife of Prœtus, a daughter of Iobates, king of Lycia, conceived a tender affection for the handsome youth, which was soon changed to hatred because it found no return on the part of Bellerophon. She basely accused him of an attempt on her honor, and enjoined her husband to avenge both her and himself. But the rites of hospitality were too sacred to allow of Prœtus killing Bellerophon; he therefore sent him to Iobates, his father-in-law, with a letter, in which he was desired to avenge the crime of which the bearer was accused, by putting him to death. Iobates. however, did not read the letter until he had hospitably received Bellerophon. after which, he also abhorred the thought of violating the sacred rites of hospitality. He therefore trusted to chance to effect his ruin, bidding him embark in the most dangerous enterprises, in which his destruction seemed inevitable.

Of the monsters which descended from Phorcys and fair Ceto, one, the terrible Gorgo, was vanquished by Perseus; but another, not less

formidable, was assigned to
Bellerophon as a trial of his
valor. It was the fire-vomiting
Chimæra, with the head of
a lion, the body of a goat,
and the tail of a dragon. To
this bold adventure the gods
lent their assistance. granting
Bellerophon the winged horse
Pegasos. The hero bestrode
him and then in the air commenced the fight. The monster defended herself to the
utmost, sending from her
mouth whole masses of fire,
and coiling her dragon tail in
formidable windings. But all this availed her not. After a persevering and obstinate struggle, the monster lay stretched on the ground
weltering in her blood.

Thus the most difficult tasks assigned to the heroes of antiquity, are
always the killing of monsters and unnatural beings, who by degrees
must vanish from the chain of things. It seems almost as if these
fictions implied that truth and dream, reality and fable, had long to
struggle with one another, before order was established. And it was
a worthy task of the heroes of humanity, to banish these unnatural
appearances and illusory exhibitions, in order to create around her
regularity, light, and truth. The Sphinx hurled from the height of
rock that she occupied, every one who could not solve her enigma; but
Œdipus had no sooner unriddled it, than she flung herself down into
the abyss.

Not enough that Bellerophontes had vanquished Chimæra, the scourge
of the land; he must now conquer the human enemies of Iobates, the
courageous Solymians, and the manlike Amazons. As he was returning victorious, the king laid an ambush for him composed of the
bravest men of Lycia, of whom not one returned home, as Bellerophontes slew them all. The king, now perceiving him to be of divine origin,
gave him his daughter in marriage and shared his kingdom with him.

But the happiness of this hero was of short duration; for when, elated
by his victories, he attempted by means of Pegasos to ascend to Hea-

ven, Zeus, incensed at his boldness, sent an insect to sting the steed, which made Pegasos bound so furiously in the air as to throw his rider to the earth, where he wandered in solitude and melancholy until death relieved him of his grief.

Though Homer makes no mention of Pegasos, this steed forms an essential part of the mythe of Bellerophontes. In the Theogony it is said of the Chimæra, that she was killed by Pegasos and the "good Bellerophontes." The poets seem all to agree in giving the winged steed to the hero, yet none of them inform us how he obtained him. But in Pindar we find a remarkable legend, which connects Bellero· phontes with Corinth.

According to this poet, Bellerophontes, who reigned at Corinth, when about to undertake his adventures, wished to possess the winged steed Pegasos, who was accustomed to drink at the fount of Peirene, on the Acrocorinth. After frequent and fruitless attempts to catch him, he applied to the soothsayer, Polyeidos, for advice, and was directed by him to go and sleep at the altar of Athena. He obeyed the injunction, and in the dead of night the goddess appeared to him in a dream, and giving him a bridle, bade him sacrifice a bull to his sire, Poseidon (*Tamer*), and then present the bridle to the steed. On awaking, Bellerophontes found the bridle lying beside him. He obeyed the injunctions of the goddess and raised an altar to her as Hippeia (*Of the Horse*). Pegasos at once yielded his mouth to the magic bit, and the hero mounting him, achieved his adventures.

HERACLES OR HERCULES.

The first Greek tragedian (Æschylus) introduces Prometheus when chained to a rock, complaining of his sufferings to the equally unfortu· nate Io, and predicting the birth of his deliverer, Heracles.

Io, transformed into a cow, was by Juno's jealousy driven in frantic fury over the whole earth. She wandered to the solitary corner where Prometheus was suffering, who revealed her future fate as well as his own, telling her, that the thirteenth of her descendants would be his deliverer. The thirteen members of the family in uninterrupted descent are, Io, Epaphos, Libya, Belos, Danaös, Lynceus, Atlas, Acrisios, Danaë, Perseus, Alcæus, Alcmena, Heracles.

The sons of Perseus, were Electryon, Sthenelos, Alcæus, and Mestor, of whom Electryon succeeded his father in the government of Mycenæ

The children of Alcæus were, Anaxo and Amphitryon. Electryon married Anaxo, and from this marriage sprung Alcmena, the mother of Heracles. Amphitryon lived at Electryon's court, and had confident hopes of becoming his uncle's successor in the government, by his marriage with Alcmena; in which he was disappointed.

Taphios, a grandson of Mestor, had founded a colony on the island of Taphos, whose inhabitants called themselves Taphians, or, from their living at a great distance from their native country, Teleboans. After the death of Taphios, Pterelaos, his son and successor, claimed a part of the inheritance of Mycenæ, on account of his descent from Mestor, a son of Perseus, and sent his children thither to enforce his claims. Upon Electryon's denying the justice of them, and refusing to restore any thing of Perseus' inheritance, the sons of Pterelaos, with their people, laid waste the country, and drove away the royal herds. The sons of Electryon immediately collecting a body of men, fought a battle with the invaders, in which the leaders on both sides were killed, with the exception of one son of Electryon, Lycimnius, and one of Pterelaos, Eueres.

Upon this, Electryon resolved on going in person against the Teleboans, to avenge the death of his children; in the mean time transferring his government to his daughter Alcmena and his nephew Amphitryon, with the promise that they should be united in marriage as soon as he should return victorious. He returned conqueror, bringing back the herds of which he had been deprived by his enemies. Amphitryon, now quite secure of his happiness, went joyfully forth to meet him; but as one of the recovered cows strayed from the herd, he, with the intention of turning her back, threw a club at her, which unfortunately hit Electryon, who fell lifeless to the ground.

This occurrence blighted his hopes of one day becoming king of Mycenæ, for though the act was unintentional, it brought upon him the hatred of the people, and Sthenelos, the brother of the slain Electryon, seized upon the royal crown of Mycenæ, without resistance, and Amphitryon was compelled to flee to Thebes, whither Alcmena followed him. Creon, who was at that time king of Thebes, took them under his protection. Alcmena, however, refused to become Amphitryon's wife, until he had avenged the death of her brothers. Amphitryon accordingly entered into an alliance with Cephalos, Eleus, and several other neighboring princes, for the purpose of waging a new war against the inhabitants of the Taphian islands. Pterelaos was vanquished, and

Amphitryon divided the conquered islands among his allies; the one of which, called in ancient times Cephalene, and in ours Cephalonia, received its name from the above-mentioned Cephalos.

Meanwhile, however, Alcmena's charms having attracted the Thunderer, he assumed the form of Amphitryon returning as victor from his expedition and came down from Olympos to see her; and was afterwards obliged to reveal his divinity to Amphitryon, in order to appease his anger against Alcmena.

On the day in which Heracles was to be born, Jupiter boastingly spoke in the assembly of the gods, " I give you to understand, all ye gods and goddesses, that to-day a hero will be born, of a race of men who derive their origin from me, who is destined to reign over all his neighbors." Brooding artifices, the cunning Juno replied, " I shall, nevertheless, very much doubt the accomplishment of thy words, unless thou swear with the inviolable oath of the gods, that he, who to-day shall be born of the race of men that derive their origin from thee, will indeed reign over all his neighbors." Scarcely had Jupiter uttered the fatal oath, ere Juno left Olympos, and hastening to Argos, forwarded the birth of Eurystheus, and retarded that of Heracles; then, returning to Olympos, she thus triumphantly accosted Jupiter, " The hero who will rule over the Argives is already born; he is descended from the race of men that sprang forth from thee; for he is Eurystheus, a son of Sthenelos, whose father Perseus was thine offspring; the promised kingdom, therefore, is fallen to the lot of no unworthy one." (Il. xix. 101.)

The luckless father of the gods, not able to recall his oath, nor to avenge himself against the wily Juno, burst out in unspeakable wrath, and seizing the bright hand of Ate, the evil breeding power, who was his own daughter, and until now a member of the divine assembly, he hurled her from heaven to earth, swearing with a great oath, that she should never return to Olympos. Since that time, Ate hovers over the heads of mortal men, every where sowing dissensions, broils, and ruin.

Alcmena became the mother of two sons; Hercules, whose father was Jupiter, and Iphicles, the son of her husband Amphitryon. Which of these was the son of the Thunderer soon became evident. While the two children were cradled in a hollow buckler (a part of the booty which Amphitryon had taken in the war against Pterelaos), Juno sent two serpents to destroy Hercules; but the divine babe stifled them

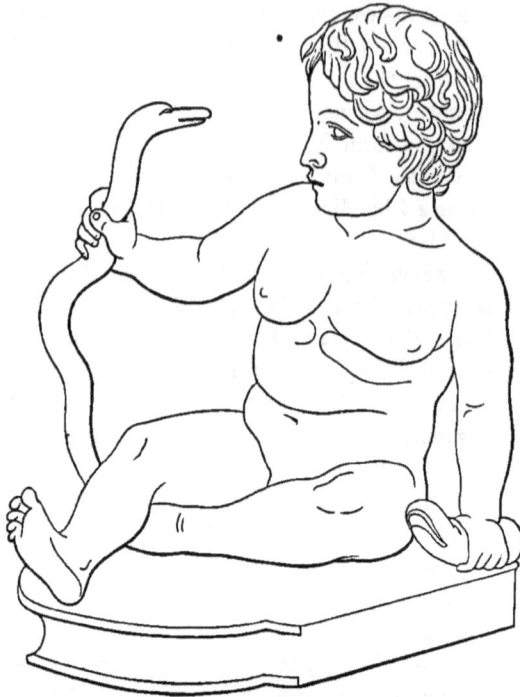

with his infant hands. Jupiter then recognized his son; and finding Juno sleeping, laid Hercules by her side, who by this means obtained the divine milk without her consent. When Juno awoke, she flung far away from her the bold suckling, sprinkling upon the vault of the sky the milk that fell from her breast, the marks of which formed the galaxy or milky way, on which the gods walk. Fiction here becomes Colossean, and the atmosphere through which the stars shine, appears therein as Juno's chief archetype.

At the command of Jupiter, Mercury committed Hercules to his tutors, who were to instruct him in warlike occupations, as well as in peaceful arts. Several of them were themselves sons of deities;—Linus, the son of Apollo, taught him to play on the lyre, and Eumolpos to sing; Castor taught him how to fight; Eurytos how to shoot with a bow and arrows; Autolicus to drive a chariot; and like the rest of his illustrious contemporaries, he became the pupil of the wise Centaur, Cheiron, and under him, perfected his accomplishments, and made himself the most valiant of the age.

When in pursuit of these occupations, Hercules one day betook himself to a lonely spot, to muse undisturbed on his future life and fate; and seating himself on a cross-way he sank into deep reflection. On this occasion two females appeared to him, the one of whom was Luxury and the other Virtue. Each endeavored to win the youth to her interest. Luxury, by promising him all the enjoyment of a cheerful, careless life, if he would follow her; Virtue, by announcing to him troublesome and laborious days, but afterwards glory and immortality, if he would choose her for his guide in the path of life. " Thee will I follow ; to thee devote my life," exclaimed the youth, with glowing heart, grasping at the same time the hand of Virtue ; and followed her with firm step, resolved to endure patiently every trial that awaited him, to bear every burden that should fall to his lot, and to shun no labor that should be appointed him, however difficult the task might be.

Two of the most terrible children of Phorcys and Ceto were vanquished by Perseus and Bellerophon, but the greatest feats of valor, as well as merit, are reserved for Hercules, who is to conquer monsters, to subdue tyrants, and to set bounds to the injustice of the Thunderer himself, by delivering Prometheus from his torments, who was still suffering for the benefits which he had conferred upon mankind. The fate of Hercules was woven in the commencement of his life's thread by the inexorable Parcæ. Born to be a ruler, he was forced by the power of the Fates to obey, and to achieve his most glorious actions at the command of one, who was in every respect his inferior, and who dreaded the strength with which he was endowed.

He was not permitted to live long in quiet at the house of his foster-father, Amphitryon ; for jealous Juno had infused into the heart of the latter dread, and suspicion against the young hero. Heracles was therefore sent by him to the court of Eurystheus, at Mycenæ, where from time to time he was charged with the most difficult labors, and the most dangerous undertakings, which put his courage and firmness to the severest test. On his journey to Mycenæ, he inquired of the oracle at Delphi concerning his future fate ; and received for answer, that twelve labors awaited him at the court of Eurystheus, after the performance of which, immortality should be his reward. For these undertakings the favors of the gods had completely armed him. From Minerva, he received a coat of arms and a helmet; from Mercury a sword; from Neptune a horse; from Jupiter a shield; from Apollo a bow and arrows; and from Vulcan, a golden cuirass and a brazen buskin.

Eurystheus, seeing so powerful a man completely subjected to him, and apprehensive of such an enemy, commanded him to achieve the most difficult and arduous enterprises ever known; generally called,

THE TWELVE LABORS OF HERCULES.

1st. *The Nemæan Lion.*—A monstrous lion, near the forest of Nemæa, whose hide no arrow could pierce, wasted the surrounding country and threatened destruction to the herds. The first of the twelve labors which Eurystheus commanded Hercules to perform was the subduing this beast of prey. The young hero did not fail to pursue the tracks of the lion, and to commence the fight as soon as he had found him; and finding that iron was too weak to wound the monster, he flung his sinewy arms around his neck and strangled him. Hercules then carried the lion to Mycenæ, but Eurystheus alarmed by this heroic feat, forbade him henceforth to come within the walls of the city, at the same time ordering him to deliver at the gates an account of his future exploits.

In memory of this deed of valor, which was a pledge of the performance of others, Hercules ever afterwards wore the skin of the lion around his shoulders, and it became, together with the club which he had cut from a knotty branch of the wild olive tree, the external mark of his extraordinary strength and invincible courage.

2d. *The Lernæan Hydra.*—In the morasses of Lerna, near Argos, was the abode of that Hydra, with many heads, which has been already mentioned in the pedigree of the monsters, descendants of Phorcys and Ceto. The time of the heroes was death to them, who were one after another extirpated from the earth by the power of Jupiter's sons. Perseus had conquered Gorgo, and Bellerophon, the Chimæra; and now, Hercules, at the command of Eurystheus, entered into the fearful struggle with the Lernæan Hydra.

He attacked the monster with his sickle-shaped sword, but no sooner had he severed one head from the trunk than a new one immediately arose in its place. At last, when the utmost peril threatened the hero, he commanded his companion, Iolaus, the son of Iphicles, to burn with a hot iron the root of the head which he had crushed with his club, before a new one could spring up. Thus the greatest danger being avoided, another presented itself ; for Juno, to render victory to Hercules difficult, if not impossible, sent a crab to gnaw at the heels of the hero while he was struggling with the monster. But this new enemy was soon dispatched, and the son of the Thunderer, after a long fight, drove the last head of the Hydra, which was invulnerable, into the ground, and covered it with an immense stone. As a reward for his labor, he dipped his arrows in the blood of the Hydra, which, by this fatal poison, became doubly dreadful, but which were destined to bring ruin on their possessor.

Juno, unable to succeed in her attempts to lessen the fame of Hercules, placed the crab among the constellations, where it is now called Cancer.

If invincible courage and perseverance in surmounting innumerable obstacles, and ever renewed dangers. can be indicated by a striking emblem, it is in this fiction of Hercules' victory over the many headed monster. For this reason, ancient and modern poets have employed this fiction of Fancy, because it is impossible to substitute one more significant.

3d. *The Erymanthian Boar.*—From the Erymanthian mountains, a monstrous boar descended, laying waste the fields of Arcadia.

This afforded Eurystheus a wished for occasion to send Hercules on a new and dangerous expedition. To the conqueror of the Nemæan Lion and the many-headed Hydra, however, it was no difficult task to catch the boar alive and carry him to Eurystheus, who, terrified at the sight of the monster, concealed himself in a brazen butt.

In this ridiculous position Eurystheus is represented upon an antique gem. The striking contrast of the strength and valor of the person who obeys, with the weakness and cowardice of the commander, gives to this fiction a more vivid interest. By the hero's conquering himself to obey, according to the will of Fate, his boldest deeds acquire the greater lustre. He first obtains the victory over himself, and then, by the command of an inferior, subdues the monsters.

4th. *The Stag of Diana.*—In order to put to the proof the swiftness and agility of Hercules, he was in his fourth labor ordered to bring alive and unhurt into the presence of Eurystheus, the stag of Diana, famous for its swiftness, its golden horns, and brazen feet.

Hercules, accepting the task, pursued the tracks of this nimble animal during a whole year, and at last caught him in a thicket, and carried him on his shoulders to the gates of Mycenæ. This celebrated stag frequented the neigborhood of Oenoë, and as Hercules was returning victorious, he met Diana, who snatched the stag from him with a severe reprimand for molesting an animal sacred to her. He pleaded necessity, and by representing the commands of Eurystheus, he appeased the goddess, and obtained the stag.

5th. *The Stymphalides.*—A kind of ghastly birds inhabited the Stymphalian lake, to which the imagination of the poets ascribes the most frightful aspect. They were represented as furnished with claws and bills of brass, enabling them to pierce any armor, and according to several fictions, were armed with darts, which they flung at their aggressors.

These monsters, which Eurystheus commanded Hercules to destroy, had taken up their abode in the deep recesses of an inaccessible morass. And here the divine hero would have been at a loss, notwithstanding his strength and courage, but for the aid of Minerva, who wished him success, and gave him a rattle of brass, the noise of which frightened the birds from their haunts, driving them into the air, where Hercules easily dispatched them with his arrows

6th. *Augias' Stables.*—Augias, a king in Elis, and called a child of the sun, from the immense number of flocks and herds which he possessed, was one of the wealthiest princes of his time. In those ages, a man's wealth was estimated in proportion to the abundance of his cattle ; and the occupations required by possessions of this kind were not degrading ; neither was it considered disgraceful to clean a stable.

According to the tale of antiquity, Augias had three thousand oxen in his stables, which had not been cleansed for thirty years, so that at last it seemed an impossibility to clear them of the prodigious accumulation. But Hercules, at the command of Eurystheus, undertook the enormous task, which was to be accomplished in the space of a few days. Augias, who doubted the possibility of the performance, promised Hercules, as a reward, the tenth part of his herds.

By turning the course of the river Alpheus through the stables, Hercules completed the task in one day. After the work was done, Augias withheld the promised reward, on the pretext that Hercules had made use of artifice ; and the son of Alcmena, enraged at this faithlessness, made war upon him, and having conquered and killed him, proclaimed his son Phyleus his successor upon the throne.

Out of the treasures which he gained in this war, he built a temple in honor of Olympian Jupiter, and renewed the Olympic games.

7th. *The Cretan Bull.*—Neptune, being angry at the inhabitants of Crete, because they were deficient in their veneration for him, sent into the island a furious bull, which exhaled fire from his nostrils, and as no one would venture to approach him, laid waste the country.

Scarcely had Eurystheus heard of this, ere he imposed on Hercules the new task of catching the beast alive. Hercules, whose bodily strength measured itself as it were with the whole animal world, subdued the bull sent by Neptune, and carried him on his shoulders to Mycenæ.

8th. *The Horses of Diomedes.*—Diomedes, a king of Thrace, and son of Mars, had in his possession four fire-vomiting horses, which were fed by him with human flesh. All strangers who fell into the hands of this barbarian, were thrown to his horses to be torn and devoured.

The report of this cruelty having spread every where, Eurystheus commanded Hercules to bring to him the fire-vomiting steeds. The hero obeyed, overpowered Diomedes, and by throwing him to the carnivorous beasts, made him suffer the just punishment of his cruelty.

Ill treatment of strangers is, in the fictions of the ancients, with whom the rites of hospitality were sacred above all other considerations, the surest mark of malicious tyranny and injustice ; and the more so, in proportion as it assumes the garb of cruelty. Those tyrants who could torment or kill strangers, were regarded as monsters, and it was the task of the divine heroes to exterminate them from the earth.

The representation of the horses of Diomedes is found upon ancient monuments of art, as they are standing before a manger, in which the body of a human being lies extended. The cruel monster stands by, gloating his eyes, as it were, on the sight.

9th. *The Girdle of the Queen of the Amazons.*—Bellerophon was compelled to fight against the Amazons, and Eurystheus did not fail to charge Hercules with the same dangerous enterprise.

The precious girdle worn by the queen of the Amazons, and which Hercules was to win, was a present from the god of war, and defended as it was by fortitude and bravery, it could only be obtained by invincible courage.

In this expedition, Hercules was accompanied by Theseus, and at the river Thermodon the fight commenced, in which the Amazons with their allies were vanquished, and the queen herself· taken prisoner. Hercules, after having on his way accomplished several other bold feats, returned to Mycenæ, and presented the girdle to Eurystheus.

10th. *The Triple-bodied Geryon.*—Geryon, the savage monarch of three islands, situated in the dusky west of the ancient world, ha·· already been mentioned in the pedigree of the monsters.

He was in possession of what, in times of antiquity, was considered the greatest treasure; and the fame of Geryon's oxen had spread so far, as to induce Eurystheus to impose upon Hercules the commission of leading them away from their pastures, and bringing them as a warlike treasure from the remotest bounds of the earth to Mycenæ.

Hercules made his way over mountains and rocks, performing on this expedition many other great exploits. After having overcome the two-headed dog, which guarded the herds, as well as Eurytion the herdsman, he took possession of Geryon's oxen. The triple-bodied monster then rushed upon him, but was killed by Hercules with his club.

11th. *The Golden Apples of the Hesperides.*—The greatest treasure which imagination transferred to the widest distance, and which was thought to be altogether unattainable, was the golden apples in the gardens of the Hesperides. These gardens were watched by a monstrous dragon, and to bring the golden fruit to Eurystheus, was one of the tasks which Hercules was to accomplish in obedience to the command of another.

The hero, ignorant of the situation of these celebrated gardens, applied to the nymphs in the neighborhood of the Po for information; and was told that Nereus, if properly managed, would direct him in the pursuit. Hercules seized Nereus as he was sleeping, and the sea-god, unable to escape from his grasp, answered all the questions that he proposed.

After reaching the gardens, Hercules gave the dragon a potion which threw him into a deep sleep; he then succeeded in killing him, gathered the apples, and returned in triumph to Eurystheus. They were afterwards carried back to the gardens by Minerva, as they could be preserved in no other place.

In the representations of Hercules, the tree which bore the golden fruit is also to be seen : the dragon coils itself around it, and Hercules stands before him with the cup that contains the somniferous potion. The Hesperides stand by, lamenting the loss of their treasure, which they had heretofore so carefully preserved.

12th. *Cerberus, the Watch-dog of Orcus.*– Hercules had now given eleven proofs of the strength and agility of his body, as well as the greatness of his soul; the last only remained. He had not done enough in conquering the monsters of the higher world.— Eurystheus also commanded him to descend into the world of shades, and drag to the light of day the triple-headed dog Cerberus, that watched the gates of Pluto. The hero is thus commanded to brave Death himself in his own dominions—to descend into the open gulf that leads to his territories, and to contend in direful fight with the king of terrors.

Before Hercules went on his way to the lower world, he was initiated in the Eleusinian mysteries, to be as it were prepared for any event, whether life or death : he then boldly entered the cavern at the Promontory of Tænarus, which led to the abode of the shades. He compelled Charon to row him across the Styx, and when reaching the opposite shore, he first beheld the three-headed dog Cerberus, and ther. chained to a rock, two well-known heroes, Theseus and Pirithoös, who had ventured to descend into Orcus, with the intention of delivering Proserpine, the Queen of the dead, from Pluto's dominions. They were overpowered, fastened to an enchanted rock, and doomed never again to see the light of the sun.

Hercules, nevertheless, succeeded in delivering Theseus. Fiction says, that when Hercules was pursuing Cerberus, whose fierceness was broken after a desperate struggle, and who was now flying with anxious wailings to the palace of Pluto, the chaplet of mallow leaves which he wore upon his head turned black. Hercules fought with Pluto himself; seized upon the triple-headed watch-dog of his dominions, loosened Theseus' bonds, and hastened out of the land of terrors. He had also endeavored to free Pirithoös from his fetters, but in vain, for Pluto defended his prey with his whole power.

Hercules brought Cerberus in triumph to the upper world. The terrified Eurystheus could not bear the sight of the monster, and Hercules, after having kept him tamed between his knees, delivered him from the pain of beholding the light of day, and the black monster slunk back to the lower world to resume his watch at its gates.

These are the proofs which Hercules gave of his strength, his perseverance, invincible courage, and patient submission to the decrees of Fate, in performing the most difficult tasks at the command of an inferior. But besides these labors imposed upon him by Eurystheus, he voluntarily achieved other deeds of valor, not less glorious, equally celebrated, and perhaps of higher merit.

1st. *The Rescue of Hesione.*—Hercules was the companion of the Argonauts in their expedition to Colchis, but he separated himself from them, and went on shore near the city of Troy, to seek for his friend Hylas, who had left the ship for water, and had not returned. In vain was the cry of the hero, Hylas! Hylas! for the Naiades had drawn him into the well. The whole shore echoed the name of Hylas, but Hylas did not return.

When Hercules found that his search was fruitless, he proceeded on his way to Troy, where, at that time, Laömedon was king ; who, when Neptune and Apollo had condescended to build a wall round the city, had cheated them of their wages. His crime did not remain long unpunished. The ruler of the waves threatened ruin to the city of Troy by an inundation, and according to the sentence of the oracle, could not be appeased, unless Laömedon would sacrifice his daughter Hesione. Like Andromeda, she also was fastened to a rock on the sea-shore, to become the prey of a sea monster, when Hercules happened to arrive there, and beheld the mournful spectacle.

He instantly offered to deliver Hesione from the cruel death that awaited her ; but not so generous as Perseus, he demanded as a reward, six beautiful horses—a demand to which Laömedon, the father of the unfortunate victim, readily agreed. But a man who had always been faithless to the gods, felt no scruples at deceiving Hercules; and after the monster was killed, and his daughter set at liberty, he refused to reward the hero's services. Hercules, incensed at his treachery, besieged Troy and put the king and all his family to the sword, except Podarces. or Priam, who had advised his father to give the promised horses to his sister's deliverer.

The conqueror gave Hesione in marriage to his friend Telamon, who had assisted him during the war, and established Priam upon his father's throne. The removal of Hesione to Greece proved fatal to the Trojans. Priam remembered with indignation, that his sister had been forcibly given to a foreigner, and sent his son Paris to Greece, to reclaim Hesione, or more probably to revenge himself upon the Greeks by carrying away Helena, which gave rise soon after to the Trojan war. Priam lived to see the future melancholy fate of Troy, together with the ruin of his royal house, then already determined by the decree of Fate.

2d. *The Victory over Antæos, Busiris, and Cacus.*—When Hercules arrived in Libya, on his expedition to the west, he met with the giant Antæos, son of Neptune and Terra.

Antæos forced all strangers who came within his reach to wrestle with him, and after having conquered them set up their skulls and bones around his dwelling as so many trophies, and boasted that he would erect a temple to his father with the skulls of his conquered antagonists. Hercules attacked him ; and having long tried his strength on him without success, at last became aware of his rising with renewed force and spirit, as often as he threw him upon his mother earth. He therefore raised him up in his mighty arms, as high as he could in the air, and squeezed him till he breathed his last. In this situation holding his foe above the ground, Hercules is often found represented upon ancient monuments.

Busiris, a king of Egypt, son of Neptune and Libya, sacrificed all foreigners to Jupiter with the greatest cruelty. When Hercules visited Egypt, Busiris carried him to the altar bound hand and foot. The hero soon disentangled himself, and offered the tyrant, with the minis· ters of his cruelty, on the altar.

Cacus, a famous robber, was a son of Vulcan and Medusa, and represented as a three-headed monster, vomiting flames. He resided in Italy, and the avenues to his caves were covered with human bones. He plundered the neighboring country; and when Hercules returned from the conquest of Geryon, Cacus stole some of his cows while he was sleeping, and dragged them backwards into his cave to prevent discovery. Hercules departed without perceiving the theft, but his oxen having lowed, were answered by the cows in the caves of Cacus, and the hero became aware of the loss that he had sustained. He ran to the place, attacked Cacus, squeezed and strangled him in his arms, though vomiting fire and smoke. In commemoration of his victory, Hercules erected an altar to Jupiter Servator; and an annual festival was instituted by the inhabitants in honor of the hero who had delivered them from such a public calamity.

Carmenta, the mother of Evander, who was then reigning over that country, presaged the apotheosis of Hercules, and here, in his life-time, the first altar was erected to him.

The representation of Hercules sleeping near his herds, while Cacus drags the oxen backwards into his caverns, is still to be found upon ancient gems.

3d. *The Deliverance of Alceste from Orcus.*—Hercules, who destroyed the tyrants that treated strangers with cruelty, was himself sensible of the benefits of hospitality, showing this sensibility in a noble manner towards king Admetos, in Thessaly.

Admetos was married to Alcestis, a daughter of king Pelias. Admetos fell sick; and according to the oracle, his life could not be saved, unless some one should be found who would voluntarily sacrifice his *own life* in his stead, and Alcestis secretly offered herself to the gods as a substitute for her husband. She in her turn fell sick, and in proportion as her illness increased, her husband's health was restored; and when Hercules entered, as a guest, the hospitable mansion of Admetos, she was dead.

The rites of hospitality were so sacred with the king, as to induce him at first to conceal his mourning in the presence of Hercules; but when the latter heard of Alcestis' tragical end, he promised his friend to bring back his beloved wife from Orcus, cost what it would.

And now Hercules embraced with his mighty arms even Death, and held him fast, until he had restored to his friend the companion of his bosom; and grief was changed into new wedding joys, and delightful conversations.

4th. *The Deliverance of Prometheus.*—In Hercules, humanity had risen, as it were, to her highest glory; as formerly in Prometheus it had sunk to the depth of humiliation. The torments of this sufferer, in whose bowels the vulture had been gnawing for centuries, now approached their termination: Hercules was to become his deliverer.

Jupiter himself gave consent to his deliverance, after Prometheus had revealed to him the prophecy, which had long been concealed, that Thetis would bear a son who should be mightier than his father

Through this revelation by the former and father of men, the power of Jupiter was a second time saved from the superiority of a mightier one, the Thunderer having entertained thoughts of marrying Thetis

Hercules killed the vulture by shooting him with his bow, and the bands with which Prometheus had been fastened to the rock fell from his limbs.

5th. *The Erection of the Pillars at the Straits between Europe and Africa.*—The fictions of the deeds of Hercules become at last colossean, losing themselves in the idea of a power, which neither men nor gods are able to resist.

When Apollo refused giving him an oracle, he took away Pythia's golden tripod, until the god had complied with his demand. The celestials complain that he once wounded Juno, and that he spared not Pluto with his arrows.

When on his expedition to the west, the sun one day emitted too vehement a heat; he drew his bow and shot an arrow at the driver of the chariot, who endeavored to reconcile him by presenting him with a golden drinking cup. On Neptune's sending a storm, he aimed at him with his arrows, and the king of the waters, to calm the hero's wrath, stilled the winds, and the waves bore on their surface that drinking vessel of gold, which, from its immense size, was used by Hercules as a bark, without apprehension of sinking, for the floods and their ruler were both submissive to him.

On his expedition to the west, having reached the remotest ends of the earth, he broke through the isthmus between Europe and Africa, thus uniting the Atlantic ocean with the Mediterranean sea. There, as a token of the exploits which he had performed, and as a mark of the termination of his wanderings, he erected two pillars upon the opposite mountains, Calpe and Abyla, which posterity called the pillars of Hercules. It is impossible for imagination to soar higher than in these pictures; for where, according to the ideas of the ancients, earth herself has her bounds—where the sun sinks into the sea—there, and there only, was the heroic course of Hercules to terminate. Only one stroke is yet wanting in the stupendous picture. It is this; he who delivered Prometheus from his protracted sufferings released Atlas also for a time from the burden that eternally pressed upon his shoulders, by taking the sky upon his own back, and thus procuring a temporary rest for the son of Iapetos.

In this posture, bearing the celestial globe upon his shoulders, Hercules is represented upon some ancient monuments.

The foregoing tales contain the most eminent of Hercules' exploits. In addition to those fictions already mentioned, the ancients ascribe to him many more; every undertaking or performance for which perseverance, heroism, and strength are requisite, is easily associated with that name which at once denoted whatever of god-like displays itself on earth in bodily strength and valor.

If, however, in any divine or heroic being, the idea of corporeal strength and undaunted courage predominates, it certainly is in the person of Heracles. Always indefatigably pursuing some object, regardless of what is standing or sinking around him, he represents, as it were, Humanity awakened from her first slumbers, feeling herself in her entire strength, and acting without any idle deliberation.

The idea of a hero in the minds of the ancients was generally not connected with that of a sage. Even in the person of Ulysses, wisdom assumes the garb of craftiness, and in that of Nestor, heroism is already lamed by old age. With the heroes, much light is mingled with the shade, and the common saying, founded upon what is constantly observed, " the greater the man the greater his shadow," finds with them its proper application. Heracles must pay the penalty of his invincible courage by many foibles, errors, and crimes. In his different marriages he found his misfortunes, and at last a painful death.

His first marriage was with Megara, the daughter of Creön, prince of Thebes, who was given to him by her father out of gratitude for having freed the city from a burdensome tribute, which had been exacted by the Orchomenians. After Megara had presented him with

four sons, he is said to have been driven distracted by Juno, and in a
fit of frenzy to have slain both mother and children. In their memory
obsequies were annually celebrated at Thebes.

In order to expiate this horrible deed, although it was not perpetrated with design, Heracles the more readily submitted to the labors
imposed upon him by Eurystheus; but when he had nearly completed
his tasks, he was enchained by a new love, and married again, notwithstanding the tragical end of his first nuptials.

Upon one of his expeditions he came to king Œneus, at Calydon,
in Ætolia, where he saw the beautiful Deianeira, the royal daughter,
who was the affianced bride of the river-god, Acheloös. Hercules
engaged in battle with him, and Deianeira was the prize of his victory.
The hero then proceeded on his way, accompanied by his wife. When
they arrived at the river Euënus, on the banks of which Nessos, the
Centaur, had his dwelling, Heracles committed to him the charge of
carrying Deianeira on his back through the river. The Centaur complied the more willingly with the request of one in whose mouth a request
amounted to a command, because he harbored the secret intention of
depriving Heracles of his wife. Accordingly, when he reached the
other bank of the river with his fair burden, he galloped off; but hearing Deianeira's cries for assistance, Heracles bent his bow, and sent
through the faithless Centaur one of those arrows which had been
dipped in the poisonous blood of the Lernæan Hydra. Nessos, brooding revenge at the very moment of his death, handed to Deianeira a
flask filled with his blood, beseeching her to keep it as a precious gift,
by means of which she could secure to herself the attachment of her
husband, as well as banish every other love from his breast, by rubbing
the blood on the garment which he wore next his body.

Heracles, pursuing his adventures, was obliged to separate himself
from time to time from Deianeira. On one occasion his absence was
unusually long; he was rambling in foreign regions without giving
her any account of himself. A new love, which afterwards afflicted
him deeper than any event of his life, because it misled him to an act
of injustice, kept him in bonds. Before his marrage with Deianeira,
Heracles had seen Iole, the daughter of king Eurytus, who reigned
over Œchalia, in Eubœa, and was conquered by her charms. He sued
for her hand from her father, but met with a refusal, at which he was
angry, and left the house of his host, meditating revenge. And soor
after, when Iphitos, the son of Eurytos, came to Heracles in quest of

his strayed horses, which the hero himself kept concealed, Heracles conducted the son of his host to the rocky walls of Tyrins, and sud-denly pitched him from the steep height.

By this deed Heracles stained his glory, and was, by the command of the gods, compelled to atone for it in a humiliating manner. He must suffer himself to be sold as a slave to the voluptuous queen Omphale, in Lydia, at whose command he was obliged to do female work.

Plastic art represents Omphale wearing the skin of the Nemæan lion round her shoulders, and holding the club in her hand, while Heracles is seen in a female dress, sitting at the distaff and spinning. The hero, who had already completed his heroic course, must never-theless become sensible of the lot of mortals, before he could take his seat in the assembly of the celestials, sinking down from his greatness in proportion to the height of his former elevation.

The fixed period of his servitude in Lydia having expired, Heracles made war upon Eurytos, because of his having refused him his daugh-ter; and carrying the city Œchalia by assault, he destroyed it, slew the king himself, and sent his daughter Iole as a slave to Deianeira, by whom she was received with kindness.

Understanding, however, that this very captive was her rival, she thought it was time to make use of the gift of Nessos. Accordingly, she took the long-preserved blood of the Centaur, and having rubbed with it a splendid tunic, she sent it to her husband by her servant Lichas, with the request not to wear the garment until he should have occasion to show himself finely dressed to the immortals at a sacred festival.

Heracles had long since received the oracle, that his death was not to be apprehended from a living being, but from a dead one. The ful-filment of this prediction was now drawing nigh.

After his victory over Eurytos, Heracles erected an altar to Jupiter upon the promontory of Cenæum, in Eubœa, and was about to kill the victims, when Lichas appeared, bringing with him Deianeira's present. The hero was the more rejoiced at the gift, because it arrived at so seasonable a time. Instantly arraying himself in the costly attire, he presented a hecatomb to the immortals, and made the flames blaze from the altars to the sky. Suddenly his newly-received tunic ad-hered to his body as if glued to it, and convulsions seized all his limbs. It was the poison of the Hydra, mingled with the blood of Nes which penetrated his body, and was now consuming the very marrow of his bones.

Suffering unspeakable pain, he called the unfortunate Lichas, who had brought him the garment, and hurled him against a rock with such force that his skull and bones were crushed to pieces. In the midst of his tortures the hero was carried to the city of Trachinia, in Thessaly. The unhappy Deianeira no sooner heard of the dreadful effect of her present than she put an end to her life.

Hyllos, the son of Heracles and Deianeira, assisting his father in his torments, at his command carried him to mount Œta, where Heracles resolved to put an end to his sufferings by a voluntary death. On Mount Œta a pile of wood was erected and kindled; it was the funeral pile of Heracles. After having recommended to his son Hyllos his much-loved Iöle, and given to Philoctetes, the son of Pœas, and his faithful companion, his bow and arrows as an inheritance, the hero ascended his fatal death-bed.

There, surrounded by the blazing flames, his face became resplendent. Heracles had finished the sufferings of humanity, and atoned for her foibles; his mortal covering, subject to pains and distress, fell off; his shade went down to Orcus, but he himself rose to Olympos, and was received into the assembly of the immortals. Juno was reconciled, and Hebe, the goddess of eternal youth, became, according to the decree of Fate, the spouse of the new deity.

Owing to the richness of Heracles' history, we find the Hero represented in many different attitudes. In a German cabinet already mentioned, two antique gems are preserved; one represents him as a youth, in the act of choking the Nemæan lion, and the other as he is resting from his labors, after having completed his course. He is sitting as if in profound meditation, drawing, with his right hand, unconsciously, as it were, a part of his lion skin round his thigh, and with his left leaning upon his club; before him an old, withered olive-trunk, with a new, flourishing shoot, is to be seen, from which his bow and quiver are suspended.

Heracles, according to the theory of Dupuis and others, is the Sun, and his twelve labors are a figurative representation of the annual course of that luminary through the signs of the zodiac. He is the powerful planet which animates and imparts fecundity to the universe; whose divinity has been honored in every quarter of the globe, by ten ples and altars, and consecrated in the religious theories of all nations; from Meroë in Ethiopia, and Thebes, in Upper Egypt, even to Britain and the very regions of Scythia; from the ancient Taprobana to Pali- bothra, in India, to Cadiz, and the shores of the Atlantic; from the forests of Germany to the burning sands of Africa; and wherever the benefits of the luminary of day are experienced, there we find estab- lished the name and worship of a Heracles.

According to Plutarch the Egyptians supposed Heracles to have his seat in the sun, and that he travelled with it around the moon; and the author of the Orphic Hymns calls Heracles the god who produced time; whose forms vary; the father of all, and the destroyer of all; the god who by turns brings back Aurora and the night, and who, moving onward from east to west, runs through the career of his twelve labors; the valiant Titan, who chases away maladies, and delivers man from the evils which afflict him.

The Phœnicians, it is said, preserved a tradition that Heracles was the Sun, and that his twelve labors indicated the Sun's passage through the twelve signs. Porphyry, who was born in Phœnicia, says, that they there gave the name of Heracles to the Sun, and that the fable of his twelve labors represents the annual path of the Sun in the heavens. The scholiast on Hesiod remarks, that "the zodiac, in which the sun performs his annual course, is the career which Heracles traverses, in the fable of his twelve labors; and his marriage with Hebe, the goddess of youth, whom he espoused after they were ended, denotes the renewal of the year."

To illustrate the fable of his labors (altering the order in which they are usually given', let us suppose the sun to commence his annual course at the summer solstice, which was indeed considered as the opening of the year, by different ancient nations.

In the first month the sun passes into the sign *Leo.* The first labor of Hercules was the slaying of the Nemæan *lion.* In the second month the sun enters Hydra. The second labor of Hercules was the killing of the Hydra, or dragon of many heads. The constellation Hydra is peculiar for its length. Its head rises with Cancer; its body extends under the sign Leo, and only ends at the later degrees of the sign Virgo. Hence the fable of the continual re-appearance of the heads of the monster whom Hercules slew. In the third month the sun enters the sign Libra, when the constellation of Centaur rises, repre- sented as bearing a wine-skin full of liquor, and a thyrsus adorned with vine-leaves and grapes. Bayer represents him with a thyrsus in one hand, and a flask of wine in the other; and the Alphonsine tables, with a goblet in his hand. At this same period, what, by some, is termed the constellation of the Boar rises. In his third labor, Hercules, after being hospitably entertained by a Centaur, encountered and slew the other Centaurs, who fought for a cask of wine. He slew also the Erymanthian Boar. In the fourth month the sun enters Scorpio, when Cassiopeia rises, who was represented, anciently, by a stag. In his fourth labor, Hercules caught the famous stag with golden horns and brazen feet, and breathing fire from its nostrils; aptly representing a constellation studded with blazing stars, and which unites itself with the solstitial fires of the sun. In the fifth month, the sun enters Sagittarius (the archer), when also appear the constellations of the vulture, swan, and eagle. In his fifth labor, Hercules destroyed, with arrows, the three birds near the lake Stymphalus. In the sixth month, the sun enters Capricornus, said to be a grandson of the luminary. At this period, the stream which flows from Aquarius sets. Its source is between the hands of Aristæus, son of the river Peneus. In his sixth labor, Hercules cleansed, by means of the river Peneus, the stables of Augias, son of Phœbus. In the seventh month, the sun enters the sign Aquarius; the constellation of the Lyre, or Vulture, sets, which is by the side of the constellation Prometheus; and the celestial bull, the bull of Pasiphaë, or of Marathon, or of Europa, passes the meridian. In his seventh labor, Hercules brought alive, into the Peloponnesus, a wild bull which laid waste the island of Crete. He also slew the vulture which preyed upon the liver of Prometheus. It should be observed that the constellation of the Vulture *sets*, and that the Vulture was *killed;* that the constellation of the bull *crosses the meridian* merely, and that Hercules brought his bull to Greece *alive.* In the eighth month, the sun enters Pisces, and the celestial horse Pegasus, or Arion, rises. Hercules, in his eighth labor, overcame and carried off the horses of Diomedes. In the ninth month the sun enters the sign Aries (sacred to Mars), the same with the ram of the golden fleece; the celestial ship Argo rises; Cassiopeia and Andromeda set; Andromeda is remarkable for its many beautiful stars, one of which is called her girdle. In his ninth labor, Hercules embarked on board the Argo in quest of the golden fleece; contended with female warriors, and took from their queen, Hippolyta, the daughter of Mars, a famous girdle. In the tenth month, the sun enters

Taurus ; the constellation Orion, fabled to have pursued the Pleiades, daughters of Atlas ; the conductor of the oxen of Icarus, and the river Eridanus, also ; the Pleiades rise, and the she-goat, fabled to have been the spouse of Faunus. The tenth labor of Hercules was restoring from pirates, employed by Busiris, the seven Pleiades to their father; slay-ing Busiris, the same as Orion ; bearing away the oxen of Geryon, and vanquishing Cacus. In the eleventh month, the sun passes into the sign of Gemini ; Procyon sets ; the Dog-star rises, and the swan. In his eleventh labor, Hercules conquered the Dog Cerberus, and tri-umphed over Cycnus (Swan), at the time when the dog-star's influence is felt upon the fields.

In the twelfth month the sun enters the sign *Cancer*, the last of the twelve, commencing with Leo. The constellations of the river and the Centaur set, that of Hercules Ingeniculus also descends towards the western regions, or those of *Hesperia*, followed by the dragon of the pole, the guardian of the golden apples of the Hesperides, whose head he crushes with his foot. In his twelfth labor, Hercules travelled to Hesperia in quest of the golden fruit, guarded by the dragon. After this, he offers up a sacrifice, and clothes himself in a robe dipped in the blood of the *Centaur*, whom he had slain in crossing a river. The robe takes fire, and the hero perishes amid the flames, but only to re-sume his youth in the heavens, and become a partaker of immortality.

The Centaur thus terminates the mortal career of Hercules ; and in like manner the new annual period commences with the passage of the sun into Leo, marked by a group of stars in the morning that glitter like the flames that issued from the vestment of Nessos.

If we regard Hercules as having actually existed, nothing can be more monstrous, nothing more at variance with every principle of chro-nology, nothing more replete with contradictions, than the adventures of such an individual as poetry makes him to have been. But, consid ered as the luminary that gives life and light to the world, as the god who impregnates all nature with his fertilizing rays, every part of the legend teems with animation and beauty, and is marked by a pleasing and perfect harmony. The sun of the summer solstice is here repre-sented with all the attributes of that divine strength which he has acquired at this season of the year. He enters proudly on his course in obedience to the eternal order of nature. It is no longer the sign Leo that he traverses ; he combats a fearful lion that ravages the plains. The Hydra is the second monster that opposes the hero, and the constellation in the heavens becomes a terrible animal on earth, to which the language of poetry assigns a hundred heads, with the power of re-producing them as soon as they are crushed by the weapon of the hero. All obstacles that array themselves against the illustrious champion are gifted with some quality or attribute that exceeds the bounds of nature ; the horses of Diomedes feed on human flesh ; the females rise above the timidity of their sex, and become formidable heroines; the apples of the Hesperides are of gold ; the stag has brazen hoofs ; the dog of Hades bristles with serpents ; every thing, even down to the crab, is formidable ; for every thing in nature is great, and must there-fore, be equally so in the various symbols that are used to designate her various powers.

Heracles, with Omphale, is the solar god descended into the Ompha-los, or navel of the world, amid the signs of the southern hemisphere ; and it was the festival of this powerful star, in some degree enervated at the period of the winter solstice, which the Lydian people celebrated by the change of vestments made between the weaker and stronger sex.

The fable of his protracted birth already announces the god of light, struggling against the powers of darkness. Long did Hera put every obstacle in the way of it, and this hostile power, after persecuting the mother, persecutes the son, and her obstinate hatred becomes the means by which the divine power of his nature is developed in all its splendor.

DIONYSOS OR BACCHUS.*

Dionysos and Heracles, although born of mortal mothers, are asso-ciated in the assembly of the immortal gods. Yet, Dionysos is by far the higher, the more divine person. From the beginning, the plenitude of his being is revealed ; and from his very birth, he is ranked among the celestials, while Heracles, by bold deeds and invincible valor, must prepare himself the path to immortality. For this reason, too, the latter, during his life-time, was ranked only among the god-like heroes; while Dionysos was always entitled to the society of the gods.

The archetype of Dionysos (the reproductive force of nature, of which wine is the symbol) was the inward swelling fulness of nature, typified in the foaming cup, from which she bestows animating enjoy-

---

* He was called Bacchus both by the Greeks and Romans; that is, the noisy or riot-ous god. It was originally a mere epithet or surname of Dionysos, and does not occur till after the time of Herodotus.

ment on the initiated. The worship of Dionysos, therefore, like that
of Demeter, was mysterious; for both deities are the emblems of the
whole of nature, which no mortal eye penetrates.

The fiction of the birth of Dionysos contains a deep meaning. The
jealous Hera, appearing to his mother in the character of an old woman,
instigated the daughter of Cadmos to express the extravagant wish of
enjoying Zeus in his divine character Semele accordingly, first desired the Thunderer to swear compliance to the request she was about
to make to him, and when he had taken the oath, she demanded that
he should appear to her in his true, divine person. Zeus, not daring
to break the terrible oath by Styx, was compelled to approach her by
thunder and lightning. The wretched Semele, killed by the thunder,
and consumed by the lightning, fell a sacrifice to her rash request.
Zeus snatched from her his son Dionysos, yet unborn, and placed him
in his thigh, where he remained till the regular time of his birth. Mortality is destroyed ere immortality rises. Man, during his life-time on
earth, not being able to bear the glory of divinity, is annihilated by its
terrible majesty.

At the birth of the child, Zeus gave him the name of Dionysos, and
sent him by Hermes to Ino, sister to Semele, with directions to rear
him; but Hera, whose revenge was not yet satiated, caused Athamas,
the husband of Ino, to go mad. Zeus, to save Dionysos from the machinations of Hera, changed him into a kid, under which form Hermes
conveyed him to the nymphs of Nysa, who were to take charge of his
education, and by whom he was reared with the greatest tenderness.

In his boyhood, Dionysos, as if yet half reeling in sweet slumber,
does not comprehend the fulness of his being, and appears apprehensive
of injuries inflicted by men, until his formidable power suddenly reveals itself through miraculous events. Lycurgus, king of the Edones,
a people of Thrace, surprised the nurses of Dionysos on Mount Nysa,
and wounded several of them. The terrified Dionysos threw himself
into the sea, when Thetis took him up in her arms; but he avenged
himself by driving Lycurgus mad, when he killed his own son, Dryas,
with a blow of an axe, mistaking him for a vine-branch His subjects
afterwards bound him, and left him on Mount Pangæon, where he was
destroyed by wild horses, for such was the will of Dionysos.

When Dionysos grew up, he discovered the culture of the vine, and
the mode of extracting its precious liquor; but Hera struck him with
madness, and in this state he roamed through a great part of Asia.

In Phrygia he was met by Rhea, who cured him, and taught him her religious rites, which he resolved to introduce into Greece. In his course he met with various adventures.

At one time a body of pirates, who took him for the son of a king, in the hope of obtaining a large ransom, carried him off and placed him on board their ship. No sooner, however, had they left the shore, than the cords with which the smiling boy was fastened fell off, and a fragrant stream of wine ran through the ship; then suddenly a vine rose to the top-sail, which expanded its branches, loaded with heavy grapes : the mast became entwined with dark ivy, and all the oars were covered with vine leaves. On the deck of the vessel a terrible lion made its appearance, casting around him fierce, threatening glances; terror seized the offenders, who leaped from the ship into the raging sea, where suddenly appearing as swimming dolphins, they bore witness to the power of the all-conquering deity.

When Dionysos reached Thebes, the women readily received the new rites, and ran wildly through the woods of Cithæron. Pentheus, the ruler of Thebes, set himself against them ; but Dionysos caused him to be torn to pieces by his mother and aunts The daughters of Minyas, Leucippe, Aristippe, and Alcathoë, also despised his rites, and continued plying their looms, while the other women ran through the mountains. Dionysos appeared to them as a maiden and remonstrated, but in vain ; he then assumed the form of various wild beasts ; serpents filled their baskets , vines and ivy twined round their looms, while wine and milk distilled from the roof; still their obstinacy was unsubdued. He finally drove them mad, when they tore to pieces the son of Leucippe, and then went roaming through the mountains, till Hermes touched them with his wand, and changed them into a bat, an owl, and a crow.

Dionysos next proceeded to Attica, where he taught Icarios the culture of the vine. Icarios having made wine, gave it to some shepherds, who, thinking themselves poisoned, killed him ; recovering themselves, they buried him. His daughter, Erigone, being shown the spot by his faithful dog Mæra, hung herself through grief.

At Argos the rites of Dionysos were received by the women as at Thebes, and opposed by Perseus, the son of Zeus and Danaë ; Zeus, however, reduced his two sons to amity, and Dionysos thence passed over to Naxos, where he met with Ariadne. Afterwards he descended to Erebos, whence he brought his mother, whom he named Thyone; and ascended with her to the abode of the gods.

The expedition of Bacchos to India, is a beautiful and sublime fiction. With an army of both men and women, who advanced with joyful tumult, he extended his beneficent conquests as far as the Ganges, teaching the conquered nations the cultivation of the vine, together with a higher enjoyment of life, and giving them laws. In the divine person of Bacchos, men revered the more cheerful delights of life, as a particular, sublime being, who, under the form of an eternally flourishing youth, subdues lions and tigers that draw his chariot, and who, in divine ecstasy, accompanied by the sound of flutes and timbrels, proceeds in triumph, from east to west, through all countries.

The victorious expedition, undertaken for the benefit of the nations of earth, was accomplished by Bacchos in three years ; for which reason the festivals afterwards instituted in remembrance of it, were always celebrated after the same interval of time. Then, the joyful tumult which accompanied the march of the god through the earth was repeated, and celebrated anew from every hill and mountain. The priestesses of the god of wine, roaming with dishevelled hair upon the mountains, filled the air with the noise proceeding from the beating of timbrels, playing upon flutes, &c., and the wild, continual cry, of Euöi ! Bacche ! The threatening thyrses in their hands, from which the colored ribbons waved, while the pine-apple on its top concealed the wounding point, is an emblem of the expedition to India ; on occasion of which, the clamor of war and din of battle were hidden under song and the sound of musical instruments.

These inspired priestesses of Bacchos afforded a sublime subject to ancient poetry. A Bacchante in her ecstasy, was as if raised above the bounds of humanity. Inspired by the power of the deity, the boundaries of human life were too narrow for her. Thus an ancient poet describes such an inspired personage, as on the top of a mountain, which she had unconsciously ascended ; she suddenly wakes from her mental slumber, and beholds, beneath her, the river Hebrus, and all Thrace covered with snow. "The danger is sweet, thus to follow the god whose temples are enriched with verdant leaves." The very straining of all the powers, thus climbing up a steep mountain, in wild inspiration, is what renders this picture so beautiful

Even old age is to be seen in the retinue of Bacchos, intoxicated by the sweet juice of the grape, and staggering about with uncertain step

The most conspicuous figure in the train, however, is old Silenos, his reputed foster-father, riding with hoary head on his ass, supported by Satyrs and Fauns, and making in this state the most charming contrast in the youthful picture. Notwithstanding the ridicule which in this manner is brought upon the person of Silenos, he is often represented in the fictions of the ancients, as being a person of high mental powers. A profound knowledge of divine things is ascribed to him, and his very drunkenness is emblematically interpreted, by the giddiness into which profound meditation on the most sublime subjects has thrown him, and not the immoderate use of the sweet juice of the grape. He was also associated with the wise centaur Cheiron, as the tutor of young Bacchus. Two youthful shepherds finding Silenos sleeping from intoxication, bound him, while the nymph Ægle painted his cheeks with the juice of red berries, in order that the god, whom mortals could fetter in his sleep, might ransom himself by granting some request. When old Silenos awoke, the swains promised him his liberty, on condition that he would give them a lay. He acquiesced, and profound wisdom flowed from those lips, which were commonly wet with the drink of the vine. He chants forth the origin of things, and their miraculous change; the swains listen with rapture to the song, which equals their highest wishes. This charming fiction shows also, how artfully the ancients veiled the ridiculous itself with dignity, and always found out that point which seems to us to be lost—the point where smiling sport and heavenly sublimity unite. At Elis, in Greece, Silenos had a temple of his own, and was worshipped as a higher being. The wantonly smiling Fauns, and the sarcastic Satyrs, also belonged to the train of Bacchos, with which, in general, were connected all those beings, who, endowed with youthful wantonness and cheerful levity, were, by a higher nature elevated above the cares and duties of mortals; and thus, were forced neither by human necessities, nor moral obligations, to keep within the bounds of moderation. Bacchos, with his train, was with the an- cients the emblem of the most cheerful enjoyment; and as such, they must consider it as absolute, and without restrictions, comprising what would destroy mankind, if found in real life.

The same ancient poet. therefore, who in enthusiastic strains sings the praises of Bacchos, cautions those who are drinking the cup which the god yields, to refrain from bloody quarrels; citing as a warning example, the affray between the Centaurs and Lapithæ, who, heated with wine, forgot the hospitable repast, and with blood thirsty desire assailed one another in furious tumult, till the ground was covered with the bodies of the slain. Notwithstanding the threatening dangers arising from the homage paid to the god of wine, with the ancients, sensual pleasure, and even wild debauchery, were numbered in the general computation of things, and by no means excluded from the feasts of their gods. With them, life was considered as a tree full of sap, which unrestrained, shot out in exuberant twigs and branches, and, as they thought, without being disfigured by its luxuriant excrescences.

In this light too, the festivals of Bacchos must be viewed ; for it was the intention of the ancients to represent, by the loud and cheerful train of Bacchos, the utmost degree of joy and pleasure ; a moderate Bacchanalian festival would be no Bacchanalian festival at all, as a placid and affectionate Juno would cease to be a Juno ; and an honest Mercury would no longer be a Mercury. Indeed, if one should attempt to divest a Bacchanalian feast of revelry and extravagance, it would immediately cease also to be an object of art; for the very wildness, the roving about with' reeling steps, the flourishing of the thyrses, and the licentiousness of the Bacchantes, are the traits which alone can render such a picture interesting to an artist.

Mythologists differ in opinion as to the origin of Bacchos. Creutzer and others consider his worship as evidently of eastern origin, and that he is identified with the Osiris of the Egyptians and the Schiva of India. The fable of his birth, and his strange translation to the thigh of the monarch of Olympos, bear the impress of oriental imagery. An ivy branch is made to spring forth from a column to cover him with its leaves when he is taken from his mother, and the Ivy was in Egypt the plant of Osiris. In like manner, the coffin of the Egyptian deity is shaded by the plant *erica*, which springs from the ground and envelopes it. Bacchos and Osiris both float upon the waters in a chest, or ark, and both have for one of their symbols the head of a bull.

The Lingam and equilateral triangle, symbols of Bacchos, were also symbols of Schiva. The two systems of worship have the same obscenities and the same emblems Schiva is represented, in the Hindoo Mythology, as assuming the form of a lion during the great battle of the gods. He seizes the monster that attacks him with his teeth and fangs, while Dourga pierces him with his lance. In the Grecian Mythology, the same exploit is attributed to Bacchos, under the same form, against the giant Rhœtos.

The manner in which the worship of Bacchos was carried into Greece will ever remain an enigma of difficult solution. The Greeks, indeed, made Thebes the birth-place of this deity; but this proves nothing for the fact of his Grecian origin. Thebes, in Bœotia, was the centre of the Cadmean-Asiatic Mythology; a god whose worship *came* to the rest of the Greeks out of Thebes, was for them a deity *born* in Thebes; and hence arose the legend of the Theban origin of Bacchos. So, when the Greek Mythology makes Bacchos to have gone on an expedition to Asia, and to have conquered India, it merely reverses the order of events, and describes as the victorious progress of a Grecian deity, what was in reality the course which the religion of an oriental deity took from the East to the West.

Voss, in his *Anti-Symbolik*, gives a history of the introduction of the worship of Bacchos into Greece, and its progress into that country, from the thirtieth to the sixtieth Olympiad. We find this worship making its first appearance in the mysteries of Samothrace; furnishing to the Ionian school Phœnician elements; enriching itself with ideas of Asiatic origin, by means of the extension of commerce; mingling with the elements of Grecian philosophy in their very cradle; presenting Lydian and Phrygian additions as a primitive basis; giving an occult meaning to the public games at Olympia; carrying back into Egypt, under the reign of Psammetichus along with the Milesian colonies, and enriched with immense developments, what the Egyptian colonies had once carried into Greece; identifying itself with the Orphic doctrine, but always remaining an object of suspicion and aversion, and contemned by the wise in the days of Zenophanes and Heraclitus, as it had been a long time before proscribed by kings and rejected by communities.

The fables of which Bacchos is made the hero, the rites which those fables elucidated—rites bearing at one time the impress of profound sadness, at another of frantic joy, and by turns bloody and licentious, mournful and frantic, never became a part of the Grecian religion. Wherever they announced themselves, they excited only horror and dread. The sufferings and destructions of various dynasties attach themselves to their frightful and sudden appearance. Agave rends in pieces her son Pentheus; Ino precipitates herself into the sea with Melicerta in her arms; and the daughters of Minyas, becoming furious, commit horrible murder, and undergo a hideous metamorphosis.

The language of the poets who relate to us these fearful traditions.

is sombre and mysterious in its character, and bears evident marks of a sacerdotal origin. The philosophic Euripides, as well as Ovid, who expresses himself with so much lightness in reference to other legends, appears, in describing the death of Pentheus, to partake of the sanguinary joy, the ferocious irony, and the fanaticism of the Bacchantes. One would feel tempted to say, that the sacerdotal spirit had triumphed over the incredulous poets; and that after the lapse of ten centuries, the frenzy of the ancient orgies had affected their senses and troubled their reason.

In the age of Homer, these mournful recitals were either unknown or treated with disdain ; for he speaks only once of Bacchos, on occasion of the victory which he gained over Lycurgos. And the scholiasts express their surprise that the poet, after having thus placed Bacchos among the divinities of Olympos, makes him take no part in the subjects that divide them. The Grecian spirit, therefore, at an early period, renounced every attempt to modify this heterogeneous conception.

The Grecian festivals, in honor of Dionysos, called Dionysia, were observed at Athens with more splendor and superstition than in any other part of Greece. The years were numbered by their celebration, the archon assisted at their solemnity, and the priests who officiated were honored with the most dignified seats at the public games. They were at first celebrated with great simplicity, and the time was consecrated to mirth. It was then usual to bring a vessel full of wine, adorned with a vine branch, after which followed a goat, a basket of figs, and other emblems. In imitation of the poetical fictions of Dionysos, his worshippers were clothed in fawn skins, fine linen, and mitres, and crowned themselves with garlands of ivy, vine, and fir, and carried thyrses, drums, pipes and flutes. Some, in the uncouth manner of their dress, and their fantastic motions, imitated Pan, Silenos, and the Satyrs ; and some rode on asses, while others drove the goats to slaughter for the sacrifice, and in this manner both sexes joined in the solemnity, and ran about the hills and country, nodding their heads, dancing in ridiculous postures, and filling the air with hideous shrieks and shouts, crying Bacche! Io! Io! Euöi! Iacche! etc.. beating on drums and sounding various instruments.

With such solemnities were the Greek festivals of Bacchos celebrated. In one of these a procession was formed, bearing the various emblems of his worship ; and among them a select number of noble virgins car ried baskets of gold, filled with all kinds of fruit; serpents were some-times put in the baskets, and by their wreathing and crawling out amused and astonished the beholders. This was the most mysterious part of the solemnity.

These festivals, in honor of the god of wine, contributed much to the corruption of morals among all classes of people. They were intro-duced into Etruria, and from thence to Rome, where both sexes pro-miscuously joined in the celebration during the darkness of the night; but their vicious excesses called for the interference of the senate, who passed a decree, banishing the Bacchanalia for ever from Rome.

The women who bore a chief part in these festivals were called *Mænades*, *Bacchæ*, *Thyiades*, and *Euades*.

As the god of wine, Bacchos is generally represented crowned with vine and ivy leaves, with a thyrse in his hand. His figure is that of an effeminate young man.

In the divine form of the eternally youthful Bacchos, similar beings veiled by grey antiquity in mysterious fables, are renewed. Upon ancient monuments we yet not unfrequently meet with an Indian, as well as an Egyptian Bacchos, both of whom are represented with beards, and not in youthful forms.

The golden horns upon the head of Bacchos, which by the plastic art of the Greeks were either entirely hidden, or partly concealed, are a token of the high antiquity of this god ; such horns having been in the remotest times connected with the ideas of inward, divine power.

Among animals, the spotted panther is sacred to Bacchos ; fierce-ness, nay, even cruelty is tamed by him, and cringes at his feet; and he is said to have been clothed in the skin of this animal on his expe-dition to India. The ever-verdant ivy, and the snake, which, casting its skin, renews itself, are pleasing emblems of perpetual youth ; in which the divine form of Bacchos resembles that of Apollo, only with this difference—the former is represented as more delicate and feminine. His beauty is compared to that of Apollo, and both are represented with fine hair flowing loosely on the shoulders.

A beautiful antique gem shows Bacchos sitting in a chariot, drawn by two panthers, on which two Cupids are riding, and one of them playing the flute. Another gem represents Silenos with a sickle in his right hand, and his left arm resting on a lyre ; an emblem of ecstasy overflowing in harmonious lays.

In his triumphs over the Indians, the captives are represented as chained, and placed on wagons or elephants, and among them is carried a large *crater* full of wine; Bacchos is in a chariot drawn by elephants or panthers, leaning on Ampelos, preceded by Pan, and followed by Silenos, the Satyrs, and Mænades, who make the air resound with the clash of their instruments, and the sound of their voices.

The thyrse was one of the most common and ancient attributes of Bacchos and his joyous crew. It consisted of a lance, the iron point of which was concealed in a pine cone, in memory of the stratagem of his followers in concealing their pikes. It was used at all the festivals held in his honor, and often twined with wreaths of ivy or bay.

MINOS, RHADAMANTHYS, AND SARPEDON.

Zeus, says the legend, becoming enamored of the beauty of Europa, the daughter of Phœnix or Agenor, changed himself into a beautiful white bull, and "breathing saffron from his mouth," he approached her as she was gathering flowers with her companions in a mead near the shore. Europa, delighted with the tameness and beauty of the animal, caressed him, crowned him with flowers, and at length ventured to mount his back. The disguised god immediately made off with his lovely burden, ran along the waves of the sea, and made no stop till he arrived at Crete, not far from Gortyna. Here he resumed his own form, and beneath a plane-tree embraced the trembling maiden. By him she had three sons, Minos, Rhadamanthys, and Sarpedon.

These three brothers fell into discord for the sake of a beautiful youth named Miletos, the son of Apollo, or of Zeus. The youth testifying the most esteem for Sarpedon, Minos chased them out of Crete. Miletos went to Caria, where he built a town which he named from himself. Sarpedon went to Lycia, where he aided Cilix against the people of that country, and obtained the sovereignty of a part of it. Zeus is said to have bestowed on him a life of triple duration.

Rhadamanthys ruled with justice and equity over the islands. Having accidentally committed homicide, he retired to Bœotia, where he married Alcmena, the mother of Heracles. According to Homer, Rhadamanthys was placed on the Elysian Plain, among the heroes to whom Zeus allotted that blissful abode. Pindar seems to make him a sovereign or judge in the island of the Blest. Later poets place him with Minos and Æacos in the under-world, where their office is to judge the dead.

Minos is chiefly remarkable for belonging to a period when history and mythology interlace; and as uniting in his own person the chief characteristics of both. He is a son of Zeus, and yet the first possessor of a navy; a judge in Hades, and at the same time a king in Crete.

It is worthy of remark, that Crete, so famous at this age, both for its naval power and for being the birth-place of the Olympian gods, should never afterwards have attained any thing like the celebrity which its position seemed to promise. Its office seems to have been that of leading the way in naval supremacy. Too isolated for power of a durable nature, it was lost in the confederate or opposing glories of Athens and Sparta; but while they were yet in their infancy, the insular form of Crete (together perhaps with some Asiatic refinement) gave it that concentrated energy, which in an early age is irresistible.

According to fiction, Minos, in a grotto on Mount Ida, had occasional secret converse with his father Zeus, the purport of which he announced to the listening people as the fundamental part of legislation. In consequence of this wise government and justice, fiction transferred to him, together with his brother and counsellor, Rhadamanthys, as the most righteous of mortals, the judicature over the dead in the lower world; associating with them Æacos, the father of Peleus, and sometimes Triptolemos too, the benefactor of mankind.

Minos, the legislator, was at the same time a warlike and valiant prince, who, sweeping the pirates from the Mediterranean sea, rendered sailing and commerce safe. But the hero, who in many respects was the benefactor of mankind, was obliged to endure misfortunes which shaded his glorious victories in gloom.

The wife of Minos was Pasiphaë, a daughter of the Sun and Perseis, and sister of Æetes. By her he had several children, the most celebrated of whom were Androgeos, Glaucos, Deucalion, Ariadne, and Phædra.

After the death of Asterion, the Cretans hesitated whether to give Minos the royal dignity; to prove his claim to it, he asserted that he could obtain whatever he chose to pray for. Then, sacrificing to Poseidon, he besought him to send him a bull from the bottom of the sea (a bull with the ancients being an emblem of power), promising to sacrifice whatever should appear. Poseidon sent the bull, and Minos received the kingdom. According to Homer, he ruled nine years at Cnossos, and was the intimate friend of Zeus. He was victorious in war, and extended his dominion over the isles of the Ægean.

The bull which Poseidon had sent out of the sea, being of a large size and brilliant white hue, appeared to Minos too beautiful an animal to be slain; he therefore put him in his herd and substituted an ordinary one in its place. This act offended Poseidon, and he caused the bull to run wild, and at the same time inspired Pasiphaë with a strange passion for him, and she became the parent of the monster, half man and half bull, which, under the name of the Minotaur, often makes its appearance in ancient fictions.

Dædalos, the most skilful artist and architect of that time, had fled to Crete, on account of a crime committed in his native city of Athens; and Minos, in compliance with an oracle, charged him with making that subterranean building, with many walks and innumerable winding passages, which is known by the name of the Cretan Labyrinth. In the middle of this Labyrinth was the abode of the Minotaur, visible only to those unfortunate victims who were thrown to the monster to be devoured, or those who had dared to enter the Labyrinth, but were unable to extricate themselves, and thus came within the reach of its terrible inmate.

In the mean while, Androgeos, a son of Minos, accompanied by many of his friends, had undertaken a voyage to Athens to participate in the celebration of the Athenian games. Having there excited the jealousy and suspicion of Ægeus, the childless king of Athens, because he had taken the prize in every combat, and gained the applause of the whole people, the promising son of Minos was basely assassinated. No sooner was his father informed of this new misfortune that had befallen him, than he went over to Athens with his whole force to avenge the murder.

He first besieged Nisa, where Nisos, brother of Ægeus, was king. Nisos, with his city, was betrayed by his own daughter, Scylla, who having an admiration for Minos, in disregard both of filial love and duty, went to her father while he was sleeping, and cut from his head a golden lock, by means of which he had been invincible. She handed this lock, the strength of her father, to Minos; but instead of gaining favor with the Cretan ruler, as she had expected, she was punished by him according to her deserts: he employed the gift to his advantage, but treated the giver with scorn and contempt.

After the attack on Nisa, which city was afterwards called Megara, Minos immediately moved with his army towards Athens, which oppressed by drought and famine, was already groaning under the wrath of the gods and its distressing fate. In addition to the miseries which they suffered, it was declared by an oracle, that the immortals would not cease to send misfortunes on the city, until it should have given to Minos ample satisfaction for the murder of his son. Upon this, the Athenians sent ambassadors to the ruler of Crete, who appeared before him with humble demeanor, and supplicated peace. Minos granted peace on this hard condition;—that Athens should send annually, seven of her handsomest youths, and as many of her most beautiful maidens to Crete, in order, as victims of their native land, to expiate the murder of Androgeos, by becoming the prey of the Minotaur.

When Theseus had at last killed this monster and fled with Ariadne, the daughter of the Cretan monarch, Minos, unable to avenge himself in any other manner, shut up the Athenian Dædalos, together with his son, Icaros, in the Labyrinth, the work of his own hands. The art of Dædalos, however, supplied him with the means of flying with his son out of prison, and of reaching Sicily, where he met with a friendly reception by Cocalos, king of the island.

Minos demanded that Dædalos should be delivered up to him; and having been invited by Cocalos to a personal interview, went to Sicily, where he was received by the king in a friendly manner; but in the end was secretly suffocated when bathing. Thus Minos, the wise Legislator, the valiant warrior, the benefactor of mankind, found his death in a foreign country, while pursuing the artist who was protected by the immortals. He was succeeded in his kingdom by his son Deucalion, whose son, Idomeneus, led the troops of Crete to the war of Troy.

THESEUS.

Theseus, king of Athens, and son of Ægeus by Æthra, the daughter of Pittheus, monarch of Trœzen, was one of the most famous heroes of antiquity. Ægeus, who was privately married to Æthra, before leaving Trœzen, concealed his sword and sandals under a stone, and told Æthra, that if she should have a son, not to send him to Athens until he had become strong enough to raise it. She obeyed the injunction, and Theseus was educated by Connidas under the supervision of his grandfather, the wise Pittheus; and as often as the Athenians celebrated a festival in honor of Theseus, the name of Connidas was mentioned with veneration.

When Theseus was grown to the proper age, his mother led him to

the stone on which he was to try his strength. Lifting it, he took
from beneath his father's sword and sandals, with which he entered
upon his journey to Athens.

Imitating the example of Heracles, whom the glowing soul of the
young hero had embraced as his model, he chose the more dangerous
way by land, where he must encounter robbers, who made the roads
unsafe, and who treated all strangers who fell into their hands in the
most cruel manner   As Theseus, armed with his father's good sword,
was passing on his way from Trœzen, through the country of Epidau-
ros, he first met with Periphates, a son of Hephæstos. This ferocious savage was famous for his cruelty, and trusting to his gigantic
strength, laid wait for travellers with no other weapon than a club,
which, however, was the terror of all the surrounding country. Theseus, assaulted by him, stretched him to the ground by the aid of his
good sword, and ever after carried the club of his foe in remembrance
of his victory.

Upon the Isthmus of Corinth he fought a still more cruel murderer,
Sinis (*Evil-doer*), who was also called the *Pine-bender*. His strength
was so great that he was able to take pine trees by the top, and bend
them to the ground. Placing himself by the road-side, he obliged all
passengers to take hold of a pine with him and bend it ; he would then
let go, and the tree flying up, the unhappy stranger was dashed to the
ground and killed. Theseus, on being challenged, though he never
before attempted such a feat, held down the tree with ease ; he then
conquered the monster, and obliged him to undergo the punishment
that his cruelty and crimes deserved, by putting him to death in the
same manner in which he had been accustomed to destroy his fellow
creatures.

Theseus likewise delivered the countries through which he passed
from the monsters by which they were infested ; killing, among others,
the Cromyonian Swine, which, wasting the fields, and threatening destruction everywhere to the inhabitants, was both a plague and a terror
to the land.

As he approached the borders of Megara, he came to the narrow
path overhanging the sea, where the robber Sciron (from whom the
pass derived its name) had fixed his abode. When any stranger
came to him, it was the custom of Sciron, instead of giving water to
wash the feet of his guest, to insist upon the guest's washing his feet.
This ceremony was performed on the pass ; and Sciron, taking advan-

tage of the opportunity it gave him, tumbled every one into the sea, where was a huge tortoise always ready to devour the bodies of those who were thrown down. Theseus conquered Sciron, and threw him down to the tortoise.

In Eleusis, Theseus fought with the robber Cercyon, whom he van quished and killed; and upon arriving a short distance further, at Hermione, he found the formidable Damastes, who, from the particular kind of cruelty with which he abused foreigners, was called Procrustes (*the Stretcher*). For this tyrant is said to have had two iron bedsteads, of different lengths, in which he placed all strangers who arrived within his reach; and in such a manner as to lay the short ones upon the long bedstead, and those who were of a larger stature, upon the short one. He then by force stretched the former to the extremity of the bedstead, and cut off the limbs of the latter to fit their couch of torture. Theseus, after having subdued him in a combat, subjected him to the same pain that he had inflicted upon others, and then delivered the earth from the monster.

It seems as if fiction here aimed at representing the violation of the rites of hospitality in its most heinous light; for what can be imagined more cruel and barbarous than to change the very place of repose into a rack! It was under the sacredness of hospitality, that men could first commune with each other, and contribute to their mutual civilization. To rid the earth of such as violated these sacred rites, and thereby hinder the progress of improvement among mankind, was a task worthy of the heroes, whose proper reward is, having their names immortalized as the benefactors of the world.

When Theseus arrived at Athens, he was recognized and acknowledged by Ægeus as his son and successor on the royal throne; upon which, the sons of Pallas, the brother of Ægeus, who had already flattered themselves with the hope of succeeding their childless uncle in the government of Athens, excited a revolt, which, however, was immediately quelled by Theseus.

It was then the third year that the Athenians had been obliged to send the sad tribute of fourteen of its handsomest children to the island of Crete, as an atonement for the murder of Androgeos, son of Minos; and as long as the Minotaur was alive, the Athenians dared not hope to be released from the tribute. When, therefore, the youths and maidens had drawn their lot of death, and as the destined victims

for the present year were departing, in spite of the entreaties of his
father to the contrary, Theseus voluntarily offered himself as one of
their number, in the hope of conquering the monster.

Before his departure, he made a vow to Apollo that, if he should be
successful in this undertaking, he would send annually to his temple
on the island of Delos, a ship laden with offerings and presents; and,
upon inquiring of the oracle what the event should be, he received for
answer, that if he chose Love for his guide, it would be successful.

The ship departed as usual, under black sails, which Theseus promised his father to exchange for white in case he should return victorious. The vessel, wafted by favorable winds, soon arrived at Crete,
where, when the victims were presented to Minos, the eyes of Ariadne,
his royal daughter, rested upon Theseus, whose beauty and noble stature made an impression on her heart. Theseus chose Love for his
guide, receiving from Ariadne the clew that made him secure of a passage out of the Labyrinth. Holding Ariadne's thread in his hand, he
confidently descended into the mazes of the subterranean building,
where, as soon as he had found the Minotaur, he began a desperate
fight with the monster, and killed him, aided by the advice which he
had received from Ariadne.

The death of the monster freed the Athenians from the horrible
tribute which they had twice paid with their own children; and their
sons and daughters, already destined to die a cruel death, owed their
preservation to Theseus. The expression of their gratitude became a
favorite subject of plastic art, in ancient as well as in modern times.
A picture, found in Herculaneum, shows the hero surrounded by tender boys, who were saved from death by his exertions, and who, in
gratitude, are embracing his knees and kissing his hands.

Ariadne fled with her beloved Theseus to the island of Naxos, where,
however, Theseus was forced by the will of the gods to desert her, because Bacchos, the deity of the island, was captivated by her charms.
The god found her sleeping at night in the open air, and when she
awoke, he, in token of his divinity, cast the golden crown which he
wore upon his head towards the sky, where it immediately appeared as
a splendid constellation, and bore witness to the marriage of Bacchos
and Ariadne.

Before returning to Athens, Theseus sailed to the island of Delos
in order to pay his vow to Apollo. At the same time, he there consecrated to Aphrodite, in gratitude for the assistance he had received from

her, a statue made by Dædalos ; and to preserve the memory of his victory over the Minotaur, he instituted a dance, which imitated the windings of the Labyrinth.

The sacred vow which Theseus had made to the god of Delos, was, long after his death, fulfilled with the greatest care by the Athenians. In the very same ship in which the hero had returned from Crete, ambassadors, crowned with olive wreaths, were sent every year to Delos ; and to make the vessel, as it were, everlasting, the injuries of time were carefully repaired, so that at last, although considered the same, she was an entirely different ship from that which had borne the hero. Neither was any criminal put to death while this ship was on its passage to and from Delos—a circumstance which long afterwards spared for a short time the life of Socrates. It was a law worthy of the sublime sentiments of the Athenians during their better times, that while celebrating the delivery of their children from destruction, no one should become the victim of a violent death.

From Delos, Theseus steered directly to Athens, to announce there the happy issue of his enterprise, which was yet to terminate in a tragical event. For when Ægeus, standing on a high rock near the sea-shore, and looking anxiously over the waters for the returning ship, descried at last a black sail, which the pilot had forgotten to exchange for a white one, in despair he threw himself into the sea. which after him is called the Ægean.

Theseus was received with loud applause by the Athenians, as their protector and deliverer from the most distressing tribute ; and, succeeding his father on the royal throne, he availed himself of the affection of his people, and introduced a wise course of government, as well as an improved code of laws. Indeed he may be called the creator of the Athenian state, because he united the people (who, until his day, had lived scattered) in small districts, and brought them into one compact body in the city, which he divided into certain sections; he also settled the borders of the Athenian territory, by treaties with the neighboring tribes. Having succeeded in modelling the people according to his views, he instituted the religious service of *Peitho*, the goddess of persuasion.

After having accomplished his task as a royal magistrate and legislator, Theseus gave an example of magnanimity which rendered him worthy the admiration of all successive ages. Voluntarily divesting himself of the greater part of his authority, in compliance with the

voice of an oracle, he endeavored to prepare Athens for becoming a
republic. In honor of Poseidon, whom Fame called his father, he renewed the Athenian games ; and as all Greece assembled at their celebration, he in this way promoted the intercourse and general improvement among his people.

Theseus' civic cares did not prevent him from engaging in warlike
occupations. He accompanied Heracles in his expedition against the
Amazons, who then dwelt on the banks of the Thermodon ; and as a
reward for his distinguished services in the conflict, Heracles, after the
victory, bestowed on him the hand of the vanquished queen. When
the Amazons in revenge afterwards invaded the Attic territory, they
again met with a signal defeat by the Athenian prince

An amiable feature in the history of this hero, is the inseparable
friendship which united him with Pirithoös, a Thessalian prince, who
ruled over the Lapithæ. Their friendship, nevertheless, originated in
arms. The renown of Theseus having spread widely over Greece,
Pirithoös became desirous not only of beholding him, but of witnessing
his exploits ; he accordingly made an irruption in the plain of Marathon, and carried off the herds of the king of Athens.

On receiving the information, Theseus went to repel the plunderers
The moment Pirithoös beheld him, he was seized with secret admiration, and stretching out his hand in token of peace, exclaimed, " Be
judge thyself! what satisfaction dost thou require ?" " Thy friendship,'
replied the Athenian, and they thereupon swore eternal fidelity.

There was now no danger too great for Theseus and Pirithoös to
brave ; none that could separate the heroes. They were present at
the Calydonian hunt, and both took part in the famous conflict between
the Centaurs and Lapithæ. The cause of the contest was as follows—
Pirithoös having obtained the hand of Hippodamia, daughter of Adrastos, king of Argos, the chiefs of his nation, the Lapithæ, were all invited
to the wedding, as well as the Centaurs who dwelt in the neighborhood
of Pelion. Theseus, Hercules, and Nestor were likewise present.
Heated by wine, the Centaurs began to quarrel during the repast, and
threatened to carry away Hippodamia ; and would have made good
their threat but for Heracles and Theseus, who valiantly assisted Pirithoös, and punished the haughty pride of the Centaurs, not only on
that occasion, but afterwards also in a regular battle. This is the famous battle between the Centaurs and Lapithæ, so often a subject of
poetry with the ancients, as well as of art.

Like faithful comrades, Theseus and Pirithoös aided each other in every project, and the death of Hippodamia having subsequently left Pirithoös free to form a new attachment, the two friends, equally ambitious in love, resolved each to possess a daughter of the king of the gods. Theseus fixed his thoughts on Helena, the daughter of Zeus and Leda, then a child of nine years old. The friends succeeded in their plan of carrying her off, and placing her under the care of his mother, Æthra, at Aphidnæ. Theseus then prepared to assist his friend in a bolder and more perilous attempt; for Pirithoös resolved to venture on the daring deed, of carrying away from the palace of the monarch of the under-world his queen, Proserpina, to take vengeance as it were on Pluto, for having deprived him of his wife, Hippodamia. There is a deep sense hidden in this latter fiction The undertaking was one which inevitably involved the most imminent danger, and Theseus, faithful to his friend even unto death, descended with him

"To the seat of desolation, void of light."

They descended together to the region of shadow; but Pluto, know-ing their design, seized them, and placed them upon an enchanted rock, at the gate of his realm. Here they sat, unable to move, till. Heracles, passing by in his descent for Cerberos, freed Theseus; but when he would have done the same for Pirithoös, the earth quaked, and he left him. Pirithoös, therefore, remained everlastingly on the rock, as a punishment for his audacious attempt, and thus death sepa-rated the most faithful of friends.

This loss was the forerunner of many misfortunes which afterwards befel Theseus, embittering the rest of his days. It was the common lot of heroes to end their lives in a tragical manner, and from this Theseus was not exempt.

When he returned to Athens, he found the fickle and ungrateful people excited against him by his enemies, and while struggling against a public enemy, a domestic foe arose in the bosom of his family. After Antiope's death, Theseus married Phædra, a daughter of Minos, and sister of Ariadne. Conceiving a hatred against Hippolytos, Antiope's son, she preferred a false charge against him, in consequence of which he lost his life. When Phædra heard of the fate which had befallen her innocent victim, in bitter repentance she put an end to her own life; and Theseus, learning too late the innocence of his son, was well nigh driven to despair.

The invasion of Attica by Castor and Pollux, for the recovery of their sister, Helena, and an insurrection of the Pallantidæ, brought on Theseus the usual fate of all great Athenians—exile. Oppressed by misfortunes, as well as the ingratitude of his people, he banished himself from Athens, uttering before he went on board the ship that was to take him to a foreign country, the bitterest curses against the Athenians. The place where this occurred was afterwards called the place of imprecations.

He retired to the isle of Scyros, where he hoped to spend the rest of his days in quiet, but the treacherous Lycomedes, who was king of the island, feared the enemies of Theseus, and violated the sacred rites of hospitality. Under the pretext of showing his guest the island, he conducted him to the summit of a steep rock, and hurled him down unawares.

Long after his death, the Athenians built temples and altars in honor of Theseus, and revering him as a demi-god, brought offerings to his altars, and instituted festivals to his memory. They also obtained his bones from the island of Scyros, and interred them beneath the soil of Attica.

"Pisistratus, tyrant of Athens, in his revision of the Homeric Poems, is said to have interpolated a verse which characterized Theseus and his friend Pirithoös as sons of the immortal gods ; and he is alleged by the same historian who makes this assertion, to have expung-ed a line from the works of Hesiod, which mentioned a fact not very creditable to the memory of the Athenian hero, namely, the reason by which he was induced, in his return from Crete to Athens, to abandon Ariadne on the island of Naxos.

That the Athenians themselves felt a personal interest in all that concerned the character of Theseus, is clear from these circumstances, as well as from other evidence. The incidents of the story which re-flected honor upon him were subjects of national pride to them ; they strove with him, as it were, in his struggles, fought by his side in his battles, and triumphed in his conquests He was, in a word, the an-cient people of Athens personified by itself.

This being the case, the narration of his exploits and adventures becomes an object of peculiar interest, not so much as presenting his-torical facts in themselves—for they rest upon evidence of too partial a kind to allow them to claim this character—but, as exhibiting to our eyes a picture of the ancient population of Attica, as drawn originally by their own hands, and retouched and embellished by those of their posterity.

It is not thereby intimated that all belief in the incidents of the biography of Theseus, as detailed in the popular records of Athenian tradition, is vain and groundless : it is, on the contrary, more rational to suppose that a people eminently distinguished for its critical perception of propriety in all the imitative arts, would not have failed, in this national portrait, to adopt a real model, and to sketch from it an outline not inconsistent with truth ; and that subsequently it would have endeavored to fill up the lineaments thus correctly drawn, with lights and shadows harmoniously adapted to them, and have been careful to introduce nothing that was not in due keeping with the tone and character of the age to which the subject of the design belonged.

As a proof of this assertion, we may refer to those particular circumstances in the life of Theseus, which exhibit him and his countrymen in an unfavorable light. His biography is not a mere panegyric. It records both his ingratitude to Ariadne, and the ingratitude of his country to him. In it, the Athenian hero leaves his benefactress on a desolate shore ; and he himself is driven by the Athenians from his kingdom into exile on the barren rock of Scyros. The heroine, indeed, is soon rescued from her distress by the appearance of Bacchos, the deity of Naxos ; but Theseus is left to die in his banishment ; and it was not until many centuries had elapsed, that his bones were dug up and brought with triumphal honors to his own city, and deposited there in that magnificent building, which still survives in its pristine beauty to this day, and thus unites the age of Theseus with our own, and was both his temple and his tomb.

We are therefore to believe, that the character of Theseus, as exhibited to us in the surviving remains of Athenian tradition, may be justly considered as a representation, partly historical and partly ideal, of the condition of the Athenian people, when the age of mythology was drawing to a close, and is founded upon a real basis of the life and exploits of an individual.

Viewed in this light, it becomes, as it were, the Athenian theory of the state in which they were wont to contemplate themselves as existing at that early period of their history ; and thus the fabulous legends of his heroic acts assume a *practical* character. They become assertions of national power exerted for great and useful purposes in that age.

His legislative enactments are expressions of their own civil policy at that time.

In these accounts, Theseus is called the founder of the Athenian form of popular government. To him, the statesmen and orators of later days ascribed the origin of the political privileges enjoyed by those whom they addressed. He was said to have organized the federal body, of which the communities of Attica were members. He united them in a civil society, of which the old Cecropian town was the head. He gave to that city, which thenceforth became the capital of Attica, the name of Athens. He instituted the Panathenaic festival, to commemorate this act of union.

All these works attributed to Theseus, seem to have been ascribed to him as the personified representative of the state. And not merely his *public* acts may be identified, as it seems, with those of the national body, but even his *private* relations appear to have been so modified as to express the connection of the Athenian people with objects analogous to those which were contemplated by those relations. Thus the inviolable *friendship* which united Theseus and Pirithoös, seems to have represented the ancient national amity which subsisted between the two countries to which these two heroes belonged, namely, Athens, and Thessaly. Again in the *rivalries* of the Athenian king was shadowed out the history of the popular jealousies. The object of his ambition is represented as a desire to emulate the deeds of his contemporary and relative, Hercules. If the latter destroyed the monsters which devastated the land of Greece, Theseus did the same. If Hercules sailed to Argo, Theseus belonged to the same crew. If he joined the hunters of the Calydonian boar, Theseus was there also ; if Hercules is clad in the skin of the lion of Nemæa, Theseus wears the hide of the Marathonian bull ; if Hercules bears a club, so does Theseus ; if the Olympian games are founded by him, Theseus institutes the Isthmian ; if Hercules erects the columns at Gades, Theseus does the same at the Isthmus of Corinth.

In all these particulars, the real competitors, whose emulation is expressed by them, are not so much Hercules and Theseus, as the *nations* of which these two heroes are the representatives. They are either Thebes and Athens, or Argos and Athens ; and thus the legends are of value, as indicating the political relation which subsisted between these nations respectively at the period when the traditions in question originated.

The antiquity of a similar feeling of jealousy which estranged Athens from Sparta, is proved by the story which represents the Spartan Helen detained as a prisoner at Aphidnæ in Attica, and committed by Theseus to the custody of Æthra, his mother, till his country is invaded by her two brothers, Castor and Pollux, who rescue her from captivity. A different feeling was entertained by Athens towards the people of Trœzen ; and this is expressed by the tradition which leaves Theseus to pass his early youth under the tuition of his father-in-law Pittheus, the wise and virtuous monarch, as he is described, of that country ; which sends him to Trœzen as a place of refuge during his temporary exile from Attica ; and which consigns Hippolyta, for his education, to the same place. In connection with these accounts, it will be remembered that Trœzen was the principal asylum of a part of the population of Attica, when driven from their country by the Persians before the battle of Salamis ; and, perhaps, the Athenian traditions *themselves* are allusive to that fact, and are grateful memorials of it. It may be added, as a future indication of this intimacy, that Sphettus and Anaphlystus, two important cities on the western coast of Attica, are said, in mythological language, to be the sons of Trœzen.

Several particulars have been referred to, in which the superiority of Theseus over his rival Hercules is evinced. Hercules indeed re mained without a competitor in deeds of physical force. The palm of greater excellence in athletic exercises was willingly conceded by Athens to Thebes ; and indeed the eminence of the latter in this respect was regarded by its more intellectual neighbor and rival as one of the causes that conduced to give it a savage character, which was neither to be envied nor admired. But Hercules was no statesman ; he framed no laws, settled no form of government, organized no religious or civil societies ; but all these things Theseus did. Above all, Hercules gave no encouragement to the arts ; but Theseus, on the other hand, was the friend—he is called the cousin and brother of Dædalos, who formed the Cretan labyrinth for Minos, and first endued statues with the power of motion and sight : he was the favorite, the son of Neptune ; he built ships and encouraged commerce ; he also worked mines and coined money. In all these respects the balance is greatly in favor of the Athenian hero ; or, as it may be expressed in other words, in all the arts and sciences which elevate the thoughts and promote the welfare of man in social and civil life, the merits of Attica are asserted by these traditions to have far eclipsed the pretensions of her Bœotian neighbor."

" The temple of Theseus, constructed of white Pentelic marble, is surrounded by a sacred inclosure, and raised upon two steps on a small isolated hill in the district of Melite. Its eastern or principal front, and its south side, are visible from our station in the Acropolis. It has six columns at each end, and thirteen on each side The eastern pediment is adorned with sculptures, as are the ten metopes on the east front ; the latter relate to the labors of Hercules ; while upon the four, both on the north and south sides, at the east end of the temple, the exploits of Theseus are represented. There is a frieze on both the pronaos and posticum ; the former exhibits a contest of men mixed with the gods, and seems to represent the war of Theseus with the Pallantidæ ; the latter represents the battle of the Centaurs and Lapithæ.

" The building of this temple was commenced under the auspices of Cimon, son of Miltiades, in the year B. C. 476, four years after the battle of Salamis, and may be considered as the first effort of great importance to restore the consecrated buildings of Athens, which were destroyed at its capture by the Persians before that event. It is a singular circumstance, and worthy of observation, that one of the first acts of the Athenians on their return to Athens, after their own temporary banishment to Salamis and Trœzen, was to restore their national hero, Theseus, who had been exiled by their ancestors, to his own native city. His remains were brought by Cimon from the island of Scyros, the scene of his banishment and death, to this place ; and as upon that occasion the Athenians were beginning to erect for themselves a new and magnificent city, so they raised for him this noble structure, in which he is buried as a man, and worshipped as a god.

·· Hercules, as its sculptures show, is associated with his kinsman and companion, Theseus, in the honors of the temple. It is an agreeable sight to witness this enduring record of friendship, and also of the alliance existing between the nations of Argos and Athens, who are represented in the present case by these two heroes ; and who entered into the confederacy at the very period when this fabric was erected : so that this temple may be considered as a treaty of peace, consecrated by the sanction of religion. Another record of the same amity is preserved in the tradition, that Hercules espoused Melite, from whom the district of Athens, in which the temple of Theseus stands, derived its name. Thus the two heroes are locally connected; nor are we surprised to find a temple to Melanippus, the son of the Athenian hero, in the same neighborhood."

CASTOR AND POLYDEUKES OR POLLUX.

Œbalus, a king of Lacedæmon, sprung from a scion of the old stem of Inachos, was the father of Tyndareos, who succeeded him in the government. Tyndareos married Leda, a daughter of Thestias, king of Ætolia.

The beauty of Leda attracted the eyes of Zeus; and, descending from his Olympian seat under the disguise of a swan, he took refuge in her lap, while Aphrodite was pursuing him in the shape of an eagle. According to the common legend, Leda produced two eggs: from the one came Pollux and Helena, children of Zeus; and from the other, Castor and Clytemnestra, children of Tyndareos. The former were immortal, the latter mortal.

Notwithstanding their different descent, Castor and Pollux were inseparable, loving one another as dear brothers and friends. Both were valiant and glowed with heroic fire, and both were skilled in every bodily exercise; with this difference only, that Castor was pre-eminent in the art of riding and managing horses, and Pollux in wrestling.

They were contemporaries of the most renowned heroes, and accompanied the Argonauts in their expedition to Colchis. On their way thither Pollux slew Amycus, a son of Poseidon, in single combat. It was also in this voyage that, in the midst of a dreadful storm, two flames were seen hovering over the heads of Castor and Pollux, whereupon the storm abated. In remembrance of this, whenever fires appeared to seamen in boisterous weather, they were called Castor and Pollux, and considered as a sure sign of health and safety. Nay, the Dioscuri (or twin sons of Zeus, under which name Castor and Pollux are generally designated) were revered above all other deities as benign beings, ever present to those who were in danger, and ready to aid them—and were addressed in every emergency, on land as well as at sea, by the prayers of such as stood in need of assistance.

After their return from the expedition to Colchis, they were informed that, during their absence, Theseus had ravished their sister, Helena,

and delivered her to the care and custody of his mother, Æthra, in Aphidnæ. Castor and Pollux conquered the city, delivered their sister, and took with them the mother of Theseus as prisoner ; they, how ever, committed no violence in the besieged city, or in the whole terri tory of Attica. This forbearing benignity, which attends the heroic deeds of the Dioscuri, is probably the chief reason why mortal men afterwards looked up to them with truth and confidence, as to friendly-assisting genii.

The fidelity, likewise, with which these inseparable brothers assisted each other in dangers, rendered them an object of love and veneration to mankind ; and their fraternal friendship is indeed one of the most beautiful circumstances which fiction has interwoven into the records of the splendid heroic age.

When Castor and Pollux sued for the daughters of Leucippus, Phœbe and Ilaïra, each of them was obliged to win his bride by a combat with a rival—Castor with Lynceus. and Pollux with Idas, the sons of Aphareus. Castor, being mortal, was conquered and slain by Lynceus. Although Pollux avenged his brother's death on Lynceus, and fought with Idas also, until the latter was struck by a thunderbolt from Jupiter, yet he could not awaken his beloved brother from death. He then implored Jupiter either to deprive him also of life, or allow his brother to share his immortality. Jupiter gave him his choice, and Pollux descended one day to his brother, in the abode of the shades, in order to enjoy life with him on the next, under the light of the sky.

Human love and veneration often dedicated temples and altars to the Dioscuri. Imagination frequently presented them to mortals, when in imminent dangers ; they then appeared in the form of two youths on white horses, arrayed in shining armor, and bearing little flames or stars upon their heads. And thus they were commonly represented in works of art, either riding side by side, or standing near together, their spears bent, the stars sparkling on their heads, and each holding a horse by the bridle. The egg-shaped caps allude to the manner of their birth.

The remarkable circumstance of the two brothers living and dying alternately, leads to the conjecture that they were personifications of some natural powers and objects. This is confirmed by the names in the myth, all of which seem to refer to light or its opposite. Thus

Leda differs little from Leto, and may be regarded as *darkness ;* she is married to Tyndareos, a name which seems to be of a family of words relating to *light, flame,* or *heat ;* her children by him or Zeus, that is, by Zeus-Tyndareos, the bright god, are Helena (*Brightness*), Castor (*Adorner*), and Polydeukes (*Dewful*). In Helena, therefore, we have only another form of Selene ; the *Adorner* is a very appropriate term for the day, whose light adorns all nature ; and nothing can be more apparent than the suitableness of *Dewful* to the night. It is rather curious that, in the legend, Helena is connected by birth with Poly-deukes rather than with Castor. The brothers may also be regarded as the sun and moon, to which their names and the form of the myth are equally well adapted.

To proceed to the other names of the legend, Idas and Lynceus, that is, *Sight* and *Light,* are the children of Aphareus or Phareus, that is, *Shiner;* and the two daughters of Leucippos, or *White-horsed* (an epi-thet of the Dioscuri), are Phœbe, *Brightness,* and Hilaeira, *Joyful,* which last is an epithet given to the moon by Empedocles. In the Cypria, they were called the daughters of Apollo.

That these were original divinities is demonstrated by their being objects of worship. The Tyndarids, Dioscuri, or *Kings* as they were named, had their temples and statues ; as also had the Leucippides, who, in perhaps the more correct form of the legend, are their wives. Helena, in like manner, had her temples ; and there is some reason to suppose that she was identified with Eileithyia. The Apharids were not objects of worship ; perhaps because they had merely been devised as opponents to the Tyndarids, to give a mythic ground for the alter-nate life and death of these last, or possibly, because in the legend they are Messenians.

JASON.

Jason was a shoot of the heroic stem of Æolus, but not the son of a god ; and Juno, while she persecuted the sons of Jupiter, took him under her especial protection.

Æolus, Deucalion's grandson, who reigned in Thessaly, was the father of Salmoneus, Sisyphos, Athamas, and Cretheus. Salmoneus was killed by Jupiter's lightnings ; Sisyphos atoned in the lower world, for the tyrannical exercise of his power while on earth ; and Athamas died in a state of madness.

Tyro, a daughter of Salmoneus, became the mother of Pelias and

Neleus, sons of Neptune. Afterwards marrying her father's brother, Cretheus, she gave him a son called Æson, who succeeded his father on the throne, and was the parent of Jason, the god-like hero, whose mother's name was Alcimede.

Æson was dethroned by his brother Pelias, but was not obliged to fly from the city of Iolcos, which was the seat of the Thessalian kings. Of young Jason, however, Pelias was anxious to rid himself; considering him as a member of the legitimate royal family who might become dangerous to him. The parents of the child, Æson and Alcimede, perceiving the intention of the tyrant, spread the rumor that Jason was sick, and soon after, that he had died. At the same time, he was taken by his mother to Mount Pelion, where the wise Centaur, Cheiron, well versed in every science, devoted himself to the education of the young hero, sheltering him in his lonely grotto.

When Jason had attained his growth, and manful courage began to awaken in his breast, following the advice of an oracle, he threw the skin of a panther over his shoulders, armed himself with a couple of darts, and went to the court of Pelias, at Iolcos.

Pelias had received an oracle, guarding him against a person who would one day appear before him with only one sandal, having the other foot bare. When Jason, on his way to Iolcos, was going to pass the river Anauras, Juno appeared to him in the shape of an old woman, and entreated him to carry her over the river. Jason readily complied with the request, but on going with his burden through the water, he lost one of his sandals in the mud, and thus presented himself before the palace of Pelias. On perceiving him, Pelias recollected, with consternation, the sentence of the oracle.

When the stranger was required to tell who he was, Jason demanded, before all the people, the royal crown which the usurper had received from the head of his father, Æson. "The revenues of the kingdom," added he, "thou mayest keep and enjoy, but of the supreme authority thou must divest thyself."

Pelias, being enabled, by this proposal, to penetrate the soul of the young hero, did not doubt that for the present he might avert the storm which was pending over his head, and remove the lion, by offering as a bait, the enticing charm of an extraordinary as well as a glorious enterprise. He therefore feigned a willingness to restore the crown to its rightful possessor, or his family, provided the manes of Phrixos, another descendant of Æolus, who had found an untimely death in Colchis, were propitiated, and that golden fleece recovered which he had deposited there.

This Phrixos, who died in Colchis, was a son of Athamas, and a grandson of Æolus. Athamas, king of Bœotia, had, by his first wife, Nephele, two children, Phrixos and Helle; but after Nephele's death, Athamas married Ino, a daughter of Cadmos, who persecuted these two children, and even resolved to deprive them of life. The shade of Nephele then appeared to her children, apprising them of the danger they were in of becoming the victims of Ino's hatred, unless they would seek safety in distant flight; and, for this purpose, a ram with a golden fleece stood ready, which, at the command of the gods, would bear them on his back over the land and through the sea.

Phrixos and Helle mounted the ram, which carried them towards the east to the distant country of Colchis, where Æetes reigned, whose father was the sun. But they were not both destined to reach that country; for, on their journey, Helle fell from the back of the animal into the sea, between Sigeon and the Chersonese, and was drowned. This sea was named from her Hellespontos (*Helle's Sea*), and still retains its name. Her brother Phrixos arrived safely in Colchis, where he sacrificed to Zeus Phyxios the ram which had borne him thither, and, as a holy token, suspended the skin, or golden fleece, in a grove sacred to Ares. He then married the daughter of Æetes, but soon died in a foreign land.

The report of the golden fleece which had spread over the earth, had for a long time excited the desire of every one who wished to obtain something particularly excellent. It was in the distant east, what the golden apples of the Hesperides were in the west—a treasure worthy of the greatest toils, pains, and perils. The image of the ram and its richly covered skin generally implies, with the ancients, the idea of wealth; and this probably gave rise to the fiction of the golden fleece, involving the ideas of riches and treasures, as well as the means of gaining them.

The miraculous which was intermingled with the tales of the golden fleece, and the adventures that were connected with an expedition to a far distant land, were most alluring calls on the heroes of yore, for a trial of courage, as well as of fortune. No sooner did the words of Pelias touch the ear of Jason, than his ardor was excited to perform the glorious deed; and, pledging his word to bring the treasure, or

never to return, he invited the most renowned heroes of Greece to
embark with him in the bold adventure.

For making the voyage to Colchis, a ship was built of pines cut from
Mount Pelion, which, although larger than any other previously constructed, moved lightly and easily, and was therefore called the Argo
(*swift-sailing*). From her name, those who embarked in her were called
Argonauts.

The mast of the Argo was taken from the forest of Dodona, where
the oaks were endowed with the power of making predictions; therefore, the ship was regarded as an animated being, in concord with Fate,
to which a man might commit himself with confidence. Among the
number of heroes who accompanied Jason, the following names are most
conspicuous: Heracles, the son of Zeus; Castor and Pollux, the Dioscuri; Calaïs and Zetes, sons of Boreas; Peleus, the father of Achilleus; Admetos, the husband of Alceste; Neleus, the father of Nestor;
Meleagros, the Calydonian; Orpheus, the divine bard of Thrace; Telamon, the father of Ajax; Menœtius, the father of Patroclos; Lynceus, the son of Aphareus; Theseus, the Athenian, and his friend
Pirithoös, the Lapithæan.

The fathers of the most renowned heroes who shone in the Trojan
war, were still in youthful vigor at the time of the voyage to Colchis.
A race of heroes, they advance with their united force to recover a
precious treasure; afterwards, a second race unites to avenge the rob-
bery of beauty by the destruction of Troy.

When the heroes were all assembled, fifty in number, the auguries
being favorable, Jason, standing at the poop, poured a libation from a
golden cup, and called on Zeus, the Winds, the Sea, the Days, the
Nights, and the Fate presiding over their return. Thunder then rolled
in the clouds, lightnings flashed through the sky; Orpheus struck his
lyre in concert with his voice, and the joyful heroes, each grasping an
oar, kept time to his harmony. The gods looked down from the sky,
the nymphs of Pelion gazed in wonder at this first of ships, and Cheiron, leaving his mountain cave, cheered them, and prayed for their
happy return. The piercing eye of Lynceus penetrated the most distant regions, and the experienced pilot, Tiphys, managed the helm with
skilful hands. For a time all things went on successfully; when suddenly a dreadful storm befel the adventurers, and forced them to seek
refuge in the harbor of Lemnos.

, is a remarkable circumstance, that while the heroes were strug-
gl.ᵣᵤ against the raging elements, several of them made a vow to consecrate themselves, by becoming initiated in the Samothracian mysteries; just as Heracles, when about to engage in the most dangerous
enterprise, was first initiated into those of Eleusis.

At Lemnos, a greater danger threatened the Argonauts than that
caused by the storm which drove them thither; for the charms of the
Lemnian women kept the heroes in bonds, protracting, for some time,
the progress of their voyage to Colchis.

Not long before the arrival of the Argonauts at Lemnos, the female
inhabitants had murdered all the males of the island, except king Thoas,
who was secreted by his daughter Hypsipyle. The anger of Venus,
whom the Lemnian women had not sufficiently honored, was the occasion of this atrocious deed. For the goddess infused into the men of
Lemnos, who were at that time warring against the Thracians, an invincible dislike to their wives, and, at the same time, a preference for
the female slaves who had become their prisoners in the Thracian war.
Such an insult the women of Lemnos could not bear; they conspired,
rose in one night upon their sleeping husbands, fathers, and brothers,
and murdered them all. Those who conducted the war in Thrace
were saved by their absence.

When the Argonauts were landing at Lemnos, they were at first
opposed by the women, who mistook them for the Lemnians returning
from Thrace to avenge the death of their fellow-citizens. But as soon
as they perceived their error, they received the strangers with hospitality, who remained on the island two years.

From Lemnos the heroes sailed to Samothrace, where they were
inspired with new courage by their initiation into the mysteries. On
landing near Troas, they were abandoned by Heracles, who with Telamon went into the country in search of Hylas. In the city of Cyzicus,
on the descent of Mount Dindymus, where the Argonauts next landed,
they were hospitably received by the king, who bore the same name as
his city, and who dismissed them with presents. But the night after
their departure, when the ship was forced back into the harbor by a
storm, king Cyzicus mistook the heroes for enemies and attacked them
in a hostile manner. In this fight, Jason had the misfortune to kill
his kind and friendly host. To atone for this deed, although unintentional, he brought offerings on Mount Dindymus to the mother of the
gᵗds, and built a temple there to her honor. The Argonauts then

proceeded on their course, and steering always towards the east, arrived
in Bebrycia, where the royal crown was worn by Amycus, who challenged every stranger to fight him with clubs, and who was at last
vanquished and slain in a combat with Pollux.

On their further course, the bold navigators were driven near the
coast of Thrace by a storm, and compelled to enter the harbor of Sal-
mydessus, where the prophesying Phineus reigned, whom the immortals
had punished with blindness. To complete his misery, he was perpetually vexed by the daughters of Thaumas, the direful Harpies. Phineus had delivered up his two sons, the children of his first wife, a
daughter of Boreas, to the hatred of their stepmother, Idaca, and at
her calumnious instigation, had even deprived them of sight;—a crime
which he was obliged to expiate by his own blindness, while the Harpies, those ghastly birds of prey, with maiden faces, seized upon his
food, or ruined and defiled whatever he was about to partake. Phineus was deprived of the external light, but with his mental vision
anticipated the future, and gave to the Argonauts prudent advice concerning their further voyage; and also furnished them with a guide
to lead them through the Cyanean rocks, or Symplegades, the dangerous passage of which now awaited the bold navigators. Grateful for
these services, the winged sons of Boreas, Calaïs and Zetes, by their
swords affrighted the Harpies from Phineus' table, pursuing them as
far as the Strophades, where, at the command of the gods, they stopped
their pursuit, and returned to their companions. From this return,
those islands derived their name.

The Cyaneæ, or Symplegades, through which the Argonauts were
obliged to sail, were two immense rocks, immediately opposite each
other, at the entrance into the Black Sea; and which seemed, accord·
ing to the different directions in which they were approached, to open
and then again to close. This phenomenon gave rise to the ancient
fiction, that the rocks really opened and closed like a pair of scissors,
crushing every thing that happened to pass between them as they were
moving together. Quite natural, therefore, is the subsequent fiction,
after the Aagonauts had successfully ventured on the passage, and the
optical illusion was thus discovered, that Neptune had made the rocks
immovable.

After having safely passed the Symplegades, the heroes next landed
in the territory of Lycus, who, being by birth a Greek, gladly received
the strangers from his native land. Here the pilot Tiphys died, and

his place was succeeded by Ancæus ; and the sacred Argo, after having long sustained the beating of the briny flood, and experienced many a storm, was at last happily conducted into the longed-for harbor of Colchis. It was here, however, that the greatest danger awaited Jason, the leader of the expedition ; a danger which could hardly be avoided without divine assistance. King Æetes received the strangers, not in a hostile or even unfriendly manner ; but he prescribed to Jason, who demanded the restitution of the golden fleece, such conditions as he thought could not be complied with ; for to the dangers which he had planned, the most undaunted hero must necessarily succumb.

In order to gain the golden fleece, Jason was, in the first place, to put two fire-exhaling bulls, sacred to Hephæstos, to an adamantine ploughshare, and to break up with them four acres of land, sacred to Ares, and which had never before been ploughed. Then he was to sow the dragon teeth of Cadmos, which yet remained in the possession of Æetes, in the newly-ploughed furrows, and the armed warriors who would immediately arise from the dreadful seed, he must kill to the last man. This done, he was at last to fight with, and conquer the dragon that guarded the golden fleece.

Medeia, a daughter of Æetes, skilled in charms and witchcraft, had scarcely beheld Jason, when, through the influence and disposal of the gods, a tender affection for the hero was raised in her bosom, which soon kindled to a flame of the most violent passion.

Jason went to the temple of Hecate to supplicate the mighty goddess, where he was met by Medeia. She disclosed her love to him, at the same time promising her assistance in the dangers which threatened him, and her powerful help in accomplishing his glorious undertaking, provided he would swear fidelity to her. Jason complied, and Medeia, reciprocating the oath, rendered the hero invincible by means of her magical incantations. She gave him a stone which he was to cast among the warriors, that would spring up from the dragon-teeth, and also herbs, and a potion for lulling to sleep the dragon that guarded the golden fleece.

On the following day, Jason, surrounded by his companions, appeared on the field of Ares in the presence of the king and a multitude of people ; the fire-breathing bulls were about to be set free, and the hearts of the assembled multitude were chilled with awe and expectation ; a deadly silence reigned, and all eyes were anxiously turned upon the hero, who alone quietly expected his fire-vomiting foes. Fierce

and snorting, the bulls rushed upon him; but the powerful charm with
which Medeia had armed him, suddenly made them tame and obedient;
without resistance they bent their necks under the yoke, suffering
Jason to put them to the plough, and quietly made the furrows into
which he sowed the dragon-teeth. No sooner were they scattered, than
a harvest of armed warriors sprang from the ground, all of them turning their swords against Jason. The hero then following the directions received by Medeia, flung the enchanted pebble, which she had
given him for that purpose, into the midst of the thronged crowd of
his enemies; this stone had the power of troubling their senses as well
as hardening their hearts, causing them to rise furiously against one
another, until the ground from which they had just sprung, was covered
with their slain bodies.

Before the king and people could recover from the amazement into
which this spectacle had thrown them, Jason was already hastening
towards the grim guardian of the fleece, to lull him to sleep. He succeeded, and afterwards killed the monster, and triumphantly held in
his hand the golden fleece. The conqueror then returned with his
companions to the ship; and Medeia, leaving in nightly silence the
house of her father, followed her lover, and went on board the Argo,
which immediately set sail.

Æetes, soon roused by the discovered flight of his daughter, went
himself with his ships in pursuit of the swift-sailing Argo. Near the
mouth of the Danube, Medeia descried the sails of her father, and to
save herself as well as her lover from the impending danger, she adopted a measure both cruel and desperate. She had taken her little
brother Absyrtus, as a kind of hostage, and in the present emergency,
seeing no other means of safety, she killed, and cut him in pieces, planting his head and hands upon a high rock, and scattering the rest of his
members upon the shore, with the view of retarding her father's pursuit, or of inducing him to desist from it altogether. In order to
mark this horrible deed in all times to come, several small islands in
that region were afterwards called Absyrtides.

Medeia's expectation was realized. Her father, first retarded by
collecting together the remains of his unfortunate son, afterwards desisted entirely from pursuit, and the Argonauts quietly proceeded on
their voyage. Having received advice from Phineus not to return to
their native land by the same course which they had pursued in coming to Colchis, they sailed up the Danube; "and when they could as-

cend the river no farther, the strong heroes," says the fiction, " took up their lightly-built vessel on their shoulders, carrying her for the space of four miles over hills and dales, as far as the Adriatic gulf." But here, when they were about to embark again, the following oracle was heard to issue from the mast of the Argo : " You are not destined to reach your home until Jason and Medeia are absolved from the murder of Absyrtus, after having atoned for their crime by a penalty imposed on them."

With a view to this atonement, the Argonauts entered the port of Ææa, the abode of Circe, a daughter of the sun, and sister of Æetes. She, however, refused to absolve Jason and Medeia, by presenting the usual offerings to the offended immortals, and by imposing a penalty on the criminals ; but announced to them, that they could not blot out their guilt until they had reached the promontory of Malea.

Thence the bold navigators steered towards the dangerous straits of Scylla and Charybdis, which they passed under the guidance of Hera. By the persuasion of Orpheus, they escaped the danger which threatened them from the Sirens, and happily reached the island of the Phæacians, where, however, they met with an unexpected enemy. After the funeral obsequies of Absyrtus had been properly celebrated, the Colchian fleet, which had desisted from its pursuit at the mouth of the Danube, took another way to intercept the fugitives ; and here, at the island of the Phæacians, it was stationed to watch for them. The anger of the Colchians against Medeia, as well as the Argonauts, having in the mean time somewhat abated, they demanded no other restitution than the person of Medeia, provided she had not yet been married to Jason. She had not yet been made the wife of Jason, but the king of the Phæacians immediately procured a private celebration of the matrimonial rites, announcing to the Colchians, on the following day, that his guests, Jason and Medeia, were lawfully married ; whereupon the former, satisfied with the answer, spread their sails to the wind and steered for Colchis.

The Argonauts, after having taken leave of their friendly host, the king of the Phæacians, endeavored to reach the promontory of Malea, when suddenly a storm cast them on the Libyan Syrtes, where the vessel would have been lost but for the appearance of a. Triton, who, for the reward of a precious tripod which Jason carried with him in the ship, promised the heroes to show them the only course by which they could escape. After having received the tripod, at the sight of which he was highly delighted, the Triton kept his word, and conducted the Argo in safety out of the surrounding Syrtes. Moreover, he presented Euphemos, one of the Argonauts, with a clod of earth, as a pledge that his descendants should reign in Libya. This pledge was afterwards redeemed.

Argo at last reached the longed-for promontory of Malea, where Ja son and Medeia, after having brought rich offerings to the immortal gods, obtained absolution of their crime committed against Absyrtus. They were now, according to the oracle which they had received from the oak of Dodona, as well as the promise of Circe, permitted to expect soon to reach their native port. And, indeed, without meeting any farther accidents, the Argonauts soon after entered the harbor of Iolcos. The good ship Argo was devoted by Jason to Poseidon, on the isthmus of Corinth, from whence fiction afterwards transported her to the vaults of the sky, where she shines as a glittering constellation.

The golden fleece was now gained ; but the purpose for which alone Jason had exposed himself, as well as his friends, to every imaginable danger, was frustrated : his father, Æson, having in the mean while become a decrepid, childish old man, unable to reign, or to enjoy the glorious feats of his son.

The first request, therefore, which Jason made to Medeia, was, to use her magic powers to renew, if possible, the mental as well as phys- ical abilities of his father. Medeia, complying with her husband's re- quest, infused a new juice of life, prepared of secret herbs, into the veins of the old man, so as to make him sensible of the return of his gay youth and the renewed strength of life. The daughters of Pelias· deprived their father of life in imitating the work of Medeia, so that Æson now reigned undisturbed, sole king of Iolcos.

Jason, with Medeia, then went to Corinth, formerly called Ephyra, where Æetes had reigned before going to the fertile Colchis. Medeia took possession of the government for her husband, and they lived there quietly during ten years. Behind this calm of peaceful life, however, a dreadful storm was lurking, which threatened Jason with a tragical fate, as was the case also with Heracles, Perseus and Bel- lerophontes.

Weary of Medeia, whom he always seems to have secretly de- spised, he was about to marry Creon's royal daughter, unmindful of the revenge of despised jealousy or disregarded faith. Medeia feigned patience and mildness, enduring with apparent resignation what she

could not prevent; she even sent to the bride a costly wedding garment. But scarcely had the latter made use of the dangerous present,
than she suddenly felt a consuming fire raging through her body, which
produced an agonizing death. Medeia, giving full scope to revenge,
rained fire upon Creon's palace, which consumed the king himself.
murdered her two children, and then hastened through the air in her
chariot drawn by two dragons, leaving Jason to grief and despair, which
embittered the remainder of his days.

MELEAGROS OR MELEAGER.

Œneus, who reigned in Calydon, was the father of renowned children ; of Deianeira, the wife of Heracles ; of Meleagros and Tydeus,
whose valorous son, Diomedes, engaged with the gods themselves in
dangerous combat during the siege of Troy.   Œneus had the misfortune to draw the wrath of Artemis upon himself as well as his country,
by having forgotten her divine personage, while he brought thank-
offerings to all the other deities, for the thriving growth of the fruits
of the field.

To punish him and his subjects for this offence, the goddess of the
forest sent a monstrous boar into the Calydonian land, which wasted the
fields, and threatened death and ruin to the inhabitants of the surrounding country.   Œneus, anxious to subdue this monster, desired the assistance of the strongest, both in his own territories and those beyond
them.   Thus the chase of Diana's Boar again united the flower of the
Greek heroes.

To hunt the Calydonian Boar, some of those heroes again assembled who had shared the dangers of the voyage to Colchis.   The most
renowned of the Argonauts who assisted Meleagros in this hunt, were
Jason, Castor and Pollux, Idas and Lynceus, Peleus, Telamon, Admetos, Pirithoös. and Theseus.   To this noble troop, the brothers of
Althæa. the wife of Œneus, and daughter of Thestius, who reigned in
Pleuron, and Atalanta, the daughter of Schœneus, associated themselves.   Atalanta, like Diana, had devoted herself to a state of virginity, and, like her, was a lover of the chase.

Atalanta first wounded the boar with her arrow ; Meleager then
cut off the head of the monster, and presented it to her as the deserved
prize of victory.   The brothers of Althæa were offended by this preference given to a woman, and disputing the prize, took it from Atalanta.   Diana setting no bounds to her wrath, kindled the spark of

24

anger between Meleager and the sons of Thestius into a flame, that burst out in a bloody fight, and gave to the Calydonian chase a tragical termination.

Meleager, in the fray, killed the two brothers of his mother, who, beholding the bodies of the slain, swore to avenge their death, even on her own son. An easy, too easy means of vengeance was in her power; for on the birth-day of Meleager, the Fates had placed a piece of wood on the hearth near the fire, with the hint that Althæa's new-born son should live as long as that piece of wood remained unconsumed. Althæa had preserved the fatal billet as a precious treasure, until the moment when she was provoked to anger by the death of her brothers. Then, seizing it in her passion, she threw it into the blazing fire. As it was gradually consuming to ashes, Meleager felt his body withering away, and the marrow of his bones drying up, until he died in convulsive agony. Scarcely had Althæa heard the cruel result of what she had done, than repenting the deed, she put a period to her own life.

CADMOS.

Poseidon, says the legend, was by Libya the father of two sons, Belos and Agenor; the former reigned in Egypt, and the latter, having gone to Europe, married Telephassa, by whom he had three sons, Cadmos, Phœnix, and Cilix, and one daughter, Europa. Zeus, becoming enamored of Europa, carried her away to Crete; and Agenor, grieved for the loss of his only daughter, ordered his sons to go in search of her, and not to return until they had found her. They went, accompanied by their mother, and by Thasos, a son of Poseidon. Their long search was to no purpose, for they could obtain no intelligence of their sister; and fearing the indignation of their father if they returned without her, they resolved to settle themselves in various countries. Phœnix therefore established himself in Phœnicia, and Cilix in Cilicia; Cadmos and his mother went to Thrace, where Thasos founded a town, calling it after himself.

After the death of his mother, Cadmos went to Delphi for the purpose of consulting the oracle about Europa. The answer was, to cease from troubling himself about her, but to follow a cow as his guide, and to build a city where she should lie down. On leaving the temple, he went through Phocis, and meeting a cow belonging to the herds of Pelagon, he followed her through Bœotia till she came to where Thebes now stands, where she laid herself down. Wishing to sacrifice her to

Athena, Cadmos sent his companions to the fount of Ares for water; but the serpent that guarded the fount killed a greater part of them. Cadmos then fought the serpent and destroyed it; by the direction of Athena he sowed its teeth, and immediately a crop of armed men sprang up, who slew each other, either quarrelling or through igno- rance; for it is said that when Cadmos saw them rising, he flung stones at them; and thinking it was done by some one of their number, they fell upon and slew each other. Five only survived; and they joined with Cadmos to build the city of Thebes.

For killing the sacred serpent, Cadmos was obliged to spend a year in servitude to Ares. At the expiration of that period, Athena herself prepared a palace for him, and Zeus gave him Harmonia, the daughter of Ares and Aphrodite. All the gods assembled in Cadmeia, the pal- ace of Cadmos, to celebrate the marriage. The bridegroom presented his bride with a magnificent robe, and a collar, the work of Hephæstos, and said to be the gift of the divine artist himself.

Cadmos endeavored to civilize the people whom he had gathered around him, and to whom he is said first to have communicated letters, brought by him from Phœnicia. The date given for the settlement of this colony is B. C. 1550.

The offspring of Cadmos and Harmonia, who is sometimes called Harmione, were Ino, Agaüe, Autonoë, Semele, and a son named Poly- doros. All these children were persecuted by an inimical fate, or the hatred of Hera, which rested upon their father's house. Semele, the mother of Bacchos, was consumed by Zeus' lightnings. Agaüe married Echion, one of those five warriors who had arisen from the dragon teeth. She became the mother of Pentheus, who opposed the worship of Bacchos, and was torn in pieces by his own mother, and the other votaries of the god. Ino was persecuted by the wrath of Hera, because she had taken care of young Bacchos. She was married to Athamas, who, seized by a sudden fury, dashed their first son, Zear- chus, against a rock, and then pursued the hapless mother, who fled with her younger son, Melicertes, to the very verge of a rock on the shore. Ino, with her son in her arms, flung herself down, and both were henceforth numbered among the deities of the sea; Ino under the name of Leucothea, and Melicertes under that of Palæmon. Both were worshipped as benign beings, who assist seafaring people in the dangers of their element. Autonoë, the fourth daughter of Cadmos, married Aristæos, son of Apollo and king of Arcadia. He was said first to have taught man how to manage bees and raise honey, as well as to use the milk of animals. Autonoë became the mother of Actæon, who was punished for the crime of beholding Diana when bathing.

After the various misfortunes which befel their children, Thebes became odious to Cadmos and his wife, and they migrated to the country of the Enchelians; who, being harassed by the incursions of the Illyrians, were told by the oracle, that if they made Cadmos and Harmonia their leaders, they would be successful. They obeyed the god, and the prediction was verified. Cadmos became king of the Illyrians, and had a son named Illyrios.

Cadmos lived with Harmonia to his latest years; and in order to ascribe to them a kind of immortality, fiction suffers them at last to be transformed into serpents, and sent by Zeus to thê Elysian Plain; or, as some say, they were conveyed thither in a chariot drawn by serpents.

When Cadmos left Thebes, he placed his son Polydoros upon the throne. Labdacos, the son of Polydoros, married Nicteis, the daughter of Nycteus, and became the father of Laïos. At the time of his father's death, Laïos was a minor, and therefore his uncle Lycos reigned in his place over Thebes.

Antiopē, another daughter of Nycteus, beloved by Zeus, and rejected by her father, fled to Epopeus, king of Sicyon, who married her. But Lycos, having given to the dying Nycteus a solemn promise to avenge him on his daughter, killed Epopeus, and carried Antiopē prisoner to Thebes, where he prepared for her the most cruel treatment, by committing her to his wife, Dirce.

Antiopē had borne Jupiter two sons, Amphion and Zethos, who were brought up secretly. As soon as she found means to escape, she hastened to her sons, bidding them avenge the injury of their mother. Amphion and Zethos immediately invaded Thebes, slew Lycos, expelled Laïos, and fastened Dirce, by whom their mother had been so cruelly treated, to the horns of a wild bull, thus devoting her to a painful death *

Amphion then built the walls of Thebes, with their seven gates; and the persuasive eloquence with which he prevailed on the rude in-

---

* The celebrated group in the museum of the king of Naples, known under the name of the Farnese Bull, represents this scene.

habitants to assist him in this undertaking, has been veiled by fiction in the fable, that he moved the stones by the notes of his lyre, so that they voluntarily united, and formed themselves into walls and turrets. After the death of Amphion and Zethos, the Thebans invited the expelled Laïos to take charge of the government, which belonged to him by hereditary right. He returned and married Jocasta, a Theban princess.

ŒDIPUS.

It had been predicted to Laïos that he should have a son who would be the murderer of his father. Therefore, when Jocasta became the mother of a son, Laïos ordered the child to be exposed in a wild desert. The servant who was intrusted with this commission, perforated the ankles of the child, in order to recognize it, if it should ever appear. In this condition it was found by Phorbas, the overseer of the herds of king Polybos, who reigned in Corinth. The latter, to whom Phorbas delivered the hapless infant, adopted it, and from its swollen feet, gave it the name of Œdipus.

The foster-parents of Œdipus kept his descent carefully concealed from him, so that until he approached to manhood, he believed them to be his real parents. But some doubts having been raised in his mind as to his birth, he resolved to inquire at the oracle of Apollo. The oracle, leaving the question of his descent untouched, confined itself to the warning never to return to his native country, because he would there slay his own father, and marry his own mother.

To escape a fate so horrible, Œdipus voluntarily banished himself from Corinth, which he supposed to be his native land, and took his way towards Thebes. Thus went the hapless youth directly to meet that doom of fate which he intended to avoid. For on his journey he encountered his father, Laïos, in a narrow pass, accompanied only by his herald, Polyphontes. Œdipus was ordered to give way; and upon his refusal, the herald killed one of his horses, which so exasperated him, that he slew the king and Polyphontes. He was unconscious of having killed his own father, but he thus made true a part of the oracle which he had received at Delphi.

Upon his arrival at Thebes, Œdipus found the Sphinx in its vicinity; a monster in the shape of a lion, with the head of a maiden, the progeny of Echidna, and sent by Juno to terrify the inhabitants of the city and surrounding country.* The monster, lying on a steep rock, proposed this riddle to all who passed by: "What animal is it that goes in the morning upon four feet, at noon upon two, and in the evening upon three?" Every one who was unable to interpret this riddle, was hurled into the abyss by the Sphinx, and hundreds had already perished in this way ere Œdipus arrived. He came and explained the riddle. "Man," said he, "as a child, in the morning of life, creeps upon hands and feet: at the noon-tide of life, when strength dwells in his members, he goes upright on two feet; and in the evening, when old age has stolen upon him, he needs a staff for his support, and goes, as it were, upon three feet."

Œdipus had scarcely spoken the last words, when the Sphinx flung herself down from the rock, or, according to another fiction, she was killed by Œdipus.

Laïos was dead, and in order to get rid of the monster that desolated the country, the Thebans had promised his widow, together with the throne of Thebes, to the man who should be able to unriddle the enigma of the Sphinx. To Œdipus this apparent fortune, envied by many, was destined, and thus was the second part of the oracle fulfilled without mercy; for in taking Jocasta, the queen of Thebes, for his wife, he ignorantly married his mother, after having slain his father. His hard and unfriendly fate, having drawn a veil over all these horrors, granted him yet for a short time the enjoyment of life. Œdipus and Jocasta had two sons, Eteocles and Polyneices, and two daughters, Antigone and Ismene; their wretched father being as ignorant of his own fate, as of the future destiny of his children.

Yet the days of this happy ignorance drew to an end. A wasting pestilence spread itself over Thebes. Œdipus himself proposed to ask the oracle whether any man had drawn down the wrath of the gods by secret crimes, and whether the whole land was suffering for the misdeeds of an individual. His advice was followed, and the dreadful sentence fell upon himself. He determined not to cease investigating until he should succeed in bringing the truth to light, or in setting the calumny to rest; but with every inquiry, the horrible story developed itself with additional evidence.

---

* The Theban Sphinx differed from the Egyptian. The former had the head of a woman, the body of a lion, and was winged; the latter had the head of a man, the body of a lion, and was not winged.

When, at length, every doubt had vanished, and Œdipus, with dreadful certainty, had found himself guilty of the worst crimes, no longer able to bear the light of day, he blinded himself. Thus deprived of his eyes, he wandered until death in foreign lands, led by the hand of his daughter, Antigone. The unfortunate Jocasta strangled herself.

Eteocles and Polyneices succeeded their father in the government, with this arrangement: that each of them should enjoy, by turns, the supreme power, every other year. But neither could they escape that hostile destiny which hung over Thebes, and the house of Cadmos

ETEOCLES AND POLYNEICES.

These two brothers became victims of their own discord, arising from envy, and the desire of despotic power. Eteocles first entered upon the government; but when his year had expired, he refused to cede the royal authority to Polyneices for the succeeding year.

Upon this, Polyneices left Thebes, retiring to Adrastos, the ruler of Argos, who kindly received him, gave him his daughter in marriage, and promised to defend his claim to the Theban throne to the utmost of his ability. Tydeus also, the son of Œneus, and brother to Meleager, came at that time as a fugitive to Adrastos, and to him the king of Argos married his second daughter.

The first step taken by Adrastos, in order to secure for his son-in-law the portion of authority that was due to him in Thebes, was to send Tydeus to Eteocles, that he might prevail on the usurper to share with his brother the throne of their common father. But before he could reach Thebes, Tydeus was treacherously attacked by armed men, who, at the command of Eteocles, lay in wait for him; and he returned to Argos, after narrowly escaping with his life. Upon relating this treachery, Adrastos immediately prepared war against Eteocles.

THE THEBAN WAR.

Adrastos and his two sons-in-law, Tydeus and Polyneices, united in the expedition against Thebes, in which several other heroes were eager to share with them the danger and the glory. The valiant Capaneus of Messene joined them, and Hippomedon, a son of Adrastos' sister ; also Parthenopæus, a handsome and brave youth from Arcadia, the son of Melanion and Atalanta.

Amphiaraös, the husband of Eriphyle, sister of Adrastos, could not

for a long time, be prevailed upon to take part in the enterprise, because, anticipating the future, his mind foreboded not only the misfortune that awaited the besiegers of Thebes, but also his own inevitable
death. He therefore retired to a private place, where he concealed
himself from Adrastos and Polyneices, until his wife, bribed by the
latter with a costly necklace, discovered his hiding-place, and thus
Amphiaraös was obliged to embark in the enterprise against his will.

The leaders in this expedition were seven in number: Adrastos,
Polyneices, Tydeus, Amphiaraös, Capaneus, Parthenopæos, and Hippomedon.

On their way to Thebes they met with an accident, which involved
unfavorable auspices. Hypsipyle, whose name has already been mentioned in the history of the Argonauts, was compelled, after the departure of Jason and his companions from Lemnos, to leave her home,
because she had spared the life of her father, Thoas. At the sea-shore,
whither she had fled and where she was wandering, she fell into the
hands of pirates, who sold her as a slave to Lycurgos, king of Nemea,
and there she was employed as nurse to the king's infant son, Opheltes.

At that time the seven heroes, with their army, were passing through
the dominions of Lycurgos, and found the royal daughter of Thoas
with her little nursling in a wood. Hastening to point out a fountain
to the Greeks, who were suffering from thirst, she left the little Opheltes alone on the turf; she returned again to the child, who, in the
mean time, had been killed by a snake. The Greeks were confounded
at this accident, but celebrated the funeral of the child in a splendid
manner, and, under the name of Archemorus, instituted sacred games
in his honor, which were afterwards periodically repeated at Nemea.

Having completed these funeral rites, the heroes proceeded on their
way, and arrived under the walls of Thebes. Here the seven leaders
distributed their army around the seven gates, so that one was to be
blocked by each of the heroes with his troop, and thus take the city, if
possible, by a regular siege.

To oppose each of the leaders in the army of Adrastos, Eteocles
placed within the walls one whom he regarded as his equal: against
Tydeus, Melanippus; against Capaneus, Polyphontes; against Hippomedon, Hyperbius; Actor against Parthenopæos; Lasthenes against
Amphiaraös; and stationed himself against his brother, Polyneices.

If the besiegers were animated by their just cause, by hatred against
the usurper, Eteocles, and by confidence in their superior power, the

besieged, on the other hand, were urged to the most desperate struggle by a still more powerful motive—the fear of hunger. They made a furious sally, and a battle ensued equally fatal to both parties. Hippomedon and Parthenopæos fell under the swords of the enemy : Capaneus, who had mounted the walls, was killed by a flash of lightning ; Tydeus fell under the hand of Melanippus ; Eteocles and Polyneices, the two unnatural brothers, killed each other in single combat ; Amphiaraös was swallowed up by the earth ; and Adrastos owed his life only to the swiftness of his good steed, Arion, whose sire was the ruler of the waves.

The sovereignty of Thebes now devolved on Creon, the brother of Jocasta. He ordered the corpse of Eteocles to be buried with the usual rites and due honors ; but commanded, on pain of death, that the bodies of Polyneices and his fallen friends should remain unburied, a prey to the fowls of the air.

Antigone, the faithful daughter of Œdipus, prompted by her sisterly love, notwithstanding the interdict of Creon and the danger to which she exposed her life, stole out of the city in a moonlight night, and with her own hands covered the body of her brother with sand.

Her disobedience to the command of the tyrant was discovered, and she was condemned to die by being buried alive ; but she prevented a public execution and a cruel death by strangling herself.

Hæmon, Creon's son, who had tenderly loved this victim of his father's cruelty, upon finding Antigone dead in her prison, plunged his sword in his breast ; neither did Hæmon's mother survive the loss of her beloved son. Thus stood Creon, bereft of all who had been related to him by the sacred ties of nature, accusing his destiny.

In the mean time, Adrastos had solicited the assistance of Theseus, who conquered Thebes, and forced the inhabitants to surrender all the slain bodies that belonged to the army of Adrastos, in order to their interment with solemn funeral rites.

The misfortunes attending this war were insufficient to extinguish the enmity that subsisted among the sons of the fallen heroes. Ten years after, it burst forth in a new war, which, from its being carried on by the descendants of the former leaders, was called the war of the Epigones.

Creon was succeeded on the throne of Thebes by Laodamas, a son of Eteocles. Thersander, the son of Polyneices, assisted by the sons of those heroes who were slain in the former war, together with Ægialeus, the son of Adrastos, undertook a new expedition against Thebes, conquered Laodamas, and seized upon the royal authority, of which his father Polyneices had been unjustly deprived. Laodamas fled to Illyria, which had formerly been also the asylum of Cadmos. In the first Theban war, Adrastos was the only one of the leaders who escaped; in the second, his son, Ægialeus, was the only one who fell.

Upon one of the rarest and most precious monuments of ancient sculpture, which is preserved in a German museum of antiquities, the heroes are represented who, under the command of Adrastos, besieged Thebes. The group consists of five persons, under each of whom the name is engraved, and both figures and letters prove the high antiquity of the work. The heroes represented are, Adrastos, Tydeus, Polyneices, Amphiaraös, and Parthenopæos. They appear to be assembled for the purpose of holding a new council on their affairs after a defeat. In the midst of them sits Amphiaraös, with dejected countenance, foreseeing his own death, as well as that of his associates. Opposite to him Polyneices is seated, leaning his head upon his hand, as if in deep, melancholy musings. On the side of Amphiaraös appears Parthenopæos, seated also on a chair, with his hands drawn round his knees in a quiet, thoughtful posture. Adrastos has risen from his seat, and seems willing to hasten again to the field of battle, being armed with a shield and spear. Tydeus, who is also armed, is following him, but with less spirit in his countenance, and with downcast look. In this beautiful group a gradation of feeling and inward emotion, as it were, is expressed from Polyneices, whose head rests upon his hand, to Adrastos, who is courageously hastening to the battle-ground.

THE PELOPIDÆ.

Pelops, a son of that Tantalos, who, after having been raised by the gods even to their own assembly, was hurled down by them into the depths of Tartaros, came from Phrygia to Œnomaos, king of Pisa, by whom he was hospitably received. Struck by the charms of the beautiful Hippodameia, the king's daughter, Pelops requested her from her father as his wife. But it had been predicted to Œnomaos that his son-in-law would deprive him of life; and he therefore proposed to every suitor for his daughter to contend with him in the chariot race, putting to death all whom he overtook in the course. The race was from the banks of the Cladios in Elis to the altar of Poseidon, at the isthmus, and was run in the following manner: Œnomaos, placing his daughter in the chariot with the suitor, gave him the start; he then followed with a spear in his hand, with which, on overtaking the suitor, he ran him through. Thirteen had already lost their lives when Pelops appeared.

"In the dead of night," says Pindar, "Pelops went down to the margin of the sea, and invoked the god who rules it. Suddenly Poseidon stood at his feet; and he conjured him by the memory of his affection, to grant him the means of obtaining the lovely daughter of Œnomaos, declaring, that even if he should fail in the attempt, he regarded fame beyond inglorious old age. Poseidon, assenting to his prayer, gave him a golden chariot, and horses of winged speed."

Pelops then went to Pisa, and by alluring promises prevailed on Myrtilos, the charioteer of Œnomaos, to adjust the king's chariot in such a manner that it would break down in the middle of the course. The king was thrown out and lost his life, when Hippodameia became the bride of Pelops. To celebrate the wedding. Poseidon assembled the Nereïdes upon the strand of the sea. and raised a bridal chamber of the waves, which arched in bright curves over the marriage bed.

After his marriage with Hippodameia. Pelops, unwilling to fulfil his promise to Myrtilos for the aid he had given him, threw him unawares from a rock into the sea, which from him derived the name of Myrtœan. One misfortune after another followed this act of injustice and cruelty, although the power of Pelops increased to such a degree, that the whole Peninsula of Greece was called after him Peloponnesus.

Hippodameia had two sons, Atreus and Thyestes, who became jealous of their father's affection for their step-brother, Chrysippos, and put him to death. Pelops supposed Hippodameia to have instigated this murder, and upon being charged with it, she destroyed herself, and her two sons fled from the wrath of their father.

Atreus went to Eurystheus, king of Mycenæ, who received him kindly, and gave him his daughter Arëope in marriage. After the death of Eurystheus, Atreus mounted the throne of Mycenæ

Thyestes followed Atreus, and shared his brother's good fortune; but soon brought reproach and misfortune upon himself by his own misdeeds. During the absence of Atreus, Arëope bore two sons to Thyestes. As soon as Atreus became apprised of it, he expelled them, as well as their father from his dominions. Thyestes, breathing revenge, contrived to get a son of Atreus into his power, and educated him as his own, at the same time instilling into his youthful heart a deadly hatred against his father, and finally sent him away to commit a murder at which the Sun veils his face.

But the youth was unsuccessful in his attempt, and upon the discov-ery of his design, he was put to death under the most cruel tortures ; and Atreus learned too late that by his command his own son, instead of his brother's, had suffered a cruel death. Atreus, now brooding over a still deeper revenge, feigned a reconciliation with his brother, and by various marks of affection induced him to come to Mycenæ and bring his sons with him. He then had them secretly murdered and their flesh served up on the table at which their father sat. After Thyestes had eaten the food prepared for him, Atreus cast their heads and hands before his eyes. " On beholding the scene," says the fiction, " the Sun swiftly turned back his course."

Thyestes then fled to Sicyon, where he had a son by his daughter Pelopia, whose name was Ægisthos, who, on attaining the years of manhood, murdered Atreus, and expelled his sons Agamemnon and Meneläos from the kingdom, when Thyestes usurped the royal throne of Mycenæ.

The fugitive sons of Atreus found a friendly reception at the court of Tyndarëos, king of Lacedæmon, where each married a daughter of their host; Agamemnon, Clytemnestra, and Meneläos, the beautiful Helena, who afterwards brought wo throughout Greece and destruc-tion on Troy. The two brothers avenged the death of their father, Atreus, and once more expelled Thyestes from Mycenæ. Agamem-non then took the reins of government in his father's dominions, while Meneläos succeeded Tyndarëos in the government of Sparta.

Meneläos and Helena had no children. Agamemnon and Clytem-nestra had two daughters, Iphigeneia and Electra, and one son, Ores-tes.

When Agamemnon afterwards took the chief command of the army destined to call Troy to account for the offence which his brother Meneläos had suffered from Paris, forgiving Ægisthos, the murderer of his father, he became reconciled to him, and even intrusted him with the care of Clytemnestra and his house during his absence. Ægisthos, however, abused this confidence, misleading Clytemnestra to infidelity and bringing ruin upon her husband. For when Agamemnon return-ed to Mycenæ after an absence of ten years, to enjoy the remainder of his days in quiet and domestic happiness, he was murdered by Ægis-thos and Clytemnestra.

With regard to the children of Agamemnon. Iphigeneia was to have been sacrificed on entering upon the expedition against Troy; but was rescued by Diana, who carried her to Tauris, where she became a priestess in her temple. Orestes, whose life was threatened with great danger from the hands of Ægisthos, was secretly sent by his sister to Strophios, king of Phocis, and the husband of Agamemnon's sister. Electra remained at home, exposed to the abuse of an unnatural mother.

After the death of her husband, Clytemnestra, fearing neither gods nor men, married Ægisthos, and put the royal crown of Mycenæ on his execrable head. But Destiny had already decreed the punishment of that guilty couple, although it was to be executed only by the means of a new crime.

In Orestes, Agamemnon's son, rose an avenger both of his father's death and his mother's infamy. A false report, intentionally circulated, had announced him as dead; and while Ægisthos and Clytemnestra rejoiced in the thought of being rid of him, Orestes was planning their destruction. As soon as Orestes felt his arm strong enough to meet a foe with his sword, he went to Mycenæ and slew the murderer of his father, not sparing his own mother who shared in the crime. But on account of this horrible deed, Orestes was punished by the Furies wherever he went ; that is to say, his conscience would not allow him any rest, and suffered him not to be reconciled to himself, until he went to Delphi and consulted the oracle of Apollo, which promised him alleviation of his torments if he would go to Tauris, and carry the statue of Diana from thence to Greece.

Orestes had been brought up with Pylades, the son of king Strophios, at Phocis, and both were so intimately and inseparably united by the tie of friendship, that their union became proverbial in antiquity, and is so even in our own times. This faithful friend, Pylades, who had never left Orestes during all his sufferings, was now his companion on the voyage to Tauris. It was there an old and barbarous custom to bring human offerings to Diana, the severe goddess who was the tutelary deity of the country, and whose image Orestes was to carry away. Orestes and Pylades had no sooner landed, than they were made prisoners, and doomed to be for ever separated by the sacrifice of one of them to Diana. In the trying hour, when the sentence of the high priest was received, each of the friends offered his life to save that of the other. A contest that was pleasing in the sight of the gods, and worthy of heavenly assistance.

Orestes recognized his sister Iphigeneia, the priestess of Diana, and made himself known to her; and she found means not only to bring the statue of the goddess on board her brother's ship, but also to rescue both the friends and fly with them to Greece. The oracle of Apollo proved true. The Furies ceased to torment Orestes, who henceforth' reigned quietly over Mycenæ, and the wrath of the gods, which had borne so long and so heavily upon the house of Pelops, seemed now to abate.

Goethe. the author of "Iphigeneia in Tauris," gives to the ancient representation a very ingenious and beautiful turn. According to him, the oracle of Apollo promises tranquillity to Orestes. " if he would carry the sister to Greece, who remained in the sanctuary at Tauris against her will." Orestes, who was not aware that his s'ster lived in Tauris, was necessarily led to apply the word *sister* to Diana. the sister of Apollo, who by way of distinction was often thus designated. But when Orestes unexpectedly found his own sister, who indeed remained in Tauris against her will, he was allowed to apply the word sister to her; and Iphigeneia was neither obliged to steal the statue of Diana, nor to commit a treason against Troas, the king of the island, who had always been her benefactor, and who dismissed her in a kind and friendly manner.

ACHILLEUS OR ACHILLES.

Achilles was the son of Peleus (a descendant of Zeus) and of Thetis, the goddess of the sea At the festivity of their marriage, the gods brought gifts, the Muses sang. the Nereïdes danced, and Ganymedes poured forth nectar for the guests.

When Achilles was born, Thetis plunged him in the river Styx, which made him invulnerable in every part except the heel, by which she held him. And in this heel he received a fatal wound.

Achilleus, like the other heroes, was reared by the wise Centaur Cheiron. A fine picture represents him as a beautiful youth, standing near Cheiron on the sea-shore, receiving a visit from Thetis, who is seated on a car drawn by dolphins With a look of the most animated delight. he is displaying to his mother the skill he has acquired in the musical art.

In the Ilias. Achilleus appears as one of the most prominent heroes.

Wì seli remarks, that " each individual of Homer forms a class, expresses and is circumscribed by one quality of heroic power; Achilleus
alone unites their various but congenial energies. The grace of Ni-
reus, the dignity of Agamemnon, the impetuosity of Hector, the magnitude, the steady prowess of the great, the velocity of the lesser Ajax,
the perseverance of Ulysses, the intrepidity of Diomede, are emanations
of energy that re-unite in one splendid centre fixed in Achilles."

When Nestor, who had lived through two ages, and was then reigning over Pylos in the third, endeavored, during the siege of Troy, to
allay the contention that existed between Achilles and Agamemnon,
he reminded them at the commencement of his speech, that he had
been living and communing with stronger men than the present age
produced ; with Ceneus, Dryas, Pirithoös, and Theseus, with whom no
man would dare to enter into combat ; and moreover, they had all lis-
tened to and been guided by his advice.   Achilleus and Agamemnon,
therefore, he added, might do the same.

Thus Nestor describes the heroes before the time of the Trojan war ;
and the bard of the Iliad in his turn represents the heroes of that war,
as having far surpassed in strength the men of his age. " Hector,"
says he, " took up a stone, which two of the strongest men living in our
times could scarcely raise from the ground, and with ease flung it
against the door of the Greek wall, and with such force, that the leaves
sprung at once from their hinges."

Men whom Prometheus had first formed of clay, though odious to
the reigning gods, and deprived by them of fire—destroyed, except a
few, by several deluges, gradually rose by their own efforts to a noble
self-esteem, and the appreciation of their inward powers, and became
assimilated to the immortal gods. Beholding the god-like heroes who
rose from the midst of her, Humanity became sensible of her worth
and her higher destination ; and the gods, now becoming, as it were,
reconciled to mankind, took more and more interest in their transactions and their fates. Thus divinity and humanity approached nearer
and nearer, till at last, in the war with Troy, the gods themselves took
part, and were wounded by mortal hands.

ILION OR TROY.

A history of Troy embraces events that are divided into three periods, Ante-Homeric, Homeric, and Post-Homeric.

Ante-Homeric.—Zeus and Electra, the daughter of Atlas, had two sons, Dardanos and Iasion The latter was the favorite of Cybele, for which reason Zeus struck him with lightning. Dardanos, afflicted with the death of his brother, left Samothrace, where they had dwelt together, and passed over to the main land, where Teucros, the son of the river Scamandros, and the nymph Idæa then reigned, from whom the people were called Teucrians. He was well received by this prince, who gave him his daughter Bateia in marriage, and a part of his territory, on which he built a town called Dardanos. On the death of Teucros, he named the whole country Dardania.

Dardanos left two sons, Ilos and Erichthonios, the former of whom died childless; the latter succeeded to the kingdom, and married Astyoche, daughter of the Simoïs, and had a son named Tros, who succeeded him on the throne. Tros married Callirrhoë, daughter of the Scamandros, and had one daughter, Cleopatra, and three sons, Ilos, Assaracos, and Ganymedes. The last was admired by Zeus for his beauty, who, in the shape of an eagle, carried him to Olympos, where he made him cupbearer to the gods. As a compensation for his loss, Zeus gave Tros some horses of the Olympian breed.

Assaracos married a daughter of the river Simoïs, and was the grandfather of Anchises, who was beloved by Aphrodite, the mother of Æneias.

Ilos went to Phrygia, and in games of wrestling given by the king, won fifty youths and as many maidens. The king also, in obedience to an oracle, gave him a spotted cow, and told him to build a city where she should lie down. Ilos followed the cow till she came to the hill of Ate (*Mischief*), where he built the town of Ilion, named from himself. He then prayed to Zeus to give him a sign ; and the following day he found the Zeus fallen Palladium, the image of Pallas Athene, lying before his tent.

Laomedon, the son of Ilos, married Strymo, the daughter of the Scamandros, by whom she had Tithonos (who was carried off by Eos), Lampos, Clytios, Hiketaon, Priamos, and Hesione. By the nymph Calybe he had a son, named Bucolion.

Priamos reigned over Ilion after the death of his father, and was the last king of Troy. When Heracles took the city of Troy, Priamos was among the number of prisoners, but was redeemed by his sister Hesione, whom Heracles had given to Telamon as a reward for his valor. She was allowed to choose one among the captives, and when she had fixed upon her brother Podarkes, Heracles replied, that he must first be made a slave, and then by some gift she might redeem him. She took the golden veil from her head, and gave it as a price for his purchase; and hence he was afterwards called Priamos (*purchased*), instead of Podarkes (*swift-foot*).

Heracles placed Priamos on his father's throne, when he employed himself with well-directed diligence in embellishing the city of Ilion. He married Hecabe (Hecuba), a daughter of Dymas the Phrygian, by whom he had nineteen children, of whom the chief were Hector, Paris or Alexandros, Deiphobos, Helenos, Troilos, Polites, Polydoros, Cassandra, Creusa, and Polyxene. Æsacos, the soothsayer, predicted that Paris would prove the ruin of his country, and recommended that the babe should be exposed to perish. He was therefore committed to a servant to be left on mount Ida, who, on returning to the place at the end of five days, found that a bear had suckled the infant. Struck with the incident, he took home the child, reared him as his own son, and named him Paris. Paris afterwards distinguished himself by his strength and courage in repelling robbers from the flocks, and the shepherds then gave him the name of Alexandros.

Ilion was the principal theatre of tragic events among those countries which lay without the boundaries of Greece. " A day was to come in which Ilion should fall, and Priam's royal race be extinguished." This was the decree of Destiny, against which neither gods nor men could prevail; all circumstances must concur to bring about its accomplishment.

Eris, the goddess of discord, enraged at being the only one of the celestials who had not received an invitation to the marriage of Peleus with the silver-footed Thetis, contrived to throw into the assembly of the gods who were celebrating the nuptials a golden apple, which bore the inscription, " Destined to the fairest." Juno, Minerva, and Venus were unanimously acknowledged the most worthy to contend for the prize.

None of the gods being willing to undertake the office of awarding it, and thereby incur the inevitable risk of offending two powerful beauties of Olympos, Jupiter commanded Mercury to lead the three deities to mount Ida, and intrust the decision to Paris, whose judg

25

ment was to be definitive. The three goddesses, consenting to this, appeared before him, each privately endeavoring to influence him by the promise of such gifts as she thought most likely to bias his judgment. The majestic Juno, while she haughtily demanded the prize as her right, signified her intention to confer the greatest riches and dignity upon the giver of it. Minerva offered him a diadem, the symbol of thrones, as well as the pure and lasting pleasure with which wisdom rewards her votaries. At last Venus advanced: "I will give thee a wife," said she, "whose exquisite beauty will induce mortals to say, were Venus to descend upon earth, she would appear in such a form as Helena's." The shepherd awarded the golden apple to Venus. Venus was intent upon the fulfilment of her promise, while Paris suffered the unrelenting enmity of her two disappointed rivals, which was extended also to his whole family, and the entire Trojan race.

Soon after this event, Priamos proposed a contest among his sons and other princes, promising to reward the conqueror with one of his finest bulls from Mount Ida. On sending to procure the animal, it was found in the possession of Paris, who reluctantly yielded it up. The shepherd, desirous of recovering his favorite, went to Ilion, and entered the lists of the combatants.

Paris proved successful against every competitor, and gained an advantage over Hector himself. The prince, irritated at finding himself vanquished by an unknown stranger, pursued*him closely, and Paris must have fallen a victim to his brother's resentment, had he not fled to the altar of Jupiter. This sacred place of refuge saved his life. Cassandra, the daughter of Priam, struck with the similarity of Paris' features to those of her own brothers, inquired his birth and age. From these circumstances she soon discovered that he was her brother, and as such, she introduced him to her father. Priamos, forgetting the alarming predictions of Æsacos, acknowledged Paris as his son, and all enmity instantly ceased between him and his brother.

Priamos, having reigned for many years in great prosperity, ex-pressed a wish to recover his sister Hesione, who had redeemed him from captivity. To carry this plan into execution, he manned a fleet, and gave the command of it to Paris, at the same time ordering him to bring back Hesione. At the instigation of Venus, Paris proceeded on his memorable voyage to Greece, from which the soothsaying Cassandra in vain endeavored to detain him.

Arriving at Sparta, where Meneläos, the husband of Helena, was reigning, he met with a hospitable reception ; but Meneläos, having soon after sailed to Crete, Paris availed himself of his absence, gained the affections of Helena, and bore her away to his native city, together with a large portion of wealth belonging to her husband.

Helena was the daughter of Jupiter and Leda, and foster-daughter of Tyndarëos, king of Lacedæmon. The fame of her beauty had spread over all Greece, and drew many kings to the court of Tyndarëos, in the hope of obtaining her as a wife. While Tyndarëos was flattered at seeing his daughter, and consequently himself who had the disposal of her. so highly honored, he entertained the well-grounded fear, that since she could be given to but one of the suitors, the pretended friend-ship of the rest might change to hatred and revenge, which would become dangerous to him.

In this dilemma he consulted Ulysses, king of Ithaca, who was re-nowned for his prudence throughout all Greece. Ulysses advised him to assemble all the suitors of Helena, and require of them a solemn oath, that they would acquiesce in her choice, and with their united power protect the preferred lover against every one who might dispute with him the quiet possession of his rightfully gained treasure

Tyndarēos followed his advice. The assembled kings submitted to his proposal, and Helena made choice of Menelãos, brother to Agamemnon, king of Mycenæ. They lived happily together until Paris entered Sparta, and repaid the kindness of Menelãos with the blackest ingratitude, by persuading Helena to leave her husband, and accompany him to Troy.

Menelãos, deprived of his adored wife, became incensed, and caused all Greece to re-echo his complaints against Priam's treacherous son. The kings were reminded of the oaths they had taken, and hastened to act accordingly. Every soul was exasperated against Paris, not only on account of his having carried off a citizen of a foreign country, but particularly for his having so grossly violated the sacred rights of hospitality. Ambassadors were immediately despatched to Priamos to complain of the offence perpetrated against all Greece, and also to reclaim the ravished Helena ; but the old, hapless king, influenced by the machinations of his son, and by his own paternal love, suffered them to return, without granting them their just demand.

The kings of Greece, with Agamemnon at their head, then formed a coalition, swearing to overthrow the city of Troy. Each one fitted out and manned as many ships as he had at his disposal, and the whole fleet assembled in the harbor of Aulis. The chief leaders in this war were—Agamemnon, king of Mycenæ ; Menelãos, king of Sparta ; Nestor, king of Pylus ; Diomedes, the son of Tydeus ; Ajax, the son of Telamon ; Odysseus, king of Ithaca ; Patroclos, the son of Menœtius : Podaleirios and Machaon, the sons of Asclepios ; Philoctetes, the last companion of Heracles ; Sthenelos, the son of Capaneus ; Thersandres the son of Polyneices ; and Idomeneus, the grandson of Minos.

The heroes wished particularly to obtain the assistance of Achilleus. His mother had seen with pleasure the warlike ardor of her son, but knowing that he must perish in the flower of his age, after having achieved the most brilliant exploits, she prevailed upon Lycomedes to receive him in the dress of a female, among the attendants of his daughter, Deidameia. The Greeks discovered the artifice, and sent Diomedes, Odysseus, and Agyrtes to the palace, disguised as merchants. They had concealed arms in their dress, and also among the articles of traffic offered to Deidameia and her attendants. Each selected what best pleased her taste. Achilleus seized upon a spear and lance, when he was recognized by Odysseus. The trumpet of Agyrtes still more excited his warlike ardor, and he left Deidameia in tears, who had conceived a tender passion for him, and joined the army of the Greeks.

Agamemnon, the most powerful of the Grecian kings, was chosen chief of the expedition. The army then offered a solemn sacrifice, during which a serpent appeared which devoured nine little birds in their nest, and afterwards their mother. Calchas interpreted the presage by saying that the siege would last ten years.

The fleet lay a long time in the harbor waiting for a fair wind. Agamemnon, having killed a deer in the chase, boasted that he was superior in skill to Diana. The offended goddess sent adverse winds to detain them, and through the mouth of the augur, Calchas, demanded Iphigeneia, Agamemnon's daughter, as a propitiatory sacrifice. Iphigeneia, accompanied by her mother, was conducted to the altar of the indignant goddess, and the sacrificial knife already flashed in the hand of the priest, when she was involved in a cloud by Diana, and transported to Tauris. A roe stood in the place of Iphigeneia.

After Diana was propitiated, the fleet steered with a fair wind out of the harbor of Aulis, and landed safely on the shores of Troas, where siege was immediately laid to the city of Troy.

Meanwhile, Priam was spending the remainder of a long and peaceful life in the midst of a numerous family. The industrious citizens, whose commerce flourished, lived in affluence and tranquillity, and the husbandman exulted in the hope that his labors would meet with a due reward. In fine, that harmony so beneficial, so requisite to the peace of society, prevailed in Troas.

An army of Greeks now makes its appearance, and universal confusion ensues. Fear takes possession of every breast The inhabitants of the country seek refuge in the city, the gates of which are instantly closed. The brave Hector flies to the ramparts. His example cheers the most disheartened. They gather round him, follow him in every sally, and for ten years resist every effort of the Greeks.

In this war all the celestials took part, espousing either the side of the Greeks or that of the Trojans. Imperial Jove sat on the top of Mount Ida, holding the balance in his mighty hand, and directing the fate of the combatants. In favor of the Greeks were the majestic Juno, the queen of the heavens; the severe Pallas-Athene, the goddess of wisdom; Neptune, the ruler of the waves; Vulcan, the god of fire; and Mercury, the swift messenger of the immortals. On the side of the Trojans stood Venus, the goddess of beauty; Apollo, the god of music; Diana, the goddess of the chase, and Latona. Mars, as the god of war, went from one army to the other, siding now with the Greeks, and now with the Trojans.

Homeric.—The cause of the detention of the Greeks for ten years before the city of Troy, without being able to get possession of it, was the wrath of Achilles against Agamemnon, who had deprived him of his slave, the fair Briseïs. Agamemnon had received the beautiful Chryseïs as a part of the booty at the taking of Thebes. Her father, who was a priest of Apollo, went to the camp of the Greeks, supplica· ting for the release of his daughter, and offering an ample ransom. Agamemnon refused to release Chryseïs on any terms; and moreover, loaded the wretched old man, who stood before him supplicating for the restitution of his beloved and only child, with ignominious words and menaces. Perceiving that his entreaties were ineffectual, the priest lifted up his hands to Apollo, praying him to avenge the injury done to his servant, and to punish the cruelty of the Greeks. Apollo heard the supplication of the wretched father, and highly incensed against Agamemnon, as well as his followers, shot several of his arrows into the camp of the Greeks, thus causing a pestilence that swept away multitudes of the people.

At length, through the augur Calchas, it was revealed by whose guilt, and for what cause, the people of Greece were suffering. Aga·memnon, at the entreaties of all his allies, could no longer refuse to restore Chryseïs to her father, but at the same time, he demanded to be indemnified for his loss, by another part of the booty, which had already been divided. Achilles, indignant at his pride and selfishness, rebuked him with great severity; and when Agamemnon threatened him, he was even on the point of drawing his sword against the chief, but was restrained by the goddess of wisdom, who grasped his yellow locks.

Agamemnon, still more enraged at the opposition on the part of Achilles, insisted with the greater obstinacy on receiving an indemnity for the loss of his slave; and to avenge himself upon the bold son of Thetis, he carried off Briseïs by force from his tent. Upon this act of violence and injustice, Achilles retired to the lonely shore of the sea, and stretching forth his hands to his mother, implored her vengeance upon the haughty king of Mycenæ, by inducing the gods to assist the Trojans, and to withdraw their aid from the Greeks; so that while he declined taking part in the war, these might feel the want of his strong arm, and experience the effects of his wrath.

Thetis heard the prayers of her son, and, hastening to the throne of Jupiter, besought the ruler of gods and men to bestow victory upon the Trojans, and thus avenge her son on the proud Agamemnon and the ungrateful Greeks, reminding him, at the same time, of the assistance he had once received from her when his sovereignty was endangered by a conspiracy of the other deities. Jupiter complied with the request of his benefactress; prohibited all the gods in the strictest terms from assisting in any manner the besiegers of Troy, and upon Hector, the chief of the besieged, who made frequent and successful sallies, he bestowed immortal glory.

Too late did Agamemnon repent of the offence which he had given to the valiant Achilles. Too late did all the Greeks repent of having suffered this offence to be committed against one, who alone was able to save them from destruction by his mighty arm. Their attempts to reconcile Achilles, and the entreaties by which they endeavored to induce him again to take up his spear in their behalf, were all in vain. He had closed his ears to all their prayers, as well as their promises; his resolution was not to be shaken. At last, however, when the Trojans, after they had vanquished the Greeks in a bloody battle, assailed their camp, and were even casting fire into their ships, Achilles, moved by the prayers and entreaties of his beloved friend Patroclos, permitted him to array himself in his own armor, and to lead on a troop of his myrmidons against his enemies.

When the Trojans beheld the armor of the hero, they supposed that the wearer was Achilles himself, and fled like a flock of sheep at the approach of the wolf. Although the death of Patroclos was decreed by Destiny, yet he was permitted, before he fell, to gain a never-fading glory; for Sarpedon, Jupiter's son, together with many other valiant heroes, were subdued by his sword, and went down to the dominions of Pluto. But his own fate was fast approaching. Apollo stood behind him covered with night, and struck him with his broad hand on his neck and shoulders, so that his eyes grew dim. The god then pulled the helmet from his head, which rolled under the feet of the horses, broke the heavy spear in his hand, mounted with brass, and stripped him of his breast-plate. While Patroclos, stunned, could scarcely support himself on his staggering limbs, Hector gave him the deadly stroke. The soul of Patroclos went down to Orcus, complaining of her fate, because she had left behind her the strength of youth.

When Achilles heard of the death of his beloved Patroclos, his wrath against Agamemnon and the Greeks gave place to nobler feelings. His soul was filled with distress and grief; and his eyes wept tears of blood over the body of his departed friend. In this mournful situation he was found by his mother, who had risen from the deep, where his lamentations had reached her ears. Although she made known to him, after her parental consolations had in some measure quieted his soul, that Hector's death would not long precede his own, yet he swore to avenge the early departure of his friend, regardless of the destiny that awaited himself. Thetis, seeing her son firm in his resolution, endeavored to comfort and animate him for the short remainder of his days; she promised and brought to him new armor of Vulcan's workmanship, and upon his reconciliation with Agamemnon, who had restored to him the fair Briseïs, he rushed forth in the din of battle, to avenge the death of his friend, and to bring sadness and grief over Priam and his whole house.

Hector, thine hour is at hand! Cover thy head, old Priam, for the best and bravest of thy numerous offspring, who has hitherto defended the walls of Troy, and Ilion, and thee, shall now fall! Pluck out thy grey hair, O Hecuba, mother of many sons and daughters, for the nearest and dearest to thy heart of all thy children—he who has been the protector of thy house, thy daughters, and thyself, is now to enter on the solitary journey to those mansions, whither soon to follow him is thine only consolation! Go into thy chamber, Andromache, best of wives and tenderest of mothers, there to weep, and mourn over the loss of the best of husbands and the tenderest of fathers, who shall no longer defend thee, nor thy little son, Astyanax! Go, thine own Hector must fall!

When Achilles appeared on the battle-ground, shaking his mighty spear, and thundering like a lion, the Trojans, terror-struck, fled back in confusion to the city. Hector alone stood firm to await the son of a goddess, and to enter with him on the decisive combat. He stood firm, till Achilles drew so near that he could see the divine armor in which he was clad. At that moment he fled with sudden consternation. Three times was he chased around the walls of Troy by the son of Thetis: so long had Apollo strengthened his knees. But as he was running round for the fourth time, Jupiter took up the balance, put into each scale a lot of death, and that of Hector sank down to Orcus. Then Apollo left him to his destiny.

The heroes fought. Hector fell. And Achilles, fastening his feet to his chariot, dragged him in triumph round the city of Troy. The old and wretched parents of the fallen hero stood upon the walls, and beheld the mournful spectacle. Hecuba filled the air with her lamentations, and Priam stretched forth his trembling hands, as if entreating forbearance.

In the camp of the Greeks, the funeral of Patroclos was celebrated with great pomp, and public games of combat, while Hector's corpse lay there unburied. In order to procure for his body the funeral rites, and bring Hector's soul to rest in the Elysian fields, the aged Priam himself, conducted by Mercury, came at night to the Grecian camp, and entering Achilles' tent, threw himself upon his knees, and conjured him, by the memory of his old father, Peleus, to surrender him the body of his son Hector, that he might procure for it an honorable interment.

This picture of Priam, as he is embracing the knees of the man who had slain his dearest son, the support of his old age, and the defender of his city and his throne, and supplicating for this son's body, is one of the most tragic, and, at the same time, one of the most touching scenes exhibited in the annals of mankind. Another scene, equally affecting, deserves to be placed beside it. It is Cassandra, the daughter of Priam, who, through the power of her presaging mind, foresees all the misery which hangs over Troy, her parents, and herself. But obtaining no credit or belief, and therefore no means of preventing that misery, she wanders in lonely places, in despair, lamenting her cruel fate.

The distress of Priam reminds Achilles of his own aged father, and touched by the thought that he also would soon be lamenting his departed son, he grants the request of the old man, who, with the corpse of Hector, hastens back to Troy, where, with his whole people, he celebrates the funeral in the most solemn manner.

Post-Homeric.—After the death of Hector, the Amazons, conducted by their queen Penthesileia, daughter of Mars, went to the aid of the Trojans. In the first engagement she was slain by Achilles, who, struck with her beauty, returned her body to the Trojans, that they might perform her obsequies. Thersites railed at the hero, who turned upon him and slew him. This caused a dissension among the army, and Achilles sailed to Lesbos, where, after having sacrificed to Latona, Apollo, and Diana, he was purified of the murder by Ulysses.

Memnon, the Æthiopian, the son of Tithonos and Aurora, now came to the aid of the Trojans. He was arrayed in Hephæstean armor, and after having slain Autilachos, he is himself slain by Achilles. His mother was much grieved at his death, and in her despair went to Jupiter to obtain immortality for him. To console her, Jupiter promised that her son should reappear under a new form, and when his body was consumed, two white birds were seen to rise from his ashes, which were called Memnonides.

Achilles himself was soon overtaken by his destiny. Pursuing the Trojans to the city, and while endeavoring to force his way in, the fatal arrow, shot by Paris, and directed by Apollo, wounded him in the heel, his only vulnerable part, and the wound proved fatal. An unfortunate contest ensued among the leaders of the Grecian army on account of his armor, the present of Vulcan. It was at length awarded to Ulysses, at which Ajax, who ranked next in valor to Achilles, was so displeased and offended, that he put a period to his life.

Paris did not long boast of his victory over Achilles. He was wounded by Philoctetes, with one of those arrows which Hercules had dipped in the blood of the Lernæan Hydra, and left as an inheritance to his friend. Paris, when a shepherd, and before he was discovered to be a son of Priam, had married Œnone, a nymph of Mount Ida, and daughter of the river Cebrenus, in Phrygia. Œnone had received the gift of prophecy from Apollo, and warned Paris against the consequences of his voyage to Greece. She had also told him, that if he was ever wounded, to come to her, as she alone could cure him. Paris accordingly went to her when wounded by Philoctetes, but Œnone, offended at his desertion of her, refused him assistance, and he died on his return to Ilion. Repenting of her cruelty, Œnone hastened to his relief, but, coming too late, she threw herself upon his funeral pile and perished.

The downfall of Troy, and the overthrow of Priam's ancient realm, now drew nearer and nearer. Yet, after all the blood that had been shed, the walls of the city and castle of Ilion were to be conquered, not by power, but by artifice. By the advice of the crafty Ulysses, a colossal horse was constructed of wood, within which several of the most courageous heroes concealed themselves, while the Greek army went on board their ships, feigning to have left the coast of Troas for ever. Sinon only remained; who, on being discovered by the Trojans, made them believe, by means of a well-studied tale, that he was a fugitive, persecuted by his own countrymen, the Greeks, and that he was on his way to implore the assistance and protection of the magnanimous Trojans. He told them, at the same time, as an important secret, that the wooden horse, at which the Trojans looked with much astonishment, not knowing for what purpose it was left, had been built by the Greeks with the view of propitiating Minerva, because they had taken the Palladium from the city, the statue of the goddess, which was looked upon as the pledge of safety for the realm of Troy. Sinon acted his part so well as nearly to disperse all doubt respecting the truth of his account, and if some distrust still remained in the breasts of one or two, it was dispelled by a singular event, which happened quite seasonably to support the fictitious tale of the treacherous Greek.

Laocoön, an old Trojan priest, who had heard that his fellow-citizens were about to transport the dangerous gift which the sons of Danaös had left behind them, to the temple of Pallas-Athene in the centre of the city, hastened before the gates, and conjured them to reflect on what they were about to do. At the close of his speech, he struck his spear against the side of the horse, from which resounded a feeble clash of arms. Laocoön then went with his sons to a neighboring temple of Neptune, to offer a sacrifice to the ruler of the waves, to thank him for the preservation of his native city, and to implore his further assistance. There, while preparing the offerings, two enormous serpents, which came from the Isle of Tenedos, over the sea, suddenly made their appearance, and ere the wretched father could warn his sons or fly with them, the reptiles had already coiled their immense folds around the tender bodies of the youths. Laocoön rushing desperately upon the monsters, to save his children, became entangled himself within the coils of the snakes. Father and sons beholding their mutual agonies, without the power to assist each other, or relieve themselves, died a doubly-painful death.

The fate of Laocoön was considered by the Trojans as a punishment inflicted on him by the gods, for violating that present, which was left by the departing Greeks to Minerva, and was destined to be the substitute for the Palladium of which her temple had been robbed. There

was now no longer any doubt of the pretended fugitive's sincerity, or of the truth of what he had related. The infatuated people hasten-ed, with triumphant exultation, to convey this Palladium, the new pledge of safety, into the city; boys and girls were delighted to touch the cords by which the horse was drawn. When it was found that the gate was not large enough for its admittance, part of the wall was broken down, and the fatal horse stood in the midst of Troy.

Rejoicing at their deliverance from the dangerous enemies who had afflicted them with many woes for the past ten years, the hapless in-habitants of the city now abandoned themselves freely to wine, dance, and joy, until a late hour of the night. At last, while they were buried in sleep and intoxication, and midnight had spread its sable mantle over the country, the Grecian fleet, which had concealed itself behind the isle of Tenedos, again landed on the shores of Troas. Sinon, the treacherous Sinon, put a ladder to the wooden horse, and opened a secret door, and thus a number of Greek heroes were already in the streets of Troy. They gave a sign to those on board the ships, by lighting a torch. Then, easily overpowering the drunken guard, they opened the gates of the city, and in rushed the Greek army. The last day of Ilion and Priam's old realm had passed. While sleep pressed upon the eyelids of the greater part of the wretched inhabitants, those few who at the first alarm endeavored to escape or to resist the enemy, were slaughtered in the streets. The enraged soldiery immolated to their fury whatever met their eye. They set fire to the four corners of the city, and while it was raging, they entered the houses in search of prey and murder. Unhappy Priam was slain at the very altar of his domestic temple, where he had sought an asylum. Pyrrhus, the son of Achilles, in his fury, revered no god, no altar, no asylum; he plunged his sword in the old man's heart. Priam had seen nearly all his sons become the prey of the sword during the unfortunate war; happy for him that his eyes could not behold the fall of the aged Hecuba, his queen, of his daughters, and of Andromache, Hector's noble spouse. They were all carried away captives, to weep as slaves in a foreign land.

Thus sunk the glory of Ilion, and thus was Priam's royal race extinguished.

ODYSSEUS OR ULYSSES.

The Greeks, on their return to their native land, were obliged to atone for their dearly-bought victory with many misfortunes. Even the greater part of those who reached their homes in safety, found their domestic affairs so changed and disordered during a ten years' absence, that the remainder of their days, instead of being passed in peace and tranquillity, were embittered by many calamities.

The hardest fate befel " the sufferer Odysseus," who in addition to the ten years which he had lain before the walls of Ilion, was now doomed to wander about on the sea another ten years before he was permitted to behold again the shores of Ithaca. On doubling the cape of Malea, in Laconia, Odysseus encountered a violent north-east wind, which for nine days drove him along the sea, till he reached the country of Lotus-eaters. His men, going on shore, were kindly entertained by the Lotus-eaters, who gave them some of their own food the Lotus-plant. The effect of this plant was such, that they lost all thought of home, and Odysseus was obliged to drag them away and fasten them to the ship.

Polyphemos, one of the Cyclopes, is represented as having but one eye in the middle of his forehead, of an enormous size, and leading a pastoral life. On leaving the country of the Lotus-eaters, and sailing further westward, Ulysses was thrown upon that part of the coast of Sicily which was inhabited by these monsters, and having with twelve of his companions entered the cave of Polyphemos during his absence, they were found by him on his return, and kept immured for the purpose of being devoured. Four of the Grecian chief's companions fell a prey to the voracity of the monster; but Ulysses escaped by the following expedient: Having intoxicated the Cyclope, he availed himself of his state of insensibility to deprive him of sight, by means of a large stake which was discovered in the cave. After having sharpened it and heated it in the fire, Ulysses plunged it into his eye.

Polyphemos roared so loud with the pain, that he roused the other Cyclopes from their mountain retreats. On inquiring the cause of his outcries, they were told by Polyphemos that *No-man* (the name which Ulysses had applied to himself) had inflicted the injury: whereupon they retired to their dens, recommending him to supplicate his father, Poseidon, for aid; since his malady came not, as he himself said, from human hands, and must therefore be a visitation from Zeus.

The monster then having removed the immense stone which blocked up the mouth of the cave, placed himself at its entrance to prevent the escape of his enemies. Ulysses, however, eluded his vigilance by fastening the sheep together three and three, with osier bands, and then tying one of his companions beneath the middle one of every three. In this manner the whole party passed out safely; the hero himself bringing up the rear, clinging to a thick-fleeced and favorite ram.

After escaping from the Cyclopes, and sailing still farther west, they reached the treacherous harbor of the Lestrigonians, a gigantic nation that fed on human flesh. After devouring one of the crew, they pursued the rest, and with huge rocks destroyed them, as well as all the vesssels within the harbor; that of Odysseus, which had not entered, alone escaping. Leaving this place, they next landed at the isle of Ææa, the abode of Circe.

By Homer, Circe is called human speaking; he also calls her the daughter of Helios by the Oceanis Persa, and own sister of the *wise*

Æetes. She seems not to have possessed the power of moving through the air or upon the water, but to have dwelt continuously in one place. She was famous for her power of enchantment.

The island of Circe was small, and her abode in the centre of it, deeply embosomed in wood. She dwelt alone, attended by four nymphs; and all persons who approached her dwelling were, by her magic art, turned into swine. Odysseus sent his companions to explore her residence; she set before them the drugged draught, and when they had tasted it, touched them with her wand, and they suffered the usual metamorphosis. Odysseus, hearing of their misfortune, resolved to release them or share their fate. On his way he was met by Hermes, who gave him a plant named *Moly*, potent against her magic, and directed him how to proceed. Circe gave him the medicated bowl, of which he drank freely, and thinking it had produced its usual effect, she struck him with her wand, and bade him join his comrades in the sty. But Odysseus, drawing his sword, threatened to kill her. The terrified goddess then bound herself by an oath to do him no injury. At his request, she restored his companions to their pristine form, and they all abode in her dwelling for an entire year.

At the end of that period they were anxious to depart; but the goddess bade the hero first cross the ocean, and enter the abode of Aïdes, where he was to consult the blind prophet, Teïresias. Accordingly, they left Æaea, and impelled by a favorable wind, soon reached the opposite coast, the land of perpetual gloom. Odysseus obeyed the direction of the goddess, and dug a small pit, into which he poured mulse, wine, water, flour, and the blood of victims. The dead came forth from the house of Aïdes, and Odysseus there saw the heroines of former days, and conversed with the shades of Agamemnon and Achilleus. Terror at length came over him; he hastened back to his ship, and reached Æaea while it was yet night.

Leaving Æaea on their homeward voyage, Odysseus and his companions came first to the island of the Sirens. These were two maidens who sat in a mead close to the sea, and with their melodious voices so charmed those who were sailing by, that they forgot home and every thing relating to it, and abode there till their bones lay whitening upon the strand. Forewarned by Circe of the evils to which he would subject himself by listening to them, he made his companions stop their ears with wax, and had himself fastened to the mast of the ship, enjoining his followers not to unbind him, even if he should desire it.

Thus he passed in safety the abode of the Sirens, hearing without dan
ger the enchanting harmony of their voices.

Hesiod described the mead of the Sirens as blooming with flowers
and their voices, he said, stilled the wind.   Their names were said to
be Aglaiophcme (*Clear-voice*), Thelxeipeia (*Magic-speech*).   It was
feigned that they threw themselves into the sea with vexation at the
escape of Odysseus.

Having passed by the dangerous Sirens, his course lay between
Scylla and Charybdis; a pass so difficult, that its danger has given
rise to the saying, "If one avoid Charybdis, he is sure to be wrecked
on Scylla."   Circe informed him of the danger, telling him that he
would come to two lofty cliffs placed opposite each other, between
which he must pass.   One of these cliffs she represents as towering to
such a height that its summit is for ever enveloped in clouds, and no
man, even if he had twenty hands and as many feet, could ascend it.
In the middle of this cliff, she said, is a cave facing the west; but so
high, that a man in a ship passing under it could not shoot up to it
with a bow.   This den was the abode of Scylla, whose voice sounds
like that of a young whelp: she has twelve feet. and six long necks,
with a terrific head, and three rows of close set teeth in each.   Ever-
more she stretches out these necks and catches the animals of the sea,
and out of every ship that passes each mouth takes a man.

The opposite rock, the goddess informs him, is much lower, for a
man could shoot over it.   A wild fig tree grows upon it, stretching its
branches down to the water; but "beneath, divine Charybdis, three
times each day, absorbs and regorges the water.   It is much more dangerous, she adds, to pass Charybdis than Scylla"

As Odysseus sailed by, Scylla took six of his crew, and when, after
having lost his companions, and floating on a part of the wreck. he was
carried between the monsters, the mast by which he supported himself
was sucked in by Charybdis.   He held fast to the branches of the fig
tree till it was thrown out again, and then resumed his voyage

Both Tciresias and Circe had charged Odysseus to shun the isle
Thrinakia, on which the flocks and herds of the Sun-god fed, under the
care of Phaëthusa and Lampetia, to which he would come immediately
after passing Scylla and Charybdis.   Odysseus was desirous of obeying
the injunctions he had received; but as it was evening when they
reached the island, his companions forced him to consent to their landing and passing the night there.   They proposed to depart in th

morning, and took an oath not to molest the cattle of the sun. During the night a violent storm came on ; and for an entire month a south-east wind (Euros and Notos) confined them to the island. They exhausted their provisions, and then lived on such birds as they could catch. At length, while Odysseus was sleeping, his companions killed several of the sacred oxen. On awaking, he was filled with horror and despair at what they had done. Apollo complained of the crime at the throne of the Thunderer, and as soon as the ship had reached the open sea, Zeus dashed her to pieces with one of his thunderbolts. Of the whole crew, Odysseus was the only survivor ; and he saved himself by swimming to Ogygia, the island of Calypso, by whom he was most kindly received and entertained. She detained him there for eight years, designing to make him immortal, and to keep him with her for ever ; but Hermes, arriving with a command from Zeus, she was obliged to consent to his departure. She then gave the hero tools to build a raft or light vessel, supplied him with provisions, and reluctantly took a final leave of him.

Calypso, that is the *Concealer* (the poet after his usual manner giving her a significant name), is called by Homer the daughter of Atlas. Hesiod makes her an Oceanis, and Apollodorus a Nereïs. Like Circe she was a *human-speaking* goddess, and dwelt in a solitary state with her attendant nymphs ; but her abode was a cavern, while the daughter of Helios possessed a mansion of cut stone. Her isle presented such a scene of sylvan beauty as charmed even Hermes, one of the dwellers of Olympos.

Odysseus once more surrendered his life to the waves of the sea on a raft which he had built with his own hands, and was now approaching the shores of Ithaca, when Poseidon cast his eye upon the bold navigator. The god being incensed against him for having deprived his son Polyphemos of his only eye, raised a sudden storm, by which Odysseus was cast back upon the open sea and upset. Exposed to the wild tempest as a prey to the raging billows, still he despaired not. Clinging to a rock, he suffered the storm to pass over, and then swam to the neighboring island of the Phæacians, where he was received with kindness and hospitality.

The Phæacians are said to have dwelt originally in Hypereia, near the Cyclopes ; but being oppressed by that savage race, they migrated to the isle of Scheria, having been led thither by their king, Nausithoös,

the son of Poseidon and Periboea the youngest daughter of Eurymidon,
king of the giants.

The Phæacians, like the Cyclopes and giants, were a people akin to
the gods, who appeared manifestly, and feasted among them when they
offered sacrifices, and did not conceal themselves from solitary wayfarers whom they might chance to meet. They are represented in the
Odyssey as having abundance of wealth, and enjoying it peacefully, for
as they "dwelt remote from gain-seeking man," no enemy ever approached their shores, and they had no occasion for bows and quivers.
Their chief employment was navigation ; their ships, which went with
the velocity of birds, or of thought, were, like the Argo, endued with
intelligence   They knew every port, and needed no pilot when impelled by the rowers.

The princess Nausicaä, when reproving the false alarm of her attendants at the sight of Odysseus, says to them, "Do you think he is an
enemy ? There is not a living mortal, nor will there be, who will come
bearing war to the land of the Phæacians ; for they are very dear to
the immortals. We dwell apart in the wave-full sea, the last ; nor does
any other mortal mingle with us ; but this is some unfortunate wan-
derer who has come hither." (Od. vi. 200.)

Alcinoös, the king of the Phæacians, furnished Odysseus with one
of their magic vessels to convey him and the gifts he had received to
his native isle.   He reached there in safety, and the sailors then departed, leaving him asleep on the shore.   On awaking, he was informed by Athena that he had reached his home ; and going to the house
of his swine-herd, Eumæos, he there met his son Telemachos, to whom
he revealed himself.   He found his old father Laertes still alive, and
his faithful wife, Penelope.

During the absence of Odysseus, Penelope had held him in faithful
remembrance, and though pressed by her numerous suitors to consider
him as dead, and make a second choice, yet she retained such faithful
love for her husband, with a full prophetic assurance that she should
once more see him, that all their efforts to influence her were vain.

In order to put them off more effectually, she commenced making a
piece of cloth, promising that when it was finished she would choose
one from among their number   This stratagem was successful ; for
she undid at night what she had wrought in the day, so that when
Odysseus arrived, she was no nearer its completion than at first.

The first care of Odysseus on returning to his native land, was to

punish those suitors who had wooed his chaste spouse during his ab
sence, and consumed his property in their daily banquets. With the
assistance of his son Telemachos, and his faithful swine-herd Eumæos,
he killed them in the porch of his palace in the midst of their revelry,
and with the assistance of his friends who gathered around him, he ob
tained possession of his throne.

Tyresias, the soothsayer, had informed him that he should be killed
by one of his sons. To avert this misfortune, he determined to forsake
the world, and retire into some solitary place, and there to end his days
in peace. But about that time Telegonos, one of his sons by Circe,
came to the city, and as he was endeavoring to enter the palace, the
officers refused admission. A tumult arose, Odysseus stepped out,
and Telegonos, not knowing him, ran him through with his lance, thus
fulfilling the prophecy of the soothsayer.

ROMULUS.

According to the old poetic legend, Romulus and Remus were the
sons of Mars and Ilia, a daughter of Numitor. Amulius, who had
usurped the throne of Alba in defiance of the right of his elder brother,
Numitor, ordered the infants to be thrown into the Tiber. The basket
in which they were placed drifted down the current, till it became entangled in the roots of a wild vine at the foot of the Palatine Hill.
There they were suckled by a she-wolf, which had come to the river to
drink, and were afterwards found in her den by Faustulus, one of the
king's herdsmen, who took them home to his wife Larentia, by whom
they were carefully nursed and named Romulus and Remus.

As the two youths grew up, they displayed superior courage and
abilities, and became the leaders of the youthful herdsmen in their
contests with robbers or rivals.

Having quarrelled with the herdsmen of Numitor, they were seized
and taken before him, when the secret of their origin was discovered.
They speedily expelled Amulius, and restored their grandfather to his
throne. But accustomed to the enjoyment of liberty, they preferred
not to remain as subjects at Alba, and requested permission of Numitor
to build a city on the banks of the Tiber, where their lives were so
miraculously preserved. This permission was no sooner granted, than
a contest arose between the two brothers in regard to the site, the
name, and the sovereignty of the new city which they were about to
found. They at length agreed to refer it to the gods by augury. Ro-

mulus took his station on the Palatine Hill and Remus on the Aventine. At sunrise Remus saw six vultures, and immediately after Romulus saw twelve. The superiority was adjudged to Romulus, against
which Remus remonstrated, on the ground that he had received the
first omen. Romulus proceeded to mark the boundaries for the wall
of the city. This took place on the twenty-first of April; the day of
the festival of Pales, the goddess of shepherds.

While the wall was beginning to rise above the surface, Remus, whose
mind was still rankling with disappointment, leaped over it, saying
scornfully, "Shall such a wall as this keep your city?" He was immediately killed, some say by Romulus. According to others, Celer, who
had charge of erecting that part of the wall, struck him with the im-
plement which he held in his hand, exclaiming, " So perish whosoever
shall hereafter overleap these ramparts."

By this event, Romulus was left the sole sovereign of the city. Yet
he felt a deep remorse at his brother's fate, buried him honorably, and
when he sat to administer justice placed a vacant seat by his side with
a sceptre and a crown, as if acknowledging the right of his brother to
the possession of equal honor.

At the close of the reign of Romulus, as he was reviewing his army
near the Lake Capra, the sky was suddenly darkened, and dreadful
thunderings and tempestuous winds scattered the people in dismay.
When the tempest was over, they made anxious inquiries for the king;
but the patricians would not allow them to search for Romulus, saying
that he had been caught up to heaven, and if they worshipped him he
would be a propitious deity to the Romans. Upon this the multitude
were satisfied and dispersed. They then offered worship to Romulus
in the hope of obtaining his favor and protection.

NUMA POMPILIUS.

This hero was born on the very day that Romulus laid the foundation of Rome. He was married to Tatia, a daughter of Tatius, who
was the associate of Romulus in the kingdom. Numa remained in the
country of the Sabines, devoting himself to the service of his father,
who was now grown old. Tatia shared his retirement, preferring the
calm enjoyments of private life with her husband, to the honor and
distinction in which she might have lived with her father at Rome.

Thirteen years after their marriage, Tatia died. Numa then left
the city, and passed his time in wandering about the sacred groves.

This habit gave rise to the popular opinion that the Nymph Egeria dictated the laws that he established, both civil and religious.

When upon the death of Romulus, he was chosen by the senators of Rome to be their ruler, it was with great difficulty that he was persuaded to accept the office. But on deciding to go, he offered sacrifices to the gods, and then set out for Rome. He was met by the people with every demonstration of honor and respect. Robes and other distinctions of royalty were offered him. when he commanded them to forbear, as his authority yet wanted the sanction of heaven. Taking with him the priest and augurs, he went up to the Capitol, which the Romans at that time called the Tarpeian rock. There the chief of the augurs covered the head of Numa, and turned his face towards the south; then, standing behind him, and laying his right hand upon his head, he offered up his devotions and looked around in hopes of seeing birds or some other signal of the gods. An incredible silence reigned among the people, anxiously lost in suspense for the event, till the auspicious birds appeared, and passed on the right hand. Numa, then taking the royal robe, went down from the mount to the people, who received him with acclamations as the most pious of men, and beloved of the gods. ·

The duties of his office were discharged to the satisfaction of his subjects. His great object was to quell the spirit of war and conquest which he found in the people, and to inculcate a love of peace, with a reverence for the deity, whose worship by images he forbade. He established a priesthood, the effect of which was to prevent any graven images, or statues, from appearing in their sanctuaries for upwards of a hundred and thirty years.

This wise monarch, aware of the power of superstition, encouraged the report that he was regularly visited by Egeria. In her name he introduced all his laws and regulations, and solemnly declared in the presence of the people, that they were sanctified by the approval of that being; an approval which gave them additional favor in the eyes of this superstitious people.

> " Egeria ! sweet creation of some heart,
> Which found no resting-place so fair
> As thine ideal breast ; whate'er thou art,
> Or wert—a young Aurora of the air,

The nympholepsy of some fond despair;
Or, it might be, a beauty of the earth,
Who found a more than common votary there
Too much adoring, whatsoe'er thy birth,
Thou wert a beautiful thought, and softly bodied forth

Here didst thou dwell, in this enchanted cover,
Egeria! thy all-heavenly bosom beating
For the far footsteps of thy mortal lover;
The purple midnight veiled that mystic meeting
With her most starry canopy, and seating
Thyself by thine adorer, what befel?
This cave was surely shaped out for the greeting
Of an enamored goddess, and the cell
Haunted by holy love—the earliest oracle!

And didst thou not, thy breast to his replying,
Blend a celestial with a human heart;
And love, which dies as it was born, in sighing,
Share with the immortal transports? Could thine art
Make them indeed immortal, and impart
The purity of heaven to earthly joys,
Expel the venom and not blunt the dart—
The dull satiety which all destroys—
And root from out the soul the deadly weed which cloys?"

Byron.

The Greeks appropriated a religious worship to those who were regarded as the founders of colonies and cities. From thus honoring
the benefactors of nations, originated the custom of rendering the same
homage to kings and princes.

During many centuries, the Romans deified no one but Romulus.
Cæsar was the first who received this distinction. After his death a
comet appeared as they were celebrating the funeral games in his hon-
or, and was regarded by the people as a sign that his soul was admitted to the society of the gods. For which reason a star was added to
his statue erected soon after in the Forum.

Divine honors were afterwards accorded to Augustus. The provinces bordering the empire demanded permission to erect a temple to
him, which he granted on condition that they associated him with the
deities of Rome; and above all, that they raised to them a common
altar. After his death, he received the honors of consecration, and a
temple was built to him in Rome. From this time the ceremony of
deification was termed consecration, and was first decreed by the senate. But the people, the army, and often-times the emperor himself

forced the decision. The same honor was also accorded to the empresses.

The ceremony of consecration was very solemn. The body was placed upon a bed of ivory, and borne to the funeral pile upon the shoulders of young men of the highest rank. This was formed of rows of columns, one placed above the other, filled in with combustible matter, and decorated with sculptures and paintings. The body, enveloped in precious spices and aromatics, was placed upon the second tier. The successor of the emperor then took a torch and set fire to the pile, from the summit of which arose an eagle, that they believed carried the soul to heaven. After this apotheosis, temples and altars were erected to the departed emperor, and he was worshipped as a god.

The symbols of consecration are usually found upon imperial medals, the head of the emperor being surrounded with rays, and on the reverse, the funeral pile with the eagle ; or on that of an empress, a peacock.

In the height of her glory, Rome was honored as a deity in Rome itself. Augustus allowed this worship only in the provinces. Hadrian was the first who erected a temple to her in the city. She is represented as robust and warlike, according to the Greek etymology of her name, which signifies *force*. Her statues, which are rare, resemble those of Pallas. On medals she is sometimes represented as seated upon the seven hills, and sometimes in her temple, holding an eagle, a trophy, or a palladium ; a globe, or a victory. The victory, or a crown, always accompanies her.

PART FIFTH.

MYTHIC FICTIONS.

MYTHIC FICTIONS.

ACCORDING to Hesiod, Triton was
a son of Poseidon and Amphitrite,
who, " keeping to the bottom of the
sea, dwelt with his mother and royal
father in a golden house." Later poets made him his father's trumpeter.
He is sometimes represented as blow-
ing the shell and holding a rudder
over his shoulder. He was also mul-
tiplied, and we read of Tritons in the plural number.

Like the Nereïdes, the Tritons were degraded to the fish form. Pausanias tells us, that the women of Tanagra, in Bœotia, going into the
sea to purify themselves for the orgies of Bacchos, were assailed by
Triton ; but on praying to their god, he vanquished their persecutor.
Others, he adds, said that Triton used to carry off the cattle which
were driven down to the sea, as well as seize all small vessels, till the
Tanagrians, placing bowls of wine on the shore, he drank of them, and
becoming intoxicated, threw himself down to sleep. A Tanagrian
then cut off his head with an axe. These legends he relates, to account
for the headless statue of Triton at Tanagra. He then subjoins :

" I have seen another Triton among the curiosities of the Romans ;
but it is not so large as that of the Tanagrians. The form of the
Tritons is this—the hair of their heads resembles the parsley that grows
in the marshes, both in color and the perfect likeness of one hair to
another, so that no difference can be perceived among them ; the rest
of their body is rough with small scales, and is of about the same hard-
ness as the skin of a fish ; they have fish gills under their ears ; their

nostrils are those of a man, but their teeth are broader, and like those of a wild beast; their eyes seem to me azure; and their hands, fingers, and nails are of the form of the shell-fish; instead of feet, they have fins, like those of the porpoise."

OTOS AND EPHIALTES.

The Aloeids, Otos and Ephialtes, were also sons of Poseidon. In their ninth year, they were nine cubits in width, and nine fathoms in height. At this early age they undertook to make war upon Zeus; and, in order to reach the heavens, they strove to place Mount Ossa upon Olympos, and Pelion upon Ossa; but (to use the graphic language of Homer) "they were destroyed by Apollo before the down had bloomed beneath their temples, and had thickly covered their chins with a well-flowering beard." According to the animated narrative of the same bard, they would have accomplished their object had they made the attempt, not in childhood, but after having "reached the measure of youth."

Such is the Homeric legend of the Aloeids, as given in the Odyssey. In the Iliad, they are said to have bound Mars, and kept him eighteen months captive, until Mercury stole him away. Later writers of course add many other particulars. Apollodorus makes Ephialtes to have aspired to a union with Juno, and Otos with Diana; and further states, that Diana effected their destruction in the island of Naxos. She changed herself, it seems into a hind, and bounded between the two brothers, who, in their eagerness each to slay the animal, pierced one another with their weapons. Diodorus Siculus gives an historical air to the narrative, making the brothers to have held sway in Naxos, and to have fallen in a quarrel by each other's hands; and the Scholiast Virgil assigns the Aloeids a place of punishment in Tartaros; and some of the ancient fabulists make them to have been hurled thither by Zeus, and others by Apollo. So in the Odyssey they are spoken of as inhabiting the lower world, though no reason is assigned by the poet for their being there, except that we may infer, from the legend itself, that they were cut off in early life, lest, if they had been allowed to attain their full growth, they might have obtained the empire of the skies.

Pausanias makes the Aloeids to have founded Ascar in Bœotia, and to have been the first who sacrificed to the Muses on Mount Helicon. Müller regards the Alocids as the mystic leaders of the old Thracian colonies, heroes by land and sea. In Pieria they appear at Aloium, near Tempe, and at Mount Helicon, and in both quarters have reference to the digging of canals and the draining of mountain dales. Creuzer, on the other hand, sees a figurative allusion to a contest, as it were, between the water and the land. Alocus is the man of the threshing-floor, whose efforts are all useless, from the infidelity of his spouse, the Earth—the very wise one. She unites with Neptune against him, and the Sea thereupon begets the energies of the tempests (Otos and Ephialtes), which darken the day; and brooding heavily over the earth, cause the waves of the Ocean to leap and dash upon the cultivated region along the shore.

At last the god of day, Apollo, comes forth, and the storm ceases; first along the mountain tops, and finally upon the shore. The other version of the fable, that the Aloeids were destroyed by DiaLa, would make it appear that the storm was hushed by the influences of the moon.

TALOS.

Minos had a brazen man named Talos, given to him by Hephæstos, or to Europa by Zeus, who compassed the island of Crete thrice in each day, in order to prevent the landing of strangers. His mode of destroying them was to make himself red-hot in the fire and then embrace them. When the Argo reached Crete, Medeia persuaded Talos that she could make him immortal; and he therefore allowed her to pull out the pin in his heel, and let the *ichor* run out from his only vein, and he thus died.

DÆDALOS.

At Athens, Minerva's sacred city, plastic art first developed itself, claiming an eminent rank among the occupations of men.

Dædalos, a descendant of the royal race of the Erechthides, is said by fiction to have infused life and motion into the statues that he made. He was the first to separate the legs of his statues, which formerly, as is yet to be seen in the Egyptian monuments, were united together. He in like manner dislodged the arms from the body, giving his figures a moving attitude. We cannot wonder that such a representation, entirely new as it was, should fill every mind with astonishment, and give rise to the saying, that Dædalos' statues were endowed with motion.

The first step of Dædalos involved something lofty and divine, which excited the admiration of posterity, and immortalized the name of the artist, although its glory was tarnished by a black and cruel deed.

Under his guidance a youth, named Talos, and son of the artist's sister, while engaged in the practice of the art, was one day cutting a piece of wood with the jaw-bone of a snake, when he conceived the idea of imitating the sharp teeth in iron, and thus became the inventor of the *saw*; one of the most useful, as well as one of the most necessary instruments to man. Another invention of Talos was the potter's wheel. Dædalos, jealous of the progress of his pupil, cherished a deadly hatred against him; thus showing in the very commencement of art, the envy of artists almost inseparable from art itself. Leading the promising youth to a steep height, Dædalos, ere the innocent victim of his jealousy and hatred was aware of his intention, hurled him down into the abyss, because he wished to take a higher flight than even his master had attained.

When this murder became known in Athens, Dædalos, although as an artist he graced Athena's mansion, was condemned to die by the court of the Areiopagos, and would have been executed, but for his flight to Crete, where his divine art contrived the Labyrinth. This wondrous abode of the Minotaur, which his hands had reared, became the prison of himself and son. But art, even while imprisoned, shakes off her shackles, and takes her flight to the sky. Dædalos attempted what appeared to all but himself impossible to be performed. There was but one outlet through which he could hope to escape, and this was in the high arched ceiling. He procured by artifice the necessary implements for making wings, and after having exercised his son, Icaros, in the use of them, and given him warning not to raise himself too high, lest the wax with which the feathers were united should be melted by the sun-beams; nor, on the other hand, to pursue too low a course, lest they should be wet with the waters of the sea, both father and son took their flight through the opening of the prison.

Icaros, overjoyed at sailing through the air like a bird, and forgetful of the counsels of his father, soared in an elevated course towards the sky, and fell from an immense height, the wax of his wings having been melted by the sun-beams. The sea in which he found his death was called after him the Icarian. Dædalos, who without pity had hurled Talos into the abyss, is now obliged, with bitterness of soul, to witness the fall of his own son, to whom he can afford no assistance.

Dædalos descended on the island of Sicily, where he was hospitably received by Cocalos, who defended him from the persecutions of Minos. Grateful for his hospitality and protection, the artist undertook several great works, both of architecture and sculpture, in the territory, and for the benefit of king Cocalos. He dug canals and ponds; built a castle upon a high rock; levelled the top of mount Eryx, and there consecrated a golden cow to the Erycinian Venus.

Long after his time, traces of his genius and art were still found in Sicily; and his name became proverbial to denote whatever is ingenious or skilful. He was the personification of the earliest developments of the arts of sculpture and architecture, especially among the Athenians and Cretans.

Upon ancient works of art, the representation of Dædalos is often found, as he is sitting and musing over the artificial wing, on which he is still laboring with skilful hand.

CENTAURS.

The Centaurs were a tribe of Thessaly, fabled to have been half men and half horse, and are always mentioned in connection with the Lapiths. The former are twice spoken of in the Iliad, under the name of *Wild-men*, and once in the Odyssey. They appear to have been a rude, mountain tribe, dwelling on and about Mount Pelion.

Cheiron, who is called by Homer "the most upright of the Centaurs," was intrusted with the care of rearing Iason, Medeios, Heracles, Asclepios, and Achilleus. Besides his knowledge of the musical art, which he imparted to his heroic pupils, he was also skilled in surgery, which he taught to Asclepios and Achilleus.

In the contest between Heracles and the Centaurs, Cheiron was accidentally wounded by one of the hero's arrows. Grieved at this unhappy event, Heracles ran to him, drew out the arrow, and applied a remedy which had been given him by Cheiron himself; but in vain. The venom of the Hydra was not to be overcome.

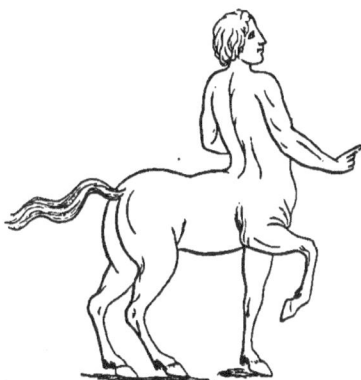

Cheiron entered a cave, longing to die, but was unable, on account of his immortality. He prayed to Zeus for relief, when he was raised to the sky, where he appears as the constellation Sagittarius.

ATALANTA.

Iasos, or Iasion, a descendant of Arcas, was married to Clymene, a daughter of Minyas. He was anxious for a male offspring, and therefore, disappointed at her birth, he exposed the babe in the mountains, where she was suckled by a bear, and at last found by some hunters, who named her Atalanta, and reared her. She followed the chase, and was alike distinguished for beauty and courage. The Centaurs, Rhœcos and Hylæos, approaching her with evil intentions, perished by her arrows. She distinguished herself in the Calydonian hunt, and at the funeral games of Pelias, she won the prize in wrestling.

Atalanta was afterwards recognized by her parents. Her father wished her to marry, to which she consented, on condition that her suitors should run a race with her, promising, if she should be vanquished, to become the wife of the victor; but the vanquished suitor should be shot by one of her own darts. As she was almost invincible in running, many of her suitors perished in the contest.

Hippomenes, venturing to enter upon this dangerous race, implored the assistance of Aphrodite, who presented him with three golden apples, which, one after another, he let slip from his hands during the course. Atalanta, whose eyes were dazzled by the glitter and beauty of this golden fruit, repeatedly stopped to take it up from the ground, and thus Hippomenes gained time to reach the goal before her.

Atalanta became the wife of Hippomenes; but unmindful of the benefit which he owed to Aphrodite, both were obliged to atone for his offence against the goddess. Upon her impulse, they profaned a sanctuary of Cybele, who, with formidable power, transformed them into two lions, that under one yoke drew her chariot.

ARACHNE.

A Mæonian maid, named Arachne, proud of her skill in weaving and embroidery, in which arts the goddess of wisdom had instructed her, ventured to deny her obligation, and challenged her patroness to a trial of skill. Athena, assuming the form of an old woman, warned her to desist from her boasting, but, finding her admonitions vain, she resumed her proper form, and accepted the challenge. The skill of

Arachne was such, and the subject she chose (the love transformations of the gods) so offensive to Athena, that she struck her several times on the forehead with the shuttle. The high-spirited maid, unable to endure this affront, hung herself; and the goddess, relenting, changed her into a spider.

> "Arachne thrice upon the forehead smote;
> Whose great heart brooks it not; about her throat
> A rope she ties; remorseful Pallas stay'd
> Her falling weight; 'Live, wretch, yet hang!'—she said."
>
> *Ovid.*

TANTALOS.

Tantalos is fabled to have been the son of Zeus and the Nymph Pluto (*Wealth*). He was the father of Pelops and of Niobe, the wife of Amphion. His residence was placed at the foot of Mount Sipylos, in Lydia, and fiction represents him as the favorite of the gods, who admitted him to their table, where he feasted on nectar and ambrosia, which made him immortal.

He once so far forgot himself as to offend Jupiter with some intemperate language, and was immediately plunged from the height of happiness to the immeasurable depths of misery. His punishment is thus described by Homer: "And I saw," says Odysseus, "Tantalos suffering grievous torments, standing in a lake, and the water dashed against his chin, but he resembled one thirsty, and could not take any to drink; for as often as the old man stooped eager to drink, so often the water disappeared, being absorbed; and about his feet the black earth appeared, for a divinity withheld him; and above his head lofty trees, pear trees, and peach trees, and apples, with their beautiful fruit, and sweet figs, and flourishing olive trees hung their fruit, which, when the old man straightened himself to reach with his hands, the wind dissipated them into dark clouds."

This punishment was, as it were, a continuance of the life he had led on earth; an emblem of that unsatisfied desire to penetrate the secrets of the gods; a desire which even induced him to kill his son Pelops, and to serve up his flesh at a banquet, in order to ascertain their divinity. If any thing can indicate the danger of inordinate curiosity, it is this shocking tale. It is the depravation that humanity commits on itself, in order to investigate the primeval cause of its existence.

The other crimes of Tantalos were encroachments upon the privileges

27

of the celestials.   He stole ambrosia from their table, that mortal lips might taste it; and assisted by Pandaros, he carried off the dog that guarded the sanctuary of Zeus in Crete.

NIOBE.

Niobe, the daughter of Tantalos, and wife of Amphion, king of Thebes, prided herself on being the mother of seven hardy sons and as many beautiful daughters; and to such an excess was she led by her maternal pride, that she scoffed at Latona, who was the parent of only one son and one daughter.

Incensed at the affront offered to their mother, Latona's twins united to avenge her; and while the arrows of Apollo pierced the heart of Niobe's sons, their sisters were shot by Diana.   The wretched parents hastened to their children's assistance, when an arrow from the bow of Apollo pierced the heart of Amphion.   Niobe, thus deprived of her children, who had been her greatest treasure as well as the pride of her heart, and at the same time of her husband, went forth into the wilderness, there in lonely solitude to shed maternal tears.   The gods beheld her sufferings, pitied her, and put an end to her grief.   The once beautiful queen, suddenly found herself deprived of motion, and gradually stiffening into stone.   She was changed into a rock, which on Mount Sipylos in Lydia, as if still conscious of sorrow, continues to shed tears, and is a perpetual monument of her grief.

IXION.

Ixion, who reigned in Thessaly, was subjected to a fate similar to that of Tantalos.

He obtained the hand of Dia, the daughter of Deïoneus, at the same time promising his father-in-law large nuptial gifts, according to the custom of the heroic ages.   He broke his engagement, when Deïoneus seized his horses and detained them as a pledge.   Ixion then sent to say that the gifts were ready if Deïoneus would come and take them. He accordingly went; but his treacherous son-in-law had prepared in his house a pit filled with fire and covered over, into which the unsuspecting prince fell and perished.   After this deed, the mind of Ixion became deranged; and his atrocity was such that neither gods nor men would absolve him   At length, Zeus himself took pity, purified him, and admitted him to the table of the gods, where the charms of the queen of heaven made him forget his mortality

Vain and presumptuous, he imagined himself to have attained the summit of his wishes, when, instead of embracing Hera, he clasped a cloud in his arms, which Zeus had purposely thrown in his way. The presumptuous attempts of this mortal to enjoy what is unattainable by man, were not only defeated, but punished. He was expelled from Olympos, and when he had the temerity to boast on earth of what he had attempted in heaven, Zeus precipitated him into Tartaros, where Hermes fastened him with brazen bands to an ever-revolving fiery wheel. Thus is he obliged to atone for indulging the wishes that induced him to transgress the boundaries allotted to humanity. His restlessness never ceases; but like the wheel of mere human endeavors, turns round and round to no purpose.

SISYPHOS.

Sisyphos, the son of Æolos, was said to be the founder of Ephyra. He married Merope, the daughter of Atlas, by whom he had four sons, Glaucos, Ornytion, Thersandros, and Halmos.

Zeus had carried off Ægina, the daughter of Asopos, and the river-god in his search for her came to Corinth. Sisyphos informed him that Zeus was her ravisher. The king of the gods then sent Death to punish him; but Sisyphos contrived to outwit Death, and even to put fetters on him; and there was great joy among mortals, for no one died. Hades, however, set Death at liberty, and Sisyphos was given up to him. When dying, he charged his wife to leave his body unburied; then complaining to Hades of her unkindness, he obtained permission to return to the light and upbraid her for her conduct. On finding himself again in his own house, he refused to leave it. Hermes, however, reduced him to obedience, and like the Danaïdes, he was condemned to perform an endless task. Hades required him to roll a huge rock up a mountain, a never-ending, still beginning toil; for as soon as he has nearly reached the top, and rejoices in the hope of being permitted to rest from his hard labor, the rock, in spite of all his endeavors, rolls back again to the plain.

Sisyphos had lived to a great age, and hence the fiction of his having refused to return to Orcus. As he endeavored in this way to prolong his days beyond the destined term, the ever-rolling rock, on which he vainly exhausts his strength in Tartaros, is, as it were, an emblem of the troublesome labor of life, which he was unwilling to abandon.

MIDAS.

Pan, favorite of Midas, king of the Phrygians in Macedonia, wished also to compete with Apollo in the art of which the latter was master. Pan commenced the contest, and Midas repeated his songs with enthusiasm, regardless of his celestial rival, when, to his surprise, the latter felt a pair of ears, long and shaggy, pressing through his hair. Alarmed at this phenomenon. Pan fled. The prince, desolate at the loss of his favorite, made his wife the confidante of his misfortune, begging her not to betray his trust. She longed to tell the secret, but dared not, for fear of punishment; and, by way of relief, sought a retired and lonely spot, where she threw herself upon the ground, and whispered, " King Midas has the ears of an ass. King Midas has the ears of an ass."

Not long after her visit, some reeds arose in this place, and as the wind passed through them, they repeated, " King Midas has the ears of an ass." Enraged, no less than terrified at this occurrence, Midas sacrificed to Bacchos, who, to console him, desired him to ask whatever he wished.

> "Give me, says he (nor thought he asked too much),
> That with my body whatsoe'er I touch,
> Changed from the nature which it held of old,
> May be converted into yellow gold !
> He had his wish. But yet, the god repin'd
> To think the fool no better wish could find.
> But the brave king departed from the place,
> With smiles of gladness sparkling in his face:
> Nor could contain; but, as he took his way,
> Impatient longs to make the first essay.
> Down from a lowly branch a twig he drew,
> The twig straight glittered with a sparkling hue.
> He takes a stone; the stone was turned to gold.
> A clod he touches, and the crumbling mold
> Acknowledged soon the great transforming power,
> In weight and substance like a mass of ore.
> He plucked the corn; and straight his grasp appears
> Filled with a bending tuft of golden ears.
> An apple next he takes, and seems to hold
> The bright, Hesperian, vegetable gold.
> His hand he careless on a pillar lays,
> With shining gold the fluted pillars blaze."

> "The ready slaves prepare a sumptuous board,
> Spread with rich dainties for their happy lord,

Whose powerful hands the bread no sooner hold,
But its whole substance is transformed to gold :
Up to his mouth he lifts the savory meat,
Which turns to gold as he attempts to eat.
His patron's noble juice, of purple hue,
Touched by his lips, a golden cordial grew,
Unfit for drink, and wondrous to behold,
It trickles from his jaws a fluid gold.
The rich, poor fool, confounded with surprise,
Staring on all his various plenty lies;
Sick of his wish, he now detests the power
For which he asked so earnestly before :
Amidst his gold with pinching famine curst,
And justly tortured with an equal thirst.
At last his shining arms to heaven he rears,
And, in distress, for refuge flies to prayers.
'O father Bacchos ! I have sinned,' he cried,
'And foolishly thy gracious gift applied ;
Thy pity now, repenting I implore ;
Oh ! may I feel the golden plague no more !' "—*Ovid.*

Bacchos directed him to wash in the river Pactolus. and hence that river has golden sands.

LETO AND THE FROGS.

While wandering from place to place with her children, Leto arrived in Lycia. The sun was shining fiercely, and the goddess was parched with thirst. Seeing a pool of water, she knelt down by it to drink, when some clowns who were there refused to allow her to slake her thirst. In vain the goddess entreated, representing that water was common to all, and appealing to their compassion for her babes. The brutes were insensible, and not only mocked at her distress, but jumped into and muddied the water. The goddess, though the most gentle of her race, was roused to indignation; and raising her hands to heaven, cried, " May you live for ever in that pool !" Her wish was instantly accomplished, and the churls were transformed into frogs.

HERMAPHRODITOS.

Hermaphroditos was the offspring of Hermes and Aphrodite. His story is thus told by Ovid.

"From both the illustrious authors of his race
The child was named; nor was it hard to trace
Both the bright parents through the infant's face.
When fifteen years in Ida's cool retreat
The boy had told, he left his native seat,

And sought fresh fountains in a foreign soil,
The pleasure lessened the attending toil.
With eager steps the Lycian fields he crossed,
And fields that border on the Lycian coast;
A river here he viewed so lovely bright,
It showed the bottom in a fairer light,
Nor kept a sand concealed from human sight.
The fruitful banks with cheerful verdure crowned,
And kept the spring eternal on the ground.
A nymph presides, nor practised in the chase,
Nor skilful at the bow, nor at the race;
Of all the blue-eyed daughters of the main,
The only stranger to Diana's train;
Her sisters often, as 'tis said, would cry
Fie! Salmäeis, what, always idle! Fie!
Or take the quiver, or the arrows seize,
And mix the toils of hunting with thy case.'
Nor quivers she, nor arrows e'er would seize,
Nor mix the toils of hunting with her ease;
But oft would bathe her in the crystal tide,
Oft with a comb her dewy locks divide;
Now in the limpid stream she viewed her face,
And dressed her image in the floating glass:
On beds of leaves she now reposed her limbs,
Now gathered flowers that grew about her streams,
And there by chance was gathering as she stood
To view the boy"——

Hermaphroditos turned a deaf ear to her love, and Salmaeis, throwing her arms around him, entreated the gods to render her inseparable from him whom she adored. The gods heard her prayer, and formed of the two a being of perfect beauty, preserving the characteristics of both sexes.

MILO.

Milo, of whose wonderful strength many curious stories are related, was a celebrated athlete of Crotona, in Italy.

He accustomed himself from early youth to bear burdens, the weight of which he gradually augmented, till at last he carried the most prodigious loads with perfect ease. Athenæus relates, that on one occasion he carried a steer, four years old, the whole length of the stadium at Olympia, and then devoured the whole in one day. Some authorities add, that he killed it with a single blow of his fist.

One day, while attending the lectures of Pythagoras, of whom he was a disciple and constant hearer, the column which supported the ceiling of the hall where they assembled, was observed to totter, when Milo, upholding the entire structure by his own strength, allowed all present an opportunity of escaping, and then saved himself.

At the Pythian games Milo was seven times crowned victor, and six at the Olympic; and only ceased to present himself at these contests when he found no one willing to be his competitor.

In B. C. 509, he had the command of an army, sent by the people of Crotona against Sybaris, and gained a signal victory.

His death was a melancholy one. He was already advanced in years, when, traversing a forest, he found the trunk of a tree partly cleft by wedges. Wishing to sever it entirely, he introduced his hands into the opening, and succeeded so far as to cause the wedges to fall out; but his strength here failing him, the separate parts suddenly reunited, and his hands remained imprisoned in the cleft. In this situation he was devoured by wild beasts.

PHILOMELA.

Philomela was a daughter of Pandion, king of Athens, and sister to Procne, who married Tereus, king of Thrace

Procne had a son named Itys. After living some time in Thrace, she became desirous of seeing her sister, from whom she had been long separated ; and at her request, Tereus went to Athens, and prevailed on Pandion to allow Philomela to accompany him to Thrace. But instead of taking her directly to her sister, he confined her under the promise of returning to marry her as soon as he should have disposed of Procne. But fearing that she might communicate his purpose, he cut out her tongue.

She, however, contrived to communicate her story to her sister, by means of characters woven into a robe. Procne, who had been informed by Tereus that Philomela had died by the way, was plunged in the deepest affliction for her loss. She now sought her out and released her. In revenge, Procne resolved to inflict the greatest possible suffering upon Tereus. She therefore killed her own son, Itys, and served up his flesh to his father. The two sisters then fled ; and Tereus, discovering the truth, pursued them with an axe. Finding themselves nearly overtaken, they prayed the gods to turn them into birds. Procne immediately became a nightingale, and Philomela a swallow. Tereus was also changed, and became a hoopoo.

This legend is one of those invented to account mythically for the habits and properties of animals. The twitter of the swallow sounds like Itys, Itys. The note of the nightingale was regarded as lugubrious, and the hoopoo chases these birds.

CEPHALOS AND PROCRIS.

Cephalos, son of Dïoneus, king of Phocis, married Procris, the beautiful daughter of Erectheus, king of Athens.

Soon after, as he was on Mount Hymettus, pursuing the deer at dawn of day, he was seen and carried off by Aurora. The society of the goddess was to Cephalos no equivalent for the loss of his beloved wife. Aurora tried every art to reconcile him to his present state, and to induce him to exchange for ever a terrestrial for a celestial abode. Still her endeavors were fruitless. Cephalos longed for Procris, and his former abode. At last, when the goddess found that all her blandishments were unavailing, that his heart was full of his wife, and her name for ever on his lips, she dismissed him; at the same time intimating, that the time would arrive when he should repent of having preferred to a goddess a mortal woman, who in the bitterness of his soul he would wish never to have seen.

These words effected the object intended by the incensed goddess, for they filled the heart of Cephalos with jealousy and suspicion towards his wife. For the purpose of trying her fidelity, he returned disguised to Procris, presenting himself to her as a lover. She received his overtures with disdain. But Cephalos, once experiencing the sting of jealousy in his heart, after having made himself known, loaded her with reproaches, and left her in a transport of rage. He was afterwards prevailed upon to become reconciled to her. Procris soon after became jealous of him, having heard that he loved the nymph Aura, with whom he held secret intervews, at the same time pretending to her that he was going to hunt.

To convince herself of the truth of this, she went to the spot which was designated as their place of meeting, and concealed herself behind some trees. Cephalos soon arrived, breathless and panting from the fatigues of the chase, and throwing himself upon the grass, exclaimed, Aura! Aura! meaning, by the words, nothing more than gentle breeze, fresh air. Procris, supposing that she heard the name of her rival, moved from behind the trees; and Cephalos, supposing the rustling that he heard to be occasioned by some wild beast, drew his bow, and the fatal arrow pierced the heart of Procris, who, when dying, was convinced of the groundlessness of her suspicions.

PHAETHON.

Phaëthon (*Gleaming*) was a son of Helios and the ocean-nymph Clymene. Venus intrusted him with the care of one of her temples. This distinguished favor of the goddess rendered him so vain and aspiring, that Epaphos, a son of Zeus, to check his pride, disputed his claims to a celestial origin. Phaëthon, to refute this bitter reproach, resolved to know his true origin ; and, at the instigation of his mother, visited the palace of the Sun, to beg that Helios, if he really were his father, would give him some proof of his paternal tenderness, and convince the world of his legitimacy. Helios swore by the Styx, that he would grant him whatever he required. The ambitious youth instantly demanded permission to guide the solar chariot for one day, in order to prove himself the undoubted progeny of the Sun-god. Not daring to violate the oath by Styx, and finding entreaties and remonstrances unavailing to dissuade him from his perilous enterprise, Helios complied with his wish, and Phaëthon courageously and joyfully mounted the chariot of the Sun.

No sooner, however, did the celestial coursers discover that they were guided by a feebler hand than that of Helios, than they disregarded the efforts of the new charioteer, and leaving their usual course, now approached too near the heavens, and now again so close to earth, that the mountains began to blaze, and the rivers and fountains dried up. Earth, in her extremity, besought Jupiter for help. Enraged at the presumption of this new driver of the celestial horses, Jupiter struck him with one of his thunderbolts, by which he was precipitated into the river Eridanos. There his three sisters, the Heliades, or daughters of the sun, Lampetia, Phaëthusa, and Ægle, who tenderly loved their brother, lamented his loss so long, that at length the gods were touched with compassion for their grief, and changed them into poplar trees. Their tears, which still continued to flow, became amber as they dropped into the stream.

Cycnos, also, the chosen friend of the ill-fated Phaëthon, lamented his death on the banks of the Eridanos, till his form, dissolved in tears, was changed to that of a swan, which always remained on the water that swallowed his beloved friend.

PHILEMON AND BAUCIS.

In Phrygia, as a beautiful ancient tale relates, Jupiter laid aside his thunderbolts and Mercury his caduceus, and assuming the form of wayfarers, wandered in disguise among men, in order to try their characters and actions.

One evening, when as weary travellers they sought for hospitality, the doors of the rich were closed against them. At length they approached the abode of Philemon and Baucis, a pious couple, but poor, and already advanced in years, and in their humble cottage they were received with hospitality and kindness. The gods were served with a supper such as the cottage afforded, and the wine bowl being spontaneously replenished, the quality of the guests was revealed.

The guests after having declared themselves to be Jupiter and Mercury, told their host that they intended to destroy the neighboring town, and desired them to leave their dwelling and ascend the adjacent hill. The aged couple obeyed, and ere they had reached its summit they turned round and beheld the waste and destruction wherewith the gods had punished the hard-heartedness of the inhabitants of the country. The houses and palaces of the rich were ruined by a deluge, while the poor, hospitable cottage still raised its roof above the floods, and before the astonished eyes of its late inhabitants, was transformed into a magnificent temple.

On being desired by Jupiter to express their wishes, they prayed that they might be appointed to officiate in that temple, bringing offerings to Jove, the patron and rewarder of hospitality, and finally be united in death as in life. Their prayer was granted; and as they were one day standing before the temple, they were changed into trees, an oak and a lime. These trees overshadowed the temple, and in their memory were long afterwards called Philemon and Baucis.

In this and similar traditions of old, the dreadful as well as beneficent power of the deities was recognized. Altars were every where erected to Jupiter Hospitalis. Strangers arriving at any place where they were destitute of friends, were under his immediate protection, and guests were considered as sacred and inviolable persons; for in strangers and guests the celestials were revered, who often came down from Olympos in human form, in order to mingle among mankind

PYRAMUS AND THISBE.

Pyramus and Thisbe were two young Thebans, whose union was opposed by their families, between whom there had been a variance for many years. They determined, however, if possible, to elude the vigilance of their persecutors, and agreed to meet outside the walls of the city, under a mulberry tree, and there to celebrate their union. Thisbe first arrived at the appointed place, when the sudden appearance of a lioness so frightened her that she fled, dropping her veil in her fright. This the lioness smeared with blood, and then disappeared, leaving it under the trysting tree.

In a short time Pyramus arrived, and found that she for whom he looked was absent. The bloody veil alone met his gaze. He instantly recognized it, and concluding that Thisbe had been torn to pieces by wild beasts, drew his sword and killed himself.

When the fears of Thisbe had passed away, she returned to the mul‑ berry tree.

> " But when her view the bleeding love confessed,
> She shrieked, she tore her hair, she beat her breast,
> She raised the body, and embraced it round,
> And bathed with tears unfeigned the gaping wound,
> Then her warm lips to the cold face applied—
> ' And is it thus, ah ! thus we meet,' she cried,
> ' My Pyramus, whence sprang thy cruel fate ?
> My Pyramus, ah ! speak, ere 'tis too late :
> I, thy own Thisbe, but one word implore,
> One word thy Thisbe never asked before !
> Fate, though it conquers, shall no triumph gain,
> Fate, that divides us, still divides in vain.
> Now, both our cruel parents, hear my prayer,
> My prayer to offer for us both I dare ;
> Oh ! see our ashes in one urn confined,
> Whom love at first, and fate at last has joined.
> Thou tree, where now one lifeless lump is laid,
> Ere long o'er two shalt cast a friendly shade.
> Still, let our loves from thee be understood,
> Still witness, in thy purple fruit, our blood.'—
> She spoke, and in her bosom plunged the sword
> All warm and reeking from its slaughtered lord."— *Ovid.*

TITHONOS.

Tithonos, a handsome youth, was a son of the Trojan king, Laomedon. Going out one day with his flocks he returned no more; and
Fiction explained his loss by saying that Aurora beheld him and carried him off for his beauty.

Aurora besought Jupiter to render him immortal. The request was
granted; and. according to the poets, Aurora rises every morning from
the bed of Tithonos to open the gates of the sky. The only offspring
of this marriage was Memnon, a king of Ethiopia, who took part in
the Trojan war, and was slain by Achilles.

Although immortal, and the husband of a goddess, the happiness of
Tithonos was incomplete. When Aurora prayed to Jupiter to grant
him immortality, she forgot to ask at the same time for exemption
from old age; and thus her husband, exhausted by years and infirmity, withered away, so that his voice was scarcely left to him. At
length he prayed for dissolution, and was changed into a grasshopper;
for the decrees of Fate, according to which he was rendered immortal,
can never be reversed.

ENDYMION.

Among all the favorites of the gods, the handsome sportsman Endymion was honored by Fiction with the highest preference. since
Diana, the severe goddess of chastity, attracted by his charms, became
sensible of the power of love.

Endymion's abode was on the lonely mountain Latmos, in Caria, a
province of Asia Minor. By moonlight he pursued the chase of the
deer through the forest, until worn out by fatigue, he sank into the
arms of sleep. Then it was that Diana, rising with glimmering torch
in the vault of heaven, beheld the slumbering youth. All was lonely
and silent. She stopped the steeds that drew her car, and gliding
slowly from the height of the sky down to the lips of the slumberer, she.
for the first time, kissed them in glowing love. Thus Endymion e-
joyed, sleeping, a happiness which had never fallen to the lot eithe.
of gods or men.

The eternal sleep of Endymion is in ancient story assigned to various causes. Some say that he begged Zeus to give him immortality.
Zeus then bestowed upon him the boon of perpetual youth, united with
perpetual sleep. Others state that Zeus threw him into everlasting

sleep as a punishment for his love for Hera. These stories are un-
questionably poetical fictions, in which sleep is personified. His name
and attributes confirm this opinion. Endymion signifies a being that
gently comes over one. He is called a king, because he has power
over all living creatures ; a shepherd, because he slumbered in the cool
caves of Mount Latmos, that is, " the Mount of Oblivion ;" and, lastly,
nothing can be more beautiful than the idea of his being kissed by the
soft rays of the Moon.

ANCHISES.

Anchises, son of Calyps and Themis, attracted Venus by his beauty,
and she introduced herself to his notice in the form of a nymph on
Mount Ida, and urged him to a union. Anchises no sooner discovered
that he had been in the company of a celestial being, than he dreaded
the vengeance of the gods. Venus then addressed him in these words:

"Dismiss all fear! Thou shalt suffer no harm because of my love. I will not supplicate for thee immortality, as Aurora did for her Titho-nos; but swift age shall steal upon thee, even as upon the rest of mor-tal men. The nymphs of the forest are to nurse thy son, and when he has reached manhood, then thine eyes shall feast on his godlike form; should any one ask thee of thy son's mother, thou art to answer, she was one of the nymphs that dwell upon these mountains. Beware thou boast not of my love, or the lightnings of Jove shall fall upon thy head! These words engrave deeply in thy heart, and beware of the celestials!"

Anchises disobeyed her injunction, and boasted of the partiality of the goddess, for which Jupiter struck him with blindness. The off-spring of this union with Venus was the celebrated Æneias. When Troy was in flames, Anchises was saved from the victorious Greeks by his son, who bore him on his shoulders away from the burning city. He afterwards accompanied Æneias in his voyage to Italy; but died at the harbor of Depranum, at the island of Sicily, before the land was reached, and was buried on Mount Eryx.

MERCURY AND HERSE.

As Mercury met the maidens that were carrying the sacred baskets to the temple of Minerva, he beheld Herse, the beautiful daughter of Cecrops. Admiring her charms, he resolved to have her for a wife, and for that purpose entered the royal abode, where dwelt the three sis-ters, Aglauros, Paudrosos, and Herse. Mercury was first met by Ag-lauros, who felt great displeasure at his preference for her sister. He entreated her good offices, which she promised on condition that he would reward her with a large quantity of gold, and immediately drove him from the palace till he should obtain it.

Minerva, incensed at the cupidity of Aglauros, and provoked with her also for other causes, sent Envy to fill her bosom with that baleful passion. Unable then to endure the happiness of her sister, she sat down at the door, determined not to permit the god to enter. He be-sought her to admit him, but his eloquence was vain. At length, pro-voked by her obstinacy, he turned her into a black stone.

NARCISSOS.

The beautiful youth Narcissos was son of the river-god Cephissos, and the sea-nymph Liriope. According to Pausanias, Narcissos had a sister of remarkable beauty, to whom he was tenderly attached. She resembled him in features, was similarly attired, and accompanied him in the hunt. She died young, and Narcissos, deeply lamenting her death, frequented a neighboring fountain to gaze upon his own image in its stream. The strong resemblance that he bore to his sister made his own reflection appear to him, as it were, the form of her whom he had lost. The gods looked with pity upon his grief, and changed him to the flower that bears his name.

The flower alluded to in this story of Narcissus is termed by botanists, the *Narcissus poeticus*. It loves the borders of streams, and is admirably personified in this touching legend; for bending its fragile stem, it seems to seek its own image in the waters that run murmuring by, and soon fades away and dies.

ACTÆON.

Actæon was the son of Aristæos and Autonoë, daughter of Cadmos. He was reared by Cheiron, and becoming passionately fond of the chase, passed his days chiefly in pursuit of wild beasts that haunted Mount Cithæron. One sultry day as he was rambling alone, he chanced to surprise Artemis and her nymphs while bathing. The goddess, incensed at his intrusion, threw some water upon him, and changed him into a stag. She also inspired with madness the fifty dogs that attended him; when they ran down and devoured their master They then roamed about, whining, till they came to the cave of Cheiron, who appeased their grief by making an image of Actæon.

HYACINTHOS

Hyacinthos, a son of Œbalos, prince of Lacedæmon, was the favorite of Apollo. Apollo and Hyacinthos contended with each other in throwing the quoit. The fatal instrument was thrown with such force by Apollo, that it rebounded and struck Hyacinthos in the face, when he fell dead to the ground. The god unable to save his life, called forth from his ashes the flower that bears his name.

Other versions of the same legend say, that Zephyros (*west-wind*), enraged at Hyacinthos having preferred Apollo to himself, blew the discus against the head of the youth, and so killed him.

A festival called the Hyacinthia was celebrated for three days in the summer of each year at Amyclæ, in honor of the god and his unhappy favorite.

CYPARISSOS.

Cyparissos, another beautiful youth, and favorite of Apollo, was doomed to an early death. A tame stag, which had been his delight from his childhood, and to which he was most affectionately attached, was shot by the hapless youth himself in the gloom of a forest. The incident so deeply affected him that he became disgusted with life, and wandered mourning through the loneliest shades of the forest, until death freed him from his grief. Apollo called forth the dark cypress from his grave, which has immortalized the name of the youth, and still continues to be a symbol of mourning.

LEUCOTHOË.

Leucothoë, the daughter of Orchamos, secretly loved Apollo; but their intercourse was betrayed to her severe father by the jealous Clytia, and Orchamos buried his daughter alive. Apollo could not save her, and he therefore caused the frankincense shrub to spring from her grave, as a lasting monument both of her tenderness and her fate.

Clytia by her treason had for ever forfeited the love of the god. Inconsolable at her loss, she turned her face nine days towards the sun, the shining archetype of Apollo, without taking either food or drink.

At last, consumed by her grief, she became metamorphosed into the sun-flower, and in that form still turns her face constantly towards the sun.

DAPHNE.

" The first love of Phœbus," says Ovid, " was Daphne, the daughter of Peneios." Apollo, proud of his victory over the Python, beholding Eros bending his bow, mocked at the efforts of the puny archer. Eros was incensed, and taking his stand on Parnassos, shot his golden arrow of love into the heart of the son of Leto, and discharged his leaden one of aversion into the bosom of the nymph of Peneios.

Daphne loved the chase, indifferent to all other pleasures, and rejected the love of Apollo, who pursued her to the banks of her father's stream. Stretching forth her hands, she called on the river-god for protection. Peneios heard her prayer. Bark and leaves covered his daughter, and she became a bay tree, which has ever since been sacred to Apollo, and its leaves always crown his brow.

ATTIS.

Even Cybele, the grave mother of the gods, chose her favorite. Her choice fell upon the handsome youth Attis, who, forsaking his paternal fields, hastened to the Phrygian forests, there to devote himself without reserve to the service of the chaste goddess. She enjoined upon him never to prefer any other female, whether goddess or mortal. Forgetting this injunction, he suffered himself to be captivated with the charms of the beautiful nymph Sangaris, and drew the wrath of the deity upon himself as well as the object of his love. For this offence he was punished by fits of frenzy, in one of which he maimed himself.

An ancient fiction represents Attis in a touching manner, as standing on the sea shore, and during a lucid interval, looking over the waves to the distant land, where, with his parents and companions, he had dreamed the sweet dream of his childhood. The goddess approached him in her chariot drawn by lions, and again, frantic fury suddenly seized him, and he hastened to the woody top of the mountain, there to roam and rage until he died in the lonely wilderness.

CEYX AND HALCYONE.

Ceyx, king of Trachis, was son of the Morning-Star. He married Halcyone, a daughter of Æolos, son of Deucalion.

In the fable of the marriage of Ceyx and Halcyone, the Thessalian princess, is expressed the pleasure which the inhabitants of Thessaly experienced, when from the lofty cliffs of Olympos or of Ossa, or from the more cultivated declivities of Pelion, they looked down upon the wide expanse of sea, and beheld the swelling waves subside after a storm, the islands appear in the distance as the dark clouds broke away, when the white sails of the many little vessels ventured forth upon the sea.

Ceyx went to Claros to consult the oracle of Apollo, and was wrecked on his return. Halcyone, finding her husband's corpse upon the shore, was about to throw herself into the sea, when both were changed by the gods into birds called Halcyons. During seven days of winter the Halcyon sits on her eggs, and during seven more, she feeds her young upon the smooth surface of the waves, which then are calm and free from storm, and are called the Halcyon days of winter.

ORPHEUS.

Thrace is represented by the poets as the seat of whatever is wild, impetuous, or cruel. There the fierce god of war was chiefly worshipped. There Diomedes, a Thracian, and a son of Mars, is said to have had every stranger who was so unfortunate as to fall into his hands, thrown to his horses, to be devoured. Tereus, another Thracian, and also a son of Mars, cut out the tongue of the unfortunate Philomela, lest she should betray the crime he had committed against her. According to fiction, Thrace was also that country where the rough, stormy Boreas had his dwelling, for which reason those unknown nations that lived beyond Thrace were called Hyperboreans.

Thrace is also fabled to have been the native place of Orpheus, son of Apollo and the muse Calliope; that divine bard, who, by his song and the tones of his lyre, tamed the fierceness of forest beasts, moved rocks and trees, and, like a being sent from heaven, first taught mortals to listen to his harmonious notes, when he was chanting the praises of the celestials. The divine bard, not less renowned for his wisdom than for his skill in poesy and music, became also the founder of religious mysteries.

His wife, a nymph named Eurydice, died from the bite of a serpent. Orpheus, disconsolate at her loss, determined to descend to the lower world, and obtain permission for his beloved Eurydice to return to the regions of light. Armed only with his lyre, he entered the realms of Hades, and gained an easy admittance to the palace of Pluto. At the music of his "golden shell," to borrow the beautiful language of an cient poetry, the wheel of Ixion stopped, Tantalos forgot the thirst that tormented him, the Vulture ceased to prey on the vitals of Tityos, and Pluto and Proserpina lent a favoring ear to his prayer.

Eurydice was allowed to return with Orpheus, on condition that he should not look back at her until she had reached the higher world, and again beheld the light of day. But when they had nearly attained the opening above, and were about to leave the gloomy abode of the shades, tender anxiety, and doubt whether his dear companion was really following him, induced Orpheus to look back. He beheld his wife close behind him, but for the last time. Falling back, she again disappeared in the nightly darkness of Orcus, and all the sweet hope of Orpheus vanished like a dream. The joy of life was now for ever lost, and his lyre was silent.

From the Thracian mountains resounded the ferocious clamor of the Mænades, at a. Bacchic festival, who, angry at the bard for the contempt shown to them by his sorrow for Eurydice, fell upon him and tore him to pieces. Thus Orpheus, the son of Apollo, the divine poet, musician, and philosopher, fell a victim to the frantic fury of the devotees of Bacchos.

CUPID AND PSYCHE.

One of the most charming fictions transmitted to us from antiquity, is that of Cupid and Psyche. It involves the most sublime ideas of life, death, and immortality, as far as we may look for such ideas among the religious heathens of ancient times. The name of Psyche signifies both a butterfly and the human soul. Therefore, when represented with the wings of a butterfly attached to her shoulders, Psyche is, as it were, the emblem of a tender spiritual being, who, freed from the coarser covering of her chrysalis, is too sublimated for this lower world, and rises to a higher existence, where, united with Love, in sacred and mutual marriage, she participates in that bliss which the immortals themselves enjoy. This fiction forms the veil, which in a most agreeable manner conceals the terrors of the lower world.

Psyche, the most lovely of mortals, was the daughter of a powerful monarch, and the youngest of three sisters. So transcendent was her beauty, that no mortal man dared sue for her hand; and her father's subjects, neglecting the worship of Venus, raised altars to Psyche. Her parents exulted in this general homage paid to their daughter, and her sisters, somewhat jealous of her superior beauty, pleased themselves with the thought that while they were married, she would never have a husband. Both parents and sisters, however, soon found themselves disappointed in the anticipations in which they had indulged. The former consulted an oracle as to her future fate and were commanded to array their daughter in festive attire, and then conduct her as if to her burial to the summit of a mountain, and there to abandon her till her destined husband should come for her.

Venus, resolving to revenge herself upon the innocent Psyche, sent Cupid to inspire her with a passion for the ugliest of mortals. But Cupid no sooner saw Psyche, than he laid aside his bow and arrows, and resolved to make her his wife. For this purpose he went to Zephyros, the god of the west-wind, and Somnus, the god of sleep, to ask their assistance. No sooner did Psyche find herself alone, than a profound sleep stole over her senses, and then she was tenderly raised by Zephyr, who carried her to the abode prepared for her by Love. She found herself transported to an unknown region, but the most charming she had ever seen. A magnificent palace, surrounded by beautiful groves and beds of flowers, was at her disposal; she was mistress of many invisible attendants, by whom her commands were instantly obeyed. But he who had bestowed upon her this delightful abode, she was not permitted to behold. He visited her only at night, telling her with a sweetly-sounding voice, that he was the husband allotted to her by the immortals, at the same time warning and entreating her never to inquire who he was, for then she would for ever lose his love, and become miserable.

But in the midst of a heavenly happiness, Psyche longed to see her parents once more. or at least her sisters, that she might dissipate the grief of her family on account of her fate. Her husband, seeing that all the entreaties and remonstrances with which he endeavored to banish this wish from her heart were vain, at last consented that she should receive a visit from her sisters. Zephyr was accordingly ordered to convey them to Psyche's abode. No sooner had they arrived and beheld the happiness which was allotted to their sister, than envy filled their hearts, destroying every better feeling; and after having heard the particular circumstances under which Psyche enjoyed her matrimonial happiness, they infused into her mind the suspicion that her husband must be a hideous monster, because he dreaded to be seen. Their malevolence even went so far as to persuade their sister, by every possible art, to transgress the positive commands of her husband, and, by the use of a dagger, to rid herself of the monster when buried in sleep.

The sisters were carried away by Zephyr, and poor Psyche, whose mind was agitated by contending passions, resolved at last to follow the malevolent counsel which they had given her. When Night had expanded her wings over her blessed abode, and her husband was buried in repose, she took the lamp, and a dagger which she had concealed, and stepped, with fainting knees and a trembling hand, to the couch of the unknown. But instead of the monster whom she had expected to see, she beheld the most beautiful of the immortals, Cupid, God of Love! She attempted gently to withdraw the lamp, but her hand trembled, and a drop of hot oil fell on the god's shoulder. Cupid started up from his sleep, and beholding his wife, with a lamp and dagger. cast a look on the wretched Psyche, in which rage, scorn, and pity were intermingled.   He then mounted on his wings, never more to return.

When Psyche felt that she had lost the love and esteem of her adored husband, despair took possession of her mind, and she attempted to put a period to her existence.   She threw herself into the neighboring stream, but the river-god feared Love, and gently carried her to the opposite bank.   Here she met with Pan, who endeavored to console her by the prediction that she was destined at a future period to be once more happy.

Psyche's sisters, who had anticipated the consequences of their fatal counsel, and who now wished to succeed their unfortunate sister, placed themselves one after the other on the summit of the mountain, from which Psyche had been carried away, hoping that Zephyros would convey them to the wished-for residence; but being hurled into the abyss by sudden blasts of wind, they atoned by their deaths for the envy and treachery which they had displayed towards their innocent sister.

Poor Psyche overran the whole earth in search of her lost husband. But finding all her endeavors vain, she at last took the resolution of applying to Venus, and imploring mercy from her.   Venus, incensed with the fair suppliant, because she had charmed Cupid, and because of her celestial beauty, received her with reproaches, imposing upon her the severest tasks, the performance of which seemed impossible. Psyche, however, assisted by beneficent beings, whom Cupid, who still loved her, sent to her aid, surmounted all difficulties; yet for a long time she was obliged to suffer the consequences of her imprudence, until she was again thought worthy of her forfeited happiness.   At last, she was ordered by Venus to descend into Orcus itself, and to fetch from Proserpina a box containing the highest charms of beauty. Psyche obeyed the command of the cruel goddess, and set out on the dreadful enterprise, despairing of success ; but the voice of her invisible protector and guide taught her every necessary precaution, and warned her of every danger.

Provided with a cake to tame the fury of Cerberos, and a sum of money to gain the good-will of Charon, she ventured down to the gloomy regions, and arrived safely at the palace of Proserpina.   The desired box was delivered to her, but with a strict injunction not to open it.   Psyche, who had surmounted so many difficulties, and sustained with heroic fortitude so many trials, suffered herself to be overpowered by this last. Scarcely had she left the dominions of Pluto, when curiosity and vanity induced her to open the box. She was instantly involved in a black and noxious vapor, which threw her into a deep sleep, from which she would never have risen, had not Cupid, her invisible protector, hastened to her assistance. He restored her to life, collected the vapor again into the box, and conducted his beloved Psyche safely to the throne of Jove, there proclaiming her as his lawful wife, and supplicating for her admission among the immortals. Jupiter complied with his request, endowed her with immortality, and Venus became reconciled to her beauteous daughter-in-law. The Hours shed roses through the sky, the Graces sprinkled the halls of Heaven with fragrant odors, Apollo played on his lyre, the Arcadian god on his reeds, the Muses sang in chorus, while Venus danced with grace and elegance, to celebrate the nuptials of her son. Thus the celestials celebrated the second, the heavenly marriage of Cupid and Psyche.

___

TRANSLATION OF PINDAR'S SECOND ODE.

The islands of the blest, they say,
  The islands of the blest,
Are peaceful and happy by night and day,
  Far away in the glorious West.

They need not the moon in that land of delight,
  They need not the pale, pale star;
The sun he is bright, by day and night,
  Where the souls of the blessed are.

They till not the ground, they plough not the wave,
  They labor not—never! oh, never!
Not a tear do they shed, not a sigh do they heave.
  They are happy for ever and ever.

Soft is the breeze, like the evening one
  When the sun hath gone to his rest;
And the sky is pure, and the clouds there are none,
  In the islands of the blest.

The deep, clear sea, in its mazy bed,
  Doth garlands of gems unfold;
Not a tree but it blazes with crowns for the dead,
  Even flowers of living gold.

Cambridge University Magazine

APPENDIX.

Oʀᴀ'ᴄᴜ-ᴜᴍ was used by the ancients to designate both the revelations made by the Deity to man, as well as the place in which such revelations were made. The Deity was in none of these places believed to appear in person to man, and to communicate to him his will or knowledge of the future, but all oracular revelations were made through some kind of medium, which, as we shall see hereafter, was different in the different places where oracles existed. It may, on first sight, seem strange that there were, comparatively speaking, so few oracles of Zeus, the father and ruler of gods and men. Although, according to the belief of the ancients, Zeus himself was the first source of all oracular revelations, yet he was too far above men to enter into any close relation with them. Other gods, therefore, especially Apollo, and even heroes, acted as mediators between Zeus and men, and were, as it were, the organs through which he communicated his will. The fact that the ancients consulted the will of the gods on all important occasions of public and private life, arose partly from the great reverence for the gods, so peculiar to them, by which they were led not to undertake any thing of importance without their sanction. It should be borne in mind, that an oracle was not merely a revelation to satisfy the curiosity of man, but, at the same time, a sanction or authorization by the deity of what man intended to do or not to do. We subjoin a list of the Greek oracles, classed according to the deities to whom they belonged.

I. ORACLES OF APOLLO.

1. *The Oracle of Delphi* was the most celebrated of all the oracles of Apollo. Some account of it has already been given. During its best period, it was believed to give its answers and advice to every one who came with a pure heart, and had no evil designs. If he had committed a crime, the answer was refused until he had atoned for it; and he who consulted the god for bad purposes, was sure to accelerate his own ruin. No religious institution in all antiquity obtained such a paramount influence, not only in Greece, but in all countries around the Mediterranean, in all matters of importance, whether relating to religion or to politics, to private or to public life, as the oracle of Delphi. When consulted on a subject of a religious nature, the answer was invariably of a kind calculated not only to protect and preserve religious institutions, but to command new ones to be established, so that it was the preserver and promoter of religion throughout the ancient world; colonies were seldom or never founded without having obtained the advice and direction of the Delphic God. Hence the oracle was consulted in all disputes between a colony and its metropolis, as well as in cases where several states claimed to be the metropolis of a colony.

The Delphic oracle had at all times a leaning in favor of the Greeks of the Doric race; but the time when it began to lose its influence must be dated from the period when Athens and Sparta entered upon their struggle for the supremacy of Greece. At his time the partiality for Sparta became so manifest, that the Athenians and their party began to lose all reverence and esteem for it, and the oracle became a mere instrument in the hands of a political party. In the times of Cicero and Plutarch, many believed that the oracle had lost the powers which it had possessed in former days; but it still continued to be consulted down to the times of the Emperor Julian, until at last it was entirely done away with by the Emperor Theodosius.

Notwithstanding the general obscurity and ambiguity of most of the oracles given at Delphi, there are many, also, which convey so clear and distinct a meaning, that they could not possibly be misunderstood. So that a wise agency at the bottom of the oracles cannot be denied; the manner in which this agency has been explained at different times, varies greatly according to the spirit of the age. During the best period of their history, the Greeks, generally speaking, had undoubtedly a sincere faith in the oracle, its counsels and directions. When the sphere in which it had most benefited Greece, became narrowed and confined to matters of a private nature, the oracle could no longer command the veneration with which it had been looked upon before. The pious and believing heathens, however, thought the god no longer bestowed his care upon the oracle, and that he was beginning to withdraw from it, while free-thinkers and unbelievers looked upon the oracle as a skilful contrivance of priest-craft which had then outgrown itself. This latter opinion has also been adopted by many modern writers. The early Christian writers, seeing that some extraordinary power must in several cases have been at work, represented it as an institution of the evil spirit. In modern times opinions are very much divided; Hüllman, for example, has endeavored to show that the oracle of Delphi was entirely managed and conducted by the aristocratic families of Delphi, which thus are described as forming a sort of hierarchical senate for all Greece. If so, the Delphic senate surely was the wisest of all in the history of the ancient world. Klausen, on the other hand, seems inclined to allow some truly divine influence, and, in all events, thinks that, even in so far as it was merely managed by men, it acted in most cases according to pure and lofty moral principles.

2. *Oracle at Abæ, in Phocis.* An oracle was believed to have existed here from very early times, and was held in high esteem by the Phocians. Some years before the Persian invasion, the Phocians gained a victory over the Thessalians, in which they obtained, among other spoils, four thousand shields, half of which they dedicated in the temple of Apollo at Abæ, and half in that at Delphi. The oracle was, like many others consulted by Crœsus, but he does not seem to have found it agreeing with his wishes. In the Persian invasion of Xerxes, the Temple of Abæ was burned down, and like several temples destroyed in this invasion, was never rebuilt. The oracle itself, however, remained, and before the battle of Leuctra, promised victory to the Thebans; but in the Phocian or sacred war, when some Phocian fugitives had taken refuge in the ruins, they were entirely destroyed by the Thebans; but even after this calamity, the oracle seems to have been consulted—for the Romans, from reverence for it, allowed the people of Abæ to govern themselves. Hadrian built a small temple by the side of the old one, the ruins of which were seen in the time of Pausanias.

3. *Oracle on the Hill of Ptoon,* in the territory of Thebes. When Alexander the Great destroyed Thebes, the oracle also perished. In the time of Plutarch the whole district was completely desolate.

4. *Oracle of Apollo at Ismenion,* in Bœotia, south of Thebes. The Temple of Apollo Ismenios was the national sanctuary of the Thebans. The oracle was here not given

by inspiration, as in other places, but from the inspection of the victims. On one occasion it gave its prophecy from a huge cobweb in the Temple of Demeter.

5. *Oracle of Apollo at Hysiæ*, on the frontiers of Attica. This place contained an oracle of Apollo with a sacred well, from which those drank who wished to become inspired. In the time of Pausanias, the oracle had become extinct.

6. *Oracle of Apollo at Tegyra*, was an ancient and much-frequented oracle, which was conducted by the prophets. The Pythia, on one occasion, declared this to be the birth place of Apollo. In the time of Plutarch the whole district was a wilderness.

7. *Oracle of Apollo in the village of Eutresis*, in the neighborhood of Leuctra. This oracle became extinct during the Macedonian period.

8. *Oracle of Apollo at Orobiæ*, in Eubœa.

9. *Oracle of Apollo in the Lyceum at Argos*. The oracle was here given by a prophetess.

10. *Oracle of Apollo at Deiradiotes*, on the acropolis of Larissa. The oracle was given by a prophetess.

11. *Oracle of Apollo at Didyma*, usually called the oracle of the Branchidæ, in the territory of Miletus. This was the oracle generally consulted by the Ionians and Æolians. The oracles were probably inspired in a manner similar to that at Delphi. The principles which it followed in its courses and directions were also the same as those followed by the Delphians. Crœsus made to this oracle as magnificent presents as to that of Delphi.

12. *Oracle of Apollo at Claros*, in the territory of Colophon. This oracle was of great celebrity, and continued to be consulted, even at the time of the Roman emperors.

13. *Oracle of Apollo at Grynea*, in the territory of the Myrinæans.

14. *Oracle of Apollo at Gonnapæus*, in Lesbos.

15. *Oracle of Apollo at Abdera.*

16. *Oracle of Apollo at Delos*, which was consulted only in summer.

17. *Oracle of Apollo at Patara*, in Lycia, was consulted only in winter. The prophetess spent a night in the temple to receive the communications of the god.

18. *Oracle of Apollo at Telmessus*. The priests of this temple occupied themselves chiefly with the interpretation of dreams.

19. *Oracle of Apollo at Mallos*, in Cilicia.

20. *Oracle of the Sarpedonian Apollo*, in Cilicia.

21. *Oracle of Apollo at Hybla*, in Caria.

22. *Oracle of Apollo at Hiera Kome*, on the Meander, a celebrated oracle, which spoke in good verses.

II. ORACLES OF ZEUS.

1. *Oracle of Zeus at Olympia*. In this as in the other oracles of Zeus, the god did not reveal himself by inspiration, but merely sent signs which were to be interpreted by men. Those who came to consult the oracle of Olympia, offered a victim, and the priest gave his answers from the nature of its several parts, or from accidental circumstances accompanying the sacrifice. In early times the oracle was much resorted to, but afterwards was almost entirely neglected, probably because oracles from the inspection of victims might be obtained any where. The spot where the oracles were given at Olympia, was before the altar of Zeus. It was especially consulted by those who intended to take part in the Olympic games, but other subjects were brought before it.

2. *Oracle of Zeus at Dodona*. Here the oracle was given from sounds produced by the wind. The sanctuary was situated on an eminence. Although in a barbarous country, this oracle was in close connection with Greece, and in early times much more

so than afterwards. Zeus himself, as well as the Dodonæans, were reckoned among the Pelasgians, which is a proof of the ante-Hellenic existence of the worship of Zeus in these parts and perhaps of the oracle also.

The oracle was given from lofty oaks covered with foliage, hence Æschylus mentions the speaking oaks of Dodona as great wonders. Beech-trees, however, are also mentioned in connection with the Dodonæan oracle, which, as Hesiod said, dwelled in the stem of a beech tree. Hence we may infer that the oracle was not supposed to dwell in any single or particular tree, but in a grove of oaks and beeches. The will of the god was made manifest by the rustling of the wind through the leaves of the trees, which are therefore represented as eloquent tongues. In order to render the sounds produced by the winds more distinct, brazen vessels were suspended on the branches of the trees, which, being moved by the wind came in contact with each other, and thus sounded till they were stopped. Another mode of producing the sounds was this ; there were two columns at Dodona, one of which bore a metal basin, and the other a boy with a scourge in his hand ; the ends of the scourge consisted of small bones, and as they were moved by the wind, they knocked against the metal basin on the other column. According to other accounts, oracles were also obtained at Dodona through pigeons, which, sitting upon oak trees, pronounced the will of Zeus. The sounds in early times were interpreted by men, but afterwards, when the worship of Dione became connected with that of Zeus, it was done by two or three old women. There were, however, at all times, priests connected with the oracle, who on certain occasions interpreted the sounds. In the historical times, the oracle of Dodona had less influence than it appears to have had at an earlier period ; but it was at all times inaccessible to bribes, and refused to lend its assistance to the Doric interest. It was chiefly consulted by the neighboring tribes, the Ætolians, Acarnanians, and Epirotæ, and by those who would not go to Delphi on account of its partiality for the Dorians. There appears to have been a very ancient connection between Dodona and the Bœotian Ismenion.

The usual form in which the oracles were given at Dodona was in hexameters; but some of the oracles yet remaining are in prose. In 219 B. C., the temple was destroyed by the Ætolians, and the sacred oaks were cut down. But the oracle continued to exist and to be consulted, and seems not to have been totally extinct until the third century of our era. In the time of Strabo, the Dodonæan prophetesses are expressly mentioned, though this oracle, like the rest, was already decaying.

3. *Oracle of Zeus Ammon*, in an oasis in Libya, not far from the boundaries of Egypt. According to the traditions current at Dodona and Thebes in Egypt, it was founded in the latter city, and the god was represented at Thebes and in the Ammonium with the head of a ram. The Greeks became acquainted with this oracle through the Cyreneans, and Sparta was the first city of Greece which formed connections with it. Its example was followed by the Thebans, Olympians, Dodonæans, Eleans and others, and the Athenians sent frequent theories to the Ammonium, even before Ol. 91, and called one of their sacred vessels Ammonis. Temples of Zeus Ammon were now erected in several parts of Greece. His oracle in Libya was conducted by men who also gave the answers. On some occasions when they carried the statue about in procession, their number is said to have been eighty. In the time of Strabo the oracle was neglected and decayed.

III. ORACLES OF OTHER GODS.

The other gods who possessed oracles were consulted only concerning those particular departments of the world and human life over which they presided. Demeter thus gave oracles at Patræ in Achaia; but only concerning the sick, whether their sufferings would end in death or recovery. Before the sanctuary of the goddess was a well surrounded by a wall. Into this well a mirror was let down by means of a rope so as to float upon the surface. Prayers were then performed and incense offered, when the image of the sick person was seen in the mirror, either in a state of recovery, or as a corpse. At Pharæ, in Achaia, was an oracle of Hermes. His altar stood in the market-place. Here, incense was offered, oil-lamps were lighted before it, a copper coin was placed upon the altar, and after this, the question was put to the god by a whisper in his ear. The person who consulted shut his own ears, and immediately left the market-place. The first remark that he heard made by any one after leaving the market-place, was believed to imply the answer of Hermes.

At Charax, or Acharaca, not far from Nysa in Caria, was an oracle of *Pluto and Cora.* The two deities had here a temple and a grove, and near the latter was a subterraneous cave of a miraculous nature, called the cave of Charon; for persons suffering from illness, and placing confidence in the power of the gods, travelled to this place and remained for some time with experienced priests, who dwelt near the cave. These priests then slept a night in the cavern, and afterwards prescribed to their patients the remedies revealed to them in their dreams. Often, however, they took the patients into the cave, where they were kept quiet for several days, and without food. They were sometimes allowed to fall into the prophetic sleep, for which they were prepared, and received advice of the priests. To all other persons the place was inaccessible and fatal. There was an annual panegyris in this place, probably of the sick who sought relief from their sufferings.

On the middle of the festive day, the young men of the gymnasium, naked and anointed, used to drive a bull into the cave, which, as soon as it had entered, fell down dead.

At Epidaurus Limera, oracles are given at the festival of *Ino.** The same goddess had an oracle at Œtylon, at which she made revelations in dreams to persons who slept a night in her sanctuary. *Hera Acræa* had an oracle between Lechæon and Pagæ.

IV. ORACLES OF HEROES.

1. *Oracle of Amphiaraus,* between Potniæ and Thebes, where the hero was said to have been swallowed up by the earth. His sanctuary was surrounded by a wall, and adorned with columns, upon which birds never settled, and birds or cattle never fed in the neighborhood. The oracles were given to persons in their dreams, who, after having fasted one day and abstained from wine for three, were obliged to sleep in the temple. The Thebans were not allowed to consult this oracle, having chosen to take the hero as their ally rather than their prophet. Another oracle of Amphiaraus was at Dropus, between Bœotia and Attica, which was most frequently consulted by the sick about the means of their recovery. Those who consulted it, were obliged to undergo lustrations, and to sacrifice a ram, on the skin of which they slept a night in the temple, where, in their dreams, they expected the means of their recovery to be revealed to them. If they recovered, they were obliged to throw some pieces of money into the well of Amphiaraus, within his sanctuary. The oracle was said to have been founded by the Thebans.

2. *Oracle of Amphilochus,* the son of Amphiaraus, who had an oracle at Mallos, in Cilicia, which Pausanias calls the most trustworthy of his time.

An ancient heroine.

3. *Oracle of Trophonius*, at Lebadeiæ, in Bœotia. Those who wished to consult this oracle, had first to purify themselves by spending some days in the sanctuary. They must also live sober and pure, abstain from warm baths, but bathe in the river Hercyna, offer sacrifices to Trophonius and his children, to Apollo, King Zeus, Hera Heniocha, and to Demeter Europa, who was said to have nursed Trophonius. During these sacrifices, a soothsayer explained, from the intestines of the victims, whether Trophonius would be pleased to admit the consulter. Before entering the cave of Trophonius, the consulter must sacrifice a ram to Agamedes, and only in case of favorable signs in this sacrifice, was the hero thought to be pleased to admit the person into his cave. What took place after this, was as follows : Two boys, thirteen years old, led him again to the river Hercyna, bathed and anointed him. The priests then made him drink from the well of oblivion, that he might forget all his former thoughts, and from the well of recollection, that he might remember the visions he should then have. They then showed him a mysterious representation of Trophonius, required him to worship it, and led him into the sanctuary dressed in linen garments, with girdles round his body, and wearing a peculiar kind of shoes, which were customary at Lebadeiæ. Within the sanctuary, which stood on an eminence, there was a cave, into which the person was now allowed to descend by means of a ladder. Close to the bottom, in the side of the cave, was an opening into which he put his feet; the other parts of the body were then drawn into the opening by some invisible power. What the persons here saw was different at different times. They returned through the same opening at which they had entered. The priests then placed them on the throne of Mnemosyne, asked them what they had seen, and then led them back to the sanctuary of " the good spirit and good luck." As soon as they had recovered from their fear, they were obliged to write down their vision on a little tablet which was dedicated in the temple. This is the account given by Pausanias, who had descended into the cave, and writes as an eye-witness. The answers were probably given by the priests according to the report of what persons had seen in the cave. This oracle was held in very great esteem, and did not become extinct until a very late period ; and though the army of Sulla had plundered the temple, the oracle was much consulted by the Romans, and, in the time of Plutarch, was the only one among the numerous Bœotian oracles that had not become silent.

4. *Oracle of Calchas*, in Dannia, in Southern Italy. Here answers were given in dreams. Those who consulted the oracle, sacrificed a black ram, and slept a night in the temple, lying on the skin of the victim.

5. *Oracles of Asclepios.*—These were very numerous. The most important and most celebrated was that of Epidaurus. His temple was here covered with votive tablets, on which persons had recorded their recovery after spending a night in the temple. In the temples of Æsculapius and Serapis, at Rome, recovery was likewise sought by *incubatio* in his temple.

6. *Oracle of Heracles*, at Bura, in Achaia. Those who consulted it, prayed and put their questions to the god, and then cast four dice printed with figures, and the answer was given according to the position of these figures.

7. *Oracle of Pasiphaë*, at Thalamiæ, in Laconia, where answers were given in dreams, while persons spent the night in the temple.

8. *Oracle of Phrizos*, in Iberia, near mount Caucasus, where no rams were allowed to be sacrificed.

V. ORACLES OF THE DEAD.

The Oracles of the Dead, were those in which the spirits of the departed were called up Sacrifices were then offered to the gods of the lower world. One of the most ancient and most celebrated places of this kind, was in the country of the Thesprotians, near lake Aornos. Another was at Heraclea on the Propontis.

VI. ITALIAN ORACLES.

Oracles in which a god revealed his will through an inspired individual, did not exist in Italy. The oracles of Calchas and Æsculapius, mentioned above, were of Greek origin, and the former was in a Greek *heroum* on mount Garganus. The Romans, in the ordinary course of things, did not feel the want of such oracles as those of Greece, for they had numerous other means to discover the will of the gods, such as Sibylline books, augury, haruspices, signs in the heavens, and the like. The only Italian oracles known to us are the following :

1. *Oracle of Faunus.* His oracles are said to have been given in the Saturnian verse, and collections of his vaticinia seem to have existed at an early period. The places where his oracles were given were two groves, the one in the neighborhood of the Tiber, round the wall of Albunea, and the other on the Aventine. Those who consulted the god in the grove of Albunea, which is said to have been resorted to by all the Italians, were obliged to observe the following points : The priest first offered a sheep and other sacrifices to the god. The skin of the victim was then spread on the ground, upon which the consulter was obliged to sleep during the night, after having his head thrice sprinkled with pure water from the well, and touched with the branch of a sacred beech tree. He was, moreover, obliged for several days previous to abstain from animal food and matrimonial connections, to be clothed in simple garments, and not to wear a ring on his fingers. After falling asleep on the skin, he was believed to receive his answer in wonderful visions, and in converse with the god himself. Ovid transfers some of the points observed to obtain the oracle on the Albunea, to the oracle on the Aventine. Both may have had much in common, but from the story which he relates of Numa, it seems clear, that on the Aventine different ceremonies were observed.

2. *Oracles of Fortuna* existed in several Italian towns, especially in Latium, as at Antium and Præneste. In Antium two sisters Fortunæ were worshipped, and their statues bent forward when oracles were given. At Præneste the oracles were derived from lots, consisting of sticks of oak with ancient characters graven upon them. These lots were said to have been found by a noble Prænestine of the name of Numerius Suffricius, inside of a rock which he had cleft open at the command of a dream by which he had been haunted. The lots, when an oracle was to be given, were shaken together by a boy, after which, one was drawn by the person who consulted the goddess. The lots of Præneste were, at least with the vulgar, in great esteem as late as the time of Cicero, while in other places of Latium they were mostly neglected.

3. *An Oracle of Mars* was, in very ancient times, according to Dionysius, at Tiora Matiena not far from Teate. The manner in which oracles were here given, resembled the pigeon oracle at Dodona ; for a woodpecker, a bird sacred to Mars, was settled upon a wooden column, where he pronounced the oracle.

Smith's Greek and Roman Antiquities.

INDEX.

THE LATIN NAMES ARE IN ITALICS.

www.ingramcontent.com/pod-product-compliance
Lightning Source LLC
Chambersburg PA
CBHW031348290326
41932CB00044B/570